THE TRUTH ABOUT
PROPHECY IN THE
BIBLE

Bryan P. Mistele

Beyond Today Publishing
Seventh Printing

Beyond Today Publishing
21311 NE 84th St.
Redmond, WA 98053

To order additional copies of this book on-line or obtain additional information about the author go to:

www.bryanmistele.com

To send comments, questions or feedback to the author, e-mail:

bryan@mistele.com

Printed in the United States of America

Library of Congress Control Number: 2005901594

ISBN 0-9766845-0-0

Dedication

To my wife, Priscilla, whose encouragement, patience
and love made this book possible.

TABLE OF CONTENTS

Appendix

INDEX OF FIGURES, MAPS & TABLES

Figures & Timelines

Maps

Tables

PREFACE

INTRODUCTION

"About the time of the end, a body of men will be raised up who will turn their attention to the prophecies, and insist upon their literal interpretation, in the midst of much clamor and opposition."

– Sir Isaac Newton

Imagine if there were a book that existed throughout history that had successfully predicted the future in over five hundred specific cases with 100 percent accuracy. Imagine now, that this book had been passed down from generation to generation and that it still contained hundreds, if not thousands, of prophecies of things yet to come. Would you read it? How about if your life (or the destiny of your life) depended on it? Would you be interested in what it said? The truth is that this book does exist; in fact, it's the world's all-time best-seller. Yet the majority of people have not read it. Indeed, many people show no interest in it at all.

The book is the Bible, which contains literally thousands of specific prophecies that have endured the test of time. What's so significant about the Bible is that the prophecies it contains, many of them given thousands of years before their fulfillment, have been fulfilled with 100 percent accuracy over time. In more than five hundred specific cases, the Bible has clearly and specifically predicted the future, with the fulfillment verified by historians and archeologists throughout the ages. In many cases, the fulfillment of these prophecies can be verified using a common encyclopedia. No other book would dare to predict future events in such great detail, and certainly no other book can come close to matching this level of accuracy. The Bible is truly unique for its track record of predicting the future that simply defies mathematical probability.

About 30 percent of the Bible is prophecy, which is part of what makes the Bible unique among other religious works such as the writings of Muhammad, Buddha, Confucius, or the Book of Mormon. Indeed, thousands of years ago, the God of the Bible made a bold challenge to all other religions and prophets claiming to be true: "'Present your case,' says the Lord. 'Set forth your arguments,' says Jacob's King. 'Bring in your idols, to tell us what is going to happen. Tell us what the former things were, so that we may consider them and know their final outcome. Or declare to us the things to come, tell us what the future holds, so we may know that you are gods'" (Isa. 41:22-23). The accuracy of prophecy is the test by which to measure all other religions. So far, there has been no credible response to God's challenge for a religion to put its reputation on the line by accurately predicting the future.

Unfortunately, the topic of prophecy is frequently misunderstood and seldom preached in most churches. Many people simply think the topic is too complicated and never bother to read the passages of the Bible that pertain to prophecy. Others see the various debates among prophecy scholars around the difficult issues and avoid the topic altogether by saying, "God wins in the end, so why bother getting into the details?" Although God certainly does win, it's obvious that He didn't intend for 30 percent of the Bible to be ignored or glossed over. Most people equate the book of Revelation with prophecy concerning the end times. This is correct, but it's probably a surprise to most people that there is more prophetic material in Matthew, Mark, and Luke than there is in the entire book of Revelation. Obviously, God considers prophecy too important a topic to be ignored.

My purpose in writing this book is fourfold:

1. To organize prophecies by topic for easier understanding. Frequently, an event or prophecy is discussed in multiple books of the Bible, which makes it difficult for people to study and see the

whole picture of what is being described without hundreds of hours of study.

2. To show how prophecies have been fulfilled in the past (or, are being fulfilled in our day); to illustrate that Bible prophecy is real, accurate, and very relevant to our lives. The Bible contains approximately one thousand prophetic passages. Of these, half have already been fulfilled in a literal way.[1] Imagine the mathematical probability—the Bible is the only book in the world that has predicted world events with 100 percent accuracy. Since this is the case, and the accuracy of these prophecies can be verified using non-biblical sources, then it's clear that we should treat the hundreds of prophecies in the Bible that have yet to occur with utmost seriousness. Clearly, the fact that Bible prophecy has been fulfilled accurately and literally in the past gives significant credibility to the prophecies that have yet to be fulfilled.

3. To show how very near the time of Christ's return actually is. The Bible provides various signs as to when the ultimate completion of God's plan for the earth will occur. Almost all of these signs have been fulfilled in just the past sixty years, with many of the final signs being completed in our day. We are at a unique point in history. Despite thousands of years since the last words of Scripture were written, prophecies are being fulfilled and are coming together in concert for the first time in history. The time of Christ's return is very close.

4. To ultimately draw readers closer to Christ. By studying prophecy, we understand more about the person of Jesus Christ and His plan for the world. This is why John introduced the last book in the Bible as "the revelation *of* Jesus Christ" and not the revelation *from* Jesus Christ (Rev. 1:1). Indeed, the Bible states: "Worship God! For the testimony of Jesus is the spirit of prophecy" (Rev. 19:10b).

The benefits for studying prophecy are many. First and foremost, God promises a blessing for all those who study it. Although prophecy, and the book of Revelation in particular, may be difficult to read and study, Revelation is nevertheless the only book of the

Bible that contains an explicit promise just for reading it (Rev. 1:3) and a second promise for those who take it to heart (Rev. 22:7)! Obviously, God considers the study of prophecy important. Another reason for studying prophecy is to open our eyes to all that God is doing. By studying prophecy, one can't help but better understand the Scriptures and God's plan for the ages. Consequently, one will better understand the various trends that are occurring in our generation that are setting the stage for God's final act. Finally, as one grows closer to God through His word and through prophecy, one can't help but become more actively involved in the work of God. A true study of prophecy will motivate one to worship and serve the central figure of all prophecy, the Lord Jesus Christ Himself.

I encourage readers to keep an open mind to the thoughts and facts that this book contains. Even though this work is written from a point of view, I have made every effort to be objective when it comes to interpreting the Scriptures and the facts surrounding the fulfillment of prophecy. To this end, I have attempted to do the following throughout this reference:

- Wherever a prophecy is stated, I provide the verses in the Bible that are the basis of that prophecy.

- I have clearly identified what is prophecy, what is a verifiable fulfillment, and what is mere speculation. Where a prophecy has not been completely fulfilled, I identify it as a partial fulfillment.

- Where there is ambiguity in Scripture (e.g., the timing of the Rapture), I have tried to present all of the differing viewpoints and the basis for each.

- Where possible, I have tried to verify the fulfillment of each prophecy using multiple, secular sources.

- I have footnoted this work extensively so that readers can reference the source material if they so desire.

This book is divided into three sections. The first section provides a broad overview of past prophecy—prophecy that was given thousands of years ago and has already been fulfilled. This section is intended to show the clear link between prophecy and how it has been fulfilled with 100 percent accuracy over time. The fulfillment of many of the prophecies can be verified using historical works and encyclopedias, so whenever possible, I've included references to these. Some may find the historical aspects of this section a bit dry. If this is the case, skip ahead to the second section. The second section discusses present prophecy—prophecy that has been fulfilled in our generation. It's probably a surprise to most people that there are over two dozen specific prophecies given in the Bible thousands of years ago that have been fulfilled in just the past sixty years. This section discusses these, many of which still make headlines in the daily newspapers. The third and final section discusses future prophecy— prophecy that has yet to be fulfilled. This section reveals what will happen in the "end times" and discusses what the future holds for mankind.

I hope that as you read this book, you will find the topic of prophecy as interesting as I have. It was not my initial intent to write a book of this magnitude; I was merely interested in seeing what the Bible had to say about prophecy and took some notes along the way. As I started to study, however, I was fascinated by how accurate prophecy had been fulfilled in the past and the number of prophecies being fulfilled in our day. The topic engrossed me, and I found myself delving deeper and deeper into the topic. I ended with a much more complete picture of the Bible, of Christ, and of God's purpose for creating mankind in general. I hope by reading this, you will come to a better understanding of these things as well.

"Set your minds on things above, not on earthly things" (Col. 3:2).

—Bryan P. Mistele

Notes

1. Dr. John F. Walvoord, "The Rapture: The Next Event on God's Calendar," *The Road to Armageddon,* n. d., 27.

CHAPTER 1

GOD'S PLAN FOR HISTORY

"I am God, and there is none like me. I make known the end from the beginning, from ancient times, what is still to come…what I have said, that will I bring about; what I have planned, that will I do"
(Isaiah 46:9-11).

The God of the Bible is all-knowing and all-powerful. He transcends time. Events do not unfold on God's timeline at random. Rather, God has a preordained plan for the earth. His plan is to establish a right relationship with His creation. Throughout the Bible, we see this recurring theme—the story of God's unfailing love and His desire to have that love reciprocated by His creation. In case after case, we see God creating (or selecting) a group of beings with free will for the purpose of returning His love through obedience and worship. Unfortunately, time and time again we see God's creation rebelling against Him and becoming disobedient. We see this happen six times through history—first with Satan and his demons; second with Adam and mankind prior to Noah; third with the descendants of Noah; fourth with the Jewish people; fifth with the Church; and sixth with the people living during Christ's kingdom on earth (referred to as the Millennium). It is after this sixth and final rebellion, at the end of the Millennium, that God will judge creation, destroy the existing heaven and earth and start over again a seventh time, by creating a new heaven and a new earth. This final time will be perfect and will last for eternity.

Understanding this plan is the key to understanding the Bible, prophecy, and God's actions throughout history. All of the events described in the Old Testament and centuries past have happened in accordance with this plan. Likewise, all of the events described in the New Testament and all the events yet to come will happen according to God's plan. The following outline captures this theme along with the key events of prophecy and creation:

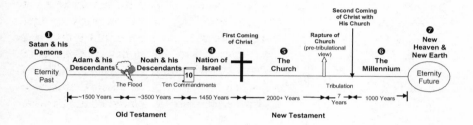

Figure 1: Timeline of History & God's Creation

Eternity Past

"Before the mountains were born or you brought forth the earth and the world, from everlasting to everlasting you are God" (Ps. 90:2).

God has always existed. He is timeless. Everything else is a creation of God. He existed before the creation of the heavens and the earth and will exist after they are destroyed. Heaven and earth are only temporary. They were created at certain points in time in the past and will be destroyed at certain points in time in the future.

What's important about eternity past is that Adam and Eve were not the first created beings to sin against God. Evidence of this is found in the fact that Satan was originally created as God's most esteemed angel—described as being "a guardian cherub" ordained by God. He was the "model of perfection, full of wisdom and perfect in beauty" and "blameless in his ways" (Ezek. 28:12-15). He was originally without sin, but Bible says he became proud, which led him to become corrupt and violent. It's at this point that he rebelled against God. God then cast Satan down to earth, along with those angels that rebelled with him (Ezek. 28:16-19, Isa. 14:12-14).

It's interesting to note that God describes Satan's fall from grace as being a "spectacle before kings" and that "nations were appalled at [Satan]" (Ezek. 28:17, 19), and Satan was known for his widespread trade (Ezek. 28:16, 18). The inference here is that there were other beings that existed prior to mankind in a civilization not unlike our own. These were not humans, but rather multitudes of angelic or immortal beings that existed prior to mankind that were capable of free will. Apparently after Satan's rebellion, God decided to create mankind as another opportunity for a race to reciprocate His love through obedience and worship.

Mankind

"In the beginning God created the heavens and the earth" (Gen. 1:1).

The story of the earth starts with God's creation. As part of this creation, God created mankind (Gen. 1-2). What then happened is that God's first creation (Satan) interacted with His second creation (mankind) and led mankind to sin and rebel against God. This is the well-known story of Satan's temptation of Adam and Eve in the Garden of Eden.

Less commonly known is what occurred next; namely, God's first creation (the fallen angels) continued to interact with mankind by intermarrying. This led to a race of people that were half-human and half-angelic. The Bible calls this race the "Nephilim,"[1] which means both "fallen ones" and "giants." The Nephilim were strong, yet full of sin. The Bible says: "The sons of God saw that the daughters of men were beautiful, and they married any of them they chose... and had children by them. They were the heroes of old, men of renown" (Gen. 6:1-4).

The term "sons of God" in this verse, translated in Hebrew, is $b^e neha^e lohim$, which is consistently used in the Old Testament for angels.[2] A good analogy to the Nephilim would be the heroes of Greek mythology such as Hercules, part human and part immortal who interacted with mankind on the earth. In fact, it is believed that Greek mythology came from the pre-flood legends that were passed down about these half-men, half-angelic beings.

Because of the Nephilim, the fallen angels of Satan, the earth became very evil. So evil, in fact, that God decided to destroy the whole earth with a flood and start over. The Bible says: "The Lord saw how great man's wickedness on the earth had become and that every inclination of the thoughts of his heart was only evil all of the time. The Lord was grieved that he had made man on the earth, and his heart was filled with pain. So the Lord said `I will wipe mankind, who I have created, from the face of the earth'... but Noah found favor in the eyes of the Lord" (Gen. 6:5-8).

This begins the well-known story of Noah and the Ark. God destroyed at least the known world at the time with a flood[3] but saved Noah, because the Bible says he was a "righteous man, blameless among the people of his time, and he walked with God" (Gen. 6:9). Essentially, destroying mankind with a flood was God's way of again trying to create a race of people to reciprocate His love and be obedient to Him. It was also His way of cleansing mankind of the Nephilim, whom He imprisoned in Hell after the flood, to be judged with all of the world's other unsaved people after the Millennium: "And the angels who did not keep their positions of authority but abandoned their own home—these he has kept in darkness, bound with everlasting chains for judgment on the great Day" (Jude 6).

Unfortunately though, mankind continued to sin and rebel after the flood starting with Noah's great grandson, Nimrod. After the flood, God commanded Noah and his sons to "be fruitful and increase in number and fill the earth" (Gen. 9:1). Nimrod, in defiance of God, attempted to unite the world together (both politically and religiously) by building a tower "whose top would reach into the heavens." This tower was known as the tower of Babel (Gen. 11:1-9). Its purpose was to facilitate the worshiping of a false god, to express pride in their own achievements, and to prevent human emigration beyond the boundaries of Mesopotamia. In essence, what God intended for good, mankind saw as a threat. By building the tower of Babel, mankind was rebelling against God's plan in favor of their own. God foiled this plan by creating different languages, but ever since, mankind has been trying to unite the world in defiance of God's explicit command.

The Nation of Israel

After the tower of Babel, God started a fourth time to create a group of beings to return His love and be obedient to Him. Instead of destroying mankind with a flood, which he promised to Noah he would never do again (Gen. 9:11-16), God decided to choose a godly man and create a nation of chosen people. These people would become His people, and He would become their God. God chose Abraham and made a covenant with him. God promised that if Abraham left his sinful country and moved to a new land, God would make him the father of a great nation and bless him.

God further refined this covenant with the people of Israel through Moses on Mt. Sinai. God promised: "If you obey me fully and keep my covenant, then out of all nations you will be my treasured possession. Although the whole earth is mine, you will be for me a kingdom of priests and a holy nation" (Exod. 19:4-6). God further directed, "I command you today to love the Lord your God, to walk in his ways, and to keep his commands, decrees and laws; then you will live and increase, and the Lord your God will bless you in the land you are entering to possess [the Promised Land]" (Deut. 30:16). Despite this opportunity to be His chosen people and to have a special fellowship with God, the nation of Israel promptly broke the covenant by making and worshiping idols (Exod. 32:1-10). But God renewed His covenant, which unfortunately, the nation of Israel promptly broke again. As punishment, and in fulfillment of prophecy that God gave to Moses, God let the Jewish people be taken into captivity and be dispersed among the nations twice—first through Babylon (which lasted seventy years) and second through the Roman Empire (which lasted almost two thousand years).

Christ and the Church

Despite God's best efforts, the nation of Israel (and mankind in general) continued to rebel against Him and be disobedient. The story of this disobedience and God's continued desire to establish an intimate relationship with His people fills the Old Testament and over two thousand years of Jewish history. But God loved His chosen people and didn't want them to perish, so he sent his only Son to earth to die as a sacrifice for their sins. Israel was very familiar with sin offerings and sacrifices; these were required as part of the program that God had established for them in the Old Testament. All the nation of Israel needed to do was to accept His son as their Savior (literally "messiah"), and they would be freed from their sins once and for all and would inherit eternity with God.

Unfortunately, the nation of Israel rejected Jesus as their messiah and had him put to death on a cross. Despite the numerous prophecies regarding His coming, they rejected Christ because they were looking for a political savior at the time and not a religious savior. Because of this rejection, God then offered the gift of His son's death directly to non-Jewish people (Acts 13:46, 18:6, 28:25-28). These people are known in the Bible as Gentiles. "Then Paul and Barnabas answered [the Jews] boldly: 'We had to speak the word of God to you first. Since you reject it and do not consider yourselves worthy of eternal life, we now turn to the Gentiles'"(Acts 13:46). If Gentiles would believe and accept Christ as their Lord, they would inherit the gift of salvation that was initially offered to the Jews. This is the heart of the Gospel message contained in the New Testament and the beginning of the modern day Church and Christianity.

For a fifth time, God tried to establish a group of people to reciprocate His love and be obedient to Him. Unfortunately, prophecy tells us the vast majority of Gentiles will also reject God's love, which will continue the theme established throughout history. Mankind will only continue to become more sinful and rebellious until God decides to bring it to and end and start again.

Many people have mistakenly thought God abandoned the Jews as His chosen people when they rejected Jesus Christ as their Messiah. This is not true. God did not abandon the Jews; rather he still desires a relationship with them. But God did offer salvation to the Gentiles, in part "to make Israel envious." "Did they stumble so as to fall beyond recovery? Not at all! Rather, because of their transgression, salvation has come to the Gentiles to make Israel envious" (Rom. 11:11).

The End Times

What happens from this point in God's plan for the world is what is known as the end times. These are a series of events (the Rapture, the Tribulation, the rise of the Antichrist, Armageddon, etc.) that lead up to the return of Jesus Christ to the earth, known as the Second Coming. The purpose of these events is to bring judgment upon the world and bring the Jewish people back into a loving relationship with Him. At the Second Coming, Christ will fulfill the Old Testament prophecies and present Himself as a political savior for the nation of Israel. The Bible tells us at this point "all Israel will be saved" (Rom. 11:26). Christ will then wipe the earth clean of all evil and unbelievers through a series of judgments. He will set up what is known as the Millennial Kingdom, which He will rule for a thousand years. This kingdom will be the fulfillment of the covenants God made with Abraham, Israel, and David. During this time, God will be the God of Israel, and they will be His people. This will be a time of great peace, prosperity, and joy, and it will be God's sixth attempt at establishing a group of people to return His love and be obedient to Him.

Eternity Future

At the end of the Millennium, mankind will once again rebel against God with the help of Satan. Despite living under the leadership of Christ in a utopian-like society, God's creation will for the sixth and final time rebel against their creator. It is at this point that God will destroy the existing heavens and earth with fire and start all over again. Just as He did in the days of Noah and of Lot, God will rescue His people (those obedient to Him during the time of the Millennium) prior to the destruction. He will then create a new heavens, a new earth, and a new Jerusalem. This is known as the Eternal State. It is in this New Jerusalem that God's people will live in obedience to Him forever more. The Bible tells us that the seventh time there will be no sin, rebellion, or disobedience. In the Eternal State, people will walk with God in a close relationship with Him.

Conclusion

It is clear from the above that God's one desire is to have His creation reciprocate His love and be obedient to Him. In many ways, this is no different than most parents, who yearn for love and obedience from their children—obedience not because they are controlling, but rather because parents have a broader perspective than young children and want what's best for them. Unfortunately, time and time again, we see God's creation turn from Him and rebel. In some way, however, this is all in accordance with God's preordained plan for the earth. God is all-powerful and all-knowing. God didn't make mistakes and then try to start over and over again with His creation. Rather, God chose to create beings with free will, capable of choosing their own destiny and whether or not to reciprocate His love. Why God would create beings that would disappoint Him time and time again is not clear. Perhaps it is the very nature of love; perhaps it is just part of God's character. Regardless, understanding this theme as it unfolds throughout time is key to understanding the Bible, prophecy, and God's actions throughout history.

Notes

1. For more background and an excellent analysis of the Nephilim, see Hugh Ross, *The Genesis Question*, Chapter 6.

2. Other examples include Job 1:6, 2:1, 38:7.

3. There is some debate among Christians whether the flood was truly worldwide in scope. Advocates put forth verses such as Genesis 6:7, 7:4, 13, 17, 21-23 as proof that the flood covered the whole earth. Opponents point to 2 Peter 3:6 as indication that it covered only the known world. Regardless of which view is true, the implications remain the same for the context of this book.

CHAPTER 2

ISRAEL, JERUSALEM & THE TEMPLE

The Jewish people, the nation of Israel, the city of Jerusalem, and the Temple on Mount Zion are central to the Bible, the study of prophecy, and God's plan for the earth. What is happening in history before our eyes in Israel, Jerusalem, and the Middle East is very significant in the entire prophetic picture—we are literally seeing prophecy being fulfilled in our own time. Understanding the significance of these events, however, requires an understanding of why Israel, Jerusalem, and the Temple are so important.

The story of prophecy in the Bible is similar to the parable Jesus told concerning the prodigal son. In this parable, the younger of two sons took the inheritance his father had given him and squandered it foolishly. When broke, and after living through some difficult times, the son returned to his father, acknowledging his sin and asking for forgiveness. Without hesitation, the father embraced his son and threw a feast in his honor, for the son he thought he had lost had returned. The older brother, who had remained obedient to his father through this time, thought the special treatment his brother received was unfair, upon which the father told him: "My son, you are always with me, and everything I have is yours. But we had to celebrate and be glad, because this brother of yours was dead and is alive again; he was lost and is found" (Luke 15:31-32).

Just as the story of the prodigal son focuses on the son who squandered his inheritance, so too the story of prophecy focuses on the people Israel, who were promised a special inheritance and position by God, but squandered it through disobedience. The Bible traces this story literally from the beginning, in the book of Genesis to the end, in the book of Revelation. The "end times" really is the story of Israel's return to God after having to go through some very difficult times. In fact, almost all prophecy concerns Israel—with less than a dozen verses in the whole Bible directed specifically toward the Church. The Church may feel this unfair at times, just as the older son did, but the restoration of Israel and the return of it to obedience with God is the central theme of prophecy. In the end, the Church will be rewarded and both Israel and the Church will jointly share in the Father's inheritance, but this is not the primary message of prophecy in the Bible.

The Jewish People

"I will make you into a great nation and I will bless you; I will make your name great and you will be a blessing. I will bless those who bless you, and whoever curses you I will curse; and all peoples on earth will be blessed through you" (Gen. 12:2-3).

The Jews are God's chosen people. Two thousand years before Christ, God made a covenant with a man named Abraham. He promised He would bless Abraham's descendants if Abraham would be obedient to Him. God further defined and sealed this covenant with one branch of Abraham's descendants (the Israelites) when he appeared to Moses on Mount Sinai. God promised to bless Israel above all other nations if they obeyed his commands, but if they disobeyed, God promised that they would encounter trials unlike any other nation. The people of Israel did disobey (see chapter three) and were consequently enslaved, persecuted, and scattered throughout the world.

The miracle of history, however, is that the Israelites have survived as a distinct race of people in spite of the most formidable odds. What other people can trace their national identity back nearly four thousand years? Twice the Jews have had their nation taken from them and were taken as slaves into other nations (first by Babylon and then by Rome); twice they miraculously survived against incomparable odds and tremendous persecution; and twice they miraculously returned to their homeland to reestablish their nation. All of these events have been in accordance with God's plan and prophecies—the most recent of which was Israel's formation of a nation in 1948 and the recapture of Jerusalem in 1967, despite over nineteen centuries of global dispersion and persecution.

There is no question that the people of Israel are one of the greatest phenomena of history. Napoleon once commented that he believed the Jews were the greatest miracle of all time, and when Frederick the Great once asked one of his close counselors to prove the existence of God, the counselor simply answered "The Jews, Your Majesty, the Jews." Certainly, what God has done *to* the Jews, *for* the Jews, and *through* the Jews is unique among all other peoples of the world. Mark Twain captured this uniqueness well in 1899:

> If the statistics are correct, the Jews represent merely one percent of humanity—an irrelevant spark in the light of the Milky Way. Normally speaking, the Jews should hardly be heard of, and yet we heard and hear of them again and again. They can rival any people on the Earth for fame, and their significance in economy and trade are in no ratio to their population. Their contribution to the list of great names in literature, natural science, art, music, finance, medicine and profound learning is just as amazing. They have done extremely well in this world—with their hands tied behind their backs. They could rightly be proud of themselves.
>
> The Egyptians, Babylonians and Persians came into power, filled the Earth with their glory, but perished. The Greeks and Romans followed, made a lot of noise, and then disappeared. Other nations arose, their torches burned for a while and then they were

extinguished, and today they sit in the twilight or are completely disappeared. The Jews saw it all. They beat them all, and are today what they always were, showing no decay, no aging, no weakening, no decline of energy, no blunting of their wide-awake dynamic spirit. Everything is mortal except the Jew. All other powers perish, but he remains. What is the mystery of his immortality? ("Concerning the Jews," Essay, Mark Twain)

The mystery that Mark Twain ponders, of course, is the covenant God made with Abraham over four thousand years ago which singled out the Jewish people as unique from all other races. God wanted a special relationship with a group of people that would reciprocate His love. He chose the Jews.

The Nation of Israel

"I will come to give rest to Israel" (Jer. 31:2).

The physical nation of Israel is tiny. It sits on the Mediterranean Sea and occupies a land about the size of Maryland. Yet, despite its insignificant size and population of only a few million, Israel has continually been at the center of world history. News reports carry daily news from this small nation, and for the last several years, almost half of all of the resolutions of the General Assembly of the United Nations have concerned this country.[1]

Why is Israel so important? There are two reasons. First, Israel is situated on a land bridge—it connects three continents and is geographically at the center of the three, great, people groups of the world: Europeans, Asians, and Africans. Israel is separated from Europe by the Mediterranean Sea, from Asia by the Euphrates River, and from Africa by the Arabian Desert. As such, the physical location of Israel is strategic because whoever controls Israel, controls the trade routes connecting these three continents. Second, and more importantly, Israel stands at the center of God's plan for the world. As mentioned in the previous chapter, Israel was chosen by God to have a special relationship with him. As such, much of history and almost all of prophecy revolve around the tiny nation of Israel and the Jewish people.

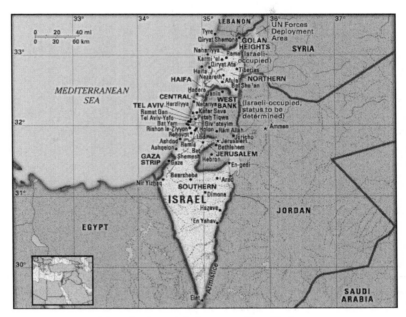

Map 1: Israel & Surrounding Nations

The nation of Israel is also at the heart of a blood feud between two groups (the Jews and the Arabs) that started with the two sons of Abraham more than four millennia ago. This feud has been perpetuated throughout the ages and was intensified when Israel was restored as a nation again in 1948, after almost two millennia of nonexistence. Unfortunately, this conflict will only continue to intensify. The Bible tells us there will be no lasting peace in the Middle East. The feud that started between two brothers and now separates two warring peoples will eventually grow so out of control that Jesus Christ will have to personally intervene to bring an end to it at the battle of Armageddon. It's only at this point that peace will be achieved in the Middle East.

Jerusalem

"This is what the sovereign Lord says: `This is Jerusalem, which I have set in the center of the nations, with countries all around her'"
(Ezek. 5:5).

Jerusalem is God's holy city. The Bible contains more than eight hundred references to Jerusalem and more than 350 prophetic passages relate to the future of this city. The prophet Ezekiel described Jerusalem as "the center of the nations" because it is so central to God's heart and plan for the world. In fact, on ancient maps, Jerusalem was frequently placed at the center of the map, signifying that it was the geographic center of all human activity. It has been common throughout history to refer to Israel as the center of the earth, Jerusalem as the center of Israel, and Mount Zion as the center of Jerusalem.

Why is Jerusalem so important? Because of its great spiritual significance. The city is sacred to three of the world's religions: Judaism, Christianity, and Islam. Each religion has strong ties to the city and has sacred sites within it. Just as New York is considered the great center of commerce and Silicon Valley the center of technology of the world, Jerusalem is considered the spiritual center of the world. One of the reasons for this significance is because it was on Mt. Zion in Jerusalem, where Abraham attempted to offer his son, Isaac, as a sacrifice to God (Gen. 22:2). Mt. Zion then became the place where the nation of Israel built the Temple of God, which is why this place is commonly referred to as the Temple Mount. The Temple Mount is shown on map 2 as a square around the Dome of the Rock – one of Islam's most sacred sites.

Of all the world's great cities, past, present, and future, only Jerusalem will be eternal. While earthquakes will level the cities of the earth in the end times and a great fire will eventually destroy the world, the city of Jerusalem alone will be preserved by God. Only Jerusalem has a divine claim that it will last forever.

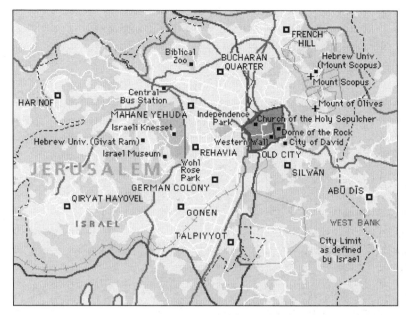

Map 2: The City of Jerusalem

As daily conflicts in the Middle East garner headlines, and diplomats negotiate new plans for peace, it's important to understand God's plan for His chosen people and His chosen city. Indeed, the Bible commands all believers to "Pray for the peace of Jerusalem" (Ps. 122:6).

The Temple

> *"And let them construct a sanctuary for me...and I will dwell among*
> *the sons of Israel and will be their God. And they shall know that I*
> *am the Lord their God who brought them out of the land of Egypt,*
> *that I might dwell among them; I am the Lord their God"*
> *(Exod. 25:8, 29:45-46).*

When Israel first became a nation in the land God had promised Abraham, God instructed the people of Israel to build a temple on

Mount Moriah (also known as Mount Zion) in Jerusalem. The inner sanctuary of this temple, known as the Holy of Holies, was built on the exact spot where Abraham was tested by God and asked to sacrifice his son Isaac.

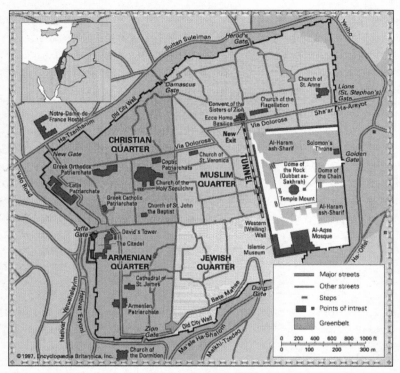

Map 3: The Old City of Jerusalem & Temple Mount

This Temple provided the Israelites with a visible symbol of God's presence. Although there have been countless temples built throughout history by many different religions, the Israelite temple was different. Rather than being a place where God's needs were met, it was a place where God met the needs of His people—God actually ruled the nation of Israel from this Temple in Jerusalem through divine authority. Ancient Israel was the world's only true theocratic form of government—a government ruled by God instead of man.

Four Israelite temples are mentioned in the Bible. Two (Solomon's and Zerubbabel/Herod's) have come and gone, but two more (frequently referred to as the Tribulation Temple and the Millennial Temple) have yet to be built. The final Temple (the Millennial Temple) will be erected by the Lord Jesus Christ Himself when He establishes His kingdom during the Millennial period (see chapter twenty-four). All of these temples have been, or will be, constructed on the Temple Mount in Jerusalem and are described in detail in the chapter that follows.

The Temple Mount is by far the most important and controversial piece of real estate in the world. As mentioned above, it's on these thirty-five acres that Abraham was willing to sacrifice his son Isaac and where the four temples of the Lord have or will be built. It's also on these thirty-five acres where Jesus made His triumphal entry on Palm Sunday to offer Himself to Israel, where Jesus was crucified (on the northernmost part in a place called Calvary), where the Antichrist will demand that the world worship him, and where Jesus will return in the last days to establish his Eternal Kingdom. In addition, it's here where Muslims believe the Prophet Muhammad ascended to heaven. Clearly the Temple Mount is unlike any other place in the world, and even today is at the heart of the issue standing in the way of Middle East peace talks.

Notes

1. Grant R. Jeffrey, *Armageddon: Appointment with Destiny,* 99.

2. Thomas Ice and Timothy Demy, *Jerusalem in Bible Prophecy,* 7-8.

Part 1

Past Prophecy

CHAPTER 3

THE HISTORY OF ISRAEL

"But you, O Israel, my servant... whom I have chosen, you descendants of Abraham my friend, I took you from the ends of the earth, from its farthest corners I called you. I said, `You are my servant; I have chosen you and have not rejected you'" (Isa. 41:8-9).

Timeline of Jewish History

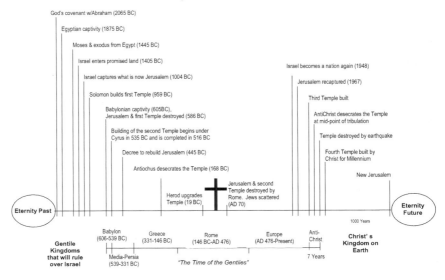

Figure 2: Timeline of the History of Israel

God's Covenant with Abraham

"The Lord said to [Abraham], `Leave your country, your people and your father's household and go to the land I will show you. I will make you into a great nation and I will bless you; I will make your name great, and you will be a blessing. I will bless those who bless you, and whoever curses you I will curse; and all peoples on the earth will be blessed through you'" (Gen. 12:2-3).

"On that day the Lord made a covenant with [Abraham] and said, `To your descendants I give this land, from the river of Egypt to the great river, the Euphrates'" (Gen. 15:18).

Abraham lived about four thousand years ago—about eighteen times longer than the history of the United States. He was the physical father of the Arab and the Jewish nations and is central to understanding three of the world's largest religions, Judaism, Christianity, and Islam. More space is given to recounting his personal life in the Bible than almost any other personality, which speaks to his importance throughout Scripture. Why was Abraham so important? Because he was obedient to God and trusted in Him.

The starting point of Israel's religion (Judaism) was the day when God spoke to Abraham. God told Abraham that if he left the land where he was living (Ur, which is in modern-day Southern Iraq) and moved to a new country, He would make Abraham the founder of a great nation and he would inherit the land that God would show him. This land is what became known as the Promised Land (Gen. 12). But Abraham and his wife Sarah were beyond childbearing age, so it was not clear how God would fulfill this promise. God fulfilled it by miraculously delivering a son to Abraham and Sarah, whom they named Isaac.

God then tested Abraham by asking Abraham to sacrifice his son on an altar, just as he would ordinarily sacrifice an animal as an offering to God. Abraham obeyed God and willingly offered up his son on an altar that he built on Mount Moriah (Gen. 22). Despite the many years of waiting for a son and the love he undoubtedly had for him, Abraham believed that God would keep His promise of making a great nation of his descendants and reasoned that God would raise his son from the dead (Heb. 11:19). God spared Isaac from death at the last minute, and Abraham was proven to be a man of faith in God's eyes because of his obedience and willingness to offer up his only son to God. As a result, Abraham served as an example of what God Himself would do two thousand years later; namely, offer His only son, Jesus Christ, to die on a cross as a sacrifice for the sin of the world. God's blessing today is for those who have faith in God and believe that Jesus Himself was resurrected from the dead.

Below are the prophecies given to Abraham by God. These are known as the "Abrahamic Covenant." It's important to note that the promises made by God to Abraham were unconditional. They did not depend on the obedience of Abraham other than Abraham's physical move from his current location to a new land—something that Abraham did. Rather, these promises were based exclusively on the will of God. God said "I will make you into a great nation," "I will bless you," "I will make your name great," and "I give this land [to you]." This is important, because many false teachings throughout history have argued that for one reason or another, the promises made by God to Abraham were nullified or transferred to a different group of people at some point. Given the unconditional nature of these promises made by God, it's clear that this can't be the case.

Prophecy: Abraham and his wife Sarah would give birth to a son, even though they didn't have any children at the time and both were past childbearing age. Abraham was eighty-five; Sarah was seventy-five (Gen. 15:4, 17:16, 19).

Fulfillment: When Abraham was 100-years-old and Sarah was ninety, they gave birth to a son—Isaac (Genesis 21:2-5). The name Isaac literally means "laughter" because both Sarah and Abraham laughed when God told them that they would bear a child at such an old age (Gen. 17:17, 18:12-15).

Prophecy: Abraham's descendants would inherit all of the land between the Wadi of Egypt (a river) and the Euphrates River (Gen. 13:14-15, 15:18-21, 17:8). This land is known as the Promised Land and roughly corresponds to modern day Israel plus parts of Syria, Lebanon, and Jordan.

Fulfillment: This prophecy was fulfilled about 660 years after it was given when the nation of Israel entered the Promised Land after their exodus from Egypt. Under King Solomon's rule (about 475 years later), Israel did control all of the land God promised to it (Josh. 1:2-6, 21:43, 1 Kings 4:21).

Note: Israel lost its empire to the Babylonians in 605 BC. Although Israel is now once again a nation, it does not control all of the land that it controlled under King Solomon's rule.

Map 4: The Promised Land & King Solomon's Empire

Prophecy: Abraham's descendants would be innumerable, becoming many great nations (Gen. 12:2, 13:16, 15:5, 17:4, 18:18).

Fulfillment: Abraham's descendants became many great nations, among them the nation of Israel and all of the Arab nations.

Prophecy: Abraham's name would become great (Gen. 12:2).

Fulfillment: Abraham is considered the father of, and revered by, three of the world's great religions: Judaism, Christianity, and Islam because he fathered two sons; Ishmael and Isaac. Ishmael's descendants became the Arab nations and their religion is Islam. Isaac's descendants became the Israelites and their religion is Judaism. Christ was descended from Abraham's lineage as well. As a result, Abraham's name has been known as one of the most famous throughout history.

Prophecy: All peoples of the earth would be blessed through Abraham's offspring (Gen. 12:3).

Fulfillment: About two thousand years after Abraham, all peoples of the earth were blessed through his offspring in the form of Jesus Christ who was descended from Abraham.[1] It is through Him that eternal salvation is found for anyone who chooses to put his or her faith in Him (John 3:16).

Prophecy: Abraham's son Ishmael would be the father of twelve rulers (Gen. 17:20).

Fulfillment: Ishmael became the father of twelve tribal rulers: Nebaioth, Kedar, Adbeel, Missam, Mishma, Dumah, Massa, Hadad, Tema, Jetur, Naphish, and Kedamah (Gen. 25:12-16). Ishmael's sons ruled over the lands stretching from Egypt to Babylon in what is now known as the Arabian Peninsula.

Prophecy: Ishmael would become the father of a great nation (Gen. 17:20).

Fulfillment: Ishmael's descendants became the Arab nations of the Middle East.

God's Covenant with Hagar

"I will so increase your descendants that they will be too numerous to count... you will have a son... and he will live in hostility toward all his brothers" (Gen. 16:10-12).

Not believing she could give birth at the age of eighty-five, Sarah ignored God's promise and instructed Abraham to sleep with her servant, Hagar. It was through Hagar that Sarah reckoned she could give Abraham a son. This practice was in accordance with the customs at the time but was not in accordance with God's will. Through Hagar, Abraham had a son who was named Ishmael. However, once Hagar became pregnant, Sarah began to despise and mistreat her, so Hagar fled into the wilderness. An angel of the Lord then appeared and instructed Hagar to return to Abraham and Sarah. It was at this time that God made several promises to Hagar about Ishmael and his descendants.

Prophecy: Ishmael's descendants would be innumerable, becoming many great nations (Gen. 16:10, 17:20, 21:18).

Fulfillment: Ishmael's descendants became the Arab nations.

Prophecy: Ishmael and his descendants would live in hostility toward Isaac and his descendants (Gen. 16:12).

Fulfillment: Isaac and Ishmael never reconciled the differences that started when they were children, and this resentment has been carried down through the ages. Throughout history, the descendants of Ishmael (the Arab nations) have fought with the descendants of Isaac (the Israelites). This family feud has been perpetuated throughout history and stands at the center of today's Middle Eastern conflict.

To fully understand this conflict however, it's important to understand the context. When Hagar bore Ishmael, it wasn't until fourteen years later when Sarah would have Isaac. Because of this, Abraham became very attached to Ishmael, his only son at the time, and Sarah became jealous. Once Isaac was born, Sarah insisted that Hagar and Ishmael be sent away. Abraham reluctantly agreed, and sent Hagar and Ishmael into the wilderness with a supply of food and water. However, when the water was gone, Ishmael approached death and Hagar began to sob over her dying son. It was then that an angel of the Lord appeared, reiterated the covenant God had made with Hagar and rescued them both from dying of thirst (Gen 21:9-18). Because of this, one can begin to understand the animosity and hatred that Ishmael must have felt toward his brother Isaac. Not only did Ishmael lose his father at the age of fourteen when he was sent away and almost die as a result of this banishment, but he also saw Abraham's temporal and eternal inheritance left to his younger brother which was not the custom at the time. Ishmael would naturally have felt betrayed, angry and jealous of Isaac.

In fact, the ongoing debate about who has the right to occupy modern day Palestine is the direct result of disagreements about which son inherited Abraham's covenant from God regarding the Promised Land. At issue is whether Ishmael was entitled to Abraham's covenant because he was the firstborn son of Abraham (and, as custom held, was entitled to it) or whether Isaac received the covenant because God specifically passed the blessing to him and not to Ishmael (Gen. 17:18-21, 21:12). The debate was intensified in AD 610 when Muhammad, the prophet of Islam, claimed that he received a divine revelation from Allah that it was Ishmael, not Isaac, who was almost sacrificed on the Temple Mount and was the one designated by God to receive Abraham's blessing. Muhammad's revelations were collected into the Koran, the Holy book of Islam, which states that the Jewish faith is based on lies and deceptions and that the Jews distorted the Holy word of God from the beginning to steal Abraham's covenant away from Ishmael and the Arab people. It is for this reason the Arab people lay claim to Palestine, the covenant of Abraham, the Temple Mount, and the one true religion of God as their own.

God's Covenant with Isaac

"I will be with you and will bless you. For you and your descendants
I will give all these lands and will confirm the oath I swore to your

father Abraham. I will make your descendants as numerous as the stars of the sky and will give them all these lands, and through your offspring all nations on the earth will be blessed, because Abraham obeyed me and kept my requirements, my commands, my decrees and my laws" (Gen. 26:3-5).

Isaac was the son of Abraham and Sarah. The Bible states that it was Isaac whom Abraham attempted to offer up as a sacrifice to God on Mount Moriah. God appeared to Isaac during his life and specifically conferred upon him the promises that he had made to Abraham. This is significant, because although Ishmael was Abraham's firstborn son (and thus entitled to the birth right), Isaac was the firstborn son of Abraham and Sarah and the one whom God chose to receive His promises. Among Isaac's descendants were many great men of the Bible including Joseph, Moses, Joshua, Gideon, and David. All of these men were able to claim Isaac's God-given covenant as their own.

God's Covenant with Jacob

"I will give you and your descendants the land on which you are lying. Your descendants will be like the dust of the earth...all peoples on the earth will be blessed through you and your offspring...I will not leave you until I have done what I have promised you" (Gen. 28:13-15).

The history of Israel as a nation began with Abraham's grandson Jacob (who was later renamed Israel) and his twelve sons, from whom the twelve tribes of Israel descended. Isaac was Jacob's father and had twin sons—Esau and Jacob. Esau was the firstborn and as the oldest, should have inherited the promises God gave to Abraham. The birthright gave the eldest son precedence over his brothers and assured him a double share of his father's inheritance. However, when Esau and Jacob were both young, Esau sold his birthright to Jacob for a bowl of soup (Gen. 25:27-34). Later, when Isaac was on his deathbed and was blind due to age, Jacob deceived him by pretending to be Esau and received the blessing that was intended for his brother. This blessing ensured that Esau's descendants would be subservient to Jacob's and that Jacob would inherit all of the promises God made to Abraham (Gen. 27, 28:3-4). Later, God appeared to Jacob in a dream (where he saw a stairway to heaven) and explicitly reaffirmed that the covenant He had made with Abraham would be inherited by Jacob and his descendants:

Prophecy: God would give Jacob's descendants the Promised Land (Gen. 28:13, 15).

Fulfillment: Roughly six hundred years after this promise was made, Moses led Jacob's descendants out of Egypt and into the Promised Land. After numerous victories in battle, the Israelites defeated the kings of Canaan and settled in what is now known as Israel. During Solomon's rule (about 475 years later), Israel did control all of the land God promised to it (Josh. 1:2-6, 21:43, 1 Kings 4:21).

Prophecy: Jacob's descendants would be very numerous (Gen. 28:14)

Fulfillment: Jacob's descendants were numerous—his sons became the patriarchs of the twelve tribes of Israel from which the Jewish people are descended.

Prophecy: All peoples of the earth would be blessed through Jacob's offspring (Gen. 28:14).

Fulfillment: All people of the earth were blessed through Jesus Christ, a descendant of Jacob. It is through Him that people receive salvation (John 3:16).

Prophecy: God would protect the Israelites and be with them wherever they went. He would not leave them until He had done all that He promised to do (Gen. 28:15).

Fulfillment: Unlike any other nation in history, Israel has maintained their unique identity as a people even though they have been enslaved, relentlessly persecuted, and frequently without a sovereign nation for most of their four thousand years of existence. Surely, God has protected the people of Israel just as He said He would do.

The Egyptian Captivity

"Know for certain that your descendants will be strangers in a country not their own, and they will be enslaved and mistreated four hundred years" (Gen. 15:13).

When God made His covenant with Abraham and promised to make his descendants a great nation, God also told Abraham of a future captivity his descendants would endure and how they would be released from this captivity.

Prophecy: Abraham's descendants would be enslaved by a foreign nation and mistreated for four hundred years (Gen. 15:13).

Fulfillment: One hundred ninety years after this prophecy was given, the Egyptians enslaved the people of Israel. This captivity lasted for 430 years (from 1875 BC when they were taken captive, to 1485 BC when they were delivered by Moses). The four hundred years in the prophecy above might have been an approximation; or it might be that the time of captivity was actually four hundred years, and the 430 year figure recorded in the Bible for the captivity includes the time between the last confirmation of the Abrahamic covenant and the giving of the Mosaic Law.

How did Jacob's descendants fall into slavery? Essentially what happened is that eleven of Jacob's sons turned on their brother Joseph and sold him into slavery at a young age. Joseph was then carried off to Egypt where he rose in favor and power under Pharaoh. God then warned Joseph of a coming famine that was going to come upon the land. Pharaoh, under the direction of Joseph, started stockpiling food in preparation for this coming famine. When the famine hit, Jacob's sons traveled to Egypt in search of food where they were reunited with Joseph. Jacob and his eleven sons then moved to Egypt where they were provided food and taken care of by Joseph (Gen. 37-47).

While in Egypt, the Israelites multiplied greatly. After the death of Joseph, a new Pharaoh rose to power in Egypt who did not know about Joseph. He perceived the growing number of Israelites as a threat. As a result, this new Pharaoh (Ahmose I) decided to enslave the people of Israel and to kill every newborn male so as to reduce the future numbers of Israelites and the perceived risk to his kingdom. The people of Israel then endured this captivity in hard labor until the time of their exodus under Moses 430 years later.

Prophecy: Abraham's descendants would come out of captivity with great possessions (Gen. 15:14).

Fulfillment: When the Israelites left Egypt, they plundered it and took with them silver, gold, flocks, herds, clothing and many other items from the Egyptians (Exod. 12:32, 35-36).

God's Covenant with Moses & the People of Israel

"Now if you obey me fully and keep my covenant, then out of all nations you will be my treasured possession. Although the whole earth is mine, you will be for me a kingdom of priests and a holy nation...the people all responded together `We will do everything the Lord has said'" (Exod. 19:4-8).

The story of Moses is well known. After more than four hundred years, God led a man named Moses to deliver the people of Israel from their captivity. He did this under the direction of God by bringing ten severe plagues upon Egypt. The tenth plague, which is what finally convinced the Pharaoh to let the people of Israel go free, caused the firstborn male of every Egyptian household to die. This plague was known as the Passover and protection from this plague is an event that Jewish people still celebrate today.

After Moses led the people of Israel out of captivity in Egypt, they wandered around the wilderness for forty years. The question of why it took forty years to travel a straight-line distance of only about 240 miles is rather startling. The answer is because the forty years wandering the wilderness wasn't so much a journey, as much as it was a death sentence for those who had refused the opportunity to enter the Promised Land. Within about one year of leaving Egypt, the Bible records that Israel reached Palestine and sent twelve scouts into the Promised Land to see what the land was like and whether the people who lived there were strong or weak. What they found was a land truly blessed with natural abundance. However, it was also occupied by formidable Canaanite forces, which caused all of the scouts, except Joshua and Caleb, to lose courage, so they gave a false report to the people. This in turn caused the people to lose heart, and actually want to return to their slavery in Egypt. At one point they were about to stone Moses, Aaron, Joshua and Caleb who desperately tried to encourage the people to remain obedient and courageous, but they wouldn't listen (Deut. 13:1-14:30).

It was a very costly mistake. As a result of their lack of faith, God declared that everyone twenty years old or older would not be able to enter the Promised land, except Caleb and Joshua: "According to the number of the days in which you spied out the land, forty days, for every day a year, you shall bear your iniquity, forty years" (Deut. 14:29-34). As a result, the generation that refused to enter the Promised Land turned back and wandered around and around in the wilderness until they all died off. For those who rebelled against God, the Exodus became a journey without a destination, and for the others, it became a matter of taking the long route home.

During this time however, God reaffirmed the covenant He made with Abraham and expanded on it. This new covenant became known as the Mosaic Covenant because it was given to the people of Israel through Moses. In this new covenant, God promised that if Israel obeyed His commandments, He would treat them as His treasured possession. He would make them a kingdom of priests, with direct access to God, and a holy nation. The people of Israel affirmed this covenant and agreed to "do everything the Lord had said" (Exod. 19:3-8). This expanded covenant included the Ten Commandments as well as various other commandments that became known as the Mosaic Law.

The Israelites, however, promptly broke God's commandments by making and worshiping idols (Exod. 32:1-10). They then repented of this sin, and God renewed the covenant He had made with them. God promised to bless them above every nation of the earth and do wonders for them never before done for any nation in the world if they remained obedient to Him (Exod. 34:10, Deut. 28:1). However, as part of this renewed covenant, God promised that if they disobeyed Him again, they would be disciplined. Moses prophesied that this discipline would take the form of two future dispersions, when the nation of Israel would be taken from their country and scattered throughout the nations:

Prophecy: The first time the Israelites disobeyed God, they would be conquered by an as-of-yet unknown nation whose language they did not understand. This nation would lay siege to Jerusalem (Deut. 28:36, 49, 52).

Fulfillment: The first conquering of Jerusalem was by Babylon in 586 BC, which laid siege to, and then destroyed Jerusalem. Babylon did not exist in 1410 BC when Moses made this prophecy, and the Babylonian language was Aramaic, not Hebrew as spoken in Jerusalem.

Prophecy: The second time the Israelites disobeyed God, the survivors would be scattered throughout the world in every nation. They would worship idols, be relentlessly persecuted and be without a country. They would be transported in ships back to Egypt and offered as slaves (Deut. 4:27-31, 28:64-68).

Fulfillment: The city of Jerusalem was rebuilt during the Media-Persian Empire but was destroyed again by Rome in AD 70 after a Jewish rebellion. When the Roman Empire invaded Jerusalem, those who survived were shipped off to slave markets in Egypt. Jews were then banished from the city of Jerusalem. In what became known as the "Diaspora," Jews fled to all parts of the known world. For the next two thousand years, the Jewish people wandered the earth with no country of their own in constant fear of persecution and death.

This was the case until 1948, when Israel was once again re-established as a nation.

The Establishment of Israel as a Nation

"Get ready [Joshua] to cross the Jordan River into the land I am about to give them—to the Israelites. I will give you every place where you set your foot, as I promised Moses. Your territory will extend from the desert to Lebanon, and from the great river, the Euphrates—all the Hittite country—to the Great Sea on the West. No one will be able to stand up against you all the days of your life...Be strong and courageous, because you will lead these people to inherit the land I swore to their forefathers to give them" (Josh. 1:2-6).

After wandering in the wilderness for forty years, the people of Israel finally entered the Promised Land in 1405 BC (Josh. 1:1-9). Just prior to entering the Promised Land, Moses died and Joshua was commissioned as his successor. Moses himself was not allowed to lead the people into the Promised Land because he at one point disobeyed God and failed to have faith in Him (Num. 20:1-12).

Under the direction of Joshua and at the instruction of God, the people of Israel then proceeded to engage in battles with the kings of Canaan in the land of Palestine. After numerous victories with the help of God, Israel eventually conquered Canaan and settled what is now known as the nation of Israel. This was in accordance with the covenant God had made with Abraham that his descendants would possess the land of Palestine.

For the first 350 years of the nation, Israel was a theocracy—a nation ruled by God and His laws as administered by a series of judges. These judges were military and civil leaders that oversaw the nation. The last of these judges was Samuel, who appeared during a very dark time in Israel's history and called the people back to faith in the one true God. As Samuel grew old, the people of Israel, in accordance with prophecy, demanded that Samuel appoint a king to succeed him. With great reluctance, Samuel conceded and appointed Saul, followed by David, as king.

Prophecy: In 1406 BC, just prior to entering the Promised Land, Moses predicted that the people of Israel would want a king to be like all of the other nations—this despite the fact the nation was being ruled by God Himself (Deut. 17:14).

Fulfillment: After the people of Israel entered the Promised Land, conquered it, and took possession of it, they asked to have a king appointed to be like all of the other nations (1 Sam. 8:5). So, in 1050 BC, about 350 years after the prophecy was made, Samuel appointed Saul as Israel's first king.

God's Covenant with David

"I will make your name great, like the names of the greatest men of the earth. Your house and your kingdom will endure forever before me; your throne will be established forever" (2 Sam. 7:9, 16).

Four hundred years after the people of Israel entered the Promised Land, David became their king. David was Israel's greatest king—the Bible describes him as "a man after God's own heart" (1 Sam. 13:14). God made several promises to David (known as the Davidic Covenant), which further defined God's plan for Israel.

Prophecy: David's name would become great (2 Sam. 7:9).

Fulfillment: David became one of the greatest heroes of ancient history. David was a great king, a great soldier, and a great poet (having written the Psalms to God). He united the kingdom of Israel and captured the city of Jerusalem, which became the political and religious center of the nation of Israel. Jerusalem became known as the City of David.

Prophecy: David would have a son who would succeed him and establish his kingdom. This son would build the Temple of God (2 Sam. 7:12-13).

Fulfillment: David had a son, Solomon, who became Israel's wisest and most magnificent king. He made Israel rich and built the first Temple to God in Jerusalem. Solomon's reign was considered Israel's golden age.

Prophecy: David's house (i.e., family line) and kingdom would be established forever (2 Sam. 7:13, 16; Ps. 89:4, 29).

Partial Fulfillment: Christ was a descendant of David (Matt. 1:6). During the Millennium, Christ will establish His kingdom, which will never end, thus fulfilling the prophecy that David's family line would be established forever.

Note: The covenant God made with David did not necessarily guarantee uninterrupted rule by David's family on the throne. In fact the covenant specified that if David's descendants sinned, God would punish them (2 Sam. 7:14-16), and He did—by interrupting the kingdom during the Babylonian exile. God did, however, promise that the right to rule would always remain with David's dynasty. Some have tried to argue that the covenant that God made with David was not literal due to the unusually long nature of this promise. David, however, specifically raised the question of the longevity of this promise himself to God, clearly indicating that he took the promise as being a literal one (2 Sam. 7:18-29).

The First Temple (Solomon's) & the Ark of the Covenant

"There, above the corner between the two cherubim that are over the ark of the Testimony, I will meet with you and give you all my commands for the Israelites...There I will meet with you and speak with you; there also I will meet with the Israelites, and the place will be consecrated by my glory" (Exod. 25:22, 29:42-43).

During the time the people of Israel were wandering in the wilderness after their exodus from Egypt, God instructed them to build the Ark of the Covenant. The Ark of the Covenant was an ornate gold overlaid box (about 4x2.5x2.5 ft.) made of acacia wood that contained three items: the tablets the Ten Commandments were written on, the rod Aaron had used to perform miracles before the pharaoh of Egypt, and a golden pot of manna—the daily bread God provided to the people of Israel for forty years while they were in the wilderness. The rod symbolized God's supernatural deliverance of Israel from Egypt; the manna symbolized God's daily provision for His people; and the tablets represented God's divine law for His people. The Ark therefore, served as a symbol of God's presence in guiding His people. The Israelites believed the Ark was the embodiment of God Himself and that the Lord dwelt in a dark cloud that existed just above the Ark. The Ark was carried by the people of Israel throughout their wanderings in the wilderness and into the Promised Land. It preceded Israel into numerous victorious battles, and God used it to perform various miracles.

Figure 3: Artist's Impression of the Ark of the Covenant

Construction of the first Temple began during the reign of David's son, King Solomon. Although it had been David's desire to build the first Temple, God did not permit it since David was a man of war rather than peace (1 Kings 5:3; 2 Sam. 7:1-13). The purpose of the Temple was to create "a house of rest for the Ark of the Covenant of the Lord." Construction of the first Temple began in the fourth year of Solomon's reign and was completed seven years later in 959 BC (1 Kings 6:1, 37-38). The Temple was built on Mount Moriah in Jerusalem. This is the same site where Abraham had offered up his son Isaac on an altar as a sacrifice to God. It is commonly believed that the holiest part of the Temple (the "Holy of Holies"—where the Ark of the Covenant rested) was built on the exact spot where Abraham had built his altar to God eleven hundred years earlier. The Bible provides detailed accounts of the Temple's construction in 1 Kings 5-8 and 2 Chronicles 2.

The Divided Kingdom

In 931 BC, after the rule of David and Solomon, the Southern tribes of Judah and Benjamin revolted against the ten Northern tribes. After this, Judah (the Southern kingdom) and Israel (the Northern kingdom) were each ruled by numerous kings, most of who disobeyed God's commandments and in so doing, violated the Mosaic Covenant. These kings ruled from 931 BC until 605 BC when Israel was taken captive by Babylon.

The First Destruction of Jerusalem and the Temple

"For when I brought your forefathers out of Egypt and spoke to them, I did not just give them commands about burnt offerings and sacrifices, but I gave them this command: Obey me, and I will be your God and you will be my people. Walk in all my ways I command you, that it may go well with you. But they did not listen or pay attention; instead, they followed the stubborn inclinations of their evil hearts. They went backward and not forward. From the time your forefathers left Egypt until now, day after day, again and again I sent you my servants the prophets. But they did not listen or pay attention. They were stiff-necked and did more evil than their forefathers. The people of Judah have done evil in my eyes" (Jer. 7:22-30).

"As you have forsaken me and served foreign gods in your own land, so now you will serve foreigners in a land not your own" (Jer. 5:19).

Because Israel disobeyed the Lord and broke the Mosaic Covenant, the Lord sent various prophets (Obadiah, Joel, Jonah, Amos, Hosea,

Isaiah, Micah, Nahum, Zephaniah, and Habakkuk) to warn the people of Israel of the consequences of their sin and to pronounce His judgment upon them. This judgment was certain destruction of the nation by the hands of foreign invaders if Israel did not turn from their ways. The people of Israel did not listen to the prophets and continued to disobey, so God sent Babylon to invade and destroy the nation (Jer. 5:19, 7:22-34). The story of Israel's disobedience, the warning given by the prophets, Israel's first dispersion into Babylon, and their return from this first dispersion fills the majority of the Old Testament. The prophets delivered their messages to the people of Israel starting 234 years prior to the invasion and right up to the year of the actual invasion. The prophecies delivered to the people included the following:

Prophecy: Babylon would invade Judah, the Southern kingdom of Israel. They would lay siege to and then destroy Jerusalem and the Temple. The country would be left desolate (Isa. 1:7, 3:1, 6:11-13, 39:6; Jer. 4:5-26, 16, 6:1, 6, 22-23, 19:8-9; Mic. 3:12).

The survivors, along with their treasures, would be carried off to Babylon as slaves (Isa. 5:13a, 22:3, 39:7, Jer. 6, 20:4-5, Ezek. 4:1-7).

Fulfillment: In 605 BC, King Nebuchadnezzar of Babylon laid siege to Jerusalem and defeated Jehoiakim, the King of Judah (the Southern kingdom of Israel). Nebuchadnezzar then carried off many Israelites (including the prophet Daniel), along with some of the articles from the Temple to Babylon (Dan. 1:1-2). Judah then became a subject state of Babylon and had to pay taxes to Nebuchadnezzar (2 Kings 24:1). Israel was now no longer a sovereign nation and for the first time since its founding, was under the control of another world power. This began what is known as the "time of the Gentiles" described in the next chapter.

In 601 BC, after a fierce battle with the Babylonians, the Egyptians encouraged Judah to rebel. Nebuchadnezzar crushed the rebellion in 597 BC. Jehoiachin, the king of Judah at the time, and many of the country's leaders, laborers, and craftsmen (including the prophet Ezekiel) were taken to Babylon in exile (2 Kings 24:10-16).

In 588 BC, despite the two prior attempts, Zedekiah, a puppet king placed on the throne of Judah by Nebuchadnezzar, appealed to the Egyptians for help and once again rebelled. On 15 January 588 BC, Nebuchadnezzar again invaded Judah and laid siege to Jerusalem. After about thirty months, the city was taken on 16 July 586 BC, and the rebellion crushed. Jewish people still commemorate this tragic day which is known as "Tisha b' Av" (the ninth of the Jewish month of Av).

Zedekiah and the remaining survivors (including the prophet Jeremiah) were carried off as slaves to Babylon. Nebuchadnezzar plundered the Temple, carrying off various articles (including the bronze pillars of the Temple). He then set fire to and destroyed the city of Jerusalem along with Solomon's Temple (Jer. 39:1-10, 52:1-23, 2 Kings 20b-25:21). Zedekiah was forced to watch his two sons being executed, and then his eyes were poked out.

Prophecy: Members of the royal family would serve in the palace of the king of Babylon (Isa. 39:5-7).

Fulfillment: Members of the royal family, including the prophet Daniel, did serve in the palace of King Nebuchadnezzar (Dan. 1:2, 2 Kings 24:15-16).

Prophecy: The captivity would last seventy years, after which, the Israelites would return to the city of Jerusalem (Jer. 25:11, 29:10).

Fulfillment: The Babylonian captivity lasted exactly seventy years (until the Media-Persian Empire conquered Babylon): from 605 BC when Nebuchadnezzar first conquered Jerusalem and carried off many Israelites to Babylon to 536 BC when the Israelites returned to Jerusalem and started reconstruction of the Temple.

Note: The Jewish year is very different than our own. It is lunar-solar and had only twelve months of thirty days each, for a total of 360 days, as opposed to the solar year used today which consists of 365.25 days (see *Appendix F*). As a result, it is necessary to convert between these two calendars when evaluating prophecies such as this one that have specific, measurable time frames that can be computed.

In this case, the seventy years given in this prophecy for the duration of the Babylonian captivity is almost exactly 69 years of time on the Jewish calendar, which maps precisely to the actual period of captivity which lasted from 605 BC to 536 BC.

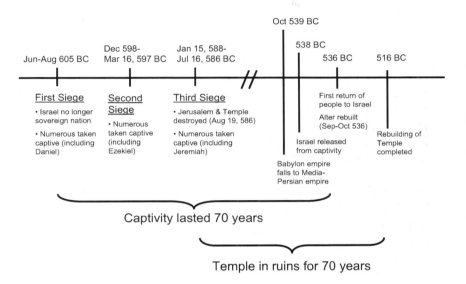

Figure 4: The Babylonian Captivity

Prophecy: The Temple would be in ruins for seventy years (Zech. 1:12-16)

Fulfillment: The Temple was destroyed and lay in ruins for exactly seventy years: from 586 BC when Nebuchadnezzar destroyed Jerusalem and the Temple, to 516 BC when reconstruction of the Temple was completed.

The Second Temple (Zerubbabel's)

"I will...bring you back from captivity. I will gather you from all the nations and places where I have banished you...and will bring you back to the place from which I carried you into exile" (Jer. 29:14).

"Of Cyrus...he will say of Jerusalem, `Let it be rebuilt,' and of the temple, `Let its foundations be laid.' He will rebuild my city and set my exiles free, but not for a price or reward" (Isa. 44:28, 45:13).

After the Medes conquered Babylon in 539 BC, Cyrus, the ruler of the Medes, permitted the Israelites to return to their homeland to rebuild the Temple. In 536 BC, fifty thousand Jews under the leadership of Zerubbabel left their captivity in Babylon and returned to Jerusalem. The rebuilding process began in 535 BC and was completed in 516 BC. Although this second Temple was approximately the same size as the original Temple, it was very modest compared to the Temple that Solomon built. It was not nearly as ornate and was missing one key component—the Ark of the Covenant. As a result, the Holy of Holies was empty, and the glory of God that was present in the first Temple seemed absent in the second. In fact, according to Roman historian Tacitus, when the Roman general Pompeii visited Jerusalem, he marched into the Temple and the Holy of Holies. He immediately came back out and declared, "It's empty. There's nothing there but darkness."

The Bible records several prophecies about this Temple and its rebuilding. These were given to the people of Israel prior to, and during, the time of their captivity in Babylon:

Prophecy: After seventy years of captivity, an as-of-yet unknown king named Cyrus would see that Jerusalem and the Temple were rebuilt by allowing the Jews to return to the land of Israel (Isa. 14:1, 44:26-45:13; Jer. 25:11-12, 29:10-14).

Fulfillment: In 538 BC, one year after Cyrus conquered Babylon, he issued a decree to free the Jewish captives and sent them to Jerusalem with a requisition for materials to help rebuild the Temple (2 Chron.

36:22-23, Ezra 1:1-11). The Israelites took with them all of their wealth, contributions from those remaining in Babylon, and according to tradition, contributions from Cyrus himself. Cyrus wasn't even born when Isaiah's prophecy was originally given (which was one hundred fifty years prior), and Isaiah died fifty years before the Babylonian captivity occurred, so the fact that his name is the same as what prophecy predicted, is astonishing.

Prophecy: Cyrus would see to it that the city of Jerusalem would be rebuilt, but not for a price or reward (Isa. 45:13).

Fulfillment: When Cyrus conquered Babylon, he released the Jewish people from captivity in Babylon in accordance with his policy of encouraging subject people to return to their homelands. This was done to win favor with his subjects and reduce the probability of rebellion. Cyrus's contributions toward the rebuilding of Jerusalem and the Temple were given as an additional token to win favor with his new subjects. Hence, Jerusalem was rebuilt, but not for a price or reward just as the Bible predicted more than 150 years before it happened.

The Rebuilding of Jerusalem

The Temple was completed by 516 BC, but the city of Jerusalem was not fully restored. It wasn't until 445 BC, when the Media-Persian ruler Artaxerxes Longimanus issued a decree to "restore and rebuild Jerusalem" that work began in earnest to restore the city itself. This work was completed in 396 BC.

Antiochus Epiphanes and The Abomination of Desolation

During the Greek Empire in 175 BC, at a time when the Jewish people were enjoying a time of relative peace, a man named Antiochus IV Epiphanes rose to power in Syria and captured Jerusalem. Antiochus was set on imposing Greek culture and religion on the Jewish people (called Hellenization). To accomplish this,

Antiochus tried to eradicate belief in and worship of, the God of Israel. He plundered the Temple, forbade worship on the Sabbath, stopped Temple sacrifices, and ordered the destruction of all ancient Jewish Scriptures. He then commanded the Jewish people to eat forbidden food and desecrated the Temple of God by sacrificing a pig on the altar. Worst of all, Antiochus stood in the Temple and declared himself to be a god (Zeus incarnate), erected an idol with his likeness, and demanded that Jewish people worship him. In the process, Antiochus massacred many Jewish people.

The Bible contains numerous prophecies about this man and his terrible actions. These prophecies were all given to the prophet Daniel more than three centuries before Antiochus was even born. Antiochus is significant because he is seen in the Bible as a forerunner of the Antichrist (a person who will arise during the end times who is described later in this book). Frequently in the Bible and throughout history, one event serves as a foreshadow, or a prototype, for a later event. Antiochus and his desecration of the Temple were this for the Antichrist.

Prophecy: In the later part of the kingdom of Greece, a king would arise that would:

• Cause deceit to prosper (Dan. 8:12; 25, 11:23).

• Consider himself superior (Dan. 8:25).

• Be destroyed—but not by human power (Dan. 8:25).

Fulfillment: Antiochus IV Epiphanes came out of Syria in 175 BC, just thirty years before the end of the Greek empire. Antiochus:

• Rose to power through deceit (Antiochus was not the rightful successor to the Seleucid throne—he seized power while the rightful heir to the throne was still very young).

• Was conceited—he took the name of "Epiphanes" which means "Select of God." His subjects however, made a pun on his name, calling him "Epinanes" or "madman."

• Died in 164 BC in Persia through illness (i.e., God destroyed him).

Prophecy: The king who would arise would be very strong. He would cause astounding devastation and be very prosperous (Dan. 8:12, 24).

Fulfillment: Antiochus IV Epiphanes was very strong and successful. He was involved in a war against Egypt from 171 to 168 BC and defeated two Egyptian kings, Ptolemy VI and Ptolemy VIII. He captured Jerusalem, slaughtered tens of thousands of Jews, and later he won victories over the Armenians and Persians.

Prophecy: The king would persecute and seek to destroy the Jews (Dan. 8:10; 24, 11:30; 33).

Fulfillment: Antiochus relentlessly persecuted the Jews during his reign—he killed fifty thousand Jews and sold an additional forty thousand into slavery. In 170 BC, he ordered the murder of the High Priest, Onias III and issued a decree outlawing the Jewish religion.

Prophecy: The king would desecrate the Temple and set himself up to be a god (Dan. 8:11, 11:31).

Fulfillment: When Antiochus invaded Jerusalem, he plundered the Temple. He then declared Mosaic ceremonies illegal and erected a statue of Zeus (which had a face that looked like Antiochus himself on it) in the Holy of Holies in the Temple. On 15 December 168 BC, Antiochus committed what is referred to as "the abomination of desolation" by dedicating the Temple to the god Jupiter Olympus and offering pig's flesh on the altar (something that was forbidden by Jewish law). He then required all Jews, under the threat of death, to sacrifice pigs to the Greek gods on their altars.

Prophecy: The king would stop the daily sacrifice in the Temple for 2300 days (Dan. 8:11, 14, 11:31).

Fulfillment: Antiochus stopped daily sacrifice in the Temple for somewhere between 2276 and 2306 days. Although the exact day sacrifices were stopped in the Temple is not known, historians identify the month as September 171 BC, when peaceful relations between Antiochus and the Jews came to an end. On 15 December 168 BC, Antiochus desecrated the Temple by sacrificing a pig on the altar of God. Three years later on 25 December 165 BC following a Jewish revolt, Judas Maccabeus restored the Temple for worship (the Jewish holidays Hanukkah and the Feast of Lights celebrate this event). Thus, the time that the sacrifices were stopped by Antiochus was somewhere between 2276 and 2306 days—most likely the 2300 days that the Bible predicted.

Note: Many other prophecies concerning this king are contained in Daniel 11:21-35.

Herod's Temple

Despite the fact the people of Israel had been allowed to return to their homeland to rebuild the Temple and the city of Jerusalem during the time of the Media-Persian Empire, Israel was not a sovereign nation—it was still under the control of a foreign power. This would be the case for centuries to come. After two hundred years, the Media-Persian Empire fell to the Greek Empire, which eventually fell to the Roman Empire (see chapter on the "Great Gentile Kingdoms of the Earth"). It is during the time of the Roman Empire that Jesus walked the earth.

When Rome conquered Judea (the territory formerly known as Israel) in 63 BC, the Jewish kingship was abolished, and Judea was required to pay taxes to Rome. Herod the Great was then installed as a puppet king by Rome to oversee the territory. During his reign, in an effort to appease and gain favor with the Jews, Herod had the Temple remodeled and greatly expanded. The initial work took about ten years and concluded in 19 BC, although some construction continued until AD 64.

It is in this second (upgraded) Temple that Jesus carried out His ministry. The upgraded Temple was magnificent and was considered one of the marvels of the ancient world. In fact, Jesus' disciples were so impressed with it that they called attention to the building at one point during Jesus' ministry. The Lord then shocked them with His prediction that the Temple would be destroyed in the future and not one stone would be left standing (Matt. 24:1-2). More significantly, Christ redefined the very purpose of the Temple. During His ministry, he was asked by the Jews to show miraculous signs. Christ answered them: "'Destroy this temple, and I will raise it again in three days.' The Jews replied, 'It has taken forty-six years to build this temple, and you are going to raise it in three days?' But the temple he had spoken of was his body" (John 2:18-21).

What Christ taught actually redefined the meaning of the Temple. With one statement, Christ claimed to be the Temple—the very presence of God among the people of Israel. He declared that "one greater than the temple is here" (Matt. 12:6). With Christ's coming, the whole purpose of the Temple—to provide a place for the Jewish people to meet with God—had become obsolete. Instead of needing a place where Jewish people could offer sacrifices to make atonement for their sins, Christ Himself became the final sacrifice and through His death, atoned for the sins of everyone.

The Second Destruction of Jerusalem and the Temple

"O Jerusalem, Jerusalem, you who kill the prophets and stone those sent to you, how often I have longed to gather your children together, as a hen gathers her chicks under her wings, but you were not willing. Look, your house is left to you desolate. For I tell you, you will not see me again until you say, 'Blessed is he who comes in the name of the Lord'" (Matt. 23:37-29).

"The days will come upon you when your enemies will build an embankment against you and encircle you and hem you in on every side. They will dash you to the ground, you and the children within your walls. They will not leave one stone on another, because you did not recognize the time of God's coming to you" (Luke 19:43-44).

During His ministry, Jesus grieved for the city of Jerusalem and wept because of the unbelief of the city's inhabitants (Matt. 23:37-39). He then clearly foretold of the devastation that was yet to come to the city and the nation of Israel—devastation also foretold by the prophet Daniel more than five hundred years earlier. This devastation would take the form of yet another destruction of the city and the Temple yet to come:

Prophecy:

• The city of Jerusalem and the Temple would be destroyed a second time—after the coming of the Messiah (Dan. 9:26).

• The destroyers would encircle the city and lay siege to it. They would then kill the Israelites within the city walls (Luke 19:43). Those who survived would be taken captive and transported back to Egypt in slave ships (Deut. 28:68).

• This would all happen in the same generation that Christ lived (Luke 21:23-24, Matt. 23:36).

Fulfillment: After a Jewish revolt in AD 66 (less than thirty-five years after the death of Christ), the Roman general Titus, the son of Emperor Vespasian, was sent to crush the Jews. He encircled the city and laid siege to it for three and a half years before it fell. When Titus and the Roman legions entered the city, they slaughtered hundreds of thousands of Jews. Those who survived were shipped off to slave markets in Egypt.

Prophecy: The destruction of the Temple would be complete—not one stone would be left on another (Matt. 24:2, Mark 13:2, Luke 19:44, 21:6). The city of Jerusalem would be plowed like a field, and the Temple Mount would be overgrown with thickets (Mic. 3:12).

Fulfillment: The city of Jerusalem and the Temple were completely leveled in AD 70 and the years that followed. The second Temple was destroyed on "Tisha b' Av" (the ninth day of the Jewish month Av), which is the same day that the first Temple was destroyed. When the Jewish Zealots saw that the Roman assault on the Temple being led by Titus was forthcoming and unstoppable, they decided to let the second Temple fall on the exact tragic day of the year when the first Temple had fallen to Babylon.

Despite Titus giving his soldiers strict orders not to destroy the Temple, which was the most beautiful building in the Roman Empire, the Roman centurions threw torches into the Temple, and it caught fire within minutes. Titus was a shocked eyewitness. Flavius Josephus (a Jewish historian) reported that General Titus made a vain attempt to save at least the inner sanctuary of the Temple from destruction. He failed, and the entire Temple was destroyed. In the inferno, the tremendous heat melted the sheets of gold that covered much of the Temple building. The gold ran into the seams between the stones. Afterward, in an attempt to recover the gold, the Roman soldiers tore apart the stone walls using wedges and crowbars, thus fulfilling precisely the prophecy of Jesus that not one stone would be left on another (Matt. 24:2).[2]

In AD 71, one year after the destruction, the Roman army plowed the city and the Temple Mount. In exact fulfillment of prophecy, weeds and thickets then grew on the Temple Mount.

When the Romans rebuilt the city in AD 135, they made every effort to erase signs of the city's ancient glory—stones from the temple were used to build the theater and to construct the city wall. The Temple Mount itself was turned into a Roman farm, with a temple to the Roman god Jupiter built on the site.

Today, the Wailing Wall is all that is left of the second Temple. The Wailing Wall is the Western Wall of Herod's Temple that stands today just off of the Temple site. It is called the Wailing Wall because of the sounds made by devout visitors when they come to the wall and mourn over the destruction of the Temple and pray for its restoration. Although this wall appears to contradict Jesus' prophecy that not one stone would be left on another, the wall was actually taken down by the Romans during the original destruction of the Temple. It wasn't until over a thousand years later that the Wailing Wall was erected using stones from the original Temple. Since the stones were so enormous, each one had to be moved one at a time to erect the wall, thereby fulfilling Christ's prophecy.

Figure 5: The Western Wall

The Diaspora

After Jerusalem and the Temple were destroyed in AD 70, the Roman Senate passed a law banishing all Jews from the city of Jerusalem. In what became known as "the Diaspora," the Jewish people who weren't taken captive or killed fled to all parts of the known world. During this time, which occurred from AD 70 to 1948, the land of Israel was occupied by one empire after another. In AD 320, Jerusalem fell under the control of Emperor Constantine and the Byzantine Empire. About three hundred years later, when Muhammad established the Muslim religion, the area became a holy site and fell under Islamic control during a Muslim attack in AD 638. It is during this time of Turkish (Arab) control in AD 691 that the Dome of the Rock was constructed. The Dome of the Rock is a domed Muslim shrine in Jerusalem that stands on the traditional site of the Temple of Solomon (the first Jewish temple). For Muslims, it is generally considered the third holiest site of pilgrimage (after Mecca and Medina), since it was also here that Muslims believe the prophet Mohammad ascended into heaven.

In 1098, the English, French, and German crusaders gained control of Jerusalem for about one hundred years until they were driven out by the warrior Saladin the Magnificent. In the thirteenth century, Jerusalem fell under the control of the Egyptians, which later fell to the Ottoman (Turkish) Empire. The Ottoman Turks ruled over the Promised Land from 1517 (the same year Martin Luther posted his theses on the church door and started the Protestant Reformation) to 1917 when the British Empire took control at the conclusion of World War I. It's interesting to note that when the British General Allenby (a devoted Christian) captured Jerusalem from the Turks in 1917, he refused to ride his horse into the city because he felt the only conquering hero who should ride into the city should be the Savior who would return to become King of Kings. In the thirty years that followed (1917-1947), Jerusalem remained under British sovereignty. Thus, for nearly two thousand years, until 1948, the Jewish people lived with no country to call their own and in constant fear of persecution and death. This was all in fulfillment of prophecy:

Prophecy: After the destruction of Jerusalem and the Temple, the Jewish people would be scattered into all nations (Deut. 28:64). During the time of the dispersion, the people of Israel would fall away from God and worship other gods (Deut. 4:28, 28:64), and be relentlessly persecuted and be without a country (Deut. 28:65-67).

Fulfillment: As the result of the Roman destruction of Jerusalem in AD 70 and a failed Jewish rebellion led by Simon Bar Cochba in AD 132, three million Jews were slaughtered and millions of Jews were sold into slavery. The rest of the Jewish people were banned from the city of Jerusalem by the Roman Senate, which led to the Diaspora. For the following two thousand years, the Jewish people were scattered around the earth and had no country to call their own.

In the two millennia that followed, the Jewish people did fall away from their true God. Although the Jewish people maintained their unique identity and still observed some of the Jewish customs, the vast majority of Jews were secular and didn't follow the Mosaic Law as commanded by God.

In fulfillment of prophecy, the Jewish people have been relentlessly persecuted throughout history including being expelled from England in 1290, expelled from Spain in 1492, and attacked in Russia during World War I. The height of Jewish persecution, however, occurred during World War II when the Nazi Holocaust put literally millions of Jews to death in concentration camps.

The Restoration of Israel as a Nation

"O my people, I am going to open your graves and bring you up from them; I will bring you back to the land of Israel. Then you, my people, will know that I am the Lord, when I open your graves and bring you up from them" (Ezek. 37:12-13).

The restoration of Israel as a nation in 1948 after two thousand years of dispersion is a hallmark event in Bible prophecy. Many Old Testament prophets foresaw this event. In one of the most graphic visions, Ezekiel saw a valley of dead bones (the house of Israel) come together and be brought back to the land of Israel to form a nation. Many look at the Holocaust, where the Nazis killed more than five million Jews and left their bodies in mass graves, as a partial fulfillment of this prophecy.

The story of how Israel became a nation again started in 1897 when a group of Jews, calling themselves Zionists, met in Switzerland. Their goal was to rebuild the nation of Israel in the ancient land of Palestine, despite the fact that Israel was under Muslim control at the time. Although the group succeeded in getting a few hearty Jews to relocate from the relative comfort of Europe to the desert of Palestine, the movement didn't gain any critical mass until two decades later when a British scientist, Dr. Chaim Weizmann, developed a new, smokeless gunpowder during World War I. This invention helped shorten the war and led England to victory, during which, it had captured Palestine from the Ottoman Empire and ended four hundred years of Turkish Muslim rule. In gratitude, the British government offered to grant Weizmann a wish, and Weizmann, who was a leader in the Zionist movement and would later become Israel's first president, asked for a homeland for his people. This request led to the issuance of the Balfour Declaration in 1917 endorsing the setting up of a national homeland for the Jews. Lord Arthur Balfour was a former Prime Minister of Britain and a believer in the literal interpretation of Bible prophecy. Because of this declaration and Britain's influence, the League of Nations divided Palestine between two peoples—the Arabs and the Jews, when it dismantled the Ottoman Empire after the war. However, the partitioning of Palestine led to conflict with the Arabs, who had become powerful due to the growing need for oil in Britain. In a move to appease them, Britain curtailed immigration of Jews into Palestine. This move essentially blocked a critical mass of Jewish people from gathering in Palestine and eliminated the ability of Israel to reestablish itself. As a result, many Jews felt betrayed by Britain. This is especially true since this refusal by Britain to allow immigration to Palestine trapped millions of Jews in Nazi occupied Europe, directly leading to the slaughter of millions during the Holocaust.

It wasn't until after World War II when the Zionist movement gained real support from the world powers. When the atrocities of the Holocaust became public, nations around the world were visibly shocked. In addition, as a result of the war, the Jews became European refugees. Most Jews had everything taken from them during the war, including their homes, their money, and all their assets. Although many people felt sorry for the Jews, most did little to right the wrongs that had been done and viewed the Jews as a people with no place to go. Pressure was then put on the allied powers to establish a permanent haven in Palestine for Jewish survivors. The establishment of Israel three years after Germany's defeat was thus a direct aftereffect of World War II and the Nazi Holocaust. As terrible as it was, the Holocaust truly was the catalyst for the rebirth of the nation of Israel.

Prophecy: Israel would be restored to a nation in its own land after a long period of dispersion (Isa. 11:11-12, Zeph. 2:1-3, Ezek. 20:34).

Fulfillment: On 14 May 1948, Israel declared its independence, and the nation of Israel was founded. This was the first time since the Babylonian captivity in 605 BC that Israel regained its status as a sovereign nation and the first time since AD 70 that the people of Israel had a place to call their own. Thus began the return of Jews from their dispersion among the nations of the world, fulfilling prophecies given thousands of years earlier.

A year prior to its founding in 1947, Britain turned control of Jerusalem over to the United Nations because it could no longer keep the peace between the growing Muslim and Jewish populations. The United Nations decided to partition Palestine into a Jewish and Arab state with Jerusalem being an international zone under U.N. jurisdiction. The Temple Mount was given to the Arabs. Jewish authorities reluctantly accepted this plan, but the Arabs rejected it.

On 15 May 1948, one day after its founding, Egypt, Jordan, Iraq, Syria, and Lebanon invaded Israel. Some forty-five million Arabs were pitted against one hundred thousand Jews. Against incredible odds, Israel managed to defend itself and eventually emerged victoriously. It was an amazing victory—at no other time in history had so few people defeated so many. Israel however, suffered dearly, losing 10 percent of its total population during the war. When the Arabs withdrew on 11 June 1948, a cease-fire was proclaimed, and the new Israeli State became a fact. In the war, Israel had managed to increase its original territory by half. East Jerusalem (where the Temple Mount is located) was left under Arab control, and West Jerusalem now came under Israeli control.

For the next two decades, the city of Jerusalem remained divided and subject to sporadic fighting and violence. In June of 1967, knowing that it was about to be attacked, Israel launched a preemptive strike against the surrounding Arab nations. In this war, known as the Six Day War, Israel won control of East Jerusalem and the Temple Mount in addition to the Gaza Strip, the West Bank, the Golan

Heights, and the Sinai Peninsula. Again, the odds of Israel winning this war were astronomical. The British Institute for Strategic Studies estimated that Israel had about sixty thousand active soldiers in its army and about 204,000 reservists. For weapons, Israel had eight hundred tanks and about 350 planes. The combined forces of Egypt, Syria, and Jordan added up to about 951,900 regular soldiers, 205,000 reservists, 1,932 tanks, and more than 1,162 planes. The fact that Israel won this war was a modern miracle and a sign that God clearly had a hand in this war.

Although Israel gained control of the Temple Mount in the Six Day War, it was returned to Muslim religious authorities ten days after its capture by Israeli authorities because it was feared that the capture of the Temple Mount (where the sacred Dome of the Rock stands) would unite the entire Arab-Muslim world against it in a holy war. King Hussein of Jordan became the custodial caretaker of the area, thus preventing any Jewish worship on the Temple Mount.

It's important to note that despite the fact Israel has had some tremendous victories in war, it does not currently hold all of the land originally promised to Abraham and occupied by Israel during Solomon's reign, nor does it presently control the land described in Ezekiel 47:13-23 that it will hold during Christ's thousand year reign on earth. This land includes parts of Lebanon, Syria, Jordan, and Egypt. The complete restoration of Israel won't take place until the Lord's Second Coming, at which time all Jews scattered throughout the world will be assembled, and God will divide the Promised Land among the tribes of Israel (Matt. 24:31, Ezek. 47:13-48:29).

Prophecy: God's punishment of Israel for their rejection of Him would last 430 years. Babylon's siege of Jerusalem would mark the beginning of the punishment (Ezek. 4:1-8).

Fulfillment: It's important to note that in this prophecy the timeline starts with the *beginning* of the siege of Jerusalem ("lay siege to it") as opposed to the end of the siege when the city itself actually fell. This leads us to use slightly different dates than Jeremiah's prophecy described in figure 3, where the fall of Jerusalem marked the beginning of the timeline.

As mentioned before, in fulfillment of prophecy, Israel was taken captive by Babylon for seventy years. If we subtract this from the 430 years of total punishment predicted in this prophecy, we end up with 360 years of punishment that should remain for the people of Israel following the Babylonian captivity. If we convert between the Jewish and Christian calendars, as before, and do the math, we would expect to see God's punishment for Israel end between 182 and 164 BC depending upon which 'siege' of Jerusalem is used. However, looking through history, these dates don't correspond to any known dates or significant events. What should we say then? Was the Bible wrong in its prediction?

To better understand this prophecy and God's punishment for Israel in more detail, we need to go back to the original covenant the people of Israel made with God at Mt. Sinai. In this covenant, God promised that if the people of Israel disobeyed Him, they would be disciplined, which Moses prophesized would take the form of two future dispersions, where the nation of Israel would be taken from their country and scattered throughout the nations (Deut. 4:27-31, 28:36, 49, 52, 64-68). What's interesting to note about these prophecies are several passages in Leviticus (Lev. 26:18, 21, 24, 28) that state that if Israel didn't obey God the first time (Babylon), He would multiply their punishment by seven. We know Israel wasn't obedient to God following the Babylonian captivity, so multiplying 360 by seven, we should then calculate 2,520 years as the expected total duration of God's punishment.

Was this prophecy fulfilled? We first have to answer the question which 'siege' to use to start calculating the timeline. Ezekiel didn't specify in his prophecy, and of the three sieges of Jerusalem that occurred at the hands of the Babylonians, both the first siege (when Israel lost its national sovereignty) and the third siege (when Jerusalem and the Temple were destroyed) were very significant to the Jewish people. Let's see what happens if we look at both.

If we consider the first siege when Israel lost its national sovereignty and was taken captive by Babylon, we should subtract the time of the captivity (the 70 years) and start from the date that Israel was released from this captivity to evaluate if multiplying the remaining punishment by seven yields a fulfillment. Although Cyrus issued an edict in 538 BC regarding Israel's release, it wasn't until July 23, 537 BC when the first group of Jewish captives organized, gathered their provisions and former Temple treasures as allowed by Cyrus's decree, and left Babylon on their "exodus" to return to their original land in Palestine. If we start from this date, we would expect the fulfillment to occur 360 years times seven – or a total of 2,520 years later on the Jewish calendar. These years add up to 907,200 days (using 360 day years, which is commonly used in prophecy because the Jewish calendar consists of twelve thirty-day months—see *Appendix G*). Converting between the calendars and adding one to account for the fact that there was no year zero on the Christian calendar, we end up with 2,483 years, 9 months and 12 days on the Christian calendar. Adding this to July 23, 537 BC, we would then expect the fulfillment to occur on the 14th day of the 5th month of 1948 or May 14, 1948.

What happened on this date? This is the *exact date* that the nation of Israel declared its independence and was reborn after almost 2,000 years of dispersion. In fact on May 14, 1948 the first Prime Minister of Israel, David Ben Gurion, cited this prophecy in the book of Ezekiel as his authority for proclaiming Israel as the new Jewish homeland. The nation of Israel was re-established on the *exact day* predicted by the Bible! The story of how Israel was reborn is a remarkable one, since no other nation in history ever has fallen off the map only to be reborn thousands of years later. The rebirth truly was a miracle of God, but even more so since He fulfilled the rebirth exactly to the day which the prophet Ezekiel predicted more than 2,500 years earlier.

Now consider what happens if we start with the third siege by Babylon when the city of Jerusalem and the Temple was destroyed. If we subtract the time of the captivity (the 70 years), we see we should start from August 16, 518 BC. Counting from this date and converting between the calendars as we did before, we would then expect the fulfillment to occur on the 7th day of the 6th month of 1967 or June 7, 1967. What happened on this date? This is *the exact date* that the nation of Israel captured the old city of Jerusalem (the site of the Temple Mount) in the Six Day War. Even though Israel was permitted to declare statehood under a plan by the United Nations in 1948, it didn't hold Jerusalem. It was only on this date that Jerusalem was fully again under the control of Israel – the first time this was the case since the original fall of the city to Nebuchadnezzar.

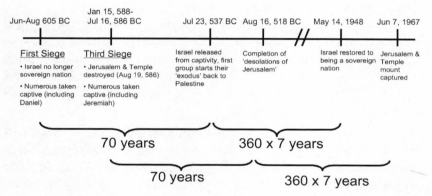

Figure 6: God's Punishment of Israel

What we see from Ezekiel's prophecy is that God fulfilled to the *exact day* the time during which Israel would be punished. And even though there were multiple sieges of the city, God's timeline still held – Israel lost its national sovereignty for "430 years" and Jerusalem and the Temple mount were out of Jewish control for "430 years". Obviously, these prophecies defy mathematical probability of occurring by random chance and certainly couldn't have been fulfilled by calculating Jews who may have been aware of these prophecies, since the Jewish people didn't control the timing of the initial sieges by Babylon or when the nation of Israel would be reborn. The later only occurred after the horrible events of World War II when Jewish refugees had nowhere to go and world sentiment was such that it was actually feasible for a new Jewish homeland to be created in the land of Palestine by the United Nations. Certainly, Israel also couldn't have predicted the timing of the Six Day War or exactly the date upon which Jerusalem would be recaptured.

So, what can we conclude? Only that once again the hand of God must have been at work in the fulfillment of these prophecies and that Ezekiel was a true prophet of God.

Prophecy: Although the nation of Israel would be restored, the people of Israel would not be spiritually reborn until a later time (Ezek. 22:17-22, 37:1-14).

Fulfillment: Despite Israel's restoration in 1948 and its miraculous victories in war, the people of Israel are, for the most part, secular. They do not follow the commandments of God and still reject Jesus Christ as their Messiah. The Bible states that Israel will not be reborn until the Tribulation period—just prior to the time of Christ's Second Coming (see chapter twenty-two).

Possible Prophecy: The generation that sees the rebirth of Israel will be the same generation to witness the fulfillment of end times prophecy (Matt. 24:32-35, Mark 13:28-31, Luke 21:29-33). In these passages, a fig tree is used as a parable of the signs of the times. When the fig tree starts sprouting leaves, it means the time of summer is near. This would mean that the same generation to see Israel's rebirth in 1948 will be the same generation to witness the events of the end times. In the Bible, a generation is typically between forty and one hundred years.

Note: The fig tree is used six times throughout the Bible as a prophetic symbol of Israel (Joel 1:7, Matt. 21:19). It's also a common symbol in Israel today—many government buildings, in fact, have a fig tree engraved on them. If this interpretation is correct and the fig tree represents Israel, then the fig tree started sprouting leaves when Israel became a nation again in 1948. However, the Bible is not specific on whether the fig tree mentioned in this passage represents

Israel specifically or the numerous other signs that are provided in the same chapter. The fig tree could just be a natural illustration for what Christ was trying to convey—namely, that the end will come when these signs are apparent. Therefore, no one should be dogmatic about this prophecy or its interpretation.

Partial Fulfillment: Over the past sixty years, the nation of Israel has been in a state of restoration and sprouting leaves. Almost all of the other signs of the times Jesus described in His discourse (Matt. 24) have been fulfilled. Only a few remain (see chapter six, "The Signs of the Times"). It is very likely we are witnessing the events of the end times.

The Third Temple (The Tribulation Temple)

Ever since its destruction in AD 70, there have been several attempts to rebuild the Temple. These endeavors have all been short-lived and have failed primarily because other countries have held control over Jerusalem. One attempt in AD 363 met with near success—building materials were provided, and Jewish people were assembled for the rebuilding effort. However, just as the builders were trying to break into the foundations of the Temple Mount, an earthquake interrupted the effort. The earthquake ignited reservoirs of trapped gases below the ground, resulting in an explosion that destroyed the building materials on the site. Despite the failed attempts, the Bible is clear that the Temple will be rebuilt and will play a key role during the Tribulation period.

As discussed in chapter eight, "Stage Setting for the Tribulation," preparations have already begun to rebuild the Temple. The biggest obstacle to the rebuilding effort has been the fact that the Dome of the Rock is built on the same location where the Temple is supposed to be built. The Dome of the Rock must either be destroyed or moved in order for rebuilding to begin—either of which would cause monumental conflict between Israel and the Arab world. However, recent discoveries indicate that the Temple could be built on a northern site, which would not require the destruction of the Dome of the Rock. The Dome of the Rock would then end up in the Temple's outer court. This would seem to fit with Revelation 11:1-2, where an angel measuring the Tribulation Temple is told not to include the outer court with its wall, because it was given to the Gentiles until the time of Christ's return. However, the Arab people would clearly not support the rebuilding of the Temple around the Dome of the Rock, so certainly something must change in the current geopolitical environment if this were to happen.

It is important to note, that unlike the other temples, the Lord will not dwell in the Tribulation Temple. Ever since the First Coming of Christ, God does not project His glory and presence through a physical temple, but through a living temple made up of every member of the body of Christ (1 Cor. 3:16-17, Eph. 2:19-22). Christ was the final sacrifice for sin (Heb. 10:18, 1 John 2:2); therefore, there is no longer need for sacrificial offerings in the Temple.

The Third Destruction of the Temple (Armageddon)

The third Temple will be short lived—it will be destroyed during the second half of the Tribulation period. Although the Bible doesn't specifically mention its destruction, the Bible is clear that Christ will rebuild the Temple at the start of the Millennium with the help of many people who will come from far away places to help in the effort (Zech. 6:13-15). Since we know that the Temple must exist at the midpoint of the Tribulation (see chapter fifteen), it can therefore be assumed that the third Temple will be destroyed at some point during the second half of the Tribulation period. This is a logical conclusion since there will be an enormous amount of destruction during the Tribulation period that will literally level all of the cities of the earth. In addition, the city of Jerusalem itself will be taken over by invading armies and ransacked, so it's reasonable to think that the Temple will be ransacked as well. See chapter thirteen, "The Tribulation Judgments" and chapter twenty-one, "Armageddon," for a more detailed description of the events that will occur during this period.

The Fourth Temple (The Millennial Temple)

The fourth and final Temple will exist during the thousand year reign of Jesus from Jerusalem, known as the Millennial period. Christ will personally be responsible for the building the Millennial Temple along with people from all nations who will come to assist in the building effort (Zech. 6:11-13,15). The Millennial Temple will be the focus of the entire world. Not only will the Temple serve as the center for priestly rituals and offerings, but Christ will also personally rule His kingdom from this Temple. The design of the Millennial Temple is described in great detail in Ezekiel 40-46, but suffice it to say this will probably be one of the most beautiful buildings in human history. A detailed description of this Temple, and all of the prophecies related to it, is contained in chapter twenty-four, "The Millennium."

The Future of Israel

During the Millennium, the glory of Israel that existed under King Solomon's rule will be restored. The nation of Israel and the city of Jerusalem will be the center of the whole world. People from all over will stream into the city year after year to see and worship the Lord. In addition, God will make a new covenant with the nation of Israel. This new covenant will replace the Mosaic Covenant that the people of Israel broke. The basis of this covenant will be a restored relationship between God and the nation of Israel—the Lord will once again be their God, and they will be his chosen people (Heb. 8:6-13).

At the end of the Millennium, Satan will lead one final rebellion against God. Satan and his forces will gather around Jerusalem in an attempt to capture it, but God will destroy them by sending fire down from heaven. After this event, God will destroy the earth by fire. The city of Jerusalem will be consumed with the rest of the earth and will be replaced by a new city, the New Jerusalem, which will descend from the heavens. This new city will be the final residence of all believers for eternity (Rev. 20:7, 21:2; 2 Pet. 3:10). Detailed descriptions of these prophecies related to the Millennial Jerusalem and Nation of Israel are contained in chapters twenty-four and twenty-five.

Notes

1. Christ was the descendant of Abraham, Isaac, Jacob, and David, among others. His complete lineage (from Abraham to Mary) is given in Matthew Chapter 1.

2. Thomas Ice & Randall Price, *Ready to Rebuild: The Imminent Plan to Rebuild the Last Days' Temple,* 55, 57.

CHAPTER 4

THE GREAT GENTILE KINGDOMS OF THE EARTH

"The great God has shown the king [Nebuchadnezzar] what will take place in the future. The dream is true and the interpretation is trustworthy" (Dan. 2:45b).

As part of the Mosaic Covenant (discussed in chapter three), God promised that if the people of Israel obeyed His commandments, He would treat them as His treasured possession and His chosen people. However, as part of this covenant, God also promised that if the people of Israel disobeyed Him, they would be disciplined—their sovereign nation would be taken from them, and they would be scattered as a people throughout all the nations of the world. As we saw in the previous chapter, Israel broke the covenant and disobeyed God. God then sent numerous prophets to warn the people of His pending judgment. Despite being warned, Israel did not turn from its ways, so God ultimately fulfilled His promise, and the nation of Israel was taken into captivity by Babylon in 605 BC. This began a period known as the "time of the Gentiles."

The time of the Gentiles was defined by Jesus as the period when the city of Jerusalem would be controlled by Gentile world powers: "Jerusalem will be trampled on by the Gentiles until the times of the Gentiles are fulfilled" (Luke 21:24). This period started with the Babylonian captivity in 605 BC. Many see the return of the Old City of Jerusalem to Jewish control in June of 1967 as being the end of the time of the Gentiles and are now awaiting the imminent return of Christ. Others believe that Israel is still under Gentile domination, because its holiest spot, the Temple Mount, is still held by Muslims and because no Davidic descendant is ruling on David's throne over David's people in Jerusalem.

The book of Daniel (written around 537 BC) provides prophecies concerning the full panorama of kingdoms that would rule during the time of the Gentiles. In a dream given to King Nebuchadnezzar of Babylon and interpreted by Daniel (an Israelite who was taken into captivity), four major Gentile world empires (and only four) were revealed to rule over the world and fall to the subsequent empire. These four empires were Babylon, Media-Persia, Greece, and Rome. What's important to note is that each empire got its power from the former: Rome got its power from Greece, Greece from Media-Persia, and Media-Persia from Babylon. Since the fall of Rome, however, there has been no leading world empire. Although many men, such as Muhammad, Charlemagne, Genghis Khan, Napoleon, Adolf Hitler, and the Russians have all attempted to build a fifth world empire. They have all failed, as the Bible predicted they would thousands of years ago.

According to Daniel's vision, the fourth empire, Rome (which broke up and became the nations of Europe), will be restored near the time of the end and will be ruled by an emperor again (Dan. 2, 7, Rev. 13:3, 4). This emperor is commonly known as the Antichrist, and this empire will be the final worldwide empire prior to Christ's return. Interestingly, this first description of the Antichrist in the Bible was given in a dream to King Nebuchadnezzar, whom scholars believe to be the most absolute and powerful dictator in world history.

What is most amazing about the book of Daniel is that it accurately predicted the rise and fall of four major world empires and provided hundreds of specific facts particular to these kingdoms. It included such detail as the name of the emperor who would conquer Babylon, the fact that the second empire would have three major conquests, the fact that the third empire would be broken into four pieces and ruled by four kings, and that the fourth empire would not be conquered, but rather would disintegrate from within. In addition, Daniel accurately predicted the wars and conspiracies of Egypt and Syria that occurred between the Greek and Roman empires. In all cases, Daniel's prophecies were fulfilled literally and exactly as they were predicted, despite the amazing odds of this happening. Non-biblical historical records confirm the fulfillment. The book of Daniel is so accurate, in fact, that many have attempted to suggest that an unknown author wrote the book after the fact, reasoning that the book must have been recording history instead of prophecy. These skeptics have been proven wrong though, by the recent archeological discovery of the Dead Sea Scrolls, which included copies of Daniel's prophecy dated from the years of the Media-Persian Empire—the time when Daniel lived. There can be no question then, that Daniel's prophecy was written in advance of the events he described and by Daniel himself, since, in the book, Daniel refers to himself in the first person numerous times (7:2, 15, 28; 8:1, 15, 27; 9:2, 22; 10:2, 7, 11-12; 12:4-5).

Clearly, Daniel passes the test of a true prophet, which states that only a prophet of God can proclaim the future with 100 percent accuracy (Deut. 18:21-22). This indicates the weight we should give to the prophecies Daniel proclaimed about the coming of Christ, the Tribulation, the restoration of the Roman Empire, the Antichrist, and the end of the age that all have yet to be fulfilled. This is especially true, since these prophecies are contained in the same text and context as the prophecies that have already been fulfilled. The following sections detail the specific prophecies related to these kingdoms and their fulfillment.

The Babylonian Empire (606-539 BC)

The first kingdom prophesied to rise to power existed during the time of Daniel. This kingdom was Babylon (Dan. 2:38) and Nebuchadnezzar was the king.

Prophecy: Babylon would be a great kingdom (Dan. 2:38).

Fulfillment: Although short lived, Babylon was one of history's greatest kingdoms. It was known as "the golden kingdom" and was the largest of the known world at its time. It became the religious and cultural center of western Asia. Babylon boasted a beautiful city with palaces, temples, and towers as well as one of the world's seven wonders, the famed Hanging Gardens of Babylon. Babylon also contained several colossal golden statues, each weighing many tons.

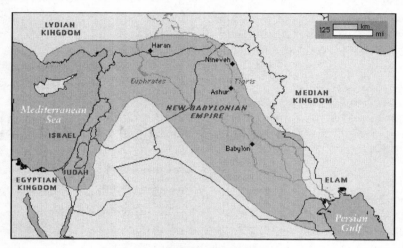

Map 5: The Babylonian Empire

Prophecy: Nebuchadnezzar would rule over all who lived (Dan. 2:38).

Fulfillment: Nebuchadnezzar did rule over the entire *known*[1] world. At its height, the Babylonian Empire extended all the way from the Persian Gulf to the Mediterranean Sea.

Prophecy: Babylon would conquer Judah (the Southern kingdom of Israel), plunder the nation and enslave the people of Israel (Jer. 20:4-5).

Fulfillment: After three campaigns, which occurred between 605 BC and 586 BC, Babylon conquered Judah (the Southern kingdom of Israel). The survivors, along with their treasures and many articles from the Temple, were carried off to Babylon where they were enslaved for seventy years.

Prophecy: Babylon would fall to a future king named Cyrus, a king of the Medes and Persians who would attack Babylon from the North. God would aid Cyrus in his conquest of Babylon as punishment for the wrongs Babylon did to Israel. Babylon would be plundered, and the people enslaved (Isa. 13:19, 45:1-13; Jer. 25:12-14, 50:2-3, 9-10, 41-42, 51:11, 24; Dan. 5:28).

Fulfillment: On 12 October 539 BC, Babylon was overrun by Cyrus, the king of the Media-Persian Empire who attacked from the north and from the east. The city of Babylon was taken without a battle— Cyrus ingeniously diverted the course of the Euphrates River (which flowed under the city walls of Babylon) to allow his armies to make their way into the city along the dried-up riverbed. The people of Babylon were enslaved, and the city was plundered just as predicted.

Prophecy: Babylon would be destroyed and would never be inhabited again (Isa. 13:20-22; Jer. 50:13, 39, 51:26, 37, 43).

Partial Fulfillment: The decline of Babylon was gradual and occurred in stages after its fall to Cyrus:

In 514 BC, Darius Hystaspes (ruler of Media-Persia at the time) put down a revolt by the Babylonians and partially destroyed the walls of the city along with the temple towers in the process. In 478 BC, his son, Xerxes, demolished the walls and temples of Babylon.

In 331 BC, the Alexander the Great (ruler of Greece) conquered the Medes and took up residence in Nebuchadnezzar's palace. He died less than eight years later. Although Babylon was a prosperous city at the time, Alexander's successor, Seleucus, built a new city (named Seleucia) nearby on the Tigris River because it had a deeper waterway for navigation. From this point on, Babylon rapidly decayed. Its structures were torn down to provide brick for building elsewhere, and the once proud city was reduced to a vast ruin.

By 20 BC, Strabo (a Greek geographer and historian) described Babylon as a "vast desolation." A few people, however, continued to live there. In fact, in AD 60 the Apostle Peter wrote his epistle from the city of Babylon (1 Pet. 5:13).

About the middle of the fifth century, Theodoret (a Greek theologian) described Babylon as only being inhabited by a few Jews.

In AD 917, Ibu Hankel (a historian) mentions Babylon as still in existence, but only as an insignificant village.

In 1898, Babylon contained only about ten thousand inhabitants.

As can be seen, Babylon was never truly destroyed. It decayed and became insignificant, but God's final prophecy of Babylon being destroyed, never to be inhabited again, has not yet been fulfilled. Indeed, the Bible predicts that the city of Babylon will be rebuilt in the end times and will once again rise to great power and prominence, only to be destroyed by God once and for all during the Tribulation period (see chapter twenty).

It has only been recently (in 1987), that the city of Babylon has been rebuilt by Saddam Hussein (see chapter eight). While the city has not yet achieved the prominence that it will under the Antichrist, it is clear that the rebuilding of Babylon is the first step toward the fulfillment of prophecy.

The Media-Persian Empire (539-331 BC)

The second empire prophesied to come to world power was the Media-Persian Empire (Dan. 5:30). Daniel lived to see the fulfillment of this prophecy, which occurred sixty-five years after he predicted it.

Prophecy: Media-Persia (the kingdom predicted by Daniel to conquer Babylon) would be inferior to Babylon (Dan. 2:39).

Fulfillment: Media-Persia was an inferior kingdom to Babylon in both its splendor and wealth. Although the kingdom wasn't inferior in military strength (since it conquered Babylon) or in size (since it held a much larger land area than Babylon), it was inferior because as a partnership between the Medes and the Persians, it lacked the absolute unity and authority that Babylon enjoyed.

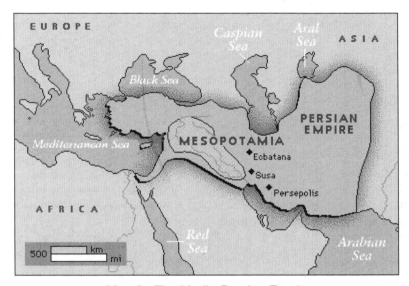

Map 6: The Media-Persian Empire

Prophecy: Media-Persia would be comprised of two different kingdoms—the younger of the two kingdoms would start out smaller, but would grow to be more powerful (Dan. 7:5, 8:3).

Fulfillment: The Media-Persian Empire was a divided kingdom consisting of the Medes and the Persians. In the beginning, the younger kingdom, Persia, was dominated by the Medes. This domination ended in 550 BC when Cyrus attained power, overthrew the Median rulers, and established the Persian Empire as the preeminent power of the world. It is because of the lopsided nature of this empire that the history books primarily describe this as the Persian Empire as opposed to the Media-Persian Empire.

Prophecy: Media-Persia would conquer three other empires (Dan. 7:5).

Fulfillment: The Media-Persian Empire had three major conquests: Lydia in 546 BC, Babylon in 539 BC, and Egypt in 525 BC.

Prophecy: Media-Persia would expand to the west, the north, and the south (Dan. 8:4).

Fulfillment: The Media-Persian Empire did expand to the west (to Lydia—what is now Asia Minor), the north (what is now Kazakhstan), and the south (to what was Babylon).

Prophecy: Media-Persia would have four kings after Cyrus. The fourth of these kings would be far richer than all the others, and would stir up everyone against the kingdom of Greece (Dan. 10:1, 11:2).

Fulfillment: After Cyrus, Persia had four more kings: Cambyses (530-522 BC), Pseudo-Smerdis (522-521 BC), Darious I Hystaspes (521-486 BC) and Xerxes (486-465 BC). The fourth king, Xerxes, was clearly the richest of all the Persian kings. He assembled perhaps the largest army ever and spent three years preparing a great fleet and army to punish the Greeks for various victories they had achieved. The Greek historian Herodotus noted that the combined strength of Xerxes' land and naval forces totaled 2,641,610 warriors, which were drawn from forty nations—an astonishing number at the time. During the spring of 480 BC, Xerxes marched with his forces through Greece and conquered various cities including Athens, which he burned.

Prophecy: The Media-Persian kingdom would fall to Greece (Dan. 8:7; 21).

Fulfillment: The Media-Persian Empire fell to Greece at the hands of Alexander the Great in 331 BC.

The Greek Empire (331-146 BC)

The third empire prophesied to come to world power by Daniel was revealed as the Greek Empire (Dan. 8:21). Greece rose to power 273 years after Daniel's original prophecy.

Prophecy: Greece would rule over the whole earth (Dan. 2:39).

Fulfillment: The Greek Empire was ruled by Alexander the Great and held control over the entire known world.

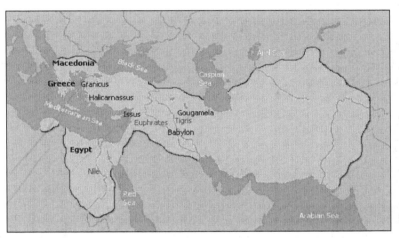

Map 7: The Empire of Alexander the Great

Prophecy: The leader of this empire would be very great and would rule with great power (Dan. 8:8, 11:3).

Fulfillment: Alexander the Great, the ruler of the Greek Empire, was one of the greatest military geniuses of all times. Arrian, a Greek historian, wrote "there was no nation, city, nor people then in being wither his name did not reach... there seems to be to have been some divine hand presiding both over his birth and actions."

Prophecy: At the height of his power, the leader of the third kingdom (Greece) would die, and the kingdom would be broken into four pieces and ruled by four kings who would not be his descendants.

The four kings would not be as great as the first (Dan. 7:6, 8:8; 22, 11:4)

Fulfillment: After the death of Alexander the Great at age thirty-two, the Greek Empire was divided among Alexander's four generals (Cassander—Macedonia, Lysimachus—Asia Minor, Seleucus—Syria, and Ptolemy—Egypt). None of these generals achieved the greatness of Alexander in wealth, power, or fame.

Prophecy: The king of the South and the king of the North would have various struggles (a very detailed prophecy of these struggles is contained in Dan. 11:5-20). Key points include:

• The king of the South would become strong, but one of his commanders would become even stronger and would rule his own kingdom (Dan.11:5).

• The daughter of the king of the South would make an alliance with the king of the North. The king of the North would not retain his power. A person from her family line would attack the king of the North and be victorious (Dan. 11:6-7).

• A king of the North will arise and defeat the kingdom of the South (Dan. 11:15-16). This king will then make an alliance with the king of the South and will give his daughter over in marriage (Dan. 11:17). He will then turn his attention to the coastlands and take many of them, but he will ultimately fail (Dan. 11:18-19). After this, the king of the North would stumble and die (Dan. 11:19). His successor would heavily tax the people (Dan. 11:20).

Fulfillment: Just as prophesied, the successors of Alexander struggled bitterly for power over his domain. This is especially true of Ptolemy of Egypt (the Southern kingdom) and Seleucus of Syria (the Northern kingdom), who fought for over 350 years. Key points include:

• Ptolemy I Sotor ruled Egypt from 323-285 BC. One of his commanders, Seleucus I Nicator, ruled his own kingdom and was the founder of the Seleucid dynasty, which would reign in the Middle

East from the fourth to the first century BC. Seleucus's empire stretched from Palestine to India and was greater than Ptolemy's.

• Ptolemy II Philadelphus, who arose after Ptolemy I, ruled Egypt from 285-246 BC. He gave his daughter, Berenice, in marriage to Antiochus I Theos of Syria as a means of making peace, but Antiochus deserted her and was later murdered by his former wife, Laodice, who conspired to have Berenice and Antiochus put to death. Ptolemy III Euergetes, Berenice's brother who ruled Egypt from 246-221 BC, invaded Syria in 246 and was successful.

• Antiochus III (called the Great) from Syria defeated the Egyptian army in Sidon. Antiochus reached a treaty with Ptolemy V and gave him his daughter, Cleopatra I, in marriage to him in 194 BC. He then annexed the coastlands of Asia Minor and unsuccessfully tried to invade Greece. He was defeated by the Romans in 190 BC and died in 187 BC while attempting to plunder a temple in the province of Elymais. He was succeeded by his son Seleucus IV Philopator (187-175 BC) who heavily taxed the people of Israel.

Although the prophecies that relate to Egypt and Syria are intricate and detailed, they are important because they were all fulfilled *exactly* as Daniel had predicted over two centuries earlier. As a result, the only reasonable explanation is that Daniel truly was an inspired prophet of God.

The Roman Empire (146 BC-AD 476)

The fourth (and final) empire prophesied to come to world power was the Roman Empire. Rome rose to power 458 years after Daniel's original prophecy.

Prophecy: Rome would be strong, crushing all others and devouring the whole earth (Dan. 2:40, 7:7, 23).

Fulfillment: Rome ruled longer than any other kingdom of the earth and became a world power, controlling all of what are now Europe, the Middle East, Asia Minor, Northern Africa, and the southwestern parts of Russia. This empire spanned the entire known world at the time. The culture, art, architecture, literature, political system, law, music, and religion of Rome spread around the world and created the basis for the modern culture of today. Rome truly was the greatest empire that has existed in the history of the world.

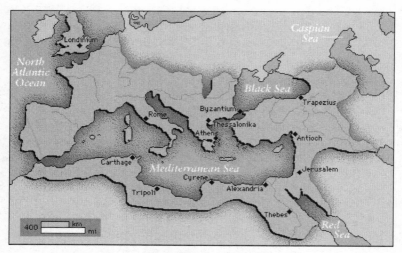

Map 8: The Roman Empire (AD 117)

Prophecy: This kingdom wouldn't be conquered by another kingdom, but rather would disintegrate from within and break into smaller kingdoms (Dan. 2:43).

Fulfillment: Rome, rather than succumbing to a succeeding empire, broke into ten smaller kingdoms in the fourth and fifth centuries AD. Rome became weak, and the Huns and the Goths from central and northern Europe swept into Rome and sacked it. The Huns and Goths did not try to unite the land that Rome had occupied. Rather, the kingdom broke up into separate identifiable nations. These nations included the Alamanni (Germany), the Franks (France), the Burgundians (Switzerland), the Suevi (Portugal), the Lombards (Italy), the Visigoths (Spain), the Anglo-Saxons (England), the Vandals (destroyed), the Heruli (destroyed) and the Ostrogoths (destroyed). These kingdoms became the nations of modern day Europe.

The Nations of Europe (AD 476-Present)

The dream God gave to king Nebuchadnezzar of Babylon didn't end with Rome. Rather, it described the breaking of the fourth empire (Rome) into pieces that would subsequently be recombined into a ten-nation federation that would arise during the end times:

Prophecy: The individual kingdoms that come out of Rome, the fourth empire, would be divided—the people would be a mixture of races and would not remain united (Dan. 2:41-43).

Fulfillment: Since the division of the Roman Empire, many men have tried to reunite the nations of Europe under one power: Charlemagne (King of the Franks) in AD 800, Charles V of Austria in 1364-1380, Louix XIV of France in 1643-1715, Napoleon of France, Kaiser Wilhelm of Germany during World War I, and Adolf Hitler of Germany in World War II. All of these have failed—the European nations have remained divided.

Note: The popular nursery rhyme "Humpty-Dumpty" was originally written as an allegorical verse referring to the fall of the Roman Empire and centuries of failed efforts at European unification. Despite the attempts, "all the king's horses and all the king's men couldn't put Humpty back together again."[2]

Prophecy: The kingdoms that would come out of Rome, the fourth empire, would be partly strong and partly brittle (Dan. 2:42).

Fulfillment: Some of the European nations did become strong—England and Germany for example. Others have remained weak—Portugal, France, Spain, and Italy for instance.

Prophecy: A federation of ten kings or nations will rise out of the countries that come out of the fourth empire (Dan. 7:24). It is out of this federation that the Antichrist will arise (Dan. 7:24). The sole purpose of this ten-nation federation will be to give its power to the Antichrist (Rev. 17:13).

Potential Fulfillment: No known federation of ten kings has yet arisen out of Europe. However, the move to create the European Union could be the start of this ten-nation federation that the Bible describes. Indeed, all of the nations that are banding together into the European Union have their roots in the old Roman Empire. Further details regarding this prophecy are contained in chapters eight and fourteen.

Notes

1. Biblical phrases such as "all that lived," "the entire world," "the whole earth," and "under the entire heavens" should be interpreted in the writer's (and most readers') context. In most cases, these phrases do not necessarily refer to the entire planet as we know it. Rather, they refer to an area that had meaning to the people living at the time to whom the Scripture was directed. Our global perspective of the twenty-first century tends to cloud our interpretation of Scripture. We must remember that the "world" was a much smaller place in biblical times. Scriptural examples of where broad phrases have obvious limited contextual meanings include Genesis 41:56, 1 Kings 10:24, Romans 1:8, and Colossians 1:6.

2. Cliff Ford, "Humpty Dumpty Stumbles," *Countdown,* April 1999.

CHAPTER 5

THE FIRST COMING OF CHRIST

"He had no beauty or majesty to attract us to him, nothing in his appearance that we should desire him. He was despised and rejected by men, a man of sorrows, and familiar with suffering" (Isa. 53:2).

"Rejoice greatly, O Daughter of Zion! Shout, Daughter of Jerusalem! See, your king comes to you, righteous and having salvation, gentle and riding on a donkey" (Zech. 9:9).

"For to us a child is born, to us a son is given, and the government will be on his shoulders. And he will be called Wonderful Counselor, Mighty God, Everlasting Father, Prince of Peace. Of the increase of his government and peace, there will be no end. He will reign on David's throne and over his kingdom, establishing and upholding it with justice and righteousness form that time on and forever"
(Isa. 9:6-7).

Because of Israel's disobedience and breaking of the Mosaic covenant, God disciplined the people of Israel by taking away their sovereign nation. This defined the "time of the Gentiles." During this period, God sent numerous prophets (including Jeremiah, Ezekiel, Daniel, Haggai, Zechariah, and Malachi) to call the people of Israel to repentance and give them hope for the future. One of the central themes of these prophecies was that a Messiah would come to redeem Israel and fulfill the promises God had made to Abraham, Isaac, Jacob, and David. This Messiah would restore Israel as the

THE TRUTH ABOUT PROPHECY IN THE BIBLE

leading nation in the world and would bring about a new time of peace and prosperity among all nations.

This message was especially compelling to the people of Israel, who were being held captive during the time these prophecies were delivered (627 BC to 400 BC). The glory that was Israel under King Solomon was gone, and the nation of Israel was enslaved in a foreign land. The promise of the Messiah gave the people of Israel hope that their former glory would return. They were looking for and end to the time of the Gentiles and were eagerly anticipating the restoration of their former nation. The Bible literally contains hundreds of prophecies related to the coming of this Messiah. What's sad is that there came a Jew who claimed to be the Messiah. He performed miracles and fulfilled many of the prophecies related to the Messiah, but the people of Israel, the very people who should have recognized Him and eagerly welcomed His arrival, rejected Him. Why?

The Old Testament prophets described two different portraits of the coming Messiah: one portrait depicts Him as a humble servant who would suffer for others, be rejected by His people, and would die to save them from their sins. This portrait of "the suffering Messiah" is primarily seen in Isaiah 53. The other portrait shows the Messiah as a king who comes to rescue the world at the point of global war and comes to reign over Israel and restore the former glory that existed under King Solomon. This portrait of "the conquering Messiah" is seen in Zechariah 14 and Isaiah 9:6-7. Writer Hal Lindsey offers an explanation of these seemingly contradictory views of the Messiah:

> Imagine a man looking at a range of mountains. He is able to see the peak of one mountain and beyond it the peak of another. However, from this vantage point, he cannot see the valley that separates these two mountains. Men viewed the two portraits of the Messiah in the same manner. They saw two different persons, but missed the connection. They did not perceive that there could be just one Messiah, coming in two different roles, and separated by a valley of time.

Jesus presented His credentials as the suffering Messiah, but many rejected Him because they were looking for a great conqueror. They were looking for a political leader who would deliver them from the Roman oppression. In their blindness they discounted more than three hundred specific predictions in their own sacred writings about this Messiah.[1]

A summary of the prophecies related to the First Coming of the Messiah appears below.

The Timing of His Coming

Prophecy: There would be 483 years between the issuing of the decree to rebuild Jerusalem until the coming of the Messiah (seven, seven-year periods plus sixty-two, seven-year periods): "Know and understand this: From the issuing of the decree to restore and rebuild Jerusalem until the Anointed One, the ruler, comes, there will be seven 'sevens,' and sixty-two 'sevens'." (Dan. 9:25) These years add up to 173,880 days (using 360-day years, which is commonly used in prophecy because the Jewish calendar consists of twelve thirty-day months—see *Appendix F*). The coming of the Messiah is described in Zechariah 9:9—the Messiah will enter Jerusalem riding on a donkey. This prophecy was given to Daniel in 538 BC.

Fulfillment: On 14 March 445 BC, the Media-Persian ruler, Artaxerxes Longimanus issued a decree to "restore and rebuild Jerusalem" (Neh. 2:1-9). Exactly 173,880 days later on 6 April, AD 32, Christ made his triumphal entry into Jerusalem on Palm Sunday riding on a donkey. The Messiah came on the *exact day* it was predicted, despite the fact that this prophecy was given ninety-three years before the decree to rebuild Jerusalem and 570 years before the actual coming of the Messiah.

Note: to replicate this calculation, remember to take into account the 116 leap years that occurred during this period and that the period between 1 BC and AD 1 is counted as one year because there was no year zero.[2] For a detailed discussion of this prophecy (known as Daniel's Seventy Weeks), see *Appendix D*.

Prophecy: The Messiah will come and then be killed. His death will take place sometime between when the Jews return from their Babylonian captivity to rebuild the Temple (at the conclusion of the sixty-two sevens) and when Jerusalem and the Temple will be destroyed for a second time (Dan. 9:25-26). This prophecy was given to Daniel in 538 BC: "After the sixty-two sevens, the Anointed One will be cut off [killed] and will have nothing. The people of the ruler who will come [Romans under Titus] will destroy the city [Jerusalem] and the sanctuary" (Dan. 9:26).

Fulfillment: The Jews were released from their captivity in Babylon to rebuild the Temple in 536 BC. Titus and the Roman legions destroyed the city of Jerusalem and the Temple in AD 70. Therefore, the Messiah that the Bible describes had to come and be killed sometime between 536 BC and AD 70. Jesus Christ fulfilled this prophecy and was the only credible one to do so during this period. He was born around 6-5 BC and was killed in AD 30. Given this, it's amazing that so many Jews continue to reject Jesus when the timing of His coming was so clearly predicted in Scripture.

A detailed discussion of this (and related prophecies) is contained in *Appendix D*.

His Lineage & Birth

Prophecy: All nations would be blessed through a direct descendant of Abraham (Gen. 12:3, 18:18, 22:18, 26:4).

Fulfillment: Jesus was a direct descendant of Abraham (Matt. 1:1-17, Luke 3:23-37, Acts 3:25) and came to save people of all nations. Paul describes the fulfillment of this prophecy in Galatians 3:8, 16.

Prophecy: The Messiah would come from the tribe of Judah and be a direct descendant of Jacob and David (Gen. 49:10, Num. 24:17, 19, 2 Sam. 7:12-14, 1 Chron. 17:11-14).

Fulfillment: Jesus was from the tribe of Judah and descended from Jacob and David (Matt. 1:1-17, Luke 3:23-37).

Prophecy: The Messiah would come as a baby, born into the world (Isa. 9:6).

Fulfillment: Jesus Christ came into the world as a baby (Matt. 1:18-2:1).

Prophecy: The Messiah would be born in Bethlehem (Mic. 5:2).

Fulfillment: Jesus Christ was born in Bethlehem (Matt. 2:1, 5-6, Luke 2:4-6).

Prophecy: The Messiah would be the Son of God (Ps. 2:7, 2 Sam. 7:14, 1 Chron. 17:13).

Fulfillment: Christ was the Son of God (Matt. 1:18, 3:17, 17:5, Luke 1:35, Acts 13:33, Heb. 5:5, 2 Pet. 1:17-18).

His Ministry

Prophecy: The Messiah would minister in Galilee (Isa. 9:1).

Fulfillment: Jesus Christ started His ministry in Galilee (Matt. 4:12-16).

Prophecy: The Messiah would be a prophet (Deut. 18:15-19).

Fulfillment: Jesus Christ was recognized as a prophet. In fact, the greatest passage of prophecy in Scripture was given by Jesus in Matthew 24. This passage predicts many things including the second destruction of the Temple, the signs that will lead up to the end times, the events of the Tribulation period, and the Second Coming of Christ. The crowds around Christ and His disciples recognized Him as a prophet in fulfillment of the prophecy given in Deuteronomy (Matt. 21:11, John 1:45, 6:14, Acts 3:22-23).

Prophecy: The Messiah would ride into Jerusalem on a donkey (Zech. 9:9, Gen. 49:11).

THE TRUTH ABOUT PROPHECY IN THE BIBLE

Fulfillment: Christ made His triumphant entry into Jerusalem on 6 April, AD 32 (Palm Sunday) riding on a donkey (Matt. 21:1-11).

Prophecy: The Messiah would perform various miracles including healing cripples and opening the eyes of the blind, the ears of the deaf and the mouths of the mute (Isa. 35:4-6).

Fulfillment: Jesus performed various miracles including those mentioned above. When asked about His identity, Jesus quoted this prophecy as proof to John the Baptist of his identity (Matt. 11:3-5, John 11:47).

His Conviction & Trial

Prophecy: The Messiah would be despised and rejected. People would mock Him and hurl insults at the Messiah (Isa. 49:7, 53:3, Ps. 22:6-8).

Fulfillment: Jesus Christ was despised and rejected. In fact, His own people, the Jews, crucified Him. At His crucifixion, people mocked Him and hurled insults at Him just as the prophecies described (Mark 15:29-32, Matt. 27:39-44, Luke 23:39).

Prophecy: A close friend would betray the Messiah (Ps. 41:9).

Fulfillment: Jesus was betrayed by one of His disciples, Judas Iscariot (Matt. 26:47-49, Mark 14:10, John 13:18-21).

Prophecy: The Messiah's value would be judged at thirty pieces of silver. This money would be cast down into the Temple, and finally, the money would be given to a potter for the graves of the poor people (Zech. 11:12-13). A "potter's field" is where potters dug clay for making pottery. These fields were frequently full of holes, so it was easy to bury people there who had no family tombs.

Fulfillment: Judas Iscariot betrayed Jesus for thirty pieces of silver. When Judas regretted what he had done, he cast the money down in front of the chief priests and elders in the Temple. The silver was blood money, so instead of returning the money to the Temple treasury, the chief priests and elders purchased a potter's field with it as a burial place for foreigners (Matt. 26:14-15, 27:3-5, 6-10).

Prophecy: The Messiah would not try to defend Himself when accused, mocked, spit on, or beaten—He would remain silent (Isa. 50:6, 53:7).

Fulfillment: Jesus Christ did not defend Himself in front of the high priest at his trial. He remained silent and allowed his accusers to mock Him, spit on Him, and beat Him (Matt. 26:62-64, 27:13-14, 30; Mark 14:60-61, 65, 15:19; Luke 22:63; John 19:1; 1 Pet. 2:23).

Prophecy: The Messiah's followers would scatter when He was "stricken" (Zech. 13:7).

Fulfillment: Jesus Christ's disciples fled when He was arrested in the garden of Gethsemane (Matt. 26:31, 56b; Mark 14:50).

His Death

Prophecy: The Messiah would be killed—He would die for the sins of mankind (Isa. 53:5-6, 8b, 10a, 11-12; Dan. 9:26).

Fulfillment: Jesus Christ was killed—He was crucified as atonement for our sins (John 19:16).

Prophecy: The Messiah's death would be extremely painful. The Messiah's bones would be pulled out of his joints, His strength would be taken away, and His hands and feet would be pierced (Ps. 22:14-17).

Fulfillment: Christ died by crucifixion, a means of execution not known until Roman times. This passage gives an account of His pain, extreme thirst, asphyxiation, and the agony of His hands and feet being nailed to the cross.

Prophecy: The Messiah's body would be pierced (Zech. 12:10, Ps. 22:16).

Fulfillment: Jesus was pierced with a spear when He was on the cross (John 19:34-37).

Prophecy: Blood and water would flow out of the Messiah's body at His death (Ps. 22:14).

Fulfillment: When Jesus was pierced with a spear, blood and water flowed out of His body (John 19:34).

Prophecy: The Messiah would be thirsty at His death (Ps. 22:15). His thirst would be quenched with vinegar (Ps. 69:21).

Fulfillment: While Christ was on the cross, He proclaimed, "he was thirsty" (Mark 15:29). Roman soldiers gave Him vinegar to quench His thirst (John 19:28-29).

Prophecy: Around the Messiah, at His death, evil men would gamble for his clothing (Ps. 22:18).

Fulfillment: When Christ was crucified, Roman soldiers did cast lots and gamble for His clothing (Mark 15:24, John 19:23-24).

Prophecy: The Messiah would be assigned a grave with the wicked and with the rich when He died (Isa. 53:9).

Fulfillment: Roman soldiers intended to bury Christ's body with the wicked since they considered Him a criminal. Instead, He was given an honorable burial in Joseph of Arimathea's (a wealthy man) tomb (Matt. 27:57-60).

Prophecy: The Messiah would be "numbered with transgressors" (i.e., considered a criminal or sinner) at the time of his death (Isa. 53:12).

Fulfillment: Christ was crucified as a criminal next to two other criminals (Luke 23:33).

His Resurrection & Ascension

Prophecy: Prior to His death, Christ predicted He would be resurrected after the third day (Matt. 12:39-41).

Fulfillment: After His crucifixion, Christ rose from the dead on the third day (Matt. 28:1-7). Over a period of forty days, many people witnessed His resurrection including 120 people at one point and at another time, five hundred people at once (1 Cor. 15:3-8).

Prophecy: The Messiah would ascend to heaven (Ps. 68:18).

Fulfillment: After His resurrection, Jesus Christ ascended into heaven (Mark 16:19, Luke 24:50-51, Acts 1:9). Paul describes this prophecy in Ephesians 4:8-10.

Probabilities

The above prophecies were all given in the Old Testament between five hundred and two thousand years prior to the coming of Christ. At the time these prophecies were written, the death and resurrection of Christ was indeed prophecy. Now, of course, it's history. The question that needs to be asked is what are the odds that Jesus Christ could have come and just pretended to be the Messiah? Could he, knowing the Jewish prophecies, manufacture His identity as the Messiah? The answer is that it would have been statistically impossible. Although Christ could have manufactured the fulfillment of some of the prophecies (for example, Jesus could have acted by not defending Himself at His trial), there are at least fifteen prophecies listed in this chapter that are quite specific and couldn't have been manufactured by Jesus Himself. For example, Jesus certainly couldn't control the city where He was born, His family lineage, or the price that was paid for His betrayal.

In statistics, the probability of any events happening together is the product of the probability of the events happening individually. So, if the probability of one event happening is one in ten and the probability of another event is one in five, then the probability of both events happening is one in fifty. If a person assigns probabilities to the above prophecies and multiplies them together, it's easy to see that it is beyond the realm of possibility that one person could come and fulfill these prophecies unless he truly was the Messiah.

For instance, if you assume the odds of the Messiah being born in Bethlehem is one in two hundred, the odds that He would be betrayed by a friend is one in ten, the odds that He would be betrayed for thirty pieces of silver one in one hundred, etc. and then multiply together for a dozen of the most common and indisputable prophecies, the combined probability quickly reaches the order of one chance in ten to the nineteenth power or one in 10,000,000,000,000,000,000. If you take the odds of any one of the above prophecies at one chance in ten and multiply together for a dozen of these prophecies, the odds are one in ten to the twelfth power or one in 10,000,000,000,000.

Regardless of the specific odds applied to any one prophecy, it's clear that the prophets could not have accurately predicted these events by chance alone and that Jesus Christ could not have come and simply pretended to be the Messiah. The odds are too astronomical.

Notes

1. Hal Lindsey, *The Late Great Planet Earth,* 17-21.

2. This calculation was originally performed in 1895 by Sir Robert Anderson, the head of Scotland Yard in *The Coming Prince,* 127.

Part 2

Present Prophecy

CHAPTER 6

THE SIGNS OF THE TIMES

"Hypocrites! You know how to interpret the appearance of the earth and the sky. How is it that you don't know how to interpret the signs of the times?" (Luke 12:56, NAS)

During his ministry, the Jewish leaders came to Jesus and tried to test Him by asking Him to show them a sign from heaven. They were looking for a physical sign that Jesus was who He said He was. Jesus scolded the Jewish leaders and said: "When you see a cloud rising in the west, immediately you say, 'It's going to rain,' and it does. And when the south wind blows, you say, 'It's going to be hot,' and it is. Hypocrites! You know how to interpret the appearance of the earth and the sky. How is it that you don't know how to interpret this present time?" (Luke 12:54-56). The Old Testament, which the Jewish leaders spent their lives studying, contained hundreds of signs, which would identify the coming of the Christ. The reason Christ scolded them was because of their inability to recognize the signs happening all around them regarding His coming.

Today there are signs all around us pointing to the approaching time of Christ's second return—newspapers, radio programs, television, and the Internet are full of growing trends that clearly indicate the time of Christ's return is near. Yet, just like the Jewish leaders two thousand years ago, most people today do not recognize these signs or take the time to discover just what the Bible says about them. The Bible is full of prophecy and after Jesus died and rose from the dead, he instructed His disciples that every prophecy must be fulfilled: "He said to them, 'This is what I told you while I was still with you: Everything must be fulfilled that is written about me in the Law of Moses, the Prophets, and the Psalms.' ...He told them, 'This is what is written: The Christ will suffer and rise from the dead on the third day'" (Luke 24:44-46).

When Jesus came, He fulfilled the role of "the suffering Messiah" as described by the Old Testament prophets. But Christ said everything must be fulfilled that was written about Him—Christ must also fulfill the role of "the conquering Messiah" described in the Old Testament. How can this be if Christ is now gone? When Christ ascended to heaven, two angels appeared to the disciples: "Men of Galilee," they said, "why do you stand here looking into the sky [where Christ ascended]? This same Jesus, who has been taken from you into heaven, will come back in the same way you have seen him go into heaven" (Acts 1:11).

The angels told the disciples that Christ would physically return to earth to fulfill the covenant God had made with the Old Testament patriarchs. The disciples knew this; during the time Christ walked on the earth, his disciples had asked Jesus the question: "What will be the sign of your [second] coming and the end of the age?" Jesus instructed them to look for various signs (Matt. 24:3-33), as they would be an indication that the end times and His return are near. The "signs" Christ provided are essentially milestones on God's calendar to indicate that the time of Christ's return is approaching. In Matthew 24:34, Christ said "I tell you the truth, this generation will certainly not pass away until all these things have happened." Many interpret this to mean the generation that sees all of the signs Jesus described come together at once will be the same generation to witness the final fulfillment of prophecy and Christ's ultimate return to the earth.

We live in exciting times! While Christians have eagerly looked for the signs that Christ described for almost two millennia, it has only been in the past sixty years that many of them have actually been fulfilled. Almost two thousand years have elapsed since any prophecy in the Bible has been fulfilled, and yet in our generation, almost all of the two-dozen or so "signs of the times" have been fulfilled exactly as the Bible described they would be. Reading through the list below, it is difficult to conclude anything other than that the time of Christ's return is very near—the second half of the twentieth century and the first few years of the twenty-first century have truly been unique. Although one could easily argue that some of these signs have been fulfilled in the past (the breakdown of morality in society, for instance, was certainly true for the cities of Sodom and Gomorrah in the days of Abraham), what's significant is that all of these signs are coming together at the same time, on a global scale, for the first time in history.

As you read through the signs below (which will be discussed in detail in subsequent chapters), it's important to keep in mind that not all signs given in the Bible are the same—different signs relate to different events that will occur in the end times. The biggest mistake frequently made by people is to confuse signs that precede the Rapture of the Church and signs that precede Christ's Second Coming. These are two very different events and will be discussed in later chapters. It is only by digging deep into passages, examining their context, and looking at related passages in the Bible that one can discern the difference between the two and properly relate the signs to the event that they are supposed to precede.

Signs Preceding the Rapture of the Church

Sign	Fulfillment	Description
Christians will abandon sound doctrine	20th Century-today	Churches have sought unity as part of the ecumenical movement, adopted 'politically correct' views and allowed New Age philosophies to permeate the culture and the Church.
People will become lovers of self & of money	Post WWII	Humanistic thinking and the 'money revolution' have permeated society; making people more materialistic and changing the way people view themselves and their money.

People will live in luxury and self-indulgence. They will fail to pay workers their fair wages	20th Century-today	The industrial revolution, modern technology and prosperity brought about by the growth in wealth have created a society where people now live in unprecedented luxury and self-indulgence.
The moral fabric of society will break down	1960s-today	The two-parent family structure, a basic tenant of civilization since the beginning of time, has broken down and is now in the minority. Basic standards of morality have also broken down.
People will deny Christ and His return	20th Century-today	Society has adopted views on Darwinism and secular humanism that have led to people denying Christ and His return.

Stage Setting for the Tribulation

Sign	Fulfillment	Description
Israel will be restored as a nation	1948	Israel became a sovereign nation for the first time since 605 BC.
Jerusalem will be the center of conflict	1948	Middle-Eastern nations continually fight over the city of Jerusalem.
Israel will be ripe for a peace treaty	1993	The first Israel/Arab peace treaty is signed – with many to follow.
Israel will be a wealthy nation	Past few decades	Israel now has achieved one of the highest living standards in the Mediterranean.
The Temple will be close to rebuilding	1967-today	Pieces for the new Temple are being brought together and a solution now exists to the problem of the Dome of the Rock.
The Ark of the Covenant will potentially be returned to Jerusalem	1991 (un-confirmed)	The Ark was potentially returned during the Ethiopian airlift referred to as 'Operation Solomon' after almost 3,000 years of being 'lost'.
Jews will return from Russia	1989	The USSR breaks up and Soviet Jews, for the first time, are free to flee to Israel. A mass exodus occurs.

Movement toward a one-world religion	1948-today	Denominations have merged and churches have sought unity with one another as part of the ecumenical movement.
Movement toward a one-world government & economy	Post WWII	'Supra-national' organizations (such as the United Nations and the IMF) have grown in power and influence.
Movement toward a European Federation	1990s-today	The European Union is formed, a common currency is created and the unification of Europe is underway.
Russia will become a world power	Post WWII	Russia rose to become a world super-power after WWII and despite losing the Cold War, still possesses an awesome arsenal of weapons.
Russia will be allied with Arab nations	1990s-today	Arab countries and Russian break-away republics draw closer, due to shared Muslim faith.
The city of Babylon rebuilt	1987	Saddam Hussein rebuilt the city of Babylon in Iraq.
Worldwide communication technology exists	Late 20th Century-today	Technology such as 24-hour cable news now allows fulfillment of prophecies where "the whole world" will see certain events occurring in Jerusalem.
Technology for the 'Mark of the Beast' exists	1990s-today	Technology advances rapidly, and electronic commerce and authentication technologies become mainstream.

The Beginning of 'Birth Pains'

Sign	Fulfillment	Description
False Christs will arise	Post WWII	False messiahs such as David Koresh, Marshall Applewhite, Sun Myung Moon and Jim Jones have led many astray.
Wars	20th Century-today	World and civil wars have created the bloodiest century in history.
Famines	Post WWII	As the world population grows, 850 million now suffer from serious famine around the globe.

Plagues	1990s-today	Rise of diseases such as AIDS and TB now cause one-third of the world's deaths each year.
Earthquakes	1970-today	The world has experienced an unprecedented growth in the frequency and intensity of earthquakes.
Persecution of Christians	20th Century-today	Persecution rises around the world. More Christians have been martyred in the 20th century than in the previous 19 centuries combined.
Spread of the Gospel	20th Century-today	The Gospel is spread around the world and 70% of all progress made toward fulfilling the 'Great Commission' occurs in the past century.
Signs in the Heavens		Not yet fulfilled.

Table 1: The Signs of the Times

Although it's apparent that the time of Christ's return is near, the Bible makes it very clear that only the Father in Heaven knows the exact date when Christ will return (Matt. 24:36, 42, 44, 25:13; Mark 13:33-37; Acts1:7). It is therefore impossible to predict and futile to speculate precisely when either the Rapture of the Church or the Second Coming of Christ will occur. Speculation has been a problem for Christendom for most of its existence. In fact, at least two recent perversions of Christianity began with setting dates for Christ's return: the Jehovah's Witnesses and the Seventh Day Adventists.

However, we do need to be watching for the signs of His return. Despite the fact we can't know the exact day, the Bible says we are accountable to know the season and recognize the signs of the times when they arise: "Now learn this lesson from the fig tree: As soon as its twigs get tender and its leaves come out, you know that summer is near. Even so, when you see all these things, you know that it is near, right at the door. I tell you the truth, this generation will certainly not pass away until all of these things have happened" (Matt. 24:33-34). "Now, brothers, about times and dates we do not need to write you, for you know very well that the day of the Lord will come like a thief in the night. While people are saying, `Peace and safety,' destruction will come on them suddenly, as labor pains on a pregnant woman, and they will not escape. But you, brothers, are not in darkness so that this day should surprise you like a thief" (1 Thess. 5:1-4).

People have been looking forward to the time of Christ's return for almost two millennia. The question is often asked, "Why has Christ delayed so long in returning to earth?" The answer is that God is a God of love, and He wants as many people as possible to have the opportunity to be saved before Christ finally returns to judge the world. The Bible says: "With the Lord a day is like a thousand years, and a thousand years are like a day. The Lord is not slow in keeping his promise, as some understand slowness. He is patient with you, not wanting anyone to perish, but everyone to come to repentance" (2 Pet. 3:8-9).

God is patient. Even though we should look for and anticipate Christ's return, we should realize that His timeline is not the same as ours. The signs of the times are coming together for the first time in history just as the Bible predicted over twenty centuries ago. While this indicates that the end times are approaching, we should be aware that if He does not return when we expect Him to, it is only because He is merciful. He is providing more time for the Gospel message to spread so that more people can come into a relationship with Him.

Probabilities

All of the aforementioned signs were predicted in the Bible thousands of years ago. Just as it was interesting to look at the probability of the prophecies related to the Messiah coming true, so too it's interesting to look at the probability of all of the above signs of the times coming together and being fulfilled in our generation.

Of the prophecies mentioned in this chapter, there are around fifteen prophecies that are quite specific and measurable. Although one could argue that Christians have abandoned sound doctrine in the past or that the moral fabric of society had decayed at prior points in history, events such as the restoration of Israel, the rebuilding of Babylon, and the movement toward globalization are undeniably unique to our generation.

In the Bible, a generation is between forty and one hundred years. If we use forty years, then there have been fifty generations since the first coming of Christ where all of these prophecies could have come together and been fulfilled in the same generation. The probability of any one of these prophecies being fulfilled in this generation then, is one in fifty. The probability of these prophecies happening together is simply the product of the individual probabilities multiplied together.

Multiplying the probabilities across the fifteen or so specific prophecies results in fifty to the fifteenth power or one chance in 50,000,000,000,000,000 (fifty quadrillion) that these prophecies could be fulfilled together in the same generation. The probability that all of the twenty-seven prophecies listed above could be fulfilled together in our generation is fifty to the twenty-seventh power or one in 500,000,000,000,000,000,000,000,000,000.

People can question specific prophecies and whether some of them may have been fulfilled in other generations. But looking at the odds, it's impossible to conclude anything other than the fulfillment of so many prophecies during our generation is truly unique. The odds that the signs the Bible gives regarding the end times coming together at the same time in our generation is absolutely astronomical, and yet that is exactly what is happening. There is no other conclusion that can be drawn, other than we are truly living in the end times that the Bible predicted thousands of years ago.

CHAPTER 7

SIGNS PRECEDING THE RAPTURE OF THE CHURCH

*"You say `I am rich; I have acquired wealth and do not need a thing.'
But you do not realize that you are wretched, pitiful, poor, blind and
naked" (Rev. 3:17).*

The Rapture refers to an event foretold in the Bible when Christ will remove His Church from the earth prior to the outpouring of His wrath during the Tribulation period. In essence, all Christians around the world will mysteriously vanish "in the blink of an eye" from the face of the earth. This will be one of the most monumental events in history and will represent the point at which it will be too late for people to escape the coming judgments. People who are left on the earth will be doomed to go through the Tribulation period. A good analogy is the point at which Noah shut the door to the Ark. Anyone alive and not on the Ark was then doomed to endure the coming flood. The key difference is that during the Tribulation period, people will still have a chance to turn from their ways and come to a relationship with God, although being a Christian during this time will be difficult. Details of the Rapture and the Tribulation are discussed in subsequent chapters.

The Bible makes it clear that the Rapture could happen any time and will occur in a split second. As such, there are no real signs that will foretell the event. By the time it happens, it will be too late for people to do anything about it. However, a number of New Testament epistles do speak of the general condition of the Church and society in "the last days." Since we know that the Church will disappear from the earth and be taken up to Heaven in Rapture, we can then conclude that these conditions must apply to the Church just prior to this event. These signs or conditions are outlined below.

Christians Abandon Sound Doctrine

Prophecy: In the last days, some Christians will abandon sound doctrine and their faith to follow their own sinful desires, false teachings, and deceiving spirits. They will find teachers who say what they want to hear. Although they will have an outer semblance of being godly, these people will not be spiritually alive (1 Tim. 4:1, 2 Tim. 3:5, 4:3-4, Jude 1:18).

Fulfillment: In the twentieth century, many Christians have abandoned sound doctrine and fallen away from the true teachings of the Church. This has led to many people who call themselves Christians, but yet lack any sort of biblical worldview or true spiritual relationship with God. In a recent survey, 87 percent of Americans said that their religious faith was either "important" or "very important" to them. Yet despite these numbers, church attendance has fallen to its lowest levels in more than a decade, with only 37 percent attending church on a regular basis.[1]

Christians have abandoned sound doctrine for three primary reasons:

1. The first reason has been the growth of liberalism. Modern churches have increasingly adopted politically correct views in order to satisfy public opinion and retain membership. As a result, it's fairly easy to find churches in any city these days that support anti-biblical doctrines such as homosexuality, abortion, and materialism. Many people attend these churches precisely because of their soft views on sin. People don't want to hear about sin, confession, and repentance. They would rather hear motivational messages that make them feel good. While many people who attend these churches have a strong semblance of being godly, they lack any real personal relationship

with God—precisely because they don't really want to hear what He has to say.

2. The second reason Christians and churches have abandoned sound doctrine has been the growth of the New Age movement which has permeated the thinking of society and the Church. The New Age movement really emerged in the 1980s as a loose conglomeration of beliefs based upon centuries-old Eastern mysticism and Gnosticism (a perversion of Christianity that the early Church fathers and apostles warned about). The modern movement arose from the counterculture of the 1960s and is opposed to organized religion in favor of direct spiritual experience and emotion. Technically, the New Age movement is pantheism—the belief that God is the sum total of all that exists. According to pantheists, there is no one God, but instead there is a god-force (or life-force). This god-force flows through all living things including plants, animals, and human beings. Since this god-force flows through all living things, the New Age movement believes that we must therefore all be gods, or at least, partly gods. Pantheists also believe that humans never die. Rather, people are reincarnated into different life forms. The New Age movement is seen as the ultimate deceiving spirit because followers are led to think they are growing closer to God, but yet are really growing closer to demonic forces. Facets of the New Age movement include the re-evaluation of traditional Western religious beliefs and morality, antimaterialism, utopianism, exaltation of nature, and fascination with the occult. As this movement has grown, it has brought feminist, occultist, ecological, and human-potential issues into the Church. In a superficial effort to become more spiritual or grow closer to God, naïve Christians have turned to these teachings and been led astray. Many have thought these New Age philosophies (either overtly or disguised) would help them realize their full potential or bring them closer to God. Unfortunately, nothing could be further from the truth. Widespread are New Age techniques for self-improvement as well as the idea that the individual is responsible for and capable of everything. These beliefs have made their way into corporate America, health care, the environment, counseling, sports, and the armed forces. Ideas frequently associated with the New Age

THE TRUTH ABOUT PROPHECY IN THE BIBLE

movement include psychic healing, holistic health, values clarification, inner transformation, reincarnation, extraterrestrial life, biofeedback, chanting, yoga, transpersonal psychology, the occult, astrology, extrasensory perception, acupuncture, massage, tarot cards, Zen, mythology, and visualization.

3. The third and primary reason that churches have abandoned sound doctrine in this century has been in the name of church unity through what is known as the ecumenical movement. The ecumenical movement has led to the creation of umbrella-like church organizations such as the World Council of Churches. As churches have sought unity as part of these organizations, it has led to watered-down doctrines and the discarding of core biblical truth in an attempt to harmonize the various belief systems. In essence, churches have resorted to a least common denominator set of beliefs, instead of holding true to biblical teaching. A detailed discussion of the worldwide religious movement is contained in chapter eight.

Because of the growth of the three elements described above: liberalism, the New Age movement, and the ecumenical movement, countless Christians have abandoned sound doctrine and their faith in recent years. They have found teachers who say what they want to hear and have been misled by false teachings and the deceiving spirits of the New Age movement. Because of this, many Christians have an appearance of being godly, yet inwardly are spiritually dead. This condition is exactly what the Bible describes will exist just prior to the Rapture of the Church. Consider the following statistics: [2, 3]

• Less than 10 percent of born-again Christians possess a biblical worldview that impacts their decisions and behaviors. The truth of the Gospel and a relationship with Christ just doesn't impact most people's attitudes and behaviors on a day-to-day basis.

• People who believe Christianity is losing its influence over society outnumber those who say it is gaining influence by more than a three-to-one margin.

• Among the people who regularly attend worship services at Christian churches, half say they have not experienced God's presence in their lives at any time during the past twelve months—and one-third of all regular churchgoers say they have never experienced His presence at all.

• Although more than four out of five churches claim that evangelism is one of their primary reasons for existence, during the past eighteen years there has been no statistically significant increase in the proportion of adults in the U.S. who are born-again—even though churches have spent more than five hundred billion dollars on domestic ministry during that period.

• More than 40 percent of the young people in Bible-believing evangelical churches are sexually active. Sixty percent of single adults, including those who attend church regularly and participate in Bible studies, are not only sexually active, but half reported having sex with more than one partner.

• Divorce rates in the Church are now actually higher than outside of the Church.

Clearly, today's Christians have become lukewarm at best, and most no longer hold to the values of Christ and the doctrines of the Bible. We have brought the world's philosophy and practices into the Church as opposed to the other way around. Many churches now are no more than social clubs—where people meet to have fellowship or to be motivated, but only if the teaching is so watered down that it doesn't impact a person's day-to-day life or their sinful pursuits.

How bad are things? Consider the following table, which compares the attitudes, opinions, and values of Christians and non-Christians. What is so surprising in these figures is the lack of any real difference between these two groups of people:

Belief	Born-Again Christians	Non-Christians
Doctrine		
There is no such thing as Satan, he's just a symbol of evil	52% (72% of Catholics)	62%
The Holy Spirit is not a living entity, just a symbol of God's presence	55%	61%
People are basically good	79%	89%
There is no such thing as absolute truth	67%	76%
Worldview		
The main purpose of life is enjoyment and personal fulfillment	53%	66%
No matter how you feel about money, it is still the main symbol of success in life	51%	54%
Freedom means being able to do anything I want	35%	42%
Nothing can be known for certain except the things I experience in my own life	61%	64%
It feels sometimes like life is not worth living	16%	20%
One person can really make a difference in the world these days	74%	71%
Morality		
What is right for one person in a given situation might not be right for another person in a similar situation	92%	90%
When it comes to matters of morals and ethics, truth means different things to different people	66%	87%
It's almost impossible to be a moral person these days	27%	33%
Occult/New Age Practices		
Have consulted a fortune-teller	16%	17%
Read astrology charts	16%	20%
Believe in reincarnation	20%	24%
Regard self as very/somewhat superstitious	22%	25%

Table 2: Comparison of Christian and non-Christian Values [4]

People Become Lovers of Self and of Money

Prophecy: In the last days, people will become lovers of themselves and of money (2 Tim. 3:2).

Fulfillment: One could easily argue that people today have become lovers of themselves (known as humanism) and lovers of money (secularism). We live in a time of unprecedented prosperity, self-indulgence, and materialism. This has actually been a fairly recent phenomenon in society that started after World War II. In the decades following the 1950s and 60s, psychology became the most popular pursuit of study in American universities. Unfortunately, just as the theories of Charles Darwin has undermined belief in God as the Creator, modern psychology tends to turn people against belief in God by turning their focus onto themselves.

In the 1980s, people's attention turned even more onto themselves in tandem with the growth of New Age thinking on self-improvement, self-healing, and self-actualization. This isn't a coincidence. One of the basic tenants of the New Age movement is that people become gods by improving themselves and their own personal experience. This thinking has caught on, and now countless magazines, books, tapes, infomercials, and seminars have arisen dedicated to self, self-improvement, self-esteem, self-identity, and self-help. Many more publications have arisen dedicated to improving one's body, love life, and appearance. Cosmetic surgery is skyrocketing (having risen by over 50 percent in just the past six years), and people are spending on themselves like never before. Instead of focusing on God, the nation, or what's best for society, people now ask "what's in it for me?" This inward focus has led society into a fascination with pleasure, emotional and sexual stimulation, and personal fulfillment instead of what God intended.

In concert with the growing focus on self, there has been a growing focus on money. There is no question that people have become "lovers of money" as the Bible described they would be in the last days. The past two decades have represented nothing less than a money revolution in mainstream society. Just twenty years ago, the daily movement of the Dow Jones Industrial average had almost no relevance to our lives, and few of us knew what a mutual fund was. Now, countless TV shows, magazines, and web sites are dedicated to making and managing money. Countless books and seminars explain how to become overnight millionaires, and people follow the daily movements of the stock market as much as they follow celebrities. In fact, the *New York Times* best-seller list almost continually has three or four books on it regarding trading strategies, how to make your first million, investing in the stock market, and money management.

As a result of this money revolution, the percentage of U.S. households that hold a stake in the stock market now stands at around 51 percent—more than five times the percentage less than twenty years ago. Thanks to the great bull market of the 80s and 90s (and despite the subsequent bursting of the high-tech bubble in the year 2000), wealth in the U.S. and in the World economy has soared—in the last fifteen years of the twentieth century the Dow Jones Industrial average surged over one thousand percent. This rise represents more than twice that of any other bull market in history.[5] As the ability to make easy money in the stock market grew, so too did people's attention and focus on making it.

Unfortunately, in an effort to have it all and keep up with the Joneses, consumerism has run rampant in the past few decades. People can now buy whatever they want, and thanks to credit cards and easy installment loans, they don't even need money in the bank to do so. This rampant consumerism has resulted in a society focused on material possessions and spending. Consider the following statistics, which support this conclusion: [6, 7, 8, 9, 10, 11]

• As of 2003, the typical U.S. family now holds thirteen credit cards and carries an average balance of over ninety-two hundred dollars—up from approximately three thousand dollars in 1990. That's an increase of 310% in a time of historically low inflation.

• Total household debt has reached the six trillion dollar mark. The share of disposable income that households must pay to service their debts has passed 18 percent. Among lower- and moderate-income families, debt is even higher.

• The percentage of U.S. households with zero or negative net worth has been steadily increasing—from 9.8 percent in 1962 to 15.5 percent in 1983 to 18.5 percent in 1995 (the last year for which data is available). This means that nearly one out of five households has more debt than they have assets, despite the booming stock market of the 80s and 90s and the low rate of inflation that has existed during this time.

• For the first time ever since the Great Depression, American households now have a negative personal savings rate. This means that Americans are spending more than they earn. The savings rate has plunged to a negative 1.4 percent in 1999 from 9 percent in 1982 and from 25 percent in 1942. Corporate debt has also spiked, and borrowing by financial institutions as a percent of gross domestic product has doubled from a decade ago. "This is historically unprecedented," says Jane D'Arista, director of programs at Virginia-based think tank Financial Markets Center. "We're in territory where no one knows what will happen."

• Once unheard of, personal bankruptcies have skyrocketed in the past decade and are now at record levels, exceeding 1.6 million in 2003 (representing about one in every 68 American families). This is seven times the rate of bankruptcies that occurred in 1980. To put this in perspective, more Americans have declared bankruptcy in recent years than graduated from college.

It's clear that the thinking of society has shifted in the past few decades. People are now more focused on themselves and on money, just as the Bible predicted they would be in the last days. This shift has created a society of people obsessed with improving themselves and with making money. As the general wealth in society grows, people who have money spend it on themselves rather than saving it. Those who don't have money obsess even more about how to keep up with those who do, and they go further into debt to do so.

People Live in Luxury, Fail to Pay Workers Fair Wages

Prophecy: In the last days, people will live in luxury and in self-indulgence. They will hoard their wealth and will not pay workers their fair wages (James 5:1-5).

Fulfillment: One could easily argue that society today lives in unprecedented luxury and self-indulgence. Thanks to the industrial revolution, modern technology, and prosperity brought about by the money revolution, people have become self-indulgent and lovers of pleasure.

In the millennia prior to the 1900s, there were few advances in the average person's standard of living. Most people were farmers and the process for growing food and living off the land didn't change much for thousands of years. In the late 1800s and early 1900s however, society underwent a fundamental change. With the advent of the steam locomotive, people no longer had to farm to feed themselves and their families. Instead, they could live in cities; food from all over the world could be brought to them. Instead of an agrarian economy, the world became an industrial economy.

As technology advanced and industrial processes for mass production were established, new types of goods could be produced. The creation of an affordable automobile, for instance, would have been impossible had it not been for the ability to ship raw materials easily and assemble them so that they could be produced in vast quantities at reasonable prices. Thanks to the industrial revolution of the 1900s and the great advances in technology that occurred after World War II, the average person living in a developed nation now enjoys a standard of living much greater than even the kings and emperors of two hundred years ago. We take for granted such conveniences as running water, electric light, education, medical care, public and private transportation, books, magazines, radio, television, the telephone, clothing, food, fuel, and the computer. We have, in the twentieth century, solved most of the major problems that once made daily living for the overwhelming majority a backbreaking routine of drudgery.

In the past two decades, the money revolution, rampant consumerism, and the great bull market of the twentieth century have caused luxury spending to grow significantly. By any measure (sales of luxury cars, travel, housing, clothing, jewelry, etc.) spending on luxury items is at an all time high. Sales of personal and corporate jets are now at near record levels, as are the sales of almost everything from vacation houses to cosmetic surgery to expensive cigars and wines.[12] People truly are living in luxury and self-indulgence just as the Bible described they would be in the last days.

Unfortunately, despite the enormous growth in wealth, the distribution of this wealth has been uneven. The rich are, in fact, hoarding their wealth as described in the Bible. The common cliché, "the rich get richer and the poor get poorer" is true. Consider the following statistics:

• Behind the hoopla of the booming nineties, most Americans actually lost wealth and now have a lower net worth (assets minus debt) than they did in 1983, when the stock market began its record-breaking climb. From 1983 to 1998, the stock market grew a cumulative 1,336 percent.[13] The wealthiest households reaped most of these gains. During this time, the inflation-adjusted net worth of the top one percent swelled by 17 percent, while the bottom 40 percent of households lost an astounding 80 percent. Their net worth shrunk from $4,400 to an even more meager $900. The wealthiest 10 percent of all households enjoyed 85 percent of the stock market's capital gains, while the wealthiest one percent reaped 40 percent. In fact, only the top 5 percent gained any net worth in this period, and now hold more than 60 percent of all household wealth. As a result, most of the benefits of the 1990s bull market bypassed the average American.[14, 15, 16]

• Using data from the Federal Reserve Survey of Consumer Finances, economist Edward Wolff of New York University says that the top one percent of households now have more wealth than the entire bottom 95 percent. Financial wealth is even more concentrated, with the top one percent of households having nearly half of all financial wealth (net worth minus net equity in owner-occupied housing).[17]

• In 1998, weekly wages were 12 percent lower than in 1973 on an inflation-adjusted basis. Productivity rose 33 percent over that period. Had pay kept pace with productivity, the average hourly wage would now be $18.10, rather than $12.77. That translates into a difference in annual pay of $11,000 for a full-time, year-round worker.[18] After the longest peacetime expansion in U.S. history, average workers are still earning less, adjusting for inflation, than they did when Richard Nixon was president. No wonder many people have been working longer hours and going deeper into debt in an effort to keep up living standards and pay for college.

• In 1999, Business Week reported that top executives in America's corporations earned 419 times the average wage of a blue-collar worker, up from 42 times in 1980.[19]

• Globally, the trends are just as bad. In 1996, the United Nations Development Program (UNDP) reported that three decades ago, the people in the most well-to-do countries were 30 times better off than those in countries where the poorest 20 percent of the world's people live. By 1998, this gap had widened to 82 times. UNDP further reported that the world's 225 richest people had a combined wealth of $1 trillion. That's equal to the combined annual income of the world's 2.5 billion poorest people. In fact, the wealth of only the three most well-do-do individuals in the world now exceeds the combined GDP of the 48 least developed countries.[20]

The industrial revolution, modern technology, and the money revolution have created a society that now lives in unprecedented luxury and self-indulgence. This is all in fulfillment of prophecy that was given almost two millennia ago to signify the approaching end times.

Breakdown of Morality in Society

Prophecy: In the last days, the moral fabric of society will break down. People will be boastful, proud, abusive, disobedient to their parents, ungrateful, unholy, without love, unforgiving, slanderous, without self-control, brutal, not lovers of good, treacherous, rash, and conceited (2 Tim. 3:1-4).

Fulfillment: There can be no question that the moral fabric of our culture has decayed. The traditional nuclear family, consisting of two parents and their own biological children, now represent the minority of families. Although the family unit has been the basic building block of society since the beginning of time, it no longer is today. Alternative family structures (the single parent household, same-sex marriages, etc.), which were originally the exception to the rule, are now more common than the traditional family. Families consisting of bread-winner dads and stay-at-home moms now account for just ten percent of all households. Married couples with kids, which made up nearly every residence a century ago, now total just 25 percent—with the number projected to drop to 20 percent by 2010, says the Census Bureau.[21]

This unprecedented demographic shift has resulted in a sea change in the way children are raised—instead of learning morality from their parents, the majority of children now learn morality from movies, TV, gangs, and the Internet. Although schools originally taught right from wrong, most schools now ban the teaching of the Ten Commandments or any Bible-based standard of morality.

The impact on society from these changes has been enormous. Think of the problems that faced the classroom teacher only a few decades ago: chewing gum, talking out of turn, tardiness, and running in the halls. Now think of the problems that face school teachers today: school shootings, drug abuse, pregnancy, suicide, assault, and rape. It is amazing how far our culture has decayed. A recent survey conducted by the MSNBC television network highlights this downward trend. In a survey of Americans it found: [22]

• Eighty-three percent of people ranked "youth violence" as their highest concern about America.

• Two out of three ranked "the influence of sexually explicit or violent media on children" as a "very serious" social problem.

• Sixty-three percent ranked "the high rate of divorce and the breakup of families" as a very serious problem for American society.

• Respondents ranked "the lack of respect for authority and elders" as their biggest concern about how American society has changed over the past fifteen or twenty years.

How bad have things become? What has been the actual impact of this shift away from the basic family structure? Consider the following statistics. Though these statistics apply to the United States, in general, statistics are similar across other Western democracies:

• Since 1960, violent crime has increased more than 560 percent.[23]

• Since 1960, illegitimate births have increased more than 500 percent. Currently, about one in every three births is to an unwed mother. This is much worse in the inner cities, where almost 70 percent of all births and 52 percent of all abortions are among unwed, poor, black women.[24]

• Since 1960, divorce rates have more than tripled, as has the number of children living in single-parent homes.[25, 26]

• Since 1960, the teenage suicide rate has increased more than 200 percent and is now the leading cause of teenage deaths in America.[27]

• Since 1976, the number of cases of child abuse has increased more than 348 percent.[28]

• Since 1973, there have been approximately thirty million abortions.[29]

• One fourth of all adolescents now contract a sexually transmitted disease before they graduate from high school.[30]

• It's now estimated that over 683,000 women are raped each year in America.[31]

• Twenty percent of suburban high school students now think it is appropriate to shoot someone "who has stolen something from you" and 8 percent believe it is acceptable to shoot a person who has "done something to offend or insult you." This is more than mere talk—at least 270,000 guns are taken to school every day, part of what has driven the recent rise in school shootings across the country in the past few years.[32, 33]

• Pornography is running rampant. Porn (excluding the Internet) is now a twelve to thirteen billion dollar a year industry—more than the annual revenues of Oracle, Marriott, or Staples. Americans now spend more money at strip clubs than at Broadway, off-Broadway, regional and nonprofit theaters, at the opera, the ballet, and jazz and classical music performances *combined.* There are now more outlets for hard-core pornography in this country (approximately twenty-five thousand) than McDonalds restaurants (approximately nine thousand). On the Internet, the situation is even worse, with pornography accounting for the majority of all e-commerce transactions. In fact, more than 70% of all e-commerce is based on some socially unacceptable if not outright illegal activity including pornography, gambling, and drugs.[34, 35, 36, 37]

• The number of high school seniors who view the institution of marriage as optional, even for purposes of child-rearing, is now the majority, while 40 percent of females in their twenties would consider having a baby on their own if they reach their mid-30s and hadn't found the right man to marry.[38]

• Although once rejected as wrong by most people, homosexuality and lesbianism are now considered mainstream. Several TV shows now run in prime time promoting these lifestyles and homosexual

THE TRUTH ABOUT PROPHECY IN THE BIBLE

marriage, once considered a contradiction in terms, has gained broader support and legal status in just the past few years.

• Moral relativism ("there are no absolutes, whatever *you* believe is right for *you*") has replaced biblical standards of morality in most of the nation's schools and in the general thinking at large.

• Churchgoing Christians, once the founding fathers of America, are now commonly labeled "intolerant religious fanatics" by the mainstream press and general population.

There is little doubt that the moral fabric of society has broken down. It should be no surprise that people have become boastful, proud, abusive, disobedient to their parents, ungrateful, unholy, without love, unforgiving, slanderous, without self-control, brutal, not lovers of good, treacherous, rash, and conceited when this is precisely what the Bible predicted almost two millennia ago.

People Deny Christ and His Return

Prophecy: People will deny Christ and His return (2 Pet. 3:3-4, 2 Tim. 3:4-5).

Fulfillment: There can be no doubt that most of society today has come to doubt the existence of God, Christ, and Christ's return. Even though some people in society and the scientific community have always sought to explain human existence independent of a creator, this belief system didn't become mainstream until the twentieth century.

Throughout history, scientists like Galileo, Copernicus, and Sir Isaac Newton all believed that their efforts were to better understand the nature of God and His creation. They viewed science as a way to better understand the character of an intelligent Creator and worshipped Him because of the order that they saw in the universe. In 1859, however, Darwin published his theory of evolution. With this, a large percentage of people have now come to believe that mankind was created by chance, independent of God. These views (frequently known as "secular humanism") have led to a society that increasingly denies the existence of God, the deity of Jesus Christ, and the imminence of Christ's return.

The secular humanist movement is growing. Although once a fringe view, it has grown over the past fifty years to be the predominant view taught in our nation's schools as truth. In fact, at a recent American Humanist Awards ceremony, it was boasted that secular humanist beliefs have now "conquered the entire public school system."[39] No longer do schools teach traditional Judeo-Christian beliefs or even attempt to present different views of creation. Today, most schools teach evolution as fact and don't even acknowledge that there could be a Divine Creator. In fact, a recent lawsuit brought on by the American Civil Liberties Union (ACLU) has sought to ban the reading of the Declaration of Independence in schools because it contains the phrase "all men are *created* equal...[and] they are endowed by their *Creator* with certain inalienable Rights."

Who are these people? What underlies their belief systems? [40]

• Secular humanists define themselves with "no belief in the supernatural, personal afterlife or system of doctrines proclaimed by a church or religion" and continually assert that they are seeking to propagate a religion to replace the "outmoded" faith in God and "belief in the Bible" idea.

• They believe "salvation...appears harmful, diverting people with false hopes of a heaven hereafter. Reasonable minds look to other means for survival."

• They are naturalists—they regard the universe as self-existing and not created.

• They believe in ethical relativism—"ethics are autonomous and situational," needing no basis in a God or theology. They believe there are no moral absolutes and that man should adjust his morals to the situations at hand.

• They believe religion unduly represses sexual conduct and believe in the right to abortion, divorce, euthanasia, and suicide.

It's no coincidence that this move away from a belief in God over the past several decades has been accompanied by the breakdown in the traditional family structure and by a decrease in morality. Christianity and Judaism taught moral truths about respect for others, honesty, sexual fidelity, honesty, the value of work, respect for the property of others, and self-restraint. With the decline of religious influence and the increase of people who deny God even exists, the constraints that religion imposes on morality are removed.

Notes

1. George Barna, *The Index of Leading Spiritual Indicators*.

2. George Barna, *The Barna Report,* November/December 1997, World Ministry Resources.

3. Billy Graham, *Storm Warning,* 170.

4. George Barna, *The Index of Leading Spiritual Indicators*.

5. "The Great Bull Market," *Business Week,* December 1997.

6. Maria Fiorini Ramirez, "Americans at Debt's Door," *The New York Times,* 14 October 1997.

7. Robin Leonard, "Money Troubles" (Nolo Press, 1997) from Microsoft MoneyInsider.

8. Ronald Blue & E. Glenn Wagner, Ph.D., "Five Keys to Financial Freedom," Promise Keepers.

9. Howard Gleckman, "How Worried Should You Be?" *Business Week,* 17 August 1998.

10. Timothy Lamer, "Is There No Tomorrow?" *World,* 7 August 1999.

11. "Is the U.S. Building a Debt Bomb?" *Business Week,* 1 November 1999.

12. "A $50,000 Car and You're Still Not Happy," *Business Week,* 15 February 1999.

13. Bloomberg L.P., Standard & Poor's. Return using capitalization weighted S&P 500 index, with dividends reinvested.

14. Edward N. Wolff, "Recent Trends in Wealth Ownership," a paper for the Conference on Benefits and Mechanisms for Spreading Asset Ownership in the United States, New York University, December 10-12, 1998, Table 2, "The Size Distribution of Wealth and Income, 1983-1997."

15. Edward Wolff, *The State of Working America,* Economic Policy Institute.

16. Robert B. Reich, "Lower Taxes? Oh, No Thanks," *Business Week,* 5 April 1999.

17. Edward Wolff, "Recent Trends in Wealth Ownership," Table 2, "The Size Distribution of Wealth and Income, 1983-1997."

18. Jeff Gates, "Statistics on Poverty and Inequality", Global Policy Forum, May 1999.

19. Ibid.

20. Ibid.

21 Michelle Conlin, "Unmarried America", *BusinessWeek*, 20 October 2003.

22. "Americans Fret About Moral Decline," MSNBC News, 24 June 1999. Based on a NBC News/*Wall Street Journal* poll.

23. Federal Bureau of Investigation statistics.

24. National Center for Health statistics.

25. Ibid.

26. Census Bureau statistics.

27. National Center for Health statistics.

28. American Humane Association and the National Committee for the Prevention of Child Abuse.

29. Billy Graham, *Storm Warning,* 234.

30. Stephen Covey, *The Seven Habits of Highly Effective Families.*

31. National Victim Center and the Medical University of South Carolina, "Rape in America."

32. Tulane University Study.

33. University of Michigan Study.

34. Laurie Hall, *An Affair of the Mind.*

35. *U.S. News & World Report,* 10 February 1997.

36. "Enough is Enough" brochure (1997) and Adult Video News (1997).

37. "The Underground Web", *BusinessWeek*, 2 September, 2002

38. Michelle Conlin, "Unmarried America". Data from the National Marriage Project, Rutgers University, Survey Research Center and the University of Michigan.

39. "What is Secular Humanism?" ChristianAnswers.Net.

40. Based on *Humanist Manifestos I and II* (1933, 1973): Bill Lockwood, "Secular Humanism, Bible Infonet, August 1997.

CHAPTER 8

STAGE SETTING FOR THE TRIBULATION

"In that day the Lord will reach out His hand a second time to reclaim the remnant that is left of His people [Israel]...He will raise a banner for the nations and gather the exiles of Israel; He will assemble the scattered people of Judah from the four quarters of the earth" (Isa. 11:11-12).

The Bible provides many, many details about the events that will occur in the end times, known as the seven-year Tribulation period. Since God has revealed what will happen during this period, we can then look to see if He is preparing the world for the fulfillment of the events that the Bible describes. In essence, we can look to see if the stage is being set for the enactment of God's final prophetic plan that will be carried out during the Tribulation period. Imagine a play about to begin. You can hear the shuffling of feet and the movement of props from behind the curtain, which indicates that there is a lot of activity going on. You know that the stage manager is in control and is directing everything to make sure that all the people and props are in place prior to the start of the play. You can see the lights starting to dim and the audience assembled. You know that the start of the drama is near.

This is the situation we find the world in today. Despite the fact many of the signs listed below are not explicit prophecy, they do speak loudly that the stage is being set. We don't know the exact time the play will start, but we can infer from the condition of the stage and the props that the time is rapidly approaching.

Israel Restored to being a Nation

Prophecy: The people of Israel will be restored to being a nation in their own land after a long period of time, but will not be spiritually reborn until later (Isa. 11:11-12, Zeph. 2:1-3, Ezek. 20:33-38, 22:17-22, 37:1-14). The restoration of Israel is a requirement for the start of the Tribulation period, because the event that starts the seven-year Tribulation clock is the Antichrist signing a seven-year peace accord with the nation of Israel (Dan. 9:27).

Fulfillment: As discussed in chapter three, "The History of Israel," the restoration of Israel as a nation after two thousand years of dispersion is a hallmark event in Bible prophecy. Many Old Testament prophets foresaw this event, and there are many prophecies related to it. When Israel became a nation again on 14 May 1948, it marked the first time since AD 70 that the people of Israel had a nation to call their own. It marked the first time since 605 BC that Israel had its own sovereign nation, which was not under the control of another world power. The importance of this event cannot be overestimated—no other nation in history has ever ceased to exist for centuries and then returned as a nation to its former land to regain its place in world history—and the Bible predicted this is exactly what would occur, thousands of years before it happened.

It wasn't too long ago that people considered this prophecy inconceivable. It was just too hard to imagine how this prophecy could be fulfilled in a literal sense. As a result, many Bible scholars tried to spiritualize prophecy to create scenarios whereby this prophecy could be fulfilled in the spiritual realm, instead of on earth. However, the rise of the Zionist movement in the late nineteenth century and the fulfillment of this prophecy in 1948 though, show that the Bible takes prophecy literally, and what may be inconceivable to man is conceivable to God.

To many students of prophecy, the restoration of Israel ended the "time of the Gentiles" that Jesus defined (Luke 21:24) and marks the imminent rise of the fifth kingdom (the Antichrist's kingdom) to world power. For more details, see chapter four, "The Great Gentile Kingdoms of the Earth."

Jerusalem the Center of Conflict

Implied Prophecy: During the war of Armageddon (described in chapter twenty-one), Jerusalem will be the center of conflict, and all nations of the world will be gathered against it. This final war, which will conclude with the Second Coming of Christ, will be fought over who will possess the Holy City (Zech. 12:2-5, 14:2). We can therefore assume that one of the signs of the times is conflict centered around who will possess the city of Jerusalem.

Fulfillment: Since its destruction in AD 70 at the hands of the Roman Empire, the city of Jerusalem has been an insignificant, minor city in the world. The city passed from people group to people group but was mostly left poor and neglected. It has only been since 1948, when Israel was re-established, that Jerusalem has become the center of world attention. Now, despite various attempts to peacefully divide the city between Arabs and Jews, the city remains at the heart of the Middle Eastern conflict. At issue is who should possess the city: the Palestinian Authority claims Jerusalem as its eternal capital, while the nation of Israel claims the same.

It's interesting to note that recent peace accords aimed at bringing peace to the Middle East (the Oslo accord, Wye River agreement, etc.) have left out the issue of who should possess Jerusalem. This has been for one simple reason—both sides have historically considered the possession of Jerusalem a nonnegotiable issue, and insist that anything short of full control over Jerusalem would be an unacceptable concession in any peace treaty.

Israel Ripe for a Peace Treaty

Implied Prophecy: The Bible warns that the Tribulation will occur when the nation of Israel is living in a time of perceived peace (1 Thess. 5:3). A treaty with the Antichrist will mark the beginning of this time of perceived peace and will start the seven-year Tribulation clock (Dan. 9:27). Therefore, we can assume that one of the signs of the times would be when the Israelites and the Palestinians are agreeable to a peace accord, since both countries are sworn enemies and have never had a history of working with one another.

Fulfillment: The nation of Israel has constantly been at war with the Arab nations since its founding in 1948. Israel and the Arab nations distrust one another and have historically been unwilling to enter into any comprehensive agreements. Events have changed, however, very recently.

Figure 7: Signing of the Oslo Accord

In 1991 the first comprehensive peace talks between Israel, the Palestinians, and neighboring Arab states began, and in 1993 a historic peace agreement between Israel and the Palestinian Liberation Organization (PLO), known as the Oslo Accord, was signed at the White House under the direction of U.S. President Bill

Clinton. This peace agreement was significant because the charter of the PLO has always called for liberating all of Palestine from the Jews (hence, the name of the organization). In fact, since its inception, the PLO Charter has contained language calling for the destruction of Israel.

Shortly after the signing of the Oslo Accord, Israel and Jordan entered into separate negotiations that led to the signing of a peace treaty in October 1994. The treaty addressed security, boundary, and other issues and established normalized relations between the two countries for the first time in history.

Following the historic Oslo Accord, several additional agreements were signed between Israel and PLO leader Yasser Arafat. These agreements included the Gaza-Jericho Accord in May 1994, the Oslo II Accord in September 1995, the Hebron Accord in January 1997, and the Wye River Accord in October 1998. The Wye River Accord was significant because (among other things) it called for a repeal of language in the Palestine National Charter calling for Israel's destruction. In exchange, Israel agreed to give part of its land in the West Bank. However, the Wye River Accord was never fully implemented by either side, and the destruction of Israel still remains very much a part of the PLO charter.

In May 1999, Binyamin Netanyahu was defeated as Prime Minister of Israel by Ehud Barak in an upset election. This election was significant because unlike Netanyahu, Barak was known for being nonreligious and was in favor of rapidly moving forward on negotiations to bring peace to Israel. In fact, the Palestinians were so thrilled with the election results that Yasser Arafat had to put a stop to plans for street celebrations in the West Bank and Gaza.[1]

Shortly after the election, Barak and Arafat announced they had reached an outline of a historic agreement on the future of Jerusalem. Jerusalem, with its holy sites sacred to Christians, Jews, and Muslims, has always been the most problematic issue in any potential peace agreement, as both sides have vowed to never compromise on having Jerusalem as their capital. Under the terms of the agreement,

Arafat would give up claims to large parts of Arab East Jerusalem (where the Temple Mount is located) in exchange for the right to declare a Palestinian state. The capital of the Palestinian state would be in Abu Dis, a village located two miles east of the Old City of Jerusalem on the eastern side of the Mount of Olives, but still technically within the historical administrative boundaries of the city. Abu Dis is also best known by Christians as the city of Bethany where Jesus raised Lazarus from the dead.[2]

Although the agreement was never signed and the leadership in both Israel and the PLO have since changed, a compromise deal along these lines would allow both sides to declare victory—Israel would regain control of all of East Jerusalem where the Temple Mount is located, and the Arabs would be able to declare a Palestinian state with its capital technically in Jerusalem.

While none of the peace agreements listed above achieved a lasting peace in the Middle East, they did signal that the nation of Israel was willing to enter into peace talks with its Palestinian enemies and make major concessions. For two thousand years the thought of Israel making a peace treaty with anyone wasn't even a possibility since Israel didn't exist, and for most of Israel's recent history there was no precedent for a treaty of any kind between Israel and the Palestinians, yet recently we have seen more than half a dozen in just the past decade.

Indeed, the desire for peace in the Middle East has spread around the world and is now a key plank in most western nations' foreign policy platforms. Although this would have been unheard of even a decade ago, it now seems quite possible that the Antichrist could enter the world stage by brokering a peace deal between Israel and their Palestinian neighbors, just as the Bible foresaw thousands of years ago. More details about the Antichrist, his seven-year peace deal with Israel, and the future of the Middle East are contained in the section on "Future Prophecy."

Israel a Wealthy Nation

Implied Prophecy: When the prophet Ezekiel describes a future attack on the nation of Israel by Russia and various other countries (described in chapter nineteen), he states that the motive for the attack will be to "plunder and loot" the nation of Israel which will be "rich in livestock and goods" (Ezek. 38:12). Thus, we can assume that one of the signs of the times is that Israel must increase in wealth and prosperity.

Partial Fulfillment: Despite being established by essentially Holocaust survivors and refugees who had almost nothing, Israel has grown to become a very prosperous nation and promises to become even more prosperous in the near future. Consider the following:

• Israel's per capita income is now comparable to England's and is greater than the largest Arab oil-producing states, including Saudi Arabia.[3]

• Israel's gross national product, which now stands at over one hundred billion dollars, is larger than the total of all its Arab neighbors, and Israel now has one of the highest living standards in the Mediterranean.[4]

• As the result of irrigation and "plant a tree" projects in Israel, what used to be a barren and desolate land is now vibrant countryside. Over two hundred million trees have been planted, which have dramatically increased the rainfall in Palestine—by over 10 percent every single decade since Israel was founded. Israeli farmers are now producing several harvests a year in the Jezreel Valley, an area that only fifty years ago was a disease-infested swamp. Because of this remarkable transformation, Israel has become the greatest source of fresh fruit in Europe, supplying 90 percent of the citrus fruit consumed by Europe's five hundred million people.[5, 6]

• Israel is now recognized as one of the key high-tech hubs in the world with many research organizations, technology companies, and venture capital firms located there.

• In 1995, oil was discovered near the Dead Sea. Unfortunately, this oil is hidden below a thick salt crust, making drilling unfeasible, but work is currently underway on methods to tap this vast reservoir.

Israel is already the envy of its neighboring countries. If the Dead Sea oil were to be extracted, the fortunes of Israel would certainly rise even further, making it an attractive target for its Arab neighbors who currently control most of the world's oil production. As Russia's economy continues to falter, it now seems quite likely that Russia, allied with the Arab nations, could attack Israel seeking to "plunder and loot" the nation just as the prophet Ezekiel described almost twenty-six hundred years ago.

Temple Close to Rebuilding

Prophecy: The Bible indicates that the Temple in Jerusalem will be rebuilt a third time. The Temple has to be rebuilt because a restored Temple exists at the midpoint of the Tribulation when the Bible indicates that the Antichrist will defile it (Dan. 9:27, 12:11, Matt. 24:15, 2 Thess. 2:3-4, Rev. 11:1-2). Details of this action are contained in chapter fifteen, "The Antichrist and His Kingdom." Note that the Bible doesn't provide timing: the Temple can be rebuilt before or during the first half of the Tribulation—it just has to be in existence and functioning at the midpoint. Therefore, one potential sign that the events of the end times are approaching would be Israel's movement toward rebuilding the ancient Temple in Jerusalem.

Partial Fulfillment: For almost two millennia, devoted Jews have turned three times a day toward Jerusalem and prayed this prayer: "Because of our sins we were exiled from our country and banished from our land. We cannot go up as pilgrims to worship Thee, to perform our duties in Thy chosen house, the great and Holy Temple which was called by Thy name, on account of the hand that was let loose on Thy sanctuary. May it be Thy will, Lord our God and God of our fathers, merciful King, in Thy abundant love again to have mercy on us and on Thy sanctuary; rebuild it speedily and magnify its glory" (*The Jewish Prayer Book*).

Facing West – The Dome of the Rock

Facing North - Toward Herod's Temple

Facing East - Toward the Mount of Olives

Facing South - Toward the Western Wall

Figure 8: Pictures of The Temple Mount [7]

Although Jewish people have believed through the ages that the Temple would be rebuilt, it has literally been unthinkable because the nation of Israel didn't exist, and for much of the time, Jews were prohibited from even visiting the Temple Mount. This all changed, however, in 1967 when Israel regained control over the old city of Jerusalem in the Six Day War. This represented the first time since the destruction of the second Temple in AD 70 that Jews have even thought it possible to actually rebuild the ancient Temple of God. However, fearful that the capture of the Temple Mount (where the sacred Dome of the Rock stands) would unite the entire Arab-Muslim world against Israel in a holy war, Defense Minister Moshe Dayan (a secular Jew) returned control of the Temple Mount area to Muslim religious authorities ten days after its capture as a bargaining chip in the peace talks. King Hussein of Jordan became the custodial caretaker of the area, thus preventing any Jewish worship on the Temple Mount. This return of the Temple Mount angered many religious Jews, who had been looking forward to rebuilding the Temple. As a result, the Temple Mount continues to be at the center of much of the contemporary Arab-Israeli conflict.

In addition to control of the Temple Mount being returned to the Muslims, there is another problem with rebuilding the Temple. It has been historically believed that the Dome of the Rock, the third holiest site in the Muslim faith, is located at the center of where the Temple would need to be built. To rebuild the Temple then, the Dome of the Rock must either be destroyed or moved—either of which would cause a monumental war between Israel and the Arab world.

However, recent discoveries indicate that the inner court of the Temple could be rebuilt without disturbing the Dome of the Rock. For almost thirteen centuries, people have believed the Dome of the Rock was built directly over the site of the original Temple and the Holy of Holies, but recent archeological discoveries have revealed otherwise. Doubt has existed on the exact location because the site of the Temple was so completely leveled after AD 70 by the Romans that few markers exist to confirm the actual location.

The new evidence revealed by Israeli archeologists, is based on the known location of the Eastern Gate ("The Golden Gate") and the newly discovered Western Gate and cornerstone of the inner court wall. These discoveries seem to confirm that the actual site of the original Temple is not where originally thought, but rather in an open area just north of the Dome of the Rock. If this is the case, the Temple and its inner court wall could be rebuilt and still clear the Dome of the Rock by one hundred and fifty feet. The Dome of the Rock would then end up in the Temple's outer court. Thus, it is possible that the Temple could be rebuilt on the original site of Solomon's Temple at any time, without actually requiring the destruction of the Dome of the Rock. If this were true, it would then seem to fit with Revelation 11:1-2, where an angel measuring the third Temple is told not to include the outer court because it was given to the Gentiles until the time of Christ's return.

Figure 9: Aerial View of the Temple Mount.
A = The newly proposed Northern Site, B = The traditional site &
Dome of the Rock

However, the Arab people would clearly not support the rebuilding of the Temple around the Dome of the Rock, so certainly something must change in the current geopolitical environment for the Temple to be rebuilt. Regardless of how these obstacles are resolved, preparations are already underway for the rebuilding of the Temple:

• A group, the Temple Mount Faithful, has cut a 4.5 ton piece of limestone to be used for the cornerstone of the Temple. Today, this cornerstone does not sit far from the Temple Mount. Architectural plans and models for the Temple have already been completed.

Figure 10: Architectural Model of the Tribulation Temple

• Utensils required for worship ceremonies have already been made. Many other items including clothing, musical instruments, architectural plans, and kosher animals have also been assembled.

• A religious school, the Ateret Cohanim, has been established for the education and training of Temple priests. According to the Bible, only descendants from the tribe of Levi can serve in this capacity. The purpose of the Ateret Cohanim is to research regulations, gather qualified Levites, and train them for future priesthood. More than five hundred descendants of Levi have already been trained for Temple service.

• In March 1997, a red heifer (a young female cow) without blemish was born on a farm near Haifa in Israel. Such an animal is necessary for the purification of the Temple site according to the Bible (Num. 19:2-7). Jewish teaching states that, since Herod's Temple was destroyed in AD 70, no flawless red heifer has been born in Israel. Twenty-five Jewish rabbinical experts confirmed the birth and acceptability of the heifer born outside of Haifa. As a result, this birth has been seen as "one of the most important signs that we are living in a special time" according to Gershon Solomon, head of a group dedicated to rebuilding the ancient Jewish Temple.[8, 9]

Clearly, the time is near when the Temple in Jerusalem will be rebuilt. Although almost twenty centuries have passed where this was unthinkable, events are now happening daily that bring Israel and the world closer to this event. It's certainly within the realm of possibility that a new peace deal (perhaps even the seven-year pact brokered by the Antichrist that signals the start of the Tribulation period) would allow the Jewish people to regain control of the Temple Mount and start the rebuilding effort. This is exactly what devoted Jews have been praying for, for almost two thousand years.

Ark of the Covenant Potentially Returned to Jerusalem

Potential Prop in the Stage Setting: As described in chapter three, "The History of Israel," the Ark of the Covenant was an ornate gold box made of wood that contained three items: the Ten Commandments, the rod of Aaron, and a golden pot of manna. It was constructed during Israel's wanderings in the wilderness and preceded Israel into numerous battles. The Israelites believed the Ark was the embodiment of God Himself and that the Lord dwelt in a dark cloud just above the Ark. King David's sole purpose for wanting to build the first Temple was to create "a house of rest" for the Ark of the Covenant.

King Solomon originally placed The Ark of the Covenant in the first Temple in 959 BC when the first Temple was completed. The Ark remained there until the final years of King Solomon's reign when it mysteriously disappeared. A close reading of the Old Testament reveals more than two hundred separate references to the Ark of the Covenant up to the time of Solomon. After his reign, however, it is almost never mentioned, and the Bible is strangely silent on what happened to it. The most important object in the world, in the biblical view, simply ceases to be in the story the Bible tells. The Bible is clear that the Temple of God must be rebuilt in the last days and that daily sacrifices will occur in the Temple before the midpoint of the Tribulation (Dan. 9:27, 12:11, Matt. 24:15, 2 Thess. 2:3-4, Rev. 11:1-2). Although the Temple could physically be rebuilt without the presence of the Ark of the Covenant (as the second Temple was), many devout Jews believe, based on scripture, that the Temple can't be built without the Ark. Furthermore, it would seem possible that if the Ark were recovered in the last days, it would lead to a renewed energy to rebuild the Temple and institute the daily sacrifices that the Bible requires. If the Ark of the Covenant were recovered, imagine the impact it would have. While there is a movement currently underway to rebuild the Temple, it has not garnered any national priority. However, imagine if the Ark were to be brought forth publicly—Jewish leadership and the nation as a whole would feel compelled to rebuild the Temple to provide a proper home for the Ark as instructed by the Torah. Furthermore, they would be required to institute the daily sacrifices in the Temple just as the Bible describes must happen in the last days, even though the concept of animal sacrifices might seem far fetched in our day and age.

Potential Fulfillment: The Bible doesn't record what happened to the Ark of the Covenant. The last reference to the Ark being in the possession of Israel is in 2 Chronicles 8:11, when Solomon asked his pagan wife to leave the area where the Ark of the Covenant was stored because she was not a believer. Shortly after this, the Ark disappeared. The Ark was not present in the second Temple, which was built when the Jewish captives returned from Babylon.

What happened to the Ark? There are various theories. Some suggest the Ark is hidden somewhere in a cave near the Dead Sea, on the Jordan River's west bank. This is the same location where the Dead Sea Scrolls were found. Another view says the Ark is buried underneath the Temple Mount, where either King Solomon, who built the first Temple, or King Josiah, one of the final kings of Judah, placed it. This later view is widely believed by most Orthodox Jewish groups who are seeking to rebuild the Temple. They state that the Ark will be revealed at the proper time—when the Temple is rebuilt.

Unfortunately, no substantial proof has ever been produced demonstrating the Ark's present whereabouts.

A third view regarding the Ark's location has garnered a lot of attention and support in the past decade and is related to Ethiopia. Based on recent events, interviews, and documentation, this view seems to be the most plausible. More significantly, this view indicates that the lost Ark of the Covenant was returned to Jerusalem in 1991, where it is now being held securely, awaiting a favorable political climate for it to be revealed. The explanation of this theory is based on two primary sources: Graham Hancock's book, *The Sign and the Seal* and Grant R. Jeffrey's book, *Armageddon: Appointment with Destiny*. Hancock was the East Africa correspondent for *The Economist,* a respected news magazine, and he based his book on personal interviews with various people, including the sacred "Guardian of the Ark." Jeffrey is a Christian researcher and based his book on external research and personal interviews, among which was Prince Stephen Mengesha, a member of the ruling family of Ethiopia and a direct descendant of King Solomon. The story developed by both authors is similar and is conveyed as follows.

The Bible states that Ethiopia's famous Queen of Sheba traveled to Jerusalem to meet King Solomon and was quite attracted to him (1 Kings 10). Ethiopian historical records and tradition indicate that King Solomon married the Queen of Sheba and had a son—Menelik I (though the Bible doesn't mention this). Menelik grew up in Jerusalem with his father, King Solomon, and became a strong believer in God while being educated by the priests of the Temple. When Menelik was nineteen, the Queen of Sheba died. Accompanied by a large group of Jews, Prince Menelik returned to Ethiopia to assume his role as king. The great distance between the two royal cities would prevent the prince from ever returning again to the Temple in Jerusalem. Before Menelik left, King Solomon ordered his craftsmen to create a perfect replica of the Ark for his son to take with him to Ethiopia. However, Ethiopian records suggest that Prince Menelik was concerned with the growing unrighteousness of Israel and the fact that his father, Solomon, was now allowing idols to be placed in the Temple to please his pagan wives. King Solomon gave the prince a going-away banquet, and after the priests were filled with wine, history records that Menelik and his loyal associates switched the replica ark with the true Ark. Menelik then took the true Ark of the Covenant home to Ethiopia, leaving the perfect replica behind in the Holy of Holies. It was Menelik's intent to return the Ark when Israel repented of their pagan idol worship and returned to the pure worship of God. Unfortunately, the people of Israel never did, and the nation was then subsequently taken into captivity by Babylon.

Menelik I became the founder of the longest-lived monarchy in history. His descendants, along with the Ethiopian descendants of Israel, formed the ruling class throughout Ethiopia's history. His dynasty lasted almost three thousand years and continued from Solomon's time until the communist takeover of Ethiopia in 1974.

During the almost three thousand years of Ethiopia's monarchy, it is believed that the Ark has been continuously stored and protected by royal priestly guards. While the Ark has been moved on occasions, it is believed to have spent most of its time in a complex set of deep underground passages beneath the church of Zion of Mary in Aksum. Priestly guards of the ancient Ethiopian, Jewish monarchy protected these passages. Only one person, the Guardian of the Ark, was allowed to enter the Holy of Holies, the room where the Ark resided. This Ethiopian priest-guard is chosen at age seven from a priestly family to give up the freedom of a normal life to guard the Ark for the rest of his life. As the guardian, he fasts, prays, meditates, and guards the sacred Ark with his life. Upon his death, another chosen Guardian replaces him. In 1986, Graham Hancock, working for *The Economist*, found and interviewed the sacred Guardian of the Ark:

> Hancock: "I have heard that the Ark of the Covenant is kept here...in this chapel. I have also heard that you are the Guardian of the Ark. Are these things true?"

> Guardian: "They are true."

Hancock: "But in other countries nobody believes these stories. Few know about your traditions anyway, but those who do say that they are false."

Guardian: "People may believe what they wish. People may say what they wish. Nevertheless we do possess the sacred Tabot, that is to say the Ark of the Covenant, and I am its Guardian..."

Hancock: "Let me be clear about this, are you referring to the original Ark of the Covenant—the box made of wood and gold in which the Ten Commandments were placed by the prophet Moses?"

Guardian: "Yes. God Himself inscribed the ten words of the law upon two tablets of stone. Moses then placed these tablets inside the Ark of the Covenant—which afterwards accompanied the Israelites during their wanderings in the wilderness and their conquest of the Promised Land. It brought them victory wherever they went and made them a great people. At last, when its work was done, King Solomon placed it in the Holy of Holies of the Temple that he had built in Jerusalem. And from there, not long afterwards, it was removed and brought to Ethiopia..."

An *Encyclopedia Britannica* article seems to confirm this tradition: "It [Aksum] contains the ancient church where, according to tradition, the Tabot, or Ark of the Covenant, brought from Jerusalem by the son of Solomon and the Queen of Sheba, was deposited and is still supposed to rest."

Besides historical records, there are other indications that seem to corroborate this story. First, in Ethiopia there is a ceremony called the Timkat. During this celebration, monks and members of the clergy carry objects called Tabots that represent the Ark of the Covenant. This religious festival in Ethiopia actually includes symbols of the Ark because they believe that is where it resides. More importantly, the actual Ark has been brought out on occasion during these festivals and has been seen by the people of Ethiopia. Ethiopian records confirm its occasional appearances. Second, in

Aksum there are various ancient murals and tapestries that depict the story of Menelik carrying the Ark off to Ethiopia. These collaborate the story that the Ark was switched in the original Temple and taken to Ethiopia.

Figure 11: Mural of Menelik traveling by sea with the Ark

Figure 12: Mural of Menelik arriving at Aksum with the Ark

Since 1975, Ethiopia has been engulfed in a civil war as the result of the Marxist takeover. Between 1976 and 1991, Israel undertook an effort to airlift the Jews of Ethiopia, called the Falashas, to Israel. During this effort, over eighty-five thousand Ethiopian Jews were transported to Israel where they would be safe from persecution. In 1991, Israel launched an extraordinary rescue operation, known as Operation Solomon, during the chaotic final days of this war. As part of this rescue, Israel flew numerous military cargo flights into the Ethiopian capital where people had gathered to escape. It is believed that during one of these cargo flights, a special team of Israeli soldiers, all handpicked from the tribe of Levi, flew an unmarked military cargo plane into the area of Aksum at night and transported the Ark of the Covenant back to Jerusalem in the final days of the civil war. According to the Law of Moses, only trained Levites were to carry the Ark (Num. 4:15). The Ark is now believed to be in Israel, in a secure place where it will be held until the time is appropriate for it to be revealed and placed into the Holy of Holies of the rebuilt Temple.

If these sets of facts are correct, the timing would be remarkable. The Menelik dynasty (a continual family of rulers that believed in the Jewish faith), lasted three thousand years. It ended in 1974, after Israel was finally restored to being a nation after two thousand years of dispersion. In essence, the Menelik dynasty lasted right up to the point when it was finally possible to return the Ark to a restored nation of Israel. All of this occurred at the same time as the fulfillment of so many other signs of the times that the Bible describes would occur near the time of the end. Surely, this cannot be coincidence.

It should be noted that the aforementioned view is not inconsistent with the view held by Orthodox Jews, who believe the Ark is currently buried underneath the Temple Mount. According to Ethiopian historical records, an identical replica of the Ark was made and placed in the Holy of Holies during the reign of King Solomon. As such, two Arks should exist—the original carried off by Menelik and now in the possession of Israel, and the replica, which could very well be buried underneath the Temple Mount. Obviously, confirmation of the Ark's presence in Israel is impossible to document or prove. Is the Ark truly in Jerusalem? Will it be revealed in the last days? Only time will tell. Regardless of its present whereabouts, a few things are certain: First, if the Ark were recovered, it would be the greatest archaeological discovery of all time. It would garner worldwide attention and would cause millions of people, especially Jews, to rethink their views of God. Second, such a discovery would lead to significant pressure to rebuild the third Temple. The Bible indicates the reason King Solomon built the first Temple was to house the Ark. If the Ark were revealed in our time, millions would demand that the government of Israel do the same. Third, although there are conflicting views on the Ark and there are potentially two Arks in existence, only one would need to be put forth as the real Ark to garner worldwide headlines and establish a need to rebuild the Temple.

Although the recovery of the Ark is not described in the Bible and cannot be considered prophecy (and therefore should not disappoint Christians if it is not recovered), it is interesting to think that God may use it as a key prop to set the stage for the final fulfillment of prophecies: the rebuilding of the Temple, the establishment of daily sacrifices, and the return of Israel to a knowledge and understanding of God. It should be noted though, that even if the Ark of the Covenant were recovered, the Lord God would not dwell in the third Temple or project His glory over the Ark of the Covenant like He did in Old Testament days. Since Christ came, God no longer requires a physical Temple on earth, but rather projects His glory and presence through a living Temple made up of every believer in Christ (1 Cor. 3:16-17, Eph. 2:19-22). Christ was the final sacrifice for sin (Heb. 10:18, 1 John 2:2); therefore from a Christian perspective, there is no longer a need for sacrificial offerings in the Temple or the Ark of the Covenant as an emblem of worship. The Jewish people, however, reject Christ and thus, still recognize the need for the Ark and the daily sacrifices that the Old Testament describes.

Jews Return from Russia

Prophecy: Near the time of the end, Jews will return to the nation of Israel from the land of the North. This migration will be so significant that the Jews will treat it as a second exodus (Jer. 16:14-15, 31:8, Zech. 2:6). In the Bible, the "land of the North" commonly refers to Russia (for more about Russia in prophecy, see chapter nineteen).

Partial Fulfillment: During the Diaspora (discussed in chapter three), Jews fled to all parts of the world following the Roman destruction of Jerusalem in AD 70. Many Jews migrated to Russia where they lived for centuries.

In the late 1700s, Russia started to impose severe restrictions on the Jewish people living within the country. Jews were forbidden to live outside specific areas, and their educational and occupational opportunities were narrowly circumscribed. In addition, the government encouraged and even financed periodic massacres of Jews, called pogroms, in order to divert the attention of the Russian people away from their discontent with the current system of government. After the communist revolution of 1917, Jews continued to endure persecution and repression from the government of Russia. During this time, Jews were prevented from immigrating to the West or to Israel.

In the late 1980s and the early 1990s, the USSR disintegrated and the fourteen former USSR republics declared their independence. When this happened, emigration restrictions were eased, and in 1989 the Jews who endured centuries of persecution under the Soviet system were finally able to flee the country. Massive waves of Soviet Jews immigrated to the newly formed country of Israel, fulfilling the prophecy predicted in the Bible thousands of years earlier. In the past decade, almost a million Jews have left Russia and returned to the homeland of their forefathers. Many believe that one of the reasons God destroyed the "evil empire" of the USSR was to free His chosen people to return to Israel.

While God has clearly opened doors for the Russian Jews to return to Israel, it should be noted that the final fulfillment of this prophecy will not occur until Christ returns and establishes His Millennial Kingdom. It is at this point that *all* Jews will return from Russia to settle in the land of Israel.

Movement Toward a One-World Religion

Implied Prophecy: The Bible indicates that during the Antichrist's reign during the Tribulation period, there will be a common, worldwide religion that will assist the Antichrist in his endeavors (see chapter sixteen). We can therefore conclude that one of the signs that the stage is being set for the end times is the movement toward the consolidation and merging of religious denominations.

Fulfillment: The movement toward global religious unity has never been stronger than in our day. Prior to the twentieth century, there were few attempts to create organizations that spanned across the various church denominations. In this century though, there have been several successful undertakings that have brought many Christian denominations closer together, most significantly the formation of the World Council of Churches, which was formed in 1948. The movement toward religious unity is referred to as the ecumenical movement, and has led to the creation of various umbrella-like church organizations that span across traditional denominations.

Although the Bible encourages Christian unity and cooperation, the problem with the ecumenical movement is that core biblical doctrine has been eroded and discarded in order to reach agreement and unity across the denominations. As churches have sought unity under these organizations, they have resorted to a least common denominator set of beliefs for the sake of compromise instead of holding true to what the Bible says. As a result, the various political pronouncements and positions produced by the ecumenical church councils now stand opposed to many core biblical doctrines. The following outlines the history and origins of the ecumenical movement and shows the progression toward the one worldwide church organization that the Bible describes will exist in the end times:

• In 1948, the World Council of Churches was founded. In the decades that followed, this organization expanded rapidly and spread into mainline denominations such as Episcopalian, Methodist, Presbyterian, Baptist, and Lutheran. By the early 1980s, the World Council of Churches included more than 295 churches spanning more than twenty-nine denominations in more than ninety countries. This organization now includes almost all Christian denominations, many of which are now involved in joint projects with one another, and others have undertaken actual merger negotiations.

• In 1950, representatives of 29 denominations formed the National Council of Churches (NCC). The NCC eventually claimed thirty-five denominations including the United Methodist Church, the Disciples of Christ, the Episcopalian Church, the United Church of Christ, the American Baptist Churches, the Presbyterian Church, and four Orthodox bodies. Although seemingly in decline as of late, the NCC represented a high-water mark for liberal Protestantism due to its liberal theology and radical positions on social issues.

• In the 1960s, the Roman Catholic Church started to cooperate with the World Council of Churches and started promoting ecumenism through the work of the Second Vatican Council that was convened by Pope John XXIII. His successors, Paul VI and John Paul II, have continued to support this movement.

• In the 1980s and 1990s, the ecumenical movement started to build increasing consensus on doctrinal questions that had once been highly disputed. This was due largely to the dialogues that took place between the various Christian churches—Anglican, Orthodox, Protestant, and Roman Catholic. Various documents were created and subsequently adopted by the churches that outlined basic, biblical principles intended to govern all aspects of society. As a result of these pronouncements and agreements between denominations, a common belief system has evolved around the following viewpoints.

The problem is that they all contradict the common, literal interpretation of the Bible traditionally taught by most churches. These beliefs include: 1) *Postmillennialism:* the belief that we are living during the Millennium and that Christ's kingdom will be established by the Church, on earth, through the evangelism of the nations. This view holds that there will be no end times, Antichrist, Tribulation, or Millennium. For a detailed discussion of this view, see *Appendix B.* 2) *Replacement theology:* the belief that the Church is the new Israel and that God's promised blessings and covenants with Israel were transferred to the Church upon Christ's death on the cross. Thus, there will be no fulfillment of the covenants God made with the patriarchs of Israel including Abraham, Isaac, Jacob, and David. 3) The belief that Satan was completely defeated by Christ at the cross and is therefore no longer the ruler of this world. According to this view, the world is getting better because Christ is ruling it from Heaven. It is not decaying and getting worse as prophecy foretells.

• On 22 June 1998 more than two hundred religious leaders from throughout the world converged on Stanford University to create a United Religions Charter. The goal was to create a permanent assembly of the world's religious leaders modeled after the United Nations to resolve lingering disputes amongst all faiths (Jews, Muslims, Christians, and pagans) and to promote global peace and cooperation between all religions in preparation for the new millennium. This group has since completed the charter and is now working toward establishing a permanent interfaith assembly.[10]

• On 31 October 1999 the Catholic Church and the Lutheran World Federation signed the Joint Declaration on the Doctrine of Justification and became united on the primary issue that has bitterly divided them for almost five hundred years—namely whether salvation comes through grace alone. And thus, according to the news media, the Reformation that began when Martin Luther nailed his ninety-five theses to the church door in Wittenberg, Germany in 1517, ended.

• On 29 August 2000 the United Nations held the Millennium World Peace Summit, which brought together more than one thousand leaders of the world's various religions and faiths. This meeting represented the largest gathering of religious leaders ever held and the first attempt by the United Nations to coordinate matters of faith. The stated goal of the summit was to "coordinate religious leadership as a driving force for building tolerance, fostering peace and encouraging interreligious dialogue among all religions of the world." In addition, the conference sought to establish a permanent council of religious leaders to "serve as an ongoing interfaith ally to the United Nations in its quest for peace, global understanding and international cooperation."[11] Interestingly, Ted Turner, a historically outspoken critic of Christianity, who served as honorary chairman for the meeting, funded a major portion of the conference.

Although none of the efforts above are the "False Religion" of the end times, we are clearly seeing the beginnings of the movement toward worldwide religious unity and consolidation that will exist during the Tribulation period. Prior to this century, the ecumenical movement didn't exist, and there were no significant gatherings of religious leaders from around the world. In the past sixty years, however, the ecumenical movement has grown to include almost all Christian denominations, and collaboration among the world's religious leaders is starting to emerge. As the United Religions Charter movement develops and the United Nations establishes a permanent council of religious leaders, the movement toward religious unity will only grow. There is no doubt that the stage is being set for the eventual creation of the false religion that the Bible describes will lead millions astray during the end times. (For more detail see chapter sixteen.)

Movement Toward a One-World Government & Economy

Implied Prophecy: The Bible indicates that during the Tribulation period, the Antichrist will be successful in uniting many nations of the earth together into a global empire (see chapter fifteen). This empire will revolve around political, economic, and religious issues. For the most part, the empire will arise voluntarily from the nations. We can therefore conclude that one of the signs of the time is the movement away from independent sovereign nations.

Fulfillment: There is no question that the world is moving quickly toward the one-world government and economy that the Bible describes. During the past sixty years, there has been a dramatic rise toward globalization and supranational organizations. Prior to the 1950s, there were almost no cross-national organizations with any significant power. In the past sixty years however, we have seen a dramatic rise in the number of these organizations and in their influence on world affairs and the support for them by very prominent people. Consider the following quotes:

"There are a lot of very brilliant people who believe that the nation-state is fast becoming a relic of the past" (President Bill Clinton).[12]

"Nationhood as we know it will be obsolete; all states will recognize a single global authority" (U.S. Deputy Secretary of State Strobe Talbott). [13]

"If we are to avoid eventual catastrophic world conflict we must strengthen the United Nations as a first step toward a world government...to do that, of course, we Americans will have to yield up some of our sovereignty" (Walter Cronkite).

"Mankind's problems can no longer be solved by national governments. What is needed is a world government. This can best be achieved by strengthening the United Nations" (Jan Tinbregen, Nobel Prize-winning economist).

"In an increasingly interdependent world, old notions of territoriality, independence, and nonintervention lose some of their meaning. National boundaries are increasingly permeable— and, in some important respects, less relevant. A global flood of money, threats, images, and ideas has overflowed the old system of national dikes that preserved state autonomy and control....It is now more difficult to separate actions that solely affect a nation's internal affairs from those that have an impact on the internal affairs of other states, and hence to define the legitimate boundaries of sovereign authority....For all these reasons, the principle of sovereignty and the norms that derive from it must be further adapted to recognize changing realities." (United Nations Commission on Global Governance)

The lives of everyone on the planet are increasingly becoming more interconnected. Even as little as a century ago, the world didn't exist as a single, interdependent unit. People on one continent had little or no knowledge of the happenings on another, and certainly what happened in one country didn't impact people around the globe. This has all changed fairly recently. Today, no one is immune to events taking place anywhere on the planet. Stock market changes in Asia send tremors around the globe in a matter of minutes. Oil prices in the Middle East can impact farmers in Central America. Wars and conflicts in the Russian Republics are televised in real-time and impact soldiers who quickly mobilize in the United States. As such, many people now see supranational organizations as essential to solving the increasingly complex problems of the world and are calling for the strengthening of these organizations. It's interesting to note that one of the key presidential campaign debates of 2004 related to whether or not the United States even had the right to start a war without the full approval of the United Nations (President George W. Bush referred to this as needing a "permission slip").

The rise of globalization and supranational organizations can be traced to the events of World War I and World War II. War has long been a good motive for the subordination of a people's freedom to achieve a great national cause. What made the two world wars of the last century unique is that they truly were worldwide in scope; they necessitated the coordination between different countries for the first time in history to achieve military dominance. Centralized planning was critical to the war effort, and it is this centralized planning that inspired both Lenin and Mussolini. After the wars ended, politicians and intellectuals everywhere were attracted to the idea that their power and intelligence could put them in control of other people's lives and wealth, which could be then be used for great purposes. This thinking has led to the rise of many of the supranational organizations that exist today.

What most people don't realize, however, is that the temporary loss of freedom that exists during a time of war will lead to inevitable decay and corruption, if the wartime controls are transformed into a permanent system of government in peacetime. Thus, the movement toward global unity will ultimately lead not to global peace and prosperity, but rather to a time of corruption and totalitarianism as prophesied by the Bible. Instead of a system of government based on the concept of "one nation under God" under which the United States was founded, we are now moving to a system of "one world under man." Why is this bad? Author Hugh Ross explains it this way:

> A marketing analogy might help explain the risks of worldwide peace and unity (under human leadership). If one corporation acquires full control over a product everyone needs, we can anticipate what will happen: the price will go up and quality will go down. Free-market economies enact antitrust laws to keep monopolies from practicing this kind of exploitation. Competition among corporations forces them, to some degree, to keep product prices low and product quality high. Typically, nations compete with one another for citizens and economic strength. "Brain drain" describes the loss of talented, well-educated citizens by one nation to another that offers such "brains" more opportunity for success and reward. Similarly, many nations constantly lure corporations to locate in their lands through tax incentives and educational programs designed to provide large pools of available, well trained, efficient, and cost-effective personnel.

> Eliminating national boundaries and uniting nations under a global banner may seem the right way to establish world peace and unity. Such peace and unity, however, eliminates competition

for citizens and corporations, and those citizens and corporations will have no recourse. If only one government exists for humanity, that government could control its citizens' lives to align with that government's goals. The government, really an elite group of people, becomes the final judge of what is "good" for itself and for everyone. Pride will command the world.

These principles help us to understand the tragedy of the Soviet Union. Soviet leaders were able to lock out competition for people and enterprises. They even locked out foreign ideas and information. Thus, for a time, they got away with oppressing their citizens.[14]

Unfortunately, the world is moving rapidly to the time of global rule that the Bible describes. Consider the following about the history and growth of these supranational organizations and the movement toward global unity:

• In 1944, the World Bank was created to help developing nations get funding for projects. The charter of this bank spanned across countries—its goal was to grant loans to various member countries to finance specific projects, and thus encourage foreign investing.

• In 1945, the United Nations was formed as a supranational organization chartered to drive toward the abandonment of the use of force and a permanent system of general security. The U.N. consists of 191 member nations, including nearly every country in the world. Since its founding, the United Nations has expanded to take on a greater role in the affairs of nations in the name of "humanitarian" and "peacekeeping" missions. Although the U.N. was originally chartered to drive toward the "abandonment of the use of force," consider the following:

1. Between 1948 and 1978, U.N. troops were called out to respond to thirteen different operations. But in the last ten years alone, more than twice that number of U.N. deployments have occurred. In fact, in the last ten years, the U.N. has engaged in more peacekeeping operations than it did in its first forty,

deploying troops to over nineteen countries at an annual cost of over three billion dollars.[15, 16]

2. In the last decade, the U.N.'s peacekeeping budget has increased by over 1000 percent, with a staggering 7000 percent increase in military personnel involved in U.N. police operations.[17]

3. In 1994, President Bill Clinton signed an executive order that would allow U.S. forces to be placed under the command of the U.N. in certain situations. This order broke with long standing military policies and would allow the U.N. access to U.S. military intelligence. In addition, this order established a U.N. military peacekeeping fund that bypasses Congress and repealed the law that limits the number of troops that the U.S. can commit without congressional approval.[18]

It's interesting that the cornerstone of the United Nations building in New York reads, "they shall beat their swords into plowshares, and their spears into pruning hooks; nation shall not lift up sword against nation, neither shall they learn war anymore." This is a direct quote from the Bible (Isa. 2:4) describing the world after Christ's return and the establishment of His Millennial Kingdom, where He will rule the world with truth and justice (see chapter twenty-four). It appears the United Nations sees its role in the world as that of Jesus Christ— seeking to be the institution that brings peace to the nations through a one-world government. Although the idea is noble, unfortunately for the U.N., the timing is wrong. The Bible indicates that nations will only be at peace after Christ returns and establishes His kingdom.

• In 1947, the International Monetary Fund (IMF) was created to promote international monetary cooperation and to facilitate the expansion of international trade. The IMF encourages its member nations to maintain an orderly pattern of exchange rates and to avoid restrictive foreign exchange practices. Membership included 183 countries in 2001 and is open to all independent nations.

• In 1949, NATO (the North Atlantic Treaty Organization) was formed as a regional defense alliance. NATO consists of twenty-six member nations with the purpose of enhancing the stability, well-being, and freedom of its member nations through collective security arrangements.

• In 1959, the World Constitution and Parliament Association (WCPA) was formed with the goal of drafting a constitution and forming a parliament for "the coming world government." This nongovernmental organization consists of intellectuals and leaders from around the world. In 1977, work on the "Constitution for the Federation of Earth" was completed and adopted by the participants of the WCPA. It is the intent that this document would eventually replace the U.N. charter. Since then, discussions of the WCPA have focused on creation of a World Disarmament Agency, a World Economic Development Organization, a Graduate School for World Problems, a World Court, an Emergency Earth Rescue Administration, a World Government Funding Corporation, a World Commission on Terrorism, A Global Ministry of the Environment, a World Hydrogen Energy System Authority, and an Earth Financial Credit Corporation. Although the WCPA is a private organization and has no real power to enact any of the efforts under discussion, it's interesting because it has prominent members from around the world and represents an organized lobbying group that is focused solely on the issue of creating a one-world government.

• In 1989, the North American Free Trade Agreement (NAFTA) was signed as a pact that calls for the gradual removal of tariffs and other trade barriers on most goods produced and sold in North America. NAFTA created the world's second largest free trade zone, bringing together 365 million consumers in Canada, Mexico, and the United States in an open market.

• In 1993, the nations of Europe came together to form the European Union dedicated to monetary and economic unity among the European states, with serious consideration toward joint policies related to defense, citizenship, and the protection of the environment.

• In 1994, the World Trade Organization (WTO) was formed to promote and enforce trade laws and regulations. The World Trade Organization has the authority to administer and police new and existing free trade agreements, to oversee world trade practices, and to settle trade disputes among member states. This organization is not accountable to any government. As of 2005, the WTO had 148 member nations.

• In 1996, the United Nations Commission on Global Governance (it's surprising to many that the UN has such a commission) published a 410-page book entitled *Our Global Neighborhood,* describing how to implement world government by establishing a World Court, a World Treasury, a U.N. Police Force, a World Bank, and various other world institutions that would be funded by a world tax.

• In 1998, the International Criminal Court (ICC) was formed in Rome. This is the first permanent global judiciary in history. The purpose of the court is to bring individuals to justice for what the treaty calls "the most serious crimes of international concern"— genocide, war crimes, crimes against humanity, and aggression. Over 137 countries signed on. Only six countries declined to participate in the court. The United States was one of these. While President Clinton supported the court, participation was blocked by Congress, which feared the court could abuse its power for political purposes, charge U.S. soldiers on frivolous charges or prosecute "hate speech" crimes such as preaching Christianity in Muslim countries like Saudi Arabia. President Clinton, however, signed the treaty during his last weeks in office despite Congressional opposition, but the Bush administration subsequently pulled out of it. The other countries which declined participation included Israel, China, India, Libya, and Qatar.[19]

• In addition to the above, many more supranational organizations have been formed around the world to promote cross-country cooperation. Some of these other organizations include the Islamic coalition, the Latin American Integration Association, the Nations of Southeast Asia, and the West African economic community.

It's important to note that the organizations listed above are not necessarily good or bad. What they indicate however, is a trend—a trend that the Antichrist will ultimately take advantage of to accomplish his purposes on the world stage. Prior to the 1950s, there were almost no supranational organizations. The dramatic rise in the number and influence of these in the past few decades speaks loudly that the stage is being set for the ultimate rise of the Antichrist. Though it would have been unheard of for a world leader like the Antichrist to rise to power and unite all of the nations of the world under one government as few as sixty years ago, we now have in place the basic building blocks for just such a government—including the legislative branch (U.N.), the judicial branch (ICC), the defense department (NATO), the finance ministry (IMF), and the treasury (World Bank). All the world needs now is an executive branch, which the Bible predicts will be led by the Antichrist in the last days.

Movement Toward a European Federation

Implied Prophecy: As described in chapter four, "The Great Gentile Kingdoms of the Earth," a federation of ten kings or nations will rise out of Europe (i.e., out of the nations that made up the Roman Empire). It is out of this federation that the Antichrist will ultimately arise (Dan. 7:24). We can therefore assume that one of the signs of the times is the movement toward the reunification of the European countries and the formation of a ten-nation federation. The Bible describes these events as preparation for the Antichrist's appearance.

Partial Fulfillment: Since the division of the Roman Empire, many men have tried to reunite the nations of Europe under one power: Charlemagne (Holy Roman Empire) in AD 800, Charles V of Austria in 1364-1380, Louix XIV of France in 1643-1715, Napoleon of France, Kaiser Wilhelm of Germany during World War I, and Adolf Hitler of Germany in World War II. All of these have failed—the European nations have remained divided.

Map 9: Nations of the European Union
(Includes 2007 Admission & Candidate Countries)

However, in 1993, with the ratification of the Maastricht Treaty, the European Union was established as a supranational organization dedicated to monetary and economic unity among the European states with serious consideration toward joint policies related to defense, citizenship, and the protection of the environment. Even though the reunification of Europe by force has been unsuccessful throughout history, the nations of Europe are now voluntarily reuniting as the result of global economic pressure. Although there are currently more than ten member nations of the European Union, it is clear that we are probably seeing the beginning of the federation referred to in the Bible. Because there are more than ten nations, we can anticipate that one of a couple different things will happen: either some members of the European Union will drop out and/or consolidate, or perhaps the ten-nation confederation will be expanded to some form of a ten-region, government, with leaders overseeing each of the various regions. Regardless, it is clear that the process of the reunification of Europe has begun.

The following quotes certainly support this:

"Once a common market interest has been created, then political union will come naturally" (Jean Monnet, one of the originators of European integration).

"We felt like Romans on that day [when the treaty of Rome was signed]... we were consciously recreating the Roman Empire once more" (Belgian Foreign Minister Henri Spaak and former secretary-general of NATO).

"The vision of a `United States of Europe' set out in Winston Churchill's famous speech at Zurich in 1946 remains our objective in the process of European unification" (German Chancellor Helmut Kohl).

"The mentality of the nation-state has been consigned to the past" (German Foreign Minister Hans-Dietrich Genscher).

"European nations are surrendering their sovereignty [to the European Union] on a scale never seen before" (U.S. Supreme Court Justice Anthony Kennedy).

"... and that means nothing less than a European Parliament and European government which really do exercise legislative and executive power" (German Foreign Minister Joschka Fischer arguing for a "United States of Europe").

The points below describe the history and advancement of the European Union:

• On 25 March 1957, the movement toward a modern European Union was started with the signing of the Treaty of Rome. This treaty created a European Court of Justice with power above that of individual member nations and mandated the elimination of trade barriers among member nations. These six nations that signed the Treaty of Rome were Belgium, Germany, Luxembourg, France, Italy, and the Netherlands. These countries had a combined population of over 220 million people. It's interesting to note that Henri Spaak, Belgium's foreign minister who signed the Treaty of Rome at the time, admitted that these leaders were consciously trying to recreate the Roman Empire through this treaty.

• In 1973, Denmark, Ireland, and Great Britain joined what was then called the European Economic Community (EEC), bringing sixty-six million more people into the union. In 1981, Greece joined the EEC, and in 1986, Portugal and Spain were added.

• On 1 January 1993, Western Europe became a single economic market linking people in twelve nations. Tariffs and customs barriers between these countries were eliminated.

• On 1 November 1993, 345 million people became citizens of the new European Union (which replaced the EEC) when the Maastricht Treaty was signed and European citizenship was granted to each of the twelve member states (Belgium, Denmark, France, Germany, Great Britain, Greece, Ireland, Italy, Luxembourg, the Netherlands, Portugal, and Spain). In 1994, the EU admitted three more members—Austria, Finland, and Sweden.

• On 1 January 2002, the Euro, for the first time in history, replaced all European national currencies and eliminated the right of individual nations to issue their own money. The European Central Bank took over monetary policy for the European Union. Six months later, all national currencies of the twelve member countries ceased to be legal tender, and only the Euro remained. The countries adopting the Euro included Germany, France, Italy, Belgium, the Netherlands, Luxembourg, Ireland, Portugal, Spain, Austria, Greece, and Finland. Great Britain, Denmark and Sweden, for various reasons, chose not to participate.

• On 1 May 2004, ten additional countries were admitted to the EU: Cyprus, the Czech Republic, Estonia, Hungary, Latvia, Lithuania, Malta, Poland, Slovakia and Slovenia. Five additional countries have since applied for membership including Bulgaria, Croatia, Romania, Turkey and the former Yugoslav Republic of Macedonia.

The impact that the creation of the European Union will have on the world cannot be underestimated. At more than 6.5 trillion dollars, the new European Union's economy will approach the U.S.'s eight trillion dollars, and the two continents' share of world trade will be almost the same at about 18 percent.[20] *Business 2.0* recently noted: "This is big. It's a major historical event, with political and economic consequences that may be felt for centuries. Three hundred million inhabitants of [the member nations]—countries that spent a significant part of the last millennium waging war upon each other—will share the same currency, the same monetary policy and the same economy."

Consider too, the following quotes from *BusinessWeek* regarding the impact that the EU and the creation of the Euro will have on the world:

The move to the Euro is expected to unleash an unstoppable market process that will sweep away structures of Old Europe. In their place will emerge the second-largest economy in the world, and will inevitably lead to talk of greater political integration. Many foresee the Euro as the "Trojan Horse" that will be "the catalyst for Europe's revival—economically, politically, and in self-confidence."[21]

Europe's impending creation of a monetary union with a single currency will be the most important change in the global economy well into the next century. The currency could pose a challenge to the supremacy of the U.S. by creating the world's second-largest economy, consisting of three hundred million people (more than either the U.S. or Japan) and a GDP of nearly 20 percent of the world's total. This threatens the U.S. because, when America's boom ends, the US will still be the world's largest debtor, whereas the European Union will be a net creditor. The U.S. will continue to run chronic trade deficits, while the European Union will amass large surpluses.[22]

The global economy wasn't supposed to look like this. After the Berlin Wall crumbled and governments throughout the world cast their lots with capitalism, it seemed logical to envision a single, seamless system. Money, goods, and eventually people... would flow south and east...Instead, the new century will begin with an eerily familiar alignment. Once again, North America and Europe are the global anchors of prosperity and stability, while the rest of the world struggles in economic limbo. Far from counting on hot emerging markets to drive global growth, companies and investors are focused on the Atlantic zone. `The big growth engines are the U.S. and Europe'...Europe? Pundits wrote it off as an also-ran in the race for global competitiveness, a continent hopelessly tangled in obsolete regulations and stubbornly refusing to change...Long considered a collection of economic has-beens clinging to outdated social systems, Europe is on the rise. The single currency, officially born on 4 January [2002], is only the latest milestone in the Continent's long journey back to global prominence.[23, 24]

Even though the promise of the new European Union centers around economic unity among member nations, the EU is now expanding its influence over other areas including education, public health, culture, consumer protection, industry, research and development, environment, social affairs, and development cooperation. *BusinessWeek* called the Euro a "Trojan Horse," and indeed that is what it is quickly becoming—a disguised beginning for the political reunification of the peoples descended from the Roman Empire that the Bible described almost three thousand years ago. As the European Union has taken shape over the past decade, we have seen more and more power being centralized into the presidency and more attention focused on non-economic issues.

Consider the implications of this—the nations of Europe are now coming together for the first time in history since the breakup of the Roman Empire. This occurs at the same time as other signs of the times are being fulfilled, such as the restoration of Israel, the Jews returning from Russia, and the movement toward a one-world religion and one-world government. There is little doubt that the pieces of the puzzle are falling into place and the stage is being set for the final enactment of God's plan. This is especially true given Europe's increasing hostility toward Israel. In poll conducted in 2000 of fifteen European Union member states sponsored by the European Commission, its citizens were asked to rank the fifteen countries they view as the biggest threats to world peace. Interestingly, Israel topped the list – even above known (then pre 9/11) terrorist states such as Iran, North Korea, Afghanistan and Iraq. In fact, Israel garnered an astounding 59 percent of the votes. In other words, Israel was viewed as bigger threat by Europeans—according to the poll—than George W. Bush's "axis of evil" countries *combined*! Given this, it's really not that hard to imagine that the Antichrist could rise to world prominence from this region and then seek to direct the affairs of Israel in the end times just as the Bible predicts.

Russia Becomes a World Power

Implied Prophecy: In the end times, the Bible describes an attack on Israel that will occur led by "Gog, of the land of Magog" (Ezek. 38-39). Chapter nineteen, "The Attack on Israel," describes this event in detail. Although a complete historical analysis is beyond the scope of this book, scholars have identified Magog as the region North and Northeast of the Black Sea and East of the Caspian Sea. Three members of the former Soviet Union now occupy this land: Russia, the Ukraine, and Kazakhstan.

The attack includes various countries, but the Bible describes Russia (Gog) as the leading country in the coalition (Ezek. 38:7), and during Armageddon, Russia is one of the major world powers that are mentioned. Therefore, we can assume that one sign of the times is that Russia must achieve a high level of power and military might in the world—enough to lead a major coalition of forces into battle against Israel.

Fulfillment: After World War II, Russia became established as one of the world's two great superpowers. This was a relatively new position for Russia—it was only after the Russian revolution in 1917 and the subsequent rise of Lenin and Stalin that Russia started to be recognized as a significant world power. Prior to that, Russia was considered a minor player on the world stage. After World War II however, the Soviet Union rapidly expanded and took over the countries of Eastern Europe. The Cold War led to the rapid buildup of military armaments in both Russia and the United States. Russia has now become recognized worldwide as one of the world's two great powers. Although Russia declined after communism fell at the end of the Cold War, Russia is still considered the world's second strongest superpower and holds much of the same nuclear arsenal that it did during its peak. While the power that was once Russia has declined, one can easily envision Russia leading a coalition of forces into a war. In fact, Russia's economic decline provides a possible motivation for just such an attack.

Regardless of the exact scenario, the point to keep in mind is that prior to the twentieth century, it would have been implausible to think pre-Lenin Russia could lead any sort of military coalition into battle. Now, however, thanks to the military buildup of the Cold War, the scenario is for the first time a possibility.

Russia Allied with Arab Nations

Implied Prophecy: In the aforementioned attack on Israel, detailed in chapter nineteen, "The Attack on Israel," the Bible describes a coalition of countries led by Russia that mount a military assault on the nation of Israel. This coalition includes Egypt, Libya, Sudan, Ethiopia, Iran, and Turkey as well as various others. The Bible mentions that Russia will be pressured to lead this coalition, seemingly against its will, by the other nations of the coalition: "I will turn you around, put hooks in your jaws and bring you out with your whole army" (Ezek. 38:2-6). The analogy describes the use of a horse's bridle, whereby a rider can direct a horse where he wants it to go. We can therefore assume that these countries must become allies at some point and that there must be some external force (or bridle) to drive Russia's entry into this battle against Israel.

Speculation: It's interesting to note that all of the allies of Russia listed in the Bible are Muslim nations. In fact, of the more that one billion followers of Islam, the vast majority live in the countries described in this prophecy, including the countries of Northern Africa (Egypt, Libya, Sudan, and Ethiopia) and the Arab nations of the Middle East (including Iran, Turkey, and Indian countries such as Afghanistan, Pakistan, and India). In addition, several of the Russian breakaway republics (including the Ukraine and Kazakhstan) have significant Muslim populations.

Even though many of these countries don't have a historical track record of working together, most are now allied with Russia and have a common enemy: Israel. As a result, they all share the fundamental Islamic belief that Palestine must be liberated from the Jews. Add this to the fact that Israel's location is very strategic, and one can easily see the scenario of Russia and the Muslim countries attacking Israel as described, playing out on the world stage today.

The City of Babylon Rebuilt

Implied Prophecy: There are many end-time prophecies that describe Babylon as God's enemy (Rev. 14:8, 17-18). Although many passages use the word "Babylon" to refer to the coming worldwide government (Rev. 13:3-4), religion (Rev. 13:11-15), or economic system (Rev. 13:16-18) under the Antichrist, there are also many references to a physical, rebuilt city of Babylon that will exist during the end times (Rev. 18). We can therefore assume that one of the signs of the times will be the physical rebuilding of the ancient city of Babylon. Why is Babylon significant? To the nation of Israel, Babylon symbolized the epitome of a powerful, evil, worldly city destined for destruction. Babylon was the first city built following the Great Flood and was built by Nimrod, a man who, in defiance of God, attempted to create the first world empire (Gen. 11:1-9). As Babylon became a world power, the city was known for its luxury and moral decadence. Under King Nebuchadnezzar, Babylon invaded Israel, destroyed the Temple and the city of Jerusalem, and took the Jewish people into captivity for seventy years (detailed in previous chapters three and four). It was here that Daniel was thrown into the lion's den and where his friends were thrown into the fiery furnace. It's also in this area where the original sin took place (Gen. 2:10-14), where Satan made his first recorded appearance (Gen. 3:1-6), where the Bible says Satan had his seat (i.e., headquarters) in ancient times (see chapter sixteen), and where the Antichrist will establish his kingdom during the Tribulation period. Throughout scripture, Babylon is seen as one of God's great enemies.

Fulfillment: The ancient city of Babylon (located just east of the Euphrates River, fifty-six miles south of Baghdad in modern-day Iraq) was overrun by the Media-Persian Empire in 539 BC. In the years that followed; Babylon decayed and was ultimately left in ruins. Since then, the city of Babylon has never been rebuilt (although an insignificant number of people occasionally lived there). This was the case for over twenty-five hundred years. This changed however, in 1987, when the city of Babylon was rebuilt and "new Babylon" was dedicated. While this event didn't gain world attention, it did have major prophetic significance and was one of the reasons for the events of the Gulf War.

The rebuilding process started in 1971, when the United Nations Educational, Scientific, and Cultural Organization (UNESCO) announced that it would help Iraq completely restore the ancient city of Babylon. Rebuilding began under the general supervision of Saddam Hussein, and in 1987, the rebuilding of the temples, the palaces, and the gardens had been completed to a point where

Hussein felt that he could declare to the world that Babylon had been restored to its former glory. The city was actually rebuilt on the original foundations of the ancient city—the bricks at the bottom of the city were actually laid by Nebuchadnezzar twenty-five hundred years earlier. On 22 October 1987, the rebuilt city and royal palace were dedicated during the Babylon International Festival.

The Great Palace

The Ishtar Gate

The Perimeter Wall

The Boundary Wall

Figure 13: Pictures of the Rebuilt City of Babylon

The festival was quite an event: during the festival, thousands of people dressed as ancient Babylonian soldiers and marched down Procession Street (the main street leading into Babylon) to promote the rebirth of the city. Various kings and queens, dancers, opera singers, movie stars, and musicians attended, including Madonna (who received a special invitation because, as was noted, "she lives in the heart of all Iraqi people"). The ceremony ended with a dedication to Ishtar, the mother goddess of Babylon, who was credited with bringing back the "eternal city of Babylon."

The total cost of the reconstruction project was over one billion dollars. Because the long war with Iran (which ended in 1988) left Saddam Hussein short of funds to complete the rebuilding process, Hussein demanded that Kuwait forgive the debt Iraq owed and give it a share of revenue from an oil field that straddled the Iraqi-Kuwaiti border. When Kuwait declined, Iraq invaded Kuwait in 1990. This event triggered the Persian Gulf War. The city of Babylon wasn't damaged during the war, and Saddam Hussein continued the rebuilding process as soon as the war was over. Saddam's stated goal was to make Babylon the most glorious city in the world, just as it was in the days of Nebuchadnezzar. It has been well documented that Saddam Hussein viewed himself as a modern-day Nebuchadnezzar who was seeking to restore the glory that was once Babylon's. Nebuchadnezzar was the ancient king (604-562 BC) who invaded Israel, destroyed Solomon's Temple in Jerusalem, and took the remaining people of Israel back to Babylon as slaves. Here are some examples that show Hussein's high regard for Nebuchadnezzar:

• The posters that appeared throughout Baghdad advertising the Babylon International Festival showed a portrait of two individuals. The first was Saddam Hussein; the other was Nebuchadnezzar. In fact, the posters were intentionally drawn so that Saddam Hussein looked like Nebuchadnezzar. Saddam's goal was to wrap himself in the glories of Nebuchadnezzar and ancient Babylon.

• On the end of each brick that was made for the rebuilt city was the name Nebuchadnezzar, and on the other end was the name Saddam Hussein.

• The plaque that was used during the dedication read, "From Nebuchadnezzar to Saddam Hussein, Babylon undergoes a renaissance."

Figure 14: Picture from Babylon International Festival Program

In 1990, Sam Donaldson and Diane Sawyer provided a tour of the rebuilt city of Babylon on their TV show, *Prime Time Live*. In it, they showed the bricks and the inscriptions from both Nebuchadnezzar and Saddam Hussein and provided a tour of this impressive city. Despite the Iraq war and the subsequent fall of Saddam Hussein, the city of Babylon was untouched by coalition bombing and stands today just it was before the war.

We can only speculate, but it is clear that God is using recent events surrounding the rebuilding of the city of Babylon, the Iraq war and the recent turmoil in this area of the world to further set the stage for the final fulfillment of His prophetic plan.

Worldwide Communication Technology Exists

Implied Prophecy: There are several events mentioned during the end times where the Bible indicates that the whole world will see certain events that take place in Jerusalem. The death of the two witnesses (see chapter seventeen) is one example. Revelation states that "for three and a half days men from every people, tribe, language and nation will gaze on their [dead] bodies and refuse them burial" (Rev. 11:9). The Second Coming of Christ is another example. The Bible states, "every eye will see him" (Rev. 1:7) and "all the nations will mourn. They will see the Son of Man coming" (Matt. 24:30). How can the whole world see events that take place in one geographic location? How could people from around the world see certain things that occur at the same time?

Fulfillment: A decade or two ago, it would have been impossible for these prophecies to be fulfilled literally. It just wasn't possible for people of all nations from around the world to view events that were occurring simultaneously. The Gulf War in 1990 changed all that. With the advent of CNN, countries from around the world experienced TV news and video of the bombing of Iraq as it happened, in real-time. This was a television first, and our generation was the first to see it. Now, with several twenty-four-hour cable news networks, satellite dishes on people's roofs, and streaming video from the Internet, these prophecies can now be fulfilled at any point. The entire world can now see events that occur in one part of the country as they happen, just as the Bible predicted almost two thousand years ago.

Technology for the Mark of the Beast Exists

Implied Prophecy: During the reign of the Antichrist, everyone on the earth will be required to have a mark on his or her right hand or forehead that will allow the buying and selling of goods. Nobody will be allowed to conduct financial or commercial transactions without this mark (Rev. 13:16-17). This mark is commonly referred to as the "mark of the Beast" and is described in detail in chapter fifteen, "The Antichrist and His Kingdom." Even though this prophecy could be fulfilled through a simple tattoo, it would be logistically difficult, if not impossible, to police the buying and selling of goods at all retail outlets around the world to ensure compliance. The Bible tells us that the Antichrist will be able to control *all* financial transactions for *everyone* in the world. We can therefore assume that a global transaction system might be employed to facilitate the mark and monitor the buying and selling of goods by all the people of the world. The technologies for such a system could include:

• A worldwide communications system, which would enable the transmission and verification of all global commercial transactions.

• Global databases, which could be used to maintain information about everyone in the world.

• Implants or tattoos that could allow people to be uniquely identified.

Partial Fulfillment: All of the technologies that would be necessary to implement a global transaction system like the one described above have been created in just the past few decades. Indeed, the world has now become reliant on electronic transactions as a means to conduct business. Most people never heard of an Automatic Teller Machine (ATM) as recently as twenty years ago; now it would be impossible for most families to live without one. Between credit card systems, ATM cards, relational databases, and the Internet, there is no doubt that technology has moved to the point where the Antichrist could easily set up a system that would prohibit individuals from buying or selling goods without a "mark" (or means of authorization). All of the key components are now in place:

• SWIFT, the International Bank Settlement System based in Brussels which is used to transmit transactions such as ATM withdrawals and debit card transactions, is now responsible for more than three trillion dollars in electronic money transfers every day among the world's three thousand largest banks. This system can validate bank balances in seconds and authorize or deny consumer transactions from a centralized processing facility.

• Relational databases, which became popular in the 1980s and 1990s, are now used by almost all companies to process orders, manage billing, and track customer accounts. What makes relational databases unique is their ability to "relate" one type of information to another. This makes it easy, for instance, to correlate a consumer's purchasing habits (as tracked by grocery stores, restaurants, or other merchants) with their personal demographics, family history, credit history, or reading habits.

• In 1995, the Internet exploded as a means to connect computers and databases around the world. What makes the Internet unique is that it knows no language barriers or national boundaries. It has only been in the last couple of years that one could even imagine a worldwide computer network that could maintain records on, and track, the buying and selling of all people on the earth. In just a few short years, electronic commerce transactions have become commonplace, with people now able to purchase anything over the Internet. Of course, all of these purchases are being tracked and stored in relational databases to help merchants better understand their customers. The popular Internet site Amazon.com, for instance, not only uses a consumer's purchase history of books, compact disks, videotapes, and consumer electronics to create a profile of a consumer, but also uses their browsing habits (i.e. the products they merely looked at) as well. They then use the profile to suggest other products the user may be interested in.

• In 1997, businesses started to develop "intranets" and "extranets" that link together all of a business's computer systems with those of the company's suppliers, buyers, and business partners. Because these networks are so efficient in communicating information, many companies are now mandating that all of their business transactions be conducted over these networks.

• Identification systems that can uniquely identify people have become pervasive. People now daily rely on Social Security numbers, barcodes, ATM cards and User IDs to prove they are who they say they are. Currently there is no means of global identification in place, but it's clear that technology has advanced to such a point where this would certainly be possible. In fact, various high-tech companies are currently working on technologies that enable users to have one, common means of identification for the Internet. This would provide users with one set of credentials that they could then use to conduct commerce—weather it is on the Internet, at a cash register or using their cellular phone. Users would then receive one, common, consolidated billing statement from the provider instead of having various different relationships with different merchants.

• Work is well underway by several companies, including Intuit, CheckFree, and Integrion Financial Network (owned by IBM, Visa International, and others), on "bill presentment" systems that enable consumers and businesses to receive billing statements through E-mail instead of through the traditional mail system. Users would then be able to receive and pay all of their bills electronically, with balances deducted from electronic bank or brokerage accounts. There would be no need for paper checks, bills, or invoices. The deployment of these systems is currently underway.

• With the enormous growth of financial transactions occurring electronically, significant attention is now being focused at improving security and reducing the potential for fraud. The problem, of course, is that it is difficult to positively identify the person initiating an electronic transaction. However, technologies have already been developed (including smart cards, fingerprint identification systems, barcodes, and smart chips) that can provide positive identification for initiators of financial transactions. These technologies are already being adopted very rapidly as businesses seek to ensure the legitimacy of the ever-increasing volume of transactions occurring. In fact, several systems using a new technology called radio-frequency ID (RFID) tags are now being deployed that use rice-grain size chips implanted under the skin of a person or animal for purposes of identification. In fact, over a million of these tags have already been implanted in pets. In 2004, the FDA approved these chips for use in humans, which are now being used for purposes of health care. The chip inserted under the skin and carries a sixteen-digit code that can be read by a scanner to unlock a medical patient's records from a secure database. Additional applications are certain to develop. Just as driver's licenses and Social Security numbers have left their highly specific originally intended purposes behind and become general-purpose ID tools, so too it is easy to imagine a biochip that unlocks personal information proving useful for a broad variety of functions.

As can clearly be seen, the components are rapidly coming together for a worldwide system that can track the buying and selling of goods all over the world, just as the Bible describes. Although it would have been unthinkable to imagine such a system as little as twenty or thirty years ago, the rapid pace of technological development in the 1980s and 1990s has made this scenario not only plausible, but also probable. Although the technologies described are not inherently good or bad, there can be little doubt that the Antichrist will exploit these technologies to control the buying and selling habits of consumers in the end times, just as the Bible foresaw almost two millennia ago.

Notes

1. "A Warrior for Peace," *U.S. News & World Report On-line*, 31 May 1999.

2. "Barak, Arafat in Accord on Jerusalem," *USA Today*, 23 May 1999.

3. Zola Levitt, "Israel on the Spot," *Foreshadows of Wrath and Redemption*, 137.

4. "Israel at 50," MSNBC News, World Wide Web, 30 April 1998.

5. Rev. Daniel Hayden, "King of the New World," *Zion's Fire*, March/April 1998.

6. Grant R. Jeffrey, *Armageddon: Appointment with Destiny*, 273.

7. Pictures from Encarta 99 Encyclopedia, Denis Tremblay/Labtex Inc.

8. London Sunday Telegraph, 16 March 1997.

9. SNS News Service, the Associated Press, 29 May 1997.

10. Carolina Wolohan, "Group Uses U.N. as its Model," *San Jose Mercury News*, 22 June 1998.

11. Taken from the *Millennium World Peace Summit Fact Sheet* posted on their web site, August 2000.

12. *New York Times,* 25 November 1997.

13. *Time*, 1992.

14. Hugh Ross, *The Genesis Question*, 170-171.

15. Hal Lindsey, *Planet Earth—2000 AD*, 54.

16. Grant R. Jeffrey, *Armageddon: Appointment with Destiny*, 282.

17. Ibid.

18. Donald S. McAlvany, "Moving the U.S. Military Under U.N. Command," *McAlvany Intelligence Advisor*, August 1994, 6.

19. "Permanent War Crimes Tribunal OK'd," MSNBC, 18 July 1998.

20. "The Atlantic Century?" *BusinessWeek*, 8 February 1999.

21. "The Euro," *BusinessWeek*, 27 April 1998, 90-94.

22. Jerrey E. Garten, Dean of the Yale School of Management: "The Euro Will Turn Europe into a Superpower," *BusinessWeek,* 4 May 1998.

23. "The Atlantic Century?" *BusinessWeek*, 8 February 1999.

24. "Europe Rising," *BusinessWeek*, 8 February 1999.

CHAPTER 9

THE BEGINNING OF 'BIRTH PAINS'

"For many will come in my name claiming, `I am the Christ,' and will deceive many. You will hear of wars and rumors of wars, but see to it that you are not alarmed. Such things must happen, but the end is still to come. Nation will rise against nation, and kingdom against kingdom. There will be famines and earthquakes in various places. All these are the beginning of birth pains" (Matt. 24:5-8).

When Jesus was asked by His disciples, "what will be the sign of Your coming and the end of the age," He listed many signs such as wars, natural disasters, famines, and increased growth and persecution of the Church (Matt. 24:3-14, Mark 13:3-13). He then stated that these signs would be like birth pains—increasing in frequency and intensity until the ultimate time of His return (Matt. 24:3-8, Mark 13:8).

Many of the signs Christ listed coincide with the Seal judgments (discussed in chapter thirteen), which will happen during the Tribulation period. However, if these events are truly to be like "birth pains" as Jesus described, then we can look to see if the contractions have started as evidence that the stage is being set for the Tribulation.

Referring to the signs, Luke 21:28 states "when these things begin to take place, stand up and lift up your heads, because your redemption is drawing near." We're instructed to take notice when these events *begin* to happen as indication that the end times are approaching. As you look at the following list of signs, it's hard to conclude anything other than that the "contractions" have already started and that the time of Christ's return truly is drawing near:

False Christs Arise

Prophecy: People will arise who claim to be the Christ or a prophet and will deceive many (Matt. 24:5, 11, 23-26, Mark 13:6, Luke 21:8).

Fulfillment: Although there have been people claiming to be the Christ starting from the very early periods of Christianity, numerous "false Christs" have arisen over the past century claiming to be the Messiah or a prophet of the Messiah. These more recent false Christs are significant because of the number of people they have misled and the consequences for their followers, which has often been death. Examples of people claiming to be the Messiah in the past century include:

• David Koresh of the Branch Davidians. Koresh claimed to be the messiah and warned his followers that the Second Coming of Christ was imminent and would be preceded by catastrophes and war. In 1993, after a fifty-one-day siege by United States federal agents, eighty-nine members of the Branch Dividian cult were killed in a fire that destroyed their headquarters near Waco, Texas.

• Marshall Applewhite of the Heaven's Gate cult. Applewhite also claimed to be the messiah. In 1998, thirty-nine members of the cult committed suicide en masse after interpreting the arrival of the Hale-Bopp comet as a sign from heaven that the earth was going to be recycled.

• Sun Myung Moon of the Unification Church. Moon says he is "Lord of the Universe" and the Messiah incarnate. Moon claims that, at the age of sixteen, he had a vision in which Jesus Christ announced that Moon had been chosen by God to complete the restoration of the kingdom of God on earth. Moon's Unification Church has a significant number of members in both Korea and in the United States.

• Jim Jones of the People's Temple. Jones claimed to be the messiah. In 1978 in Jonestown, Guyana, more than nine hundred cult members committed suicide by drinking poisoned Kool-Aid on the orders of Jones.

• Rabbi Schneerson. Schneerson misled hundreds of thousands of Jewish followers into believing that he was the promised messiah and that he would rise from the dead after his death in 1991.

• Lord Maitreya of England. Every few years Maitreya publicizes claims that he is the Christ by taking out full-page ads in major newspapers around the world announcing that he is the Christ.

• Shoko Asahara of Japan. Shoko claims to be the messiah and is suspected by police for masterminding a chemical attack on a Japanese subway, which killed ten people and injured five thousand.

• Father Divine. George Baker (aka Father Divine) claimed that he was "God Almighty...the Holy Spirit personified . . . the Prince of Peace" which led to a movement called the Peace Mission. He died in 1965.

• Elizabeth Clare Prophet of the Church Universal and Triumphant. Elizabeth says, "I am that I am" (a statement made by God in identifying himself to Moses). She and her followers are awaiting the end of the world in Montana.

• Meher Baba of the Sufism Reoriented faith. Meher claimed that he was "Christ personified." He died in 1969.

• David Berg of the Children of God. Berg claims to be God and is revered by his followers as David incarnate and God Himself.

• John Robert Stevens of The Walk movement. His followers claim to be the one true Church and denounce others as "the harlot of Babylon" (see chapter sixteen).

• Herbert Armstrong of the Worldwide Church of God. Armstrong claims that his followers will become more like God until the time of the resurrection when they shall become gods.

• Numerous Hindu-based cult leaders who have claimed to be incarnations of deity. This includes Sai Baba, who says he is "the living incarnation of both Jesus and Hare Krishna."

In addition to the above, there has been no shortage of other people claiming divine revelation that have also misled many believers:

• In 1923, Joseph Smith claimed to receive angelic revelations that led to the creation of Mormonism, which is a perversion of Christianity. Mormonism, which claims to be the fastest growing religion in the world with now over ten million members, was founded on the assumption that Christianity is more or less corrupt and that restoring the "true" Christian gospel was necessary. Mormons believe that God was a man who evolved into a god and that worthy Mormon males can evolve into gods as well.

• In the late 1800s and early 1900s, Charles Russell and Joseph Rutherford published a series of works that led to the creation of the Jehovah's Witnesses movement. Jehovah's Witnesses deny all major teachings of biblical Christianity (the Trinity, the deity of Jesus, the bodily resurrection, his visible Second Coming, a physical heaven and hell, etc.). They believe that Christ returned secretly in 1914 to establish His Millennial Kingdom. Although the actual date has moved several times and the world didn't end as they predicted in 1975, this movement still has a significant following.

• In the late 1800s, while recovering from severe injuries due to a fall, Mary Baker Eddy claimed that she received visions and was inspired of God to write her books and create the Christian Scientist movement—yet another perversion of Christianity. Mary Baker Eddy even went so far as to claim that her discovery of Christian Science was the fulfillment of Christ's Second Coming! The Christian Science movement believes that faith is all that is necessary for healing, and thus, Christian Scientists turn to prayer rather than conventional medicine to heal illness.

Clearly, we are living in a time full of false christs and false prophets who are, in fact, deceiving many in the end times just as the Bible predicted. Although there have been other false christs in times past, it's not surprising to see the rise of so many in recent years at the same time so many other prophecies are being fulfilled.

Wars

Prophecy: There will be wars and rumors of wars. Nation will rise against nation, and kingdom against kingdom (Matt. 24:6-7, Mark 13:7-8, Luke 21:9-10).

Fulfillment: Although mankind has always been at war (ever since Cain, the first child of Adam and Eve, killed their second child, Abel), the twentieth century has been different—it has been the bloodiest in the history of mankind. More people have died due to wars in this century than in the previous nineteen centuries *combined*. Despite the literally thousands of peace treaties that have been signed in this century, the last one hundred years truly have been the "century of war."

Why was the twentieth century so different? Prior to this century, the weapons used to wage war were perhaps spears and muskets. Battle was essentially based on one-on-one combat. In the twentieth century however, mankind developed the technology to wage war on a massive scale. The inventions of tanks, battleships, submarines, missiles, aircraft carriers, airplanes, and nuclear bombs all occurred during this century. As such, war evolved to the point where one person and one weapon could cause massive destruction to the enemy. This advancement of technology made world wars a possibility for the first time, which is significant given the phrase Christ used to describe this sign of the time. Christ stated, "*Nation* will rise against *nation*, and *kingdom* against *kingdom*" (italics added). This very specific phrase implies more than just two countries going to war—it implies that the real sign that Christ was referring to was when two countries would go to war and then other countries would join in. Indeed, this is just what has occurred during this century.

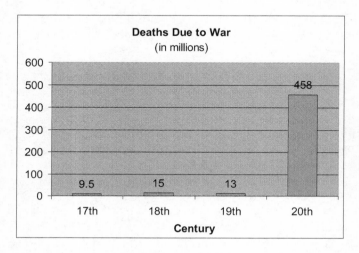

Figure 15: Increase in Deaths Due to War [7]

In 1914, a Serbian zealot assassinated Francis Ferdinand, the Archduke of Austria. This led Serbia and Austria into war and, due to alliances and interlocking treaties, eventually brought the rest of the world into World War I as well. More than 8.5 million soldiers were killed in this war with the total casualties totaling more than thirty-seven million. This figure doesn't count the close to ten million civilian deaths that were caused indirectly by the war. World War I was supposed to be the "war to end all wars," but as we know, that didn't happen. Less than twenty-five years after the start of World War I, Adolf Hitler began his conquest of Europe in an effort to reunite the German-speaking people. As Hitler started to "annex" the countries of Europe, the world was quickly brought back again into a war that would impact almost every country of the world. World War II was the most devastating war in human history. More than thirty million soldiers were killed, not including the more than twenty million civilian deaths and the more than seven million Jews that were killed in the Nazi Holocaust. Just as occurred during World War I, nation did rise against nation and then kingdom against kingdom as Christ's prophecy predicted.

As the destiny of nations become more intertwined through global commerce, treaties, and communications, it's hard to see how this trend toward global conflicts will not continue to exist. In fact, as we saw in the Persian Gulf War and in the Iraq War, one tiny nation's actions can quickly bring the nations of the world together into a war to protect each nation's self-interest. While most people think there has been relative peace since WWII, the truth is that the world has not known a single day since WWII when some nation has not been waging a war or a conflict somewhere on earth. In fact, of the two hundred members of the United Nations, one-third of them (more than sixty) have waged war in the past sixty years.[2] The death toll for the twentieth century only continued to rise with the advent of the Cold War and the rise of communism. Communism claimed almost one hundred million lives in the Soviet Union, China, Cambodia, Cuba, Ethiopia, and dozens of other totalitarian police states where it spread.

The ultimate "rumor of war" (Matt. 24:6) in the past sixty years has been caused by the advent of nuclear weapons—and the possibility that mankind could destroy the whole earth several times over. For the first time in history, nations now have the means to totally annihilate an entire enemy country. Although the Cold War between the United States and the Soviet Union has ended, there are currently over fifteen other nations that now have nuclear technologies of one kind or another, and more than half of these possess nuclear armaments. As many as twenty-five additional countries are now scrambling to achieve nuclear capability as well. Despite the end of the Cold War, the developing nuclear arms race between countries such as China, India, and Pakistan will ensure that the threat of nuclear war persists. It's interesting to note that a nuclear threat or "rumor of war" has been one of the forces driving the strengthening of the United Nations and the reunification of Europe—two other signs the Bible identifies as milestones that will mark the approaching end times.

Famines

Prophecy: There will be famines in various places (Matt. 24:7, Mark 13:8, Luke 21:11).

Fulfillment: Due to the world's growing population, natural disasters, and war, there are currently numerous famines in various places throughout the world. More than 850 million people on earth now face serious malnutrition and about one-third of the world's six billion are malnourished in some way.[3] Hunger and malnutrition claim ten million lives every year, 25,000 lives every day and one life every five seconds. In fact, hunger and malnutrition have now become the number one risk to global health, killing more than AIDS, malaria & TB combined. [4]

Most people are familiar with the pictures on TV of children whose bodies are so malnourished that they look like skeletons wrapped with skin. Indeed, the pictures are so sickening that most people would have to admit that they quickly change the channel when they see these haunting images. Unfortunately, famine is real and has become a series problem in many places around the world. The following are some examples:

• In North Korea, one-third of the population is suffering from severe famine due to floods, drought, and years of communist mismanagement. Over three million people have died of starvation and another three million are at risk.[5]

• In Sudan, food shortages are currently threatening the lives of over a million people, which is in addition to the 1.3 million people that have already died from famine and fighting wars. It's estimated that presently two hundred people are dying per day, not necessarily due to of lack of world aid, but because food can't be distributed due to the poor condition of roads and a shortage of transportation following fifteen years of civil war.[6]

• In Somalia, over one million people are facing food shortages and four hundred thousand of them are at risk of starvation. One-quarter of the children under five have now died due to starvation.[7, 8]

• In Ethiopia, drought and poor harvests have left eight hundred thousand people in need of famine relief.[9]

• In the Philippines, three hundred thousand families are hungry because of severe drought.[10]

• In Africa, nearly ten million people are currently in need of emergency food. Malnutrition and starvation have recently reached epic proportions due to a drought and civil wars.[11]

What's probably more disturbing than the current famines occurring around the world is the fact that most of the world is less than one year away from critical starvation in the event of a serious crop failure or natural disaster. Even the United States, with all its surpluses, is no more than two years away. This is primarily due to the world's growing population. Over the past two millennia, the world's population has increased thirty-fold, from approximately two hundred million at the time of Christ to over six billion today. This translates into more than 225 thousand people added to the world's population every single day—the equivalent of adding an additional, medium-size city to the earth's population every twenty-four hours. To put this growth rate in perspective, it took the entire time from the creation of man until World War I to produce a population of two billion people. That same number of new people will be added to our current population over the next forty years.

Unfortunately, while the world's population continues to increase, food production is growing at its slowest rate in four decades and is on the decline in ninety countries. Grain stocks are at their lowest levels in thirty-five years. By the year 2030, it's estimated that China alone will require all of the world's current exports of grain.[13]

Clearly, famine is a serious problem around the world. Despite modern technology and the rise of wealth in developed countries, the number of famines around the world is increasing, not decreasing. A growing number of nations now lack for food—the essential element of life. The Bible indicates that famines will increase until the time of the end and also during the Tribulation period; when more than one fourth of the earth will be killed by "sword, famine and plague" (Rev. 6:8—see chapter thirteen). We are currently seeing the initial signs of the contractions of increasing famine around the world, just as the Bible predicted.

Plagues

Prophecy: There will be plagues (disease) in various places (Luke 21:11).

Fulfillment: Despite the enormous advances of modern medicine and the use of antibiotics and vaccines, there has been a dramatic increase in the number and impact of new infectious diseases in recent years. In fact, the World Health Organization now reports that more than thirty, dangerous, new, infectious diseases with no known treatment, cure, or vaccine have been discovered in just the past two decades.

"We are seeing a global resurgence of infections diseases" (U.S. Surgeon General David Satcher. Congressional testimony, 3 March 1998). This seems counterintuitive. With all the advancement in modern science, shouldn't the spread of disease be decreasing around the world instead of increasing? One would think so, but there are at least three forces working against science. The first is the changing morality associated with sex and drug use. This has contributed to the spread of highly lethal diseases such as AIDS. The second is the increase in air travel, which is now more affordable and common than ever before. Air travel allows infectious agents, which were once confined to one corner of the world, to be spread across continents relatively easily, which speeds the spread of new disease. With the steady rise of global trade, business travel, and tourism, the rapid spread of infectious disease will only get worse. The third factor is the over use of antibiotics. It's estimated that fifty million unnecessary prescriptions are written for antibiotics every year.[14] With each new prescription, bacteria become more resistant to the antibodies. In fact, it's recently been reported that "super bugs" have emerged that have literally changed their genetic structure to ward off antibiotics. As such, antibiotics are becoming less and less effective in the war against disease.

Experts say mankind is now at a critical turning point in the millennia-old war against microbes. With AIDS, malaria, tuberculosis (TB), and dengue fever on the rise, microbes are causing one-third of the world's fifty million-plus deaths each year.[15] In fact, according to the World Health Organization, one-third of the world's population is currently infected with TB and over two million people die annually from it, making it the fifth-largest cause of death globally and the number one killer of women. In 1998, the World Health Organization warned that TB could infect one billion more people over the next twenty years. All this from a disease that only twenty years ago scientists thought had been beaten.

Even the United States, with its abundance of hospitals and quality medical care, is seeing a dramatic increase in deaths due to disease. In fact, a federal study released in 1996 and published in the *Journal of the American Medical Association*, showed that the death rate due to infectious diseases increased 58 percent in the United States between 1980 and 1992. This dramatic increase vaulted infectious diseases to third place among leading killers of Americans, behind heart disease and cancer.[16] "This new report dashes the historical prediction that the occurrence of infectious diseases would dwindle in this country" (Dr. Robert Pinner, research team leader, Center for Disease Control).

One of the leading causes for the increase in the death rate is AIDS, which is truly becoming an epidemic. Since the epidemic began, twenty-five million people have died from AIDS and more than forty-two million people around the world have become infected by the virus, which now strikes an additional fourteen thousand every day.[17] Despite the enormous efforts made by the medical community, no cure is in sight. *BusinessWeek* noted "medicine's arsenal of drugs and governments' limited policies have barely made a dent in the spread of HIV."[18]

In the United States, AIDS is now the leading cause of death among men ages twenty-five to forty-four in over sixty-four cities. Unfortunately, the situation is far worse in developing countries. In Central Africa, at least one in three people are infected with AIDS in addition to the 11.5 million who have already died.[19, 20] The situation has gotten so bad that for the first time in recorded history, the death rate on the African continent is actually greater than the rate of birth.[21] Twenty African nations are now refusing to publish accurate AIDS infection rates because the devastating information is treated as a national security risk. In addition to AIDS, other viral diseases (including SARS, West Nile, cholera, the ebola virus, yellow fever, legionnaires disease, lyme disease, polio, hanta virus and "mad cow") are also on the rise. Clearly, mankind is losing the war against disease. Around the globe, infectious diseases are spreading more than ever before and the death toll continues to rise. Not surprisingly, this is exactly what the Bible predicted would happen as mankind approaches the last days.

Earthquakes

Prophecy: There will be great earthquakes in various places (Matt. 24:7, Mark 13:8, Luke 21:11).

Fulfillment: There is no question that earthquakes are increasing in frequency and intensity just as the Bible described they would in the end days. In the first half of the twentieth century, major earthquakes that caused great damage and loss of life (measuring 6.0 or greater on the Richter scale) remained fairly constant in number, averaging between two to four each decade. In the last half of the twentieth century, however, there has been a sharp increase in the number of earthquakes each decade. In just the past decade, there have been more than 150. In fact, earthquakes in the twentieth century killed more than two million people—half the toll of all natural catastrophes put together. Just as the Bible predicted, earthquakes have been increasing in frequency and intensity. The graph below tells the story. "We've gone back and looked at events ten years ago in comparison to today and the events today are more intense, much more devastating and they're much more frequent" (James Lee Witt, FEMA Director).

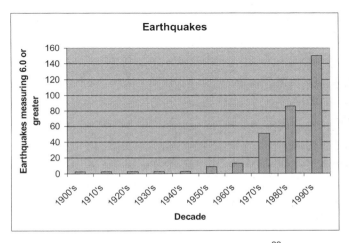

Figure 16: Increase in Earthquakes [22]

Persecution of Christians

Prophecy: Christians will be increasingly persecuted, martyred and hated (Matt. 24:9-10, Mark 13:9, 12-13, Luke 21:12,16).

Fulfillment: Just as the Bible describes, Christians are increasingly being persecuted, martyred, and hated. In fact, more Christians have been killed in the twentieth century for the name of Jesus than in the previous nineteen centuries *combined*.[23] It has been calculated that since the death of Jesus in AD 33, at least forty-one million

Christians have been martyred. According to the World Evangelization database, over 81 percent of these (twenty-seven million) have been killed since 1950 alone! Christians have become the most persecuted religious group in the world today. Right now, over two hundred million Christians live under the threat of persecution in more than thirty-five countries around the world. Below are some examples of the tremendous persecution that is occurring around the world today: [24, 25, 26, 27, 28, 29]

• In China, the communist government has called for the eradication of the independent Christian movement, which has between seventy and one hundred million Christians. Christians are regularly arrested or beaten to death by Chinese police. Because of the crackdown, there are currently more Christians in prison in China than in any other nation in the world.

• In Cuba, Fidel Castro continues to restrict Christian activity. Churches can't run schools or use television, radio, or other mass media. Missionary activity is forbidden, and the distribution of religious literature is tightly controlled. In 1996, the Castro government ordered the closure of all house churches, which numbered between three and ten thousand. Hundreds complied, but thousands of others did not and now live in fear of reprisal.

• In Sudan, after the National Islamic Front seized power in 1989, the government declared war against Christianity. To date, more than one million Sudanese Christians have been executed for their faith. Others have been sold into slavery, sent to re-education camps, or forced to participate in the war against Christians. Over 140 villages inhabited by Christian tribes have been burned down, and there is evidence that, in certain villages, every male age nine and up has been crucified.

• In Somalia, all churches have been destroyed, and Bibles are being burned. Believers are forbidden from buying certain goods, or they are charged ten times the price others pay for the same goods due to their faith.

• In Saudi Arabia, Christianity is against the law. Christians cannot even worship privately in their own homes. Believers are jailed, put to death, or tortured. There have been public beheadings and drownings of those who have converted from Islam to Christianity.

• In Pakistan, entire villages have being wiped out by Islamic forces because they harbored Christian missionaries. In 1986, a law was passed making it a capital crime to insult the Prophet Muhammad by any imputation, innuendo, or insinuation. This law has been used repeatedly to justify a reign of terror against Pakistani Christians and to sentence many Christians to death.

• In Nigeria, hundreds of churches have been vandalized or burned, and hundreds of Christians have been killed by Muslim mobs.

• In North Korea, Christians practice their faith in deep secrecy and constant danger due to the communist government's continued attempt to stamp out Christianity.

• In Vietnam, the communist party government has resumed its brutal repression of Christianity. Christians who openly profess their faith have been arrested, imprisoned, and sentenced to cultural re-education. Many die in prison, some after being tortured.

• In Iran, persecution of Christians began the day after the overthrow of the Shah by the Ayatollah Khomeini. The Christian faith is now against the law, and practicing it is punishable by death. Churches have been attacked, Christian property has been confiscated, and many believers have been killed.

These are just a few of the countries where persecution against Christianity exists. Other examples include Afghanistan, Algeria, Azerbaijan, Bangladesh, Belarus, Bhutan, Brunei, Egypt, India, Indonesia, Iraq, Kuwait, Laos, Libya, Malaysia, Maldives, Mauritania, Morocco, Myanmar (Burma), Nepal, Nigeria, Oman, Qatar, Syria, Tajikistan, Tibet, Tunisia, Turkey, Turkmenistan, United Arab Emirates, Uzbekistan and Yemen.

There is little doubt that Christians have seen in the second half of the twentieth century the worldwide rise in persecution that the Bible predicted almost two thousand years ago. While 70 percent of Christian persecution is from radical Islamic groups who reject Christianity, there has also been a change in attitude toward Christians in Western democracies that have traditionally been considered Christian countries. Due to the growth of liberalism and political correctness, Christians are increasingly being portrayed as intolerant bigots by society. In the United States, prayer in school is now a banned practice, and Bibles are no longer allowed in most school libraries. Courts have ruled that public nativity scenes are unconstitutional, and employees have being fired from their jobs for sharing their faith with co-workers. Graduates are frequently barred from making reference to their faith in valedictory addresses, and judges have been sued for opening their courts with prayer or for displaying the Ten Commandments. Despite the fact America was founded by Christians for the sake of religious freedom, there is no doubt the culture of the country has now changed to the point where Christian beliefs are being shunned, and Bible-believing Christians are increasingly becoming the hated minority. Jesus Christ foretold that during the Tribulation period, Christians would be "handed over to be persecuted and put to death, [they] will be hated by all nations because of me" (Matt. 24:9). It's apparent that the shift in attitude toward Christians has already begun, and the hatred and persecution will only intensify, just as the Bible predicted.

Spread of the Gospel

Prophecy: The Gospel will be preached around the whole world (Matt. 24:14, Mark 13:10, Acts 2:17). This will be the fulfillment of the Great Commission, where Christ instructed His disciples to "go and make disciples of all nations" (Matt. 28:19).

Fulfillment: The Gospel has been preached around the world in the past century with amazing success. In fact, 70 percent of all progress made toward fulfilling the Great Commission has taken place since

1900. Ever since the first century, the Christian percentage of the population has remained fairly low. This was the case for the first half of the twentieth century as well. However, in the past couple of decades, not only has the number of conversions per day risen dramatically, but so too has the number of Christians as a percentage of the total world population. This rate has increased so rapidly, that the number of people coming to know Christ every day has doubled in the past decade. Although there are approximately seventeen hundred groups of people in the world who have not heard God's word, it is estimated that these groups could be reached with the Gospel within the next couple of years.

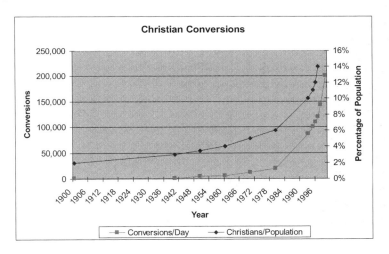

Figure 17: Growth of Christianity [30]

This recent success in spreading the Gospel is primarily the result of modern, communication technology. It is now far easier to translate the Bible, print Christian publications, and distribute Gospel information than it ever was before. Furthermore, broadcast media such as radio, TV, and the Internet are now making is possible to reach people groups that were impossible to reach before. As an example, one of Billy Graham's most recent messages was carried by video to an estimated 281 million people in countries all around the world. Because of modern communication technology, Graham has probably reached more people with the gospel of Christ than all the evangelists in history combined. Even countries that have traditionally shut out Christian missionaries have experienced a transformation. In the Soviet Union for instance, the Gospel is now being freely preached across the country; this would have been unheard of even a decade ago.

In China, where Christianity is illegal and believers must worship in underground churches, the total number of believers has grown dramatically. In 1948, when the communists in China forced out missionaries, there were perhaps one to two million believers. Today, there are between fifty and 150 million believers and thirty to thirty-five thousand new ones are being added each day.[31]

In West Africa, twenty thousand believers are being added daily. This represents twice the growth of the population as a whole. Because of this, it's now projected that over 45 percent of the five hundred million people living in Africa have become born-again Christians.[32,33] The list could go on and on. The fact is, the number of new countries where the Gospel is being spread and where God is working is staggering. For almost two thousand years, Christians have been praying and working toward the fulfillment of the Great Commission. It's awesome to think that this generation will probably be the one to see its fulfillment. It is hardly a coincidence that the spread of the Gospel occurs in the same generation as the fulfillment of other signs of the times that the Bible predicted. God is opening doors for the spreading of the Gospel in preparation for the last days, just as He said He would.

Signs in the Heavens

Prophecy: There will be fearful events and great signs from the heavens (Luke 21:11).

Speculation: The Bible is not clear about the types of signs referred to in this prophecy. It *is* clear, however, that these signs must be significant enough to strike fear into the hearts of many. While there have been no shortage of unique astronomical phenomena over the past decade (including a rare passing of the Moon in front of both Venus and Jupiter in 1998, a cosmic explosion on the sun in 1998, the arrival of the Hale-Bopp comet in 1997, a rare alignment of eight bodies in our solar system in 2000, numerous large solar flares between 2001 and 2003, and the passing of a city-sized asteroid by the earth in 2005), these would hardly qualify as a fulfillment of this prophecy.

"Great signs from the heavens," would be events or signs that would truly alarm mankind. Possible candidates might include a threat of meteors colliding with the earth or alien encounters (likely demons masquerading as aliens). It's interesting that many recent films have centered on fears such as these. Imagine the impact that scenarios like these would have on bringing the world together under a worldwide government or worldwide religion as people struggled with the basic philosophical questions these events would raise. Major events such as these might lead to other possible explanations for the Rapture (besides the Bible's explanation), when millions of Christians mysteriously disappear from the face of the earth. We know from the Bible that the world will be looking for answers during the end-times and that the Antichrist will succeed in deceiving the world through lies and powerful delusions (2 Thess. 2:11-12).

Perhaps these great signs will play a part. Regardless of what these signs from the heavens turn out to be, it's clear that these signs must occur in the end times just as the Bible predicts. It is possible that these events will be confined to the seven year Tribulation period, especially since the reference to this sign is not listed in the same passage along with the others in the book of Matthew that are labeled as birth pains. However, it seems logical that mankind will see the beginning of these fearful events in our present day, just as we have already experienced a rise in earthquakes and famines. If this is the case, then these fearful events and great signs from the heavens will be the final indication from God that the end times are at hand, since all of the other signs of the times predicted by the Bible have been fulfilled in our generation.

Notes

1. Data from the *Journal of the American Medical Association,* August 1991.

2. Dr. Mark Bailey, "The Tribulation," *The Road to Armageddon,* 49.

3. The World Health Organization, *World Health Report*, 2002.

4. Ibid.

5. MSNBC and Reuters.

6. CNN.

7. The World Game Institute.

8. The United Nations Food and Agriculture Organization.

9. CNN.

10. Weekend News Today.

11. The United Nations Food and Agriculture Organization.

12. Grant R. Jeffrey, *Armageddon: Appointment with Destiny*, 243.

13. Hal Lindsey, *Apocalypse Code,* 84.

14. The World Health Organization

15. "War against the Microbes," *BusinessWeek,* 6 April 1998, 106.

16. "Deaths by Infectious Diseases Increase Dramatically," Microsoft Encarta 99 Encyclopedia.

17. John Carey, "HIV: Sobering News from the Front," *BusinessWeek,* 6 July 1998, 86.

18. Ibid.

19. "Prophecy and Current Events," To His Glory Ministries.

20. "We Have to Find a Solution," *BusinessWeek,* 6 September 1999, 98.

21. Hal Lindsey, "Death of a Continent," *Countdown*, October 1999.

22. U.S. Geological Survey, Boulder, CO.

23. United States House of Representatives Resolution, September 1996.

24. Dr. Bob Moorehead, "Now is the Time," Overlake Christian Church, 1998.

25. Melissa J. McClard, "Religious Persecution: Long Ago in Places Far Away?" Family Research Council.

26. "The Coming Persecution," *Van Impe Intelligence Briefing,* February 1997.

27. "Family News from Dr. James Dobson," *Focus on the Family* letter, April 1997.

28. "The Beginning of Birth Pains," His Glory Ministries.

29. "Prayer Journal," The International Day of Prayer for the Persecuted Church, 1997.

30. Graph generated with data provided by Dick Eastman, Every Home for Christ, 1998 and Dr. Bob Moorehead, "Now is the Time," Overlake Christian Church, 1998.

31. Don Argue, President, Northwest College, "Who is this Jesus?" Overlake Christian Church, 1998.

32. Dr. Bob Moorehead, "Now is the Time," Overlake Christian Church, 1998.

33. Grant R. Jeffrey, *Armageddon: Appointment with Destiny,* 261.

Part 3

Future Prophecy

CHAPTER 10

THE END TIMES

"In the last days, God says, I will pour out my Spirit on all people. Your sons and daughters will prophesy, your young men will see visions, your old men will dream dreams...I will show wonders in the heaven above and signs on the earth below, blood and fire and billows of smoke. The sun will be turned to darkness and the moon to blood before the coming of the great and glorious day of the Lord. And everyone who calls on the name of the Lord will be saved"
(Acts 2:17-21).

The Bible contains approximately one thousand passages on prophecy. Of these, half have already been fulfilled.[1] Most of these prophecies and their fulfillments were discussed in Section One, Past Prophecy, and it was made clear that God has literally fulfilled prophecies in the past. Whether it be the seventy-year captivity Israel would endure under Babylon, the name of the king who would assist in rebuilding the Temple after its first destruction, the destruction of Jerusalem at the hands of the Roman Empire, or the restoration of Israel as a nation, God has always brought about the things He said He would—and always in an accurate and precise manner. There can be little doubt that the Bible is truly inspired. No other book in history besides the Bible has ever predicted the future with 100 percent accuracy.

In Section Two, Present Prophecy, it was made clear that all of the major prophecies and themes that lead up to the end times are occurring in our generation. Although some of the signs have not been completely fulfilled, it is clear that we are living at a unique time in history—a time when God is setting the stage for the final act of His plan for the earth. This final act is commonly referred to as the end times.

But what are the end times or last days? Movies frequently portray the end of the earth occurring after a collision with a meteor or as the result of a nuclear war. Global warming, pollution, or overpopulation are frequently mentioned as trends that might lead to the end of mankind. The Bible however, paints a different picture. Throughout dozens of books of the Bible, both in the New Testament and the Old, the events of the end times are described in great detail. Believers don't have to wonder what might happen to the earth—the Bible describes these events and provides a precise timeline for when certain events will occur:

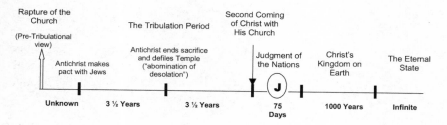

Figure 18: Timeline of the End Times

The end times that the Bible describes centers around the following key events:

The Rapture: The Rapture is an event described in the Bible where all Christians will be removed from the earth. The Christians living at the time of this event will not die. Rather, they will be taken directly to heaven to be with Christ. There are various different views on when this event will actually occur. These views, and the arguments for each, are described in the next chapter. For simplicity's sake, the Pre-Tribulation view of the Rapture is the one shown on the timelines throughout this book since this view is most widely held.

The Tribulation: The Tribulation is a seven-year period during which most of the events of the end times will take place. This period will start with the Antichrist signing a seven-year pact (treaty), with the nation of Israel. The middle of this period will be marked by what is referred to as the "abomination of desolation," an event where the Antichrist will defile the rebuilt Temple in Jerusalem. It is during this seven-year Tribulation period that God will pour out three different sets of judgments upon mankind. These judgments are known as the Seal, Trumpet, and Bowl judgments and will be reminiscent of the plagues that God poured out on the people of Egypt in the days of Moses. It is during this time of Tribulation that the Antichrist will rise to power and establish a one-world government and a one-world religion. The Tribulation will ultimately end with the nations of the world gathering together against Israel for the war known as Armageddon.

The Second Coming: Just before the nations of the world destroy themselves at the battle of Armageddon, Jesus Christ will return to the earth. He will destroy the armies gathered against Israel and capture the Antichrist and Satan. He will then cast them, along with all of the unbelievers at the time, into Hell. Christ will then judge mankind during what is known as the Judgment of the Nations.

The Millennium: The Millennium is the ultimate fulfillment of the promises God made to Abraham, Isaac, Jacob, and David. It refers to a thousand-year period after the Judgment of the Nations during which Christ will physically rule the earth from the capital city of Jerusalem. This will be a time of great peace and prosperity unlike the world has ever known.

The Eternal State: After the thousand-year Millennium, there will be a rebellion on the earth. God will immediately put a stop to this rebellion and will then destroy the heavens and the earth by fire. It is at this point that He will recreate the earth in a perfect manner for His people to live in. This will begin the Eternal State, which will last forever and will be free from the sin of mankind.

These key events will be explored in more detail in the chapters that follow. To most people, these events sound farfetched. The idea that approximately one billion people will suddenly disappear from the earth in the Rapture or that Christ will return to physically rule the earth from the city of Jerusalem sounds like science fiction. It is for this reason that many people discard the prophecies related to the end times or try to spiritualize them into celestial battles between good and evil rather than viewing them as actual events that will occur on earth in the future.

As was already pointed out, however, half of the prophecies in the Bible have already been fulfilled just as they were predicted—and in a very literal and accurate manner. The remaining half, which pertain to the end times, were written by many of the same authors and are contained in the same passages as the first half. How then should we treat these prophecies? Some people may discount these prophecies because they sound farfetched, rather than taking them at face value and anticipating that God will bring about their fulfillment in the same manner as He has the various other prophecies of the Bible. But remember, as little as one hundred years ago, the idea that the Jewish people would reclaim the nation of Israel in the land of Palestine was an absolutely absurd thought. For this reason, many early Bible teachers tried to discount the prophecies related to this event. These people were proven wrong, for God fulfilled these prophecies just as the Bible promised and restored Israel to its former land exactly as predicted. It's for this reason we should anticipate that the farfetched prophecies related to the end times will be fulfilled just as God said they would be, especially since we live in the generation where literally dozens of signs related to the end times are currently being fulfilled.

Notes

1. Dr. John F. Walvoord, "The Rapture: The Next Event on God's Calendar," *The Road to Armageddon,* 27.

CHAPTER 11

THE RAPTURE

"Watch and pray, therefore, that you would be counted worthy to escape the judgment that is coming upon the earth" (Luke 21:36).

"For the Lord himself will come down from heaven with a loud command, with the voice of the archangel and with the trumpet call of God, and the dead in Christ will rise first. After that, we who are still alive and are left will be caught up together with them in the clouds to meet the Lord in the air" (1 Thess. 4:16-17).

"Listen, I tell you a mystery: We will not all sleep, but we will all be changed—in a flash, in the twinkling of an eye, at the last trumpet. For the trumpet will sound, the dead will be raised imperishable, and we will be changed" (1 Cor. 15:51-52).

The word "Rapture" is never used in the Bible. The word comes from the Latin word *"rapare,"* which means to "take away" or "snatch out" and is based on 1 Thessalonians 4:17. The Rapture refers to the event foretold in the Bible when Christ will remove His Church from the earth prior to the outpouring of His wrath during the Tribulation period. In essence, all Christians around the world will mysteriously vanish "in the twinkling of an eye" from the face of the earth. This will be one of the most monumental events in history and will represent the point at which it will be too late to escape the coming judgments—people who are left on the earth will be doomed to go through the Tribulation period.

Although the Rapture may sound far-fetched, it is not without precedent in scripture. The Bible records similar events where people did not die, but rather were "snatched away" from the earth and taken to heaven by God. These individuals include (among others) Enoch, Elijah, and Paul. Enoch was the first. The Bible records that "Enoch walked with God; then he was no more, because God *took him away*" (Gen. 5:24, emphasis added). The New Testament expands on this to say, "By faith Enoch was taken from this life, so that he did not experience death; he could not be found, because God had *taken him away*" (Heb. 11:5, emphasis added). This is the same terminology as used in 1 Thessalonians to describe the Rapture. Likewise, the Bible states that Elijah was "taken to heaven" and did not die (2 Kings 2:11). In Paul's case, Paul himself wrote that he was "*caught up* to the third heaven" where he was given visions and revelations of the Lord (2 Cor. 12:1-4, emphasis added). These examples provide sufficient evidence to conclude that the Rapture described in the Bible will be a real and literal event. The Rapture of the end times however, will be different in that it will be the first time that a group of people will be "snatched away" to heaven.

The Rapture is analogous to when God rescued Noah from the flood and spared Lot and his family from the destruction of Sodom and Gomorrah (2 Pet. 2:4-9). God doesn't want His people to live through His judgments, so He provides a means of escape to those who are faithful to Him. The key difference is that in the case of the Rapture, the people of the earth will still have a second chance to turn from their ways and become obedient to God, although being a Christian during the Tribulation period will be difficult.

The Rapture is one of the most controversial topics in the entire Bible. There are various different interpretations of the details of the Rapture, but the following points are commonly agreed upon.

• The Rapture is imminent and will happen unexpectedly—no one knows when it will happen, not even Christ or the angels (Matt. 24:36, 44, Mark 13:32-36, James 5:8-9, Rev. 3:11; 22:7, 12, 20, Titus 2:13). Chapter seven, "Signs Preceding the Rapture of the Church," describes how all of the signs that must occur prior to the Rapture have already taken place. Although some of the signs of the times have not been completely fulfilled; yet (e.g., signs from the heavens or the establishment of the ten-nation European Federation), they are not signs that *must* precede the Rapture. The Rapture could happen tomorrow, and then there could be a period of ten, twenty, or even fifty years for the completion of the stage setting prior to the start of the Tribulation period.

• The Lord will come down from heaven with a loud command and with a trumpet call (1 Cor. 15:51, 1 Thess. 4:16). The Bible is not clear on this point, but some believe that only Christians will physically hear the call.

• In a split second, believers in Christ who have died will be raised from the dead. This is referred to as the "Resurrection of the Righteous" (Luke 14:14, John 5:28-29, 1 Cor. 15:52, 1 Thess. 4:16).

• After the dead are raised, the Christians who are living on the earth at the time will be changed from mortal to immortal without physically dying. They will then be taken to meet Christ in the air (1 Cor. 15:51-52, 1 Thess. 4:17). For a discussion of the differences between "mortal bodies" and "eternal bodies," see chapter twenty-three, "The Judgments of Mankind."

• The people that are raptured will remain with the Lord forever (1 Thess. 4:17, John 14:3).

• The Rapture will occur prior to the "coming wrath" (1 Thess. 1:10, 5:9) or "hour of trial" (Rev. 3:10, 2 Pet. 2:9). God will rescue His people from having to live through His judgment on mankind just as He rescued Noah before the flood and saved Lot prior to the destruction of Sodom and Gomorrah (2 Pet. 2:4-9, Jer. 30:7, 11). A point of debate though, is the exact period of time that the phrase "the coming wrath" refers to (see discussion below).

Many people confuse the Rapture of the Church with the Second Coming of Christ. It's worth pointing out that these are two separate events.

The Rapture	The Second Coming
Key Passages: 1 Corinthians 15:51-52, 1 Thessalonians 4:15-17	**Key Passages**: Zechariah 14:4-5, Matthew 24:27-31, Revelation 19:11-21
Characteristics:	**Characteristics**:
• Transformation of all believers from mortal to immortal bodies	• No transformation. Believers who are alive will remain mortal thru Millennium.
• Christians are taken to heaven (Christ comes *for* the Church)	• Christians return to the earth with Christ (Christ comes *with* His Church)
• The earth is not judged	• The earth is judged
• Imminent event	• Follows definite series of events
• Not mentioned in the Old Testament	• Predicted often in the Old Testament
• Affects only believers	• Affects all people on the earth
• Before the 'day of wrath'	• After the 'day of wrath'
• No references to Satan	• Satan is bound
• Christ comes in the *air*	• Christ comes to the *earth*
• Only Christians will see Him	• Every eye shall see Him
• Occurs to save believers from wrath	• Occurs to save Israel from the Antichrist
• Marks the beginning of God's outpouring of wrath during the Tribulation	• Marks the beginning of the Millennium

Table 3: Comparison of the Rapture and Second Coming [1]

The Rapture refers to the event when Christ removes His Church from the earth at some point prior to His physical return to earth. The Church, along with deceased believers, will be taken up into the air to meet the Lord. The Bible says this event will come like a thief in the night—it will come unexpectedly and will take people by surprise. It's most likely that non-Christians will not even see this event, but rather will just suddenly discover that approximately one billion people have disappeared from the face of earth. Imagine the chaos that will ensue—Christian airline pilots will suddenly disappear from their planes; Christian drivers will be removed from their cars; Christian policemen will just disappear. No doubt there will be a great deal of confusion and destruction after this event, as the world grapples with the question of what happened to roughly 15 percent of the earth's population.

The Second Coming of Christ, on the other hand, will be very different. Everyone on the earth will see this event. Christ will descend from heaven with His saints at the climax of Armageddon to put an end to the war and establish His kingdom on earth. It's at this point that the Antichrist and Satan will be stopped and Christ's Millennial Kingdom will begin. This event is described in detail in chapter twenty-two, "The Second Coming of Christ."

Timing of the Rapture

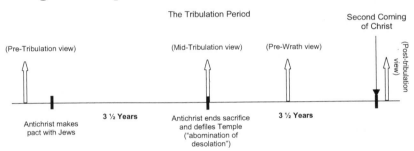

Figure 19: Different Views on the Timing of the Rapture

The Bible does not state specifically when the Rapture will occur in relation to the Tribulation period. Will it happen before? At the midpoint? Sometime during? If it happens before, how long before? Although clues are given, the Bible does not provide a definitive answer to these questions. Because of this, there has been an enormous amount of debate among Christians throughout the ages on precisely when the Rapture will occur. Four main views have emerged. These views are referred to as the pre-tribulational, mid-tribulational, pre-wrath, and post-tribulational positions:

Pre-Tribulation View: This view teaches that the Rapture will occur prior to the seven-year Tribulation period. All members of the body of Christ (both living and dead) will be caught up in the air to meet Christ and then be taken to heaven. This is by far the most popular view held by mainstream Christians.

Mid-Tribulation View: This view teaches that the Rapture will occur in the middle of the seven-year Tribulation period. This view is held by a very small group of Christians.

Pre-Wrath View: This view teaches that the Rapture will occur approximately three-fourths of the way through the Tribulation period just prior to Christ's Second Coming. This view is very new and has yet to gain any significant following within the Christian community.

Post-Tribulation View: This view teaches that Christians will be raptured at the end of the Tribulation. This view is only held by a small group of Christians.

These different views, as well as the various arguments for and against each position, are explored in detail in *Appendix C*. For simplicity's sake, the Pre-Tribulation view of the Rapture is the one shown all on timelines throughout this book since it is the most widely held view.

The Wedding of the Lamb

"For the wedding of the Lamb has come, and His bride has made herself ready" (Rev. 19:7).

Throughout the New Testament, the analogy of a wedding is used to describe the uniting of Christ with the Church after the Rapture. This event is frequently called the "Wedding of the Lamb" and describes the enormous celebration that will occur after the Church is "caught up in the clouds" during the Rapture and united with Christ for the first time.

The Wedding of the Lamb the Bible describes will be a real event. Although it won't be a wedding in the traditional sense; it will be a great time of celebration as the groom (Christ) is united with His bride (the Church). To understand this event to its fullest, one must first understand ancient Jewish marriage customs. First, a marriage contract was arranged by the two sets of parents, usually when the bride and groom-to-be were still too young to be considered adults. The marriage contract was considered a binding agreement and meant that the bride and groom-to-be were legally married even though they probably wouldn't consummate their marriage for perhaps years to come. This period of time was known as a betrothal, but it represented a much stronger tie between a couple than we experience in our present-day engagement periods. The betrothal gave the couple a chance to grow in their relationship with one another before the actual marriage vows took place. The second step in the marriage process, the actual marriage, took place when the couple had reached a suitable age of maturity.

There were two phases to an actual Jewish marriage ceremony. In the first stage, the groom went to the bride's home to collect his bride and observe various religious customs. In the second stage, the groom took the bride to his own home for more festivities and the wedding feast. The parallels to Christ and the Church are many: When a person accepts the gift of forgiveness though Christ's death on the Cross, he enters into a contract, or union, with Jesus. Through the betrothal, a person grows in his or her relationship with Christ. At the time of the Rapture, Christ will come to His betrothed and take His bride, the Church, to the place He has prepared in heaven. There, they will complete their marriage vows. At the time of the Second Coming, Christ will return with His bride for the marriage feast. Below are the prophecies related to the Wedding of the Lamb that the Bible describes.

Prophecy:

• Jesus will be the groom (Matt. 9:15, 22:2, Mark 2:19).

• The Church will be the bride (Eph. 5:25-27, 32, 2 Cor. 11:2).

• The good works of believers will constitute the `wedding dress' (Rev. 19:8).

• There will be no father of the Bride—Christ Himself will present the Church at the wedding (Eph. 5:25-27).

• Although not specifically stated, the wedding guests will most probably be the Old Testament saints and the Tribulation saints who have died before the end of the Tribulation (Rev. 19:9).

• The residence of the married `couple' will be the New Jerusalem (Rev. 21:2, 9-10).

Clearly, the Wedding of the Lamb—the uniting of Christ with His church after the Rapture—will be one of the most wonderful celebrations in all of history.

Notes

1. Table based on Thomas Ice and Timothy Demy, *The Rapture*, 30.

CHAPTER 12

TIMELINE OF THE TRIBULATION

"There will be a great tribulation, such as has not occurred from the beginning of the world until now, nor ever will be. And if those days had not been cut short, no human being would be left alive"
(Matt. 24:21-22).

The Tribulation will be the greatest period of agony and suffering the world has ever known. It will last seven years and will be divided into two periods, each lasting three and one-half years (Dan. 9:27, Rev. 11:2-3). The first half is sometimes called the "beginning of sorrows." The second half is frequently called "the Great Tribulation." The Bible has more to say about these seven years than about any other prophetic time period. During these seven years, the Antichrist will emerge, God will pour out His wrath through three sets of judgments, persecution of Israel will ensue, multitudes will become Christians, the great battle of Armageddon will be fought, and the Second Coming of Christ will transpire.

The Tribulation is frequently referred to as "Daniel's seventieth seven" by Bible scholars because the timing and major milestones of this period were given to the prophet Daniel in a vision that consisted of seventy, seven-year periods (Dan. 9:20-27). A detailed description of Daniel's *seventy sevens* is contained in *Appendix D*. The first sixty-nine of these *sevens* describes the timeline of events that will occur prior to the First Coming of Christ, including the rebuilding of Jerusalem. The seventieth *seven*, which is distinct from the first sixty-nine, described events yet to come. It is this seventieth *seven* that makes up the Tribulation period. The following chart shows the major milestones of this final seven-year period based on Daniel's prophecies:

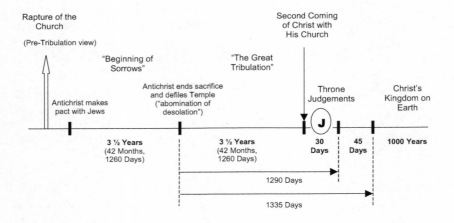

Figure 20: The Tribulation Period

The Bible says "He [the Antichrist] will confirm a covenant with many for one 'seven.' In the middle of the 'seven' he will put an end to sacrifice and offering. And on a wing of the temple he will set up an abomination that causes desolation, until the end that is decreed is poured out on him" (Dan. 9:27). The signing of a peace agreement between the Antichrist and Israel will mark the beginning of the Tribulation period. The "abomination of desolation" will mark the midpoint of the Tribulation, and the Second Coming of Christ will mark the end.

The Beginning of the Tribulation

Prophecy: The seven-year Tribulation period will begin with the Antichrist, making a firm seven-year covenant or peace treaty with the Jewish people to protect Israel. This treaty will bring a time of perceived peace to Israel and the Middle East (Dan. 9:27, Isa. 28:15, 18, Ezek. 38:11).

Speculation: It is quite possible that this treaty will allow the people of Israel to rebuild the Temple, since rebuilding it prior to some sort of Middle East peace agreement is almost impossible to imagine in today's political climate (see chapter three). It is also quite possible that this treaty is what allows the Antichrist to rise to world fame and power as the great statesman who brings peace to the Middle East, since the Bible doesn't mention any role that the Antichrist plays prior to the signing of this treaty.

The Midpoint of the Tribulation

Prophecy: The second half of the Tribulation period will be very different from the first. While the first half will be marked by various judgments (see chapter thirteen), the second half will be marked by complete chaos, destruction, and terror.

At the mid-point of the Tribulation period, Satan will physically be cast down to earth by God, and will personally possess the Antichrist. The Bible says that Satan will give the Antichrist his power, throne and authority (Rev. 13:2). The Antichrist will then break the covenant he made with the Jewish people, invade Israel and take over the Temple (Dan. 9:27, 11:41, Isa. 28:18). He will turn from being an extremely popular statesman to being a Hitler-like dictator bent on world conquest and change from being an ally of Israel to being their archenemy.

The Antichrist will then:

• Turn against the false, one-world, religious system that exists at the time (described in a chapter sixteen).

• Put an end to sacrifice in the Temple (Dan. 9:27).

• Set up a statue of himself in the Temple (Dan. 9:27). This idol, which will be erected by the False Prophet, will be able to speak (Rev. 13:15).

• Claim to be god (Daniel 11:16, 2 Thessalonians 2:4).

• Say blasphemous things against the true God (Dan. 7:8; 11; 25, 11:36; Rev. 13:6).

• Demand that people worship him.

These events are known in scripture as "the abomination of desolation" and are described in more detail in chapter fifteen.

The Antichrist will then begin to persecute the Jews (Rev. 12:13). Upon seeing and recognizing these as the events prophesied by Daniel, residents of Israel who believe in Jesus will flee for Divine Protection. They will be transported to a mountainous place in the desert that will be prepared by God where they will be safe from persecution by the Antichrist. Here, they will be taken care of for the last three and a half years of the Tribulation (Isa. 26:20-27:1, Matt. 24:16-20, Rev. 12:6, 14). This flight will be reminiscent of Israel's flight from the Egyptians in the days of Moses (compare Exod. 19:4 with Rev. 12:14). Details of this flight are contained in chapter fifteen, "The Antichrist & His Kingdom."

Everyone on the earth will then start worshiping the Antichrist (Rev. 13:8), except those who become Christians during the Tribulation period. Those who resist worshiping the Antichrist will be persecuted. Many will be killed (Matt. 24:16-22).

The End of the Tribulation

Prophecy: The Bible states that the Great Tribulation (or second half of the Tribulation period) will last "a time, times and half a time" (Dan. 12:7). In prophecy, this phrase represents three and one-half years (or half of the entire seven-year period). The Bible describes the end as the time in which "all these things [the events of the Tribulation] will be completed" (Dan. 12:7). From this, we can most likely assume that the Second Coming of Christ will occur 1,260 days after the mid-point of the Tribulation period since His return will bring the events of Daniel's prophecy to completion. The Bible then goes on to say that there will be 1,290 days from the abomination of desolation (i.e., when the Antichrist defiles the Temple) to the end (Dan. 12:11). Normally, three and one half years (using 360 days per year as per the Jewish calendar) would include only 1,260 days. The extra thirty days mentioned here most likely allows for the Judgment of the Nations that will take place after the Second Coming of Christ.

The Millennium will occur seventy-five days after the Second Coming of Christ. The Bible states "blessed is the one who waits for and reaches 1,335 days" after the abomination of desolation (Dan. 12:11). Because these people are called blessed, this likely marks the actual beginning of Christ's Millennial Kingdom. Since thirty days are allotted for judgment, the remaining forty-five likely allows time for Christ to setup and prepare His kingdom.

It's interesting to note that there are exactly seventy-five days between the Jewish holidays "the Day of Atonement" and "Hanukkah." On the Day of Atonement, the high priest would offer a sacrifice for the nation, foreshadowing the spiritual rebirth of the Jewish people at Christ's Second Coming. Hanukkah celebrates the rededication of the Temple to God after it was desecrated by Antiochus Epiphanes. Given the fact that many prophetic events in the past have occurred on Jewish holidays, and that these two holidays seem to parallel the events described at the end of the Tribulation, it's highly likely that the seventy-five days described in this passage will indeed occur between the Day of Atonement and Hanukkah.

CHAPTER 13

THE TRIBULATION JUDGMENTS

"I will punish the world for its evil, the wicked for their sins. I will put an end to the arrogance of the haughty and will humble the pride of the ruthless. Therefore I will make the heavens tremble; and the earth will shake from its place at the wrath of the Lord Almighty, in the day of His burning anger" (Isa. 13:11, 13).

During the Tribulation period, God will bring various judgments upon the earth. The book of Revelation describes these judgments as three distinct sets of seven judgments each. These judgments are physical or supernatural events that God will bring to the earth and are presented in chronological order in chapters six through nineteen of Revelation. The breaking and unrolling of a scroll sealed with seven seals depicts the first of these series of judgments. The second series is announced by the successive sounding of seven trumpets, and the third, by the pouring out of seven bowls full of God's wrath. With each successive series of judgments, the severity is increased. Each judgment is more terrible than the last. The final series will be the most severe of all and will conclude with the Second Coming of Christ. The three series of judgments are known as the Seal, Trumpet, and Bowl judgments respectively. Suffice it to say, these judgments will mark a time that will be unparalleled in human history.

In the Bible, the common term used for the Tribulation period is "the Day of the Lord." This term is used twenty-six times in Scripture and has historical significance. According to the Jewish calendar, a day begins at sundown and progresses from darkness to daylight. It is helpful to think about the Day of the Lord in these terms as well. Although the Tribulation will represent a terrible time of judgment, it will be followed by a time of restoration for Israel. In essence, the Tribulation, like the Jewish calendar, will progress from darkness to light. In this case, there will be truth to the axiom, "it's always darkest just before the dawn." The Tribulation Judgments will come with the purpose of bringing the eventual light of God's Day to the world.[1]

Purpose of the Tribulation Judgments

It is difficult for most people to understand why God would bring such terrible judgments to the world. After all, isn't God a God of love? He is, but the Bible also describes God as being a God of justice who must eventually bring judgment upon those who reject Him. This is in keeping with God's character. Although God loves the world and doesn't want anyone to perish (John 3:16), He has brought judgments to the world before—examples include the great flood that destroyed the world in the days of Noah, the destruction of Sodom and Gomorrah, the plagues that God brought upon Egypt, and the destruction of many cities during the time of Israel's entrance into the Promised Land.

Unfortunately, mankind doesn't like to view God in this manner. We would like to believe that God sends His judgments through Satan or through an angel or through a demon. We don't want to admit that God is personally responsible for death and destruction. A good example of this is the tenth plague of Egypt where the firstborn male of every Egyptian household was killed (Exod. 11-12). It was this plague that led to the Passover and the release of the Israelites from captivity. In Sunday School lessons and in the movies, we are frequently told that an angel of death caused the plague, but this is inconsistent with the Bible, that says "*the Lord* struck down all of the firstborn in Egypt." God personally brought the plague to Egypt and caused the deaths, not an angel (Exod. 11:1, 4, 12:29). It's important to note though, that God doesn't take any pleasure from these judgments. Rather, they are the result of mankind's sin and disobedience: "As surely as I live, declares the Sovereign Lord, I take no pleasure in the death of the wicked, but rather that they turn from their ways and live. Turn! Turn from your evil ways" (Ezek. 33:11). Just as parents do not enjoy disciplining their children, so, too, God doesn't take pleasure in bringing judgments upon mankind. It is just the inevitable consequence of the sinful actions of mankind. Daily, our court systems make determinations on what is right and what is wrong and dole out punishment. Everyone recognizes the need for justice in society. Is God any different? Imagine the moral outrage and sense of injustice you feel when just one terrible murder, rape, or act of terrorism goes unpunished. Then imagine how God must feel after seeing all the injustice that has gone on since the beginning of time! All of these acts have gone unpunished and injustice has triumphed. During the end times, God will say, "No more!" and will bring final justice and judgment to the world.

The Bible provides the following reasons for the terrible Tribulation period that God is going to bring upon the world in the end-days:

• To pour out His wrath on Israel for their disobedience, stubbornness, and sin: God will punish Israel for their rejection of Him just as He did when He let Israel fall into captivity at the hands of Babylon. However, the Tribulation period will also prepare the people of Israel for their restoration and time of putting their faith in Jesus prior to the Second Coming of the Lord. The Bible indicates that the Tribulation will lead to a mass-conversion of Jews to Christianity (see chapter twenty-one). When the Lord returns, He will then set up His Millennial Kingdom for all the saved Jews (and Gentiles) who accepted Him during the Tribulation period (Deut. 4:29-30, Zeph. 2:1-3, Ezek. 20:34-35, 22:17-22, Dan. 9:24, 12:7, Amos 3:2, Luke 21:23b).

• To punish the world for its wickedness and its sins against Him: The Tribulation will not only serve as a time of punishment for Israel, but also for the world as a whole. Just as God punished the wicked people of Noah's day and the people of Sodom and Gomorrah in Lot's day, so, too, will He use the Tribulation to punish the wicked people living during the end-times (Isa. 13:11, 24:5-6, 26:21, 34:2).

• To punish unbelievers for their refusal to accept Him (2 Thess. 2:10-12).

• To answer the prayers of martyrs who have died for the name of Christ: God will bring justice to His followers who have been killed by the world and will bring revenge on their behalf (Rev. 6:9-11, 15:1-4, 16:5-6).

• To bring about a worldwide revival: The Bible indicates that there will be "great multitudes" of people coming to know Christ during the Tribulation period (Matt. 24:14, Rev. 7:1-17). People will recognize the Tribulation for what it is, namely judgments from God prior to the Second Coming of Christ and will turn to Christ in record numbers, acknowledging that this is their last chance for salvation. The number of believers always grows during times of persecution as people are forced to choose sides and stand up for their beliefs. The Tribulation will be no different. All people of the earth will be forced to either identify themselves as being on the side of the Antichrist, or on the side of God. There will be no sitting on the fence.

In addition to the above reasons for the Tribulation period, the following reasons were revealed to Daniel for the *seventy sevens* that God decreed for Israel: "Seventy `sevens' are decreed for your people [Israel] and your holy city [Jerusalem] to finish transgression, to put an end to sin, to atone for wickedness, to bring in everlasting righteousness, to seal up vision and prophecy and to anoint the most holy" (Dan. 9:24).

Note a couple of things from this passage: First, the "seventy weeks" are directed to the nation of Israel and the city of Jerusalem specifically. They are not described as applying to mankind in general, but rather to the Jewish people. Second, these reasons don't pertain just to the Tribulation period alone (Daniel's seventieth seven). Rather, they pertain to the whole period of time that God will punish Israel for breaking the covenant they made with Him (the full *seventy sevens*). These *seventy sevens* span the time from Israel's first destruction at the hands of Babylon, through to the completion of the Tribulation period. A detailed discussion of Daniel's `seventy sevens' is contained in *Appendix D*. Since the Tribulation concludes Daniel's *seventy sevens* and is the climax, the following reasons can be interpreted as completing God's plan for Israel, which is to restore the Jewish people back to a close, personal relationship with their Creator. These reasons include:

• To end (or stop) transgression: The dictionary describes transgression as the "infringement or violation of a law, command, or duty" (*Webster's Ninth New Collegiate Dictionary*). This is a good definition, but the Hebrew brings a little more clarity. Translated literally, the Hebrew word for transgression means "to rebel." When Israel broke the covenant they made with God, they rebelled against Him. God essentially sentenced them to *seventy sevens* (seventy, seven-year periods) of punishment, which is why the Jewish people have had to endure difficult times and trials ever since their nation was originally taken captive by Babylon. The Tribulation period will conclude at the end of these *seventy sevens*.

• To put an end to sin: At the end of the Tribulation period, the nation of Israel will repent of its sins and turn back to God. Christ will then return and establish His Millennial Kingdom, where He will live together with Israel for a thousand years. This will be a time of obedience—Israel will no longer sin or rebel against God. The Tribulation period will end the time of Israel's rebellion and mark the beginning of a restored relationship with Him.

• To atone for wickedness: The Hebrew word for atonement has the same root meaning as the word "kippur," as in Yom Kippur. On this holiday, the nation of Israel confesses their sin and asks for God's forgiveness and cleansing. In the times of the Temple, it is the only day in the year when the high priest went into the Holy of Holies— the most sacred part of the Temple. Here, he would lay his hands on a goat (known as a "scapegoat") and then send it off into the desert as a sign that the sins of Israel had been taken away. At the Second

Coming, Christ will return to a repentant Israel and take away the sins of His people in a perfect analogy to Yom Kippur.

• To bring in everlasting righteousness: More literally translated, this phrase could be "to bring in the age of righteousness," since the Hebrew *olam* is better-translated "age" than "everlasting." This clearly refers to the start of the Millennial Kingdom, which will begin after Israel turns back to God (Jer. 23:5-6). The Millennial Kingdom will begin a time of peace, prosperity, and righteousness for Israel (see chapter twenty-four).

• To seal up vision and prophecy: When the Millennial Kingdom is established and people live in the presence of the Lord, there will no longer be any need for vision or prophecy. Prophecy will have been completely fulfilled with the coming of the Lord and the establishment of His kingdom.

• To anoint the most high: A better translation from the Hebrew would be "to anoint a most holy place." This refers to the anointing of the Holy of Holies in the Millennial Temple which will be built when the Messiah returns.

Characteristics of the Judgments

Each of the judgments that God will pour out upon the earth during the Tribulation period are described in detail in the following section. The Bible outlines some general characteristics that apply to the judgments as a whole.

• Unless specifically described as such, the judgments that God brings will affect the entire earth (Isa. 24:1, 4, Zeph. 1:2, 18). They are not limited to any specific geographic region.

• They will affect all classes of people and wildlife on the earth (Isa. 24:2, Zeph. 1:3). Although God will protect some of His followers during certain judgments, there is no distinction made between groups of people of the earth. "Good people" will be impacted in the same manner as "bad people." The rich will endure the same trials as the poor. Kings and rulers, the same as commoners.

• The judgments God brings will remove all pleasures from the earth (Isa. 24:7-13). The Tribulation will be a terrible time to be alive. There will be no escape from the trials of this period.

• Only a small few will survive the judgments (Isa. 24:6, 13). In the fourth Seal judgment, one-fourth of the world's population will be killed. In the sixth Trumpet judgment, another one-third of mankind will die. Both of these don't include the countless number of people who will die from the earthquakes, famines, wars, and lack of clean water. There is no doubt that by the end of the Tribulation period, only a small fraction of the earth's current population of around six billion will be left alive.

• Finally, at the end of the judgments, the earth will be completely laid to waste (Isa. 24:3, Zeph. 1:3). The land will be scorched, the cities of the world will lie in ruins, the seas and waterways will be contaminated and most of civilization will have been destroyed.

Clearly, the judgment that God will bring to the earth will be severe. There never has been anything like it and never will be again after this period. The Tribulation will be a unique time in the history of mankind.

Timing of the Tribulation Judgments

The Bible is not clear on the exact timing of the Tribulation Judgments as it relates to the other events of the Tribulation period. As a result, we are left to guess about when the judgments will occur based on anecdotal evidence taken from other passages of Scripture. For example, it makes sense that the fifth Seal judgment, which consists of persecution and martyrdom, relates to the time in which the Antichrist takes over the Temple and starts his campaign of persecution against Christians. Therefore we can assume that the fifth Seal judgment occurs after the midpoint of the tribulation.

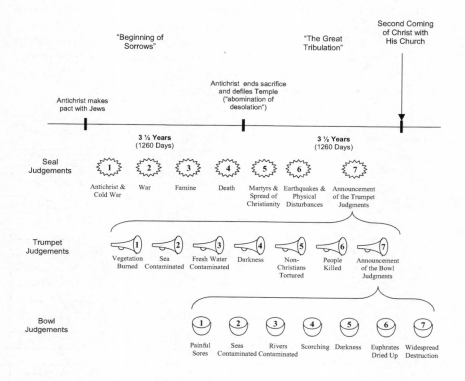

Figure 21: The Tribulation Judgments

What is known for sure about the judgments is that they are sequential—they follow a set order. In addition, it's clear from Scripture that the seventh Seal judgment contains all of the Trumpet judgments, and the seventh Trumpet judgment contains all the Bowl judgments. What does this mean? It means that the seventh Seal judgment is really just another name for the Trumpet judgments and the seventh Trumpet judgments is really just a synonym for the Bowl judgments.

Relation to the Plagues of Egypt

It's very interesting to note that many of the judgments God brings during the Tribulation period are similar, if not identical, to the nine plagues that God brought to Egypt in the days of Moses. The following table shows the relationship:

Tribulation Judgment	Plague of Egypt
Trumpet Judgment	
#1 – Vegetation burned	#7 – Destruction of crops by hail
#2 – Sea contaminated	#1 – Nile turned to blood
#3 – Fresh water contaminated	
#4 – Darkness	#9 – Darkness
#5 – Non-Christians tortured by locusts	#8 – Destruction of crops by locusts
#6 – Earthquakes	
Bowl Judgment	
#1 – Painful sores	#6 – Painful sores
#2 – Seas contaminated	
#3 – Rivers contaminated	#1 – Nile turned to blood
#4 – Scorching	
#5 – Darkness	#9 – Darkness
#6 – Euphrates dried up	
#7 – Widespread destruction (including hail)	#7 – Destruction of crops by hail

Table 4: Comparison of Tribulation Judgments to Plagues of Egypt

It is probably no coincidence that the Tribulation judgments are similar to the plagues of Egypt. God is consistent and works in consistent ways, so it shouldn't be a surprise that God repeats judgments that He has already poured out upon the earth. In addition, prophecy is full of foreshadowing, where one event may be a prototype for a later event. For example, Antiochus Epiphanes (mentioned in chapter three) was a foreshadow of the Antichrist. So too, the plagues of Egypt foreshadowed the Tribulation Judgments. Furthermore, the plagues of Egypt had a very specific purpose—for God to bring judgment upon the unbelieving Egyptians and for the

Israelites to recognize the power of God. The purpose for the Tribulation Judgments is similar if not identical—God wants to punish unbelievers for their wickedness and their sins against Him, and He wants to bring the nation of Israel back into belief in Him. By repeating judgments that the nation of Israel is already familiar with, it seems logical that many would recognize them as being from God. It's worth pointing out that the plagues of Egypt were literal judgments—they actually happened. History records these plagues as real events. So, too, we should expect that the Tribulation judgments of the end times will be actual events that will be fulfilled as literally as God fulfilled the plagues of Egypt.

The Seal Judgments

The Tribulation judgments start with seven Seal Judgments. The judgments are named the "Seals" because they are depicted in the Bible as being delivered as Christ opens successive seals on the "Scroll of Redemption." The Seals and the Scroll are figurative—nobody on earth will see them, but it's interesting to understand the reference. Author Hal Lindsey writes:

> In biblical times, sealing a scroll was a common and important practice. A scroll would be written on parchment and then rolled up and sealed using wax. An impression would then be pressed into the wax to identify the author. If the document was received with the seal intact, the person who received it knew that it had not been read or tampered with." Sometimes, to seal up really important or private documents, multiple seals were used. The wills of both Emperor Vespasian and Caesar Augustus, for example, were secured with seven seals. For such a document, a scribe would procure a long roll of parchment and begin writing. After a period of writing, he would stop, roll the parchment enough to cover the words, and seal the scroll at that point with wax. Then he would resume writing, stop again, roll the scroll, and add another seal. By the time he was finished, he would have sealed the scroll seven times. The scroll would be read a section

at a time, after each seal was opened. This process was used to prevent tampering and to ensure that the contents had not been read by anyone but the intended recipient.

The scroll described in the Bible for the Seal judgments most likely represents man's original inheritance from God being forfeited to Satan. In Old Testament days, when a Jewish family was required to forfeit its land and possessions, the property could not be permanently taken from them. Their losses were listed in a scroll and sealed seven times, then the conditions necessary to repurchase the land and possessions were written on the outside of the scroll. When a qualified redeemer was found to meet the requirements of reclamation, the one to whom the property had been forfeited was obligated to return the possessions to the original owner. The analogy is straightforward. When mankind sinned, God's inheritance for mankind (i.e., eternal life) was forfeited and passed onto Satan. In the Bible, only Christ is seen as a worthy redeemer who is able to open the Scroll of Redemption and redeem mankind because He died in the past to pay the ransom price for the sins of the world (Rev. 5:9-10). If this analogy is correct, the Seal Judgments would then represent the conditions through which mankind is ultimately redeemed and is again entitled to the original inheritance.[2]

Regardless of the meaning behind the use of the word Seals, the Bible is clear that the Seal judgments will be devastating. They will most likely start at the beginning of the Tribulation period, and extend through the end.

The first four Seal Judgments are frequently referred to as "the four horses of the Apocalypse." This is because these judgments are figuratively described in Revelation as being delivered by four different riders atop four different color horses. The following table summarizes the Seal Judgments judgments:

THE TRUTH ABOUT PROPHECY IN THE BIBLE

Seal	Judgment	References
One	The Antichrist & Cold war	Revelation 6:1-2, Matthew 24:4-5, Luke 21:8
Two	War	Revelation 6:3-4, Matthew 24:6-7, Luke 21:9-10
Three	Famine	Revelation 6:5-6, Mark 13:8, Luke 21:11
Four	Death	Revelation 6:7-8
Five	Martyrs & Spread of Christianity	Revelation 6:9-11, Matthew 24:9-13, Mark 13:9-13, Luke 21:12-24
Six	Earthquakes & Physical Disturbances	Revelation 6:12-17, Matthew 24:29-30, Mark 13:24-25, Luke 21:25-26
Seven	Announcement of the Trumpet Judgments	Revelation 8:1-6

Table 5: The Seal Judgments

First Seal: The Antichrist & Cold War

"I looked, and there before me was a white horse! Its rider held a bow, and he was given a crown and he rode out as a conqueror bent on conquest" (Rev. 6:2).

The first Seal judgment (also known as the first horse of the apocalypse) brings the rise of the Antichrist's power through cold war and deceit. Although it is not explicitly stated, the rider of the first horse is often seen as the Antichrist because he is "a conqueror bent on conquest" which parallels the description of the Antichrist given by Daniel (Dan. 11:38-39). In addition, the Bible says, "a crown was given to him" which symbolizes the rise to power of a ruler. The passage also indicates that the rider on the horse is male (he) and in the singular form (meaning one). In this passage, the Antichrist is described as riding a white horse, holding a bow and wearing a crown (Rev. 6:2). The white horse represents conquest, the bow symbolizes the Antichrist's control over the weapons of war, and the crown represents the power and authority that the Antichrist will obtain from the world. Although the Antichrist is "bent on conquest," peace is not removed from the earth until the second seal is opened. The Bible indicates that people will be proclaiming "peace and safety" at this time (1 Thess. 5:3), which implies that the Antichrist will gain power through cold war and deception. Perhaps this is why this passage describes the rider as carrying a bow, but doesn't mention any arrows. This would then be consistent with other passages in Scripture that describe the Antichrist coming to power peaceably (2 Thess. 2:9-12) and that he will deceive many (Matt. 24:5), as opposed to rising to power through outright war or conquest.

Second Seal: War

"Then another horse came out, a fiery red one. Its rider was given power to take peace from the earth and to make men slay each other. To him was given a large sword" (Rev. 6:4).

The second Seal judgment (also known as the second horse of the apocalypse) brings outright war to the earth. The rider of the second horse is "given power to take peace from the earth and to make men slay each other." The rider is described as carrying a great sword and riding a red horse. The red horse represents blood, and the sword is a symbol of war. Because this judgment represents war, it seems to imply that the Antichrist will not have everything his own way, and his methods will lead to rebellion and wars among the nations. First Thessalonians 5:3 says "while people are saying `peace and safety,' destruction will come on them suddenly, as labor pains on a pregnant woman, and they will not escape." Clearly, the peace deal that the Antichrist signs with Israel at the start of the Tribulation period will be short-lived, and the Antichrist's attempt to unite the world under his control will meet with resistance. Jesus describes this time by saying, "you will hear of wars and rumors of war...nation shall rise against nation and kingdom against kingdom" (Matt. 24:6-7). Although some of these wars will occur prior to the start of the Tribulation (see chapter nine), it's clear that the climax will occur during the seven-year Tribulation period. It's even possible that this time of war will start with the attack on Israel described in a subsequent chapter. In this scenario, Russia would be the rider that snatches peace from the earth when it invades the Middle East and attacks the nation of Israel.

Third Seal: Famine

"I looked, and there before me was a black horse! Its rider was holding a pair of scales in his hand. Then I heard what sounded like a voice...saying, `A quart of wheat for a day's wages, and three quarts of barley for a day's wages, and do not damage the oil and the wine!'" (Rev. 6:5-6)

The third Seal judgment (also known as the third horse of the apocalypse) brings famine to the earth. The rider of the third horse is told to measure out "a quart of wheat for a day's wages." Thus, an average daily wage will buy food enough for about one person. The rider is also told to measure out "three quarts of barley for a day's wages." Barley is a coarse grain that was normally used to feed cattle in biblical days. Only the poorest people made bread out of barley. Thus, if a person has to spend money for something other than food, they will be forced to eat what is essentially cattle food.

The rider is described as carrying a pair of scales and riding a black horse. The black horse signifies famine, and the scales symbolize the scarcity of food. The rider of the third hose is told, "not to damage the oil and the wine" which were the luxury foods of the biblical period. This seems to imply that although working men will face food shortages, the rich will still be able to function economically.

A worldwide famine would be the ultimate result of the war that the second Seal judgment brings. Food, fuel, and other life-supporting commodities would become more and more scarce.

Fourth Seal: Death

"I looked, and there before me was a pale horse! Its rider was named Death, and Hades was following close behind him. They were given power over a fourth of the earth to kill by sword, famine and plague, and by the wild beasts of the earth" (Rev. 6:8).

The fourth Seal judgment (also known as the fourth horse of the apocalypse) brings death to one-fourth of the world's population. The rider of the fourth horse was given power to kill over a fourth of the earth by sword, famine, and plague (Rev. 6:8, Ezek. 14:21). The rider is named Death and is riding a pale horse with Hades following close behind. The pale horse probably represents the inevitable result of disease that accompanies war and famine. Death claims the bodies, and Hades (a temporary holding place for the unsaved) claims the souls of one-fourth of the world's population.

So great will be the destruction of human life during this judgment that the Bible says that Hell will have to enlarge itself to accommodate all of the people (Isa. 5:13-16). The current population of the world is estimated at six billion. For one-fourth of these to die, would mean 1.5 billion people would have to be slain in this judgment. This is more than the current population of Europe, South America, and North America combined.

Fifth Seal: Martyrs & The Spread of Christianity

"When he opened the fifth seal, I saw under the altar the souls of those who had been slain because of the word of God and the testimony they had maintained" (Rev. 6:9).

The fifth seal represents the martyrdom of Christians who will be slain during the Tribulation period because of their beliefs. The Bible says that during this time, Christians will be intensely persecuted, hated by all nations, and killed (Matt. 24:9-13, Luke 21:17). As a result, many Christians will turn away from the faith and betray one another (Matt. 24:10, Luke 21:16). Accompanying this intense persecution, however, will be the dramatic preaching of the Gospel, which will be preached throughout the whole world (Matt. 24:14, Luke 21:13-15). Evidently, many will respond and turn to Christ during these difficult times (Rev. 7:9-10).

Although the persecution of believers will occur throughout the Tribulation period, it will become most intense at the midpoint (see chapter fifteen). This would seem to indicate that the fifth Seal judgment occurs at the midpoint of the Tribulation period.

Sixth Seal: Earthquakes & Physical Disturbances

"I watched as he opened the sixth seal. There was a great earthquake. The sun turned black like sackcloth made of goat hair, the whole moon turned blood red, and the stars in the sky fell to the earth, as late figs drop from a fig tree when shaken by a strong wind. The sky receded like a scroll, rolling up, and every mountain and island was removed from its place" (Rev. 6:12-14).

The sixth seal judgment will bring great physical destruction to the earth. This destruction will include:

• A great earthquake, so severe that the heavens will tremble and the earth will shake (Rev. 6:12, Matt. 24:29, Isa. 13:13).

• Probably as a result of the earthquake, the sea will roar and toss, causing anguish among the nations (Luke 21:15). Given the magnitude of the earthquake the Bible describes, one can easily imagine the tidal waves and the subsequent destruction that would result.

• The sun will turn black (Rev. 6:12, Matt. 24:29, Joel 2:31, 3:15, Isa. 13:10). This could possibly be caused by the destruction and smoke that would result from the earthquake.

• The moon will turn to a blood red color (Rev. 6:12, Matt. 24:29, Joel 2:31, 3:15, Isa. 13:10).

• Stars will fall from the sky and will no longer shine (Rev. 6:13, Matt. 24:29, Joel 3:15, Isa. 13:10, 34:4).

• The sky will "recede like a scroll" (Rev. 6:14, Isa. 34:4).

• Every mountain and island will be moved from its place (Rev. 6:14).

• Men will faint from terror and apprehension from these events and hide in caves (Luke 21:26, Rev. 6:15).

It's quite possible that this judgment describes a nuclear exchange— the fallout from which would darken the sun and moon and would surely shake the earth. The "stars falling from the sky" could refer to intercontinental ballistic missiles (ICBMs). Also, in a nuclear explosion, the atmosphere rolls back on itself as air rushes back into the vacuum created by the explosion. It's this tremendous rush of air that is known to cause much of the actual destruction of a nuclear blast. This could be what the Bible is referring to when it describes "the sky receded like a scroll, rolling up" (Rev. 6:14).

Seventh Seal: Announcement of the Trumpet Judgments

> *"When he opened the seventh seal, there was silence in heaven for about half an hour...and there came peals of thunder, rumblings, flashes of lightning earthquake. Then the seven angels who had the seven trumpets prepared to sound them" (Rev. 8, 5b-6).*

The seventh Seal judgment initiates the second set of judgments upon the earth—the Trumpet judgments. It is important to note that the seventh Seal judgment includes all of the Trumpet judgments, which includes all of the Bowl judgments, so that the seventh Seal ends with the Second Coming of the Lord and the start of the Millennium.

The Trumpet Judgments

The Trumpet judgments will be the second set of judgments poured down upon the earth by God. Why is the symbol of a trumpet used for these judgments? G. R. Beasley-Murray writes:

> Trumpets that herald the end of the age are a tradition "with roots deep in the history of Israel." Trumpets were used to warn the people of an emergency and to summon them to battle, so it was natural for the prophets to use them as a symbol to warn the people of approaching judgment (Ezek. 33:1-6, Joel 2:1). In addition, the trumpet on the last day heralds the deliverance of God's people (Zech. 9:14) and therefore the resurrection (Matt. 24:31, 1 Cor. 15:52, 1 Thess. 4:16). Just as trumpets preceded God's revelation to Moses at Mount Sinai (Exod. 19:11-13), so the Jews expected His appearance at the end of the age to be heralded with trumpets. All this and more may be behind God's choice of trumpets to launch this series of judgments on the earth's inhabitants.[3]

The Trumpet judgments will be extremely severe. They will increase in scope and magnitude with each sequential judgment. The Bible says that the enormity of these judgments will cause silence in heaven for about half an hour when they are announced (Rev. 8:1). Imagine how terrible these judgments must be if even the angels in heaven are shocked by the magnitude of them!

The Bible says that these judgments will be the result of "the prayers of all the saints" (Rev. 8:1). It can only be assumed that these prayers are for justice, judgment, and vengeance upon the enemies of God. As mentioned previously, the Trumpet judgments will be preceded by thunder, rumblings, flashes of lightning, and an earthquake, which will serve as a warning that these judgments are about to begin (Rev. 8:5). The first four Trumpet judgments will be directed toward the earth's ecology, but the last three judgments will be directed toward mankind. Although many of these judgments sound impossible or implausible, there is no reason that they shouldn't be taken literally. In fact, four of the six Trumpet judgments are repeats of the plagues that God poured out upon Egypt in the days of Moses. The following is a table that summarizes these judgments:

Trumpet	Judgment	References
One	Vegetation Burned	Revelation 8:7, Joel 2:30
Two	Sea Contaminated	Revelation 8:8-9
Three	Fresh Water Contaminated	Revelation 8:10-11, Jeremiah 9:13-15
Four	Darkness in the Heavens	Revelation 8:12
Five	Non-Christians Tortured	Revelation 9:1-12, Joel 2:1-11
Six	People Killed	Revelation 9:13-21
Seven	Announcement of the Bowl Judgments	Revelation 11:15-19

Table 6: The Trumpet Judgments

First Trumpet: Vegetation Burned

"The first angel sounded his trumpet, and there came hail and fire mixed with blood, and it was hurled down upon the earth. A third of the earth was burned up, a third of the trees were burned up, and all the green grass was burned up" (Rev. 8:7).

The first Trumpet judgment will cause one-third of the earth, and all the trees and grass that are on it, to be burned up through hail and fire, which will be poured down from heaven (Rev. 8:7, Joel 2:30). This judgment is very similar to the seventh plague that God brought upon Egypt, when hail and lightning was poured down from heaven, destroying trees and crops (Exod. 9:22-26). The result of this plague was that Pharaoh, for the first time, acknowledged his sin and the righteousness of the Lord (Exod. 9:27).

Some see this judgment as a reference to a nuclear attack. To the eyes of John, the first century disciple to whom God revealed the events of the end times and subsequently wrote the book of Revelation, hail, fire and blood being poured down from heaven could very easily fit today's description of a nuclear explosion. Obviously, modern technology, such as nuclear weapons, would have been unfamiliar to

John's first-century eyes. Regardless of whether this judgment is a literal judgment from God or the result of a nuclear attack, the implications of this judgment on the world's economy will be tremendous. The destruction of one-third of the world's trees and vegetation would inevitably result in famine, soil erosion, floods, and mudslides.

Second Trumpet: Sea Contaminated

"The second angel sounded his trumpet and something like a huge mountain, all ablaze was thrown into the sea. A third of the sea turned into blood, a third of the living creatures in the sea died, and a third of the ships were destroyed" (Rev. 8:8-9).

The second Trumpet judgment will cause a huge flaming mass to fall into the sea, destroying one-third of sea animals and one-third of the ships on the sea. The Bible is unclear on the exact nature of the mass or the scope of the destruction. It's possible that the huge mass mentioned here will be a meteor or a hydrogen bomb and that the sea mentioned refers to the Mediterranean, since this is only sea commonly referred to in the Bible and is the one that borders Israel. Alternatively, the sea could refer to all water on the earth, but this seems less likely given the context. The ships mentioned in this verse could possibly be destroyed by a tidal wave that would result from this event, or it could be that this mass falling from the sky may fall on a fleet of naval vessels. This judgment is similar to the first plague that God brought upon Egypt where the Nile River was turned to blood (Exod. 7:19-21). The implications of this judgment on the world economy would only add to the disaster caused by the first Trumpet judgment. Regardless of whether this judgment is limited in scope to just the Mediterranean or not, losing one-third of all marine life would only add to the famine caused by losing one-third of all vegetation in the previous judgment. Furthermore, losing one-third of all ships would have enormous consequences on the distribution of food.

Third Trumpet: Fresh Water Contaminated

"The third angel sounded his trumpet, and a great star, blazing like a torch, fell from the sky on a third of the rivers and on the springs of the water—the name of the star is Wormwood. A third of the waters turned bitter, and many people died from the waters that had become bitter" (Rev. 8:10-11).

The third Trumpet judgment will cause a star (referred to as 'Wormwood' in the Bible after a strong, bitter herb which grows in Palestine) to fall from the sky. This star will contaminate one-third of all the fresh water on the earth, causing many people to die from drinking the contaminated water (Rev. 8:10-11, Jer. 9:13-15). It is quite possible that the star mentioned in this judgment will be a meteor. It is also possible that this star is some sort of nuclear or chemical weapon, which would certainly explain the contamination of the water supply. The lack of fresh water, combined with lack of food resulting from the prior two judgments, would only further add to the worldwide famine and death.

Fourth Trumpet: Darkness in the Heavens

"The fourth angel sounded his trumpet, and a third of the sun was struck, a third of the moon, and a third of the stars, so that a third of them turned dark. A third of the day was without light, and also a third of the night" (Rev. 8:12).

The fourth Trumpet judgment will cause one-third of the sun, moon, and stars to be darkened, so that the total light on the earth (during day and night) will be reduced by one-third. This judgment is similar to what happened during the sixth Seal judgment, where the sun turned black and stars fell from the sky. It's possible that this darkness will be the result of the nuclear exchange referred to previously. Air pollution and darkness would be the consequence of nuclear fallout. This judgment will be followed by a warning to all inhabitants of the earth about the three Trumpet judgments to come

(Rev. 8:13). The Bible doesn't state specifically, but it's most likely that everyone on the earth will hear this verbal warning from heaven. This judgment is similar to the ninth plague of Egypt where darkness was brought upon Egypt for three days (Exod. 10:21-23).

Fifth Trumpet: Non-Christians Tortured

"The fifth angel sounded his trumpet... the sun and sky were darkened by smoke from the Abyss. And out of the smoke locusts came down upon the earth and were given power like that of scorpions of the earth. They were told not to harm the grass of the earth or any plant or tree, but only those people who did not have the seal of God on their foreheads. They were not given the power to kill them, but only to torture them for five months. And the agony they suffered was like that of the sting of a scorpion when it strikes a man" (Rev. 9:1-5).

The fifth Trumpet judgment will bring torture to everyone on the earth for a five-month period except for the 144,000 witnesses (described in chapter eighteen), who will be given a "seal of protection" by God. The Bible refers to this judgment as "the first woe" (Rev. 9:12). Demonic creatures that will resemble locusts will cause the torture. The Bible describes the appearance of these creatures as follows: "The locusts looked like horses prepared for battle. On their heads they wore something like crowns of gold, and their faces resembled human faces. Their hair was like women's hair, and their teeth were like lions' teeth. They had breastplates like breastplates of iron, and the sound of their wings was like the thundering of many horses and chariots rushing into battle. They had tails and stings like scorpions, and in their tails, they had power to torment people for five months" (Rev. 9:7-10).

Clearly, these creatures were unlike anything that John had ever seen because he often had to use the word `like' to make comparisons so we could visualize the creatures ourselves. Another potential description of these creatures is found in the book of Joel: "It has the teeth of a lion, the fangs of a lioness...they have the appearance of horses; they gallop along like cavalry. With a noise like that of chariots they leap over the mountaintops, like a crackling fire consuming stubble, like a mighty army drawn up for battle. At the sight of them, nations are in anguish; every face turns pale. They charge like warriors; they scale walls like soldiers. They all march in line not swerving from their course. They do not jostle each other; each marches straight ahead. They plunge through defenses without breaking ranks. They rush upon the city; they run along the wall. They climb into the houses; like thieves they enter through the windows" (Joel 1:6b, 2:4-9).

Most Bible scholars interpret these passages literally and see these creatures as some sort of supernatural beings. Will we actually see these strange creatures? Probably not. If they are truly demonic or supernatural in nature, then they will most likely be invisible to the human eye just as supernatural beings such as angels are invisible to mankind today. Others however, interpret these passages symbolically and see similarities in this description to elements of modern warfare. One must remember that the apostle John was a first century man who viewed events that would happen over two thousand years later. Concepts such as tanks, helicopters, and missiles would have been completely foreign to John, since machines did not exist in his time. Therefore, John's description could simply be using concepts he was familiar with: "locusts" could refer to helicopters, "horses" could refer to tanks, "fire and brimstone" could refer to bombs, and so on.

Regardless of the interpretation, the creatures described will:

• Have the power to sting like scorpions (Rev. 9:3).

• Will not kill people, but will cause great agony and suffering (Rev. 9:5).

• Will only afflict those who do not have the `seal of God' (Rev. 9:4).

• Will not harm any plant life or vegetation (Rev. 9:4).

• Will have a king (named 'the destroyer'), which clearly implies that these are no ordinary locusts, but rather some form of demonic beings possessing intelligence (Rev. 9:11).

The Bible says that these demonic scorpion-locusts will be released from out the Abyss (Rev. 9:2-3). The Abyss is used in Scripture to refer to the dwelling place of demons (see definition in the Glossary), which is why these creatures are · commonly thought to be supernatural in origin. When the Abyss is opened, smoke will rise from it and further darken the sun and sky (Rev. 9:2). This may be actual smoke or the appearance of the swarm of creatures filling the sky. During this five month period of torture, suicide will be desired, but will be impossible (Rev. 9:6). People will attempt to kill themselves to alleviate the pain of this torture, but their attempts will fail. This judgment is somewhat similar to the eighth plague where locusts were brought upon the nation of Egypt (Exod. 10:3-20). The locusts in this judgment, however, are obviously quite different and much more powerful than ordinary locusts.

Sixth Trumpet: People Killed

"The sixth angel sounded his trumpet, and I heard a voice commanding...'Release the four angels who are bound at the great river Euphrates.' And the four angels who had been kept ready for this very hour and day and month and year were released to kill a third of mankind. The number of the mounted troops was two hundred million... A third of mankind was killed by the three plagues of fire, smoke and sulfur that came out of their mouths" (Rev. 13-18).

The sixth Trumpet judgment will bring death to one-third of all the people on the earth. Added to the one-fourth who were killed under the fourth Seal judgment, these two judgments alone will destroy one-half of the world's population (over three billion people). This does not include those people killed by wars, famines, and diseases. The sixth Trumpet judgment is also referred to in the Bible as "the second woe."

A two hundred million-person-supernatural army will do the killing through fire, smoke, and sulfur (Rev. 9:16, 18). The Bible describes the appearance of this army as follows: "The horses and riders...looked like this: Their breastplates were fiery red, dark blue and yellow as sulfur. The heads of the horses resembled the heads of lions, and out of their mouths came fire, smoke and sulfur...the power of the horses was in their mouths and in their tails; for their tails were like snakes, having heads with which they inflict injury" (Rev. 9:17-19).

Like the scorpion-locusts in the prior judgment, John clearly had trouble describing these creatures because he used words such as "like" and "resembled" to make comparisons. Most scholars see these creatures as supernatural beings. In fact, the Bible cites several cases of supernatural armies (2 Kings 2:11, 6:14-17, Rev. 19:14), so it would certainly not be without precedent. Given the enormous size of this army (about as large as the entire population of the United States), this is probably the most plausible explanation, especially given the enormous number of deaths that will have occurred during this time, making such a large army almost impossible to amass. Just as it was with the scorpion-locusts in the previous judgment, most believe this army will be invisible to the human eye. Others, however, interpret this army to be the soldiers from the armies of the East (i.e., the Oriental nations) mentioned in Revelation 16, which will cross the Euphrates on their way to Armageddon.

This army will be led by four angels who will be released from their bondage in the Euphrates River for this task (Rev. 9:14-15). Clearly these angels are bad angels as seen from the fact that they were bound, and the angels are leaders or commanders of this supernatural army of destruction. The fact they were bound in the Euphrates River is significant because of the history of the Euphrates. It is near this river where the first sin was committed in the Garden of Eden, where the first murder occurred, and where the first war was fought. This is also where the first great revolt against God occurred at the tower of Babel and where the Bible says Satan's had his seat (i.e., headquarters) in ancient times (see chapter sixteen). When the

Antichrist establishes his kingdom during the Tribulation period, it will be near this river (specifically, in the restored City of Babylon, near modern Baghdad in Iraq). Clearly, the Euphrates River has great significance in the spiritual world and is a center for evil spirits and rebellion.

Seventh Trumpet: Announcement of the Bowl Judgments

"The seventh angel sounded his trumpet, and there were loud voices in heaven, which said: `The kingdom of the world has become the kingdom of our Lord and of his Christ, and he will reign forever and ever'... And there came flashes of lightning, rumblings, peals of thunder, an earthquake and a great hailstorm" (Rev. 11:15, 19).

The seventh Trumpet judgment (Rev. 11:15-19) initiates the third set of judgments upon the earth—the Bowl judgments. It is important to note that the seventh Trumpet judgment includes all of the Bowl judgments, just as the seventh Seal judgment included all of the Trumpet judgments, so that the seventh Seal judgment and the seventh Trumpet both end with the Second Coming of the Lord and the start of the Millennium. The Bowl judgments will be preceded by thunder, rumblings, flashes of lightning, a great hailstorm, and an earthquake (Rev. 11:19), which will serve as a warning from God that the Bowl judgments are about to begin. This judgment is also referred to as "the third woe" in the Bible. Prior to the Bowl judgments, three angels will be sent to preach the Gospel to the world one last time before God unleashes His final judgments. These angels will proclaim that the hour of judgment has come, that the kingdom of the Antichrist is over, and that those who have taken the mark of the beast are eternally doomed to Hell. They will call upon the world to worship the one true God (Rev. 14:6-11). This is the first and only time in the Bible where angels are charged with preaching the Gospel.

The Bowl Judgments

The Bowl judgments will be the third and final set of judgments poured down upon the earth by God. Why is the symbol of a bowl used for these judgments?

The word bowl, as it's used in Revelation, refers to an ancient drinking bowl or goblet. Bowls are used symbolically because they will be filled with the wrath of God which is to be poured out on the world (Rev. 15:7). In Isaiah 51:22-23, God promises that the bowl of His wrath will be taken away from Israel and given to Israel's enemies. Thus, the seven Bowl judgments represent God's wrath, which is to be poured out onto those that rejected Him (Rev. 14:10). The following table summarizes these judgments:

Bowl	Judgment	References
One	Painful Sores	Revelation 16:2
Two	Seas Contaminated	Revelation 16:3
Three	Rivers Contaminated	Revelation 16:4-7
Four	Scorching	Revelation 16:8-9, Malachi 4:1-2
Five	Darkness	Revelation 16:10-11, Joel 2:1-2, Mark 13:24
Six	Euphrates Dried Up	Revelation 16:12-16, Isaiah 11:15-16
Seven	Widespread Destruction	Revelation 16:17-21

Table 7: The Bowl Judgments

The Bowl judgments will be the most severe of the whole Tribulation period and will complete the outpouring of God's wrath (Rev. 15:1b). They will occur in the second half of the Tribulation, devastate the Antichrist's kingdom, and prepare the way for the Second Coming of Christ. The Bible says the Bowl judgments will be the result of the prayers of the saints (i.e., Christian martyrs who die during the Tribulation) who will pray for God to take revenge on their behalf (Rev. 6:9-11, 15:1-4, 16:5-6).

Just prior to the start of the Bowl judgments, the earth will be "harvested" (Rev. 14:14-20) and the Temple in heaven will be "closed" so that no one in heaven will be able to enter the Temple until the Bowl judgments are completed (Rev. 15:8). Although the Bible doesn't state exactly what these two events mean, it's quite possible that the harvesting of the earth is a reference to mankind's final chance to accept or reject the Lord, since the act of people coming to know the Lord is frequently referred to in the Bible as a harvest. After the harvest is complete, the closing of the Temple could be a reference to God closing His ears to the cries of those who had rejected Him and are now about to be judged. Essentially, what the Bible is saying is that, at this point in the Tribulation period, it will be too late for people to turn to God. God will have provided many chances for people to accept His grace during this terrible time in history, but, at this point, the destiny of everyone on the earth will have been decided once and for all.

Throughout the Bowl judgments, the Bible indicates the people of the earth who rejected God will curse His name for bringing the plagues of the Bowl judgments upon them. What's amazing though, is that despite their recognition that these judgments are from God, people will still refuse to repent (Rev. 16:9b, 11, 21b).

First Bowl: Painful Sores

"The first angel went and poured out his bowl on the land, and ugly and painful sores broke out on the people who had the mark of the beast and worshiped his image" (Rev. 16:2).

The first Bowl judgment brings painful, ugly sores to people who have the mark of the beast. Some speculate that these sores could be brought about by nuclear fallout, since thousands of people developed hideous sores as a result of the radioactive fallout following the bombings of Nagasaki and Hiroshima. Most believe, however, that these sores will be inflicted supernaturally like the sixth plague that God brought upon Egypt where boils inflicted the Egyptian people (Exod. 9:8-12). Throughout this judgment, believers in God (those who refused to take the mark of the beast) will be supernaturally protected from any harm, just as the Israelites were spared during the plague that God brought upon Egypt.

Second Bowl: Seas Contaminated

"The second angel poured out his bowl on the sea, and it turned into blood like that of a dead man, and every living thing in the sea died"
(Rev. 16:3).

The second Bowl judgment brings contamination to all of the seas of the earth. The seas will be turned to blood, and every living thing in the seas will die. This judgment is the completion of the second Trumpet judgment, when one-third of the sea was contaminated and one-third of the living creatures died. Now, the entire sea becomes contaminated and all living creatures die.

Third Bowl: Rivers Contaminated

"The third angel poured out his bowl on the rivers and springs of water, and they became blood" (Rev. 16:4).

The third Bowl judgment brings contamination to all of the rivers and springs of the earth. These, too, will be turned to blood. This judgment is similar to the first plague brought upon Egypt where the rivers, streams, and water of Egypt were turned to blood (Exod. 7:19-21). The reason God turns the seas and rivers into blood is stated in Revelation 16:6—the people of the earth deserve to drink blood because they shed the blood of God's saints and prophets.

Fourth Bowl: Scorching

"The fourth angel poured out his bowl on the sun, and the sun was given power to scorch people with fire" (Rev. 16:8).

The fourth Bowl judgment scorches people with the heat of the sun (Rev. 16:8, Mal. 4:1-2). It's possible that the scorching heat mentioned in this judgment is the result of the destruction of the ozone layer following a nuclear exchange.

Fifth Bowl: Darkness

"The fifth angel poured out his bowl on the throne of the beast and his kingdom was plunged into darkness" (Rev. 16:10).

The fifth Bowl judgment brings darkness to the Empire of the Antichrist (Rev. 16:10, Joel 2:1-2, Mark 13:24). This judgment is the completion of the fourth Trumpet judgment where one-third of the sun, moon, and stars were darkened so as to reduce the earth's light by one-third. Now, the entire sky is darkened, at least over the Antichrist's Empire. This judgment is similar to the ninth plague where darkness was brought upon the nation of Egypt (Exod. 10:21-23).

Sixth Bowl: Euphrates Dried Up

"The sixth angel poured out his bowl on the great river Euphrates, and its water was dried up to prepare the way for the kings from the East" (Rev. 16:12).

The sixth Bowl judgment will cause the river Euphrates to dry up (Rev. 16:12, Isa. 11:15-16). The purpose of this judgment is to prepare the way and make it easy for the kings of the East (i.e., the Oriental nations) to cross the river Euphrates on their way to the battle of Armageddon (see chapter twenty-one). It is after this judgment that the nations of the world will be gathered together at Armageddon. Without denying the potential of God to accomplish the supernatural, it's interesting to note that Turkey has recently completed work on a dam project that literally allows that nation to turn off the headwaters to the Euphrates at any time. In fact, in tests already conducted at the huge Ataturk Dam, Turkey, has at times, reduced the mighty Euphrates to a mere trickle—causing tensions between Ankara, Turkey's capital, and Damascus, which relies so heavily on the flow of water.[4]

Seventh Bowl: Widespread Destruction

> *"The seventh angel poured out his bowl into the air, and out of the temple came a loud voice from the throne, saying `It is done!' Then there came flashes of lightning, rumblings, peals of thunder and a severe earthquake. No earthquake like it has ever occurred since man has been on earth, so tremendous was the quake. The great city split into three parts, and the cities of the nations collapsed...every island fled away and the mountains could not be found. From the sky huge hailstones of about a hundred pounds each fell upon men"*
> *(Rev. 16:17-21).*

The seventh Bowl judgment brings widespread destruction to the earth: lightning, thunder, hailstones, and the most severe earthquake that has occurred since the beginning of time. This event will mark the climax of God's judgments upon the earth and will leave the entire planet completely devastated. During this judgment, the cities of the world will literally be destroyed. Imagine New York, Los Angeles, Tokyo, and London completely leveled! The city of Babylon, referred to as the great city (Rev. 18:2), will be split into three parts (Note: in Rev. 11:8, Jerusalem is also referred to as the great city, and although it's possible that this verse refers to Jerusalem, it's more likely that this reference is to the city of Babylon, given its context and the reference to Babylon in the same verse).

Due to the strength and magnitude of the earthquake that will occur during this judgment, the Bible indicates that islands and mountains will physically disappear from the earth. The Bible also says that hailstones, weighing about one hundred pounds each, will fall from the heavens, causing even more devastation. It's interesting to note that the Old Testament law of Israel required the stoning to death of any accused blasphemer (Lev. 24:16). In this judgment, the blasphemers of the end times will literally be stoned to death from heaven! This judgment is similar to the seventh plague where God brought thunder, hail, and fire upon the land of Egypt (Exod. 9:22-26), although obviously this seventh Bowl judgment will be much more severe.

Notes

1. Based on David Brickner, *Future Hope,* 17.

2. Hal Lindsey, *There's a New World Coming,* 74-75.

3. G. R. Beasley-Murray, *The Book of Revelation,* 152-155.

4. Hal Lindsey, *Apocalypse Code,* 230.

CHAPTER 14

THE TEN-NATION EUROPEAN FEDERATION

"The ten horns you saw are ten kings who have not yet received a kingdom, but who for one hour will receive authority as kings along with the beast. They have one purpose and will give their power and authority to the beast" (Rev. 17:12-13).

The book of Daniel, written around 537 BC, contains prophecies concerning the kingdoms that would rule over the earth during the "time of the Gentiles." These kingdoms: Babylon, Media-Persia, Greece, and Rome are explored in detail in chapter four, "The Great Gentile Kingdoms of the Earth." The prophecies in this book reveal that in the end times, the fourth empire, Rome (which broke up and became the nations of Europe) will be restored and will be ruled by an emperor again (Rev. 13:3, 4). This emperor is known as the Antichrist.

Throughout history, many men have tried to reunite the nations of Europe under one leader. All of these have failed—the European nations have remained divided and no known federation of ten kings has yet arisen out of Europe. However, as explained in chapter eight, "Stage Setting for the Tribulation," the move to create the European Union could be the start of the revived Roman Empire the Bible predicts. Indeed, all of the nations that are banding together into the European Union have their roots in the old Roman Empire.

Although it will be interesting to see how the nations of the European Union evolve into the ten-nation European federation that the Bible predicts, the following is certain about the role of this entity in the last days:

Prophecy: A federation of ten kings or nations will rise out of Europe (i.e., out of the nations that made up the Roman Empire, Dan. 7:24). It is out of this federation that the Antichrist will arise (Dan. 7:24). The sole purpose of the ten-nation European federation will be to give power to the Antichrist (Rev. 17:13). After his death and resurrection (see chapter fifteen, "The Antichrist and His Kingdom"), the Antichrist will consolidate his worldwide rule by killing three of the ten kings of the European federation. This will lead to the other seven kings submitting voluntarily to his rule. This event will provide the political power from which the Antichrist will begin his program of world conquest (Dan. 7:8, 24; Rev. 17:12-13). The details of this program are discussed in the next chapter. The Antichrist will then lead the European federation during the Tribulation period (Dan. 7:7, 24; Rev. 12:3, 13:1, 17:12).

Speculation: Most students of prophecy believe that the headquarters of the European federation will be Rome. The thinking goes that since Rome was the capital of the old Roman Empire, so, too, Rome will be the capital of the revived Roman Empire (i.e., the ten-nation European federation).

CHAPTER 15

THE ANTICHRIST & HIS KINGDOM

"And [the Antichrist] was given authority over every tribe, people, language and nation. All inhabitants of the earth will worship the beast—all whose names have not been written in the book of life belonging to the Lamb" (Rev. 13:7-8).

"We do not need another committee; we have too many already— what we want is a man of sufficient stature to hold the allegiance of all people, and to lift us out of the economic morass into which we are sinking. Send us such a man, and be he god or devil, we will receive him" (Paul Henri Spaak, Secretary General of NATO, 1957).

The word "Antichrist" evokes many different images and ideas—it has been used throughout history in various contexts and now means many different things to different people. Contrary to some views, the Antichrist mentioned in the Bible is not a general term that refers to any opponent of Christ or a term that refers to paganism in general. Rather, the term refers to a specific person who will arise near the time of the end. Throughout history, many people have tried to identify the Antichrist. Proposals that have been offered include various Roman emperors, Muhammad (the founder of Islam), Napoleon, Kaiser Wilhelm (the German emperor who intended to conquer Europe and reunite the Roman Empire), Benito Mussolini (the Roman who threatened the world after WWII), Adolf Hitler (who persecuted the Jews and tried to conquer Europe), Joseph Stalin (the atheistic leader of the Soviet Union), John F. Kennedy (because of his Catholic background and his softness on communism), Ronald

Wilson Reagan (for having six letters in each of his three names—a reference to the mark of the beast), Saddam Hussein (for rebuilding Babylon and his hostilities toward Israel), and Bill Clinton (for being a master of deceit). Each attempt to identify the Antichrist has so far proven wrong. The Bible speaks of a very different person than the ones listed above, someone who has yet to rise to power. The Antichrist cannot be identified through current events or the cultural lens of our own time. Rather, the Antichrist can only be identified through the Scriptures and what we know about him through the passages that God has given.

The Antichrist will be a real human being whom Satan will control during the Tribulation period. He will be Satan's front man. The Bible provides great detail on the Antichrist, his rise to power, and his activities. He will arise out of Europe during a time of political chaos. When he signs a seven-year covenant with the nation of Israel, it will officially mark the beginning of the Tribulation period. He will pose as a great humanitarian and will pretend to be a great friend of Israel for the first three and one-half years of the Tribulation. The Jewish race will receive him (and the False Prophet described below) as a sort of messiah who has come to usher in the "Golden Age of Israel" as pictured by the prophets. The Antichrist will have remarkable powers and will possess an irresistible personality and superhuman wisdom. He won't be called the Antichrist, but rather will have a politically correct title. People won't run *from* him, but rather will flock *to him* as a man of peace, genius, and power. He will be clever, eloquent, and very smart. He will be received by almost everyone as a man for the times who will solve the world's enormous problems. The quote at the beginning of this chapter, spoken as far back as 1957 by the former Secretary General of NATO, captures the essence of how the Antichrist will come to power—in a time of economic and political morass, the people of the world will readily flock to a man who can gain the allegiance of the world's nations and rescue them from the troubles of their time. The Antichrist will be readily accepted as the world's savior.

At the midpoint of the Tribulation, however, things will change dramatically as Satan himself will personally give his power and authority to the Antichrist. It's at this point that the Antichrist will turn on the Jews, enter the newly rebuilt Temple, place a statue of himself in the Holy of Holies, and proclaim himself to be God. This will be the ultimate sacrilege and is known as the "abomination of desolation" in Scripture. From that point, the Antichrist will demand that all people on the earth worship him and his statue. Those who don't will be persecuted and killed. The Antichrist will then seek to conquer the world. He will be very successful but will ultimately meet his demise at the hands of Christ when He returns during the battle of Armageddon.

To Christians, the Antichrist should be readily identifiable at the beginning of the Tribulation period that is, if Christians are around to see it. If the pre-tribulational view of the Rapture holds true, then Christians will be removed from the earth prior to the rise of the Antichrist. This means that almost everyone on the earth who would have been readily able to identify the Antichrist for who he really is, will be gone. This might explain how the Antichrist will be able to rise to power without significant opposition. If the pre-tribulational view of the Rapture is not the correct interpretation, then Christians should be able to readily identify the Antichrist, and should be a significant force working against the activities of the Antichrist during the Tribulation.

With the exception of one verse (1 John 2:18), the Bible never directly refers to this coming leader as the Antichrist. Christians throughout the ages have used the word Antichrist because it concisely captures the essence of who this person is and what this person will stand for. Webster's *Ninth New Collegiate Dictionary* describes the prefix *anti* as meaning, "of the same kind but situated opposite, exerting energy in the opposite direction, or pursuing an opposite policy." That is exactly what the Antichrist will be all about—the Antichrist will "be of the same kind" as Christ in the sense that he will be both a deliverer and a king, but the two will, of course, have vastly different motives and agendas. Instead of Christ, who will establish God's kingdom on earth, the Antichrist will attempt to establish a satanic kingdom on earth. Although Scripture only directly references the Antichrist once, it does use several other phrases to describe this person including the following:

Names for the Antichrist	
• The little horn (Daniel 7:8) • The insolent king (Daniel 8:23) • The prince who is to come (Daniel 9:26a) • The one who makes desolate (Daniel 9:27) • The worthless shepherd (Zechariah 11:16-17)	• The abomination (Matthew 24:15) • The man of lawlessness (2 Thessalonians 2:3) • The lawless one (2 Thessalonians 2:8) • The antichrist (1 John 2:18) • The beast (throughout Revelation)

Table 8: Names for the Antichrist

The word "antichrist" itself can have two meanings: *antichristos*, which means to oppose or to deny that there is a Christ, and *pseudochristos*, which means to come instead of Christ. In the context of the Bible, the Antichrist will do both. Initially the Antichrist will be an atheist, denying that there is a God or a Christ (Dan. 11:37-38). At the midpoint of the Tribulation, however, he will himself claim to be God and demand that people worship him. It's interesting to note that the rise of the Antichrist has many similarities to Adolf Hitler. Author Gerhard L. Weinbert writes:

> During the early years, Hitler appealed to a wide variety of people by combining an effective and carefully rehearsed speaking style with what looked like absolute sincerity and determination. He found a large audience for his program of national revival, racial pride in Germanic values, hatred for France and of Jews and other non-German races, and disdain for the Weimar Republic. Hitler asserted only a dictatorship could rescue Germany from the depths to which it had fallen. His views changed only minimally in subsequent years and attracted increasingly larger audiences.[1]

The parallels are many: the Antichrist will most likely be very eloquent and will speak with sincerity and determination. At a time of political chaos, the Antichrist's message of global and religious unity will resonate with the people of the world. The Antichrist will then grab more and more power as he asserts that a global dictatorship will be the only way to rescue the world from the depths to which it has fallen. As times goes on, the Antichrist will increasingly blame the Jews and Christians for the world's troubles and turn on them through a campaign of intense persecution, just as Hitler did during the Holocaust. The Antichrist will then turn from being a peacemaker to a warmonger set on world conquest. As his empire expands, he will meet with some resistance but will be enormously successful. At the end of his campaign, though, there will be a great battle—one that the Antichrist will lose. This battle will spell the end of the Antichrist and the beginning of a great time of peace and prosperity.

His Description and Traits

"The [Antichrist] will do as he pleases. He will exalt and magnify himself above every god and will say unheard of things against the God of gods. He will be successful until the time of the wrath is completed, for what has been determined must take place"
(Dan. 11:36).

The Antichrist will be a complex person. He will appear at times to be a great peacemaker and statesman, while at other times a madman set on world domination. The Bible provides much insight into this person and his character.

Prophecy: The Antichrist will be human. Although there have been many attempts throughout history to spiritualize away the humanity of the Antichrist, the Bible states that the number used to identify the Antichrist will be a human number or that of man (Rev. 13:18). This would exclude philosophical systems, demonic beings, political movements, empires, or the like.

• The Antichrist will have an insignificant beginning (Dan. 7:8—the reason he is called "the little horn"). In essence, no one will pay attention to him initially; he will rise to power out of nowhere.

• The Antichrist will arise out of the political chaos among the nations (Rev. 13:1—note the word "sea" in the Bible refers to nations as defined in Rev. 17:15, and the description of the sea as "churning" in Dan. 7:2).

• The Antichrist will come out of Europe (Daniel 7:24—i.e., out of the ten-nations which come out of Rome—see section on Europe described in chapter four). Some people have speculated that because America was formed out of the countries of Europe, it is possible that the Antichrist could arise out of America. However, if this were the case, it would seem odd that the Antichrist could then come to lead the ten-nation European Federation.

• The Antichrist will receive his power from Satan (Rev. 13:2).

• God himself will send a powerful delusion so that people will believe the Antichrist's lies (2 Thess. 2:11). In essence, God will, in some ways, aid the Antichrist by helping him lead people astray. Many wonder why God would cause people to be led astray by the Antichrist. The reason is that these people have continually rejected the Lord as God. In essence, God will close the minds of those who have rejected the truth as part of the punishment He will pour out during the Tribulation period (2 Thess. 2:10, 12). Such action is not without precedent in the Bible. During the days of Moses, God "hardened Pharaoh's heart" ten times (Exod. 4:21, 77:3, 9:12, 10:1, 20, 27, 11:10, 14:4, 8, 17). This hardening caused Pharaoh to reject Moses' pleas to release the Israelites from their captivity, which brought about the ten plagues of Egypt. What's important to note, however, is the Bible indicates Pharaoh first hardened his own heart ten times before God intervened (Exod. 7:13, 14, 22, 8:15, 19, 32, 9:7, 34, 35, 13:15). Pharaoh first rejected God, and then God 'hardened his heart' to ensure that Pharaoh would have to endure the consequences of his rejection. So, too, God will harden the hearts of those who reject Him in the end times, so that they will also have to endure the consequences of their rejection.

• The Antichrist will be able to perform miracles and supernatural acts (2 Thess. 2:9).

• He will be boastful and will blaspheme the true God (Dan. 7:8, 11, 25, 11:36; Rev. 13:6).

• He will be insensitive to the needs of others: he will not care for the needy, show an interest in the young, heal the injured, or help feed the hungry (Zech. 11:16).

• He will try in some way to change the set times and seasons in order to promote his anti-Christian agenda (Dan. 2:21, 7:25). The Bible is not clear on what "set times" specifically refers to. It is possible that this reference is to the redefinition of the basic Christian calendar, which counts years based upon the time that has elapsed since Christ's birth. Evidence of the movement toward this redefinition is already being seen today—the acronym BC which, for the past two millennia has been an abbreviation for "Before Christ," has recently been redefined by liberal scholars to be BCE which means "Before the Common Era," omitting any reference to Christ. Likewise AD, which is an abbreviation for "*anno Domini*" or "in the year of our Lord [Jesus Christ]," has been changed to CE which simply stands for the "Common Era". It's possible that the Antichrist will attempt to redefine the way years are counted and omit the reference to Christ in an effort to achieve global religious unity among the various faiths of the world.

• He will be an atheist—he will show no regard for any god, except the god of military power and conquest (Dan. 11:37-38).

• He will have no desire for women (Dan. 11:37). The King James and New American Standard versions interpret it this way. The NIV and Revised Standard versions interpret this verse as "He will have no regard for the one desired by women." In this latter translation, it is not clear to what this verse would be referring.

• He will reward those loyal to him by making them rulers (Dan. 11:39). This would be similar to the practice today, where an incoming president frequently rewards those who helped him get elected by appointing them to cabinet posts, staff positions, and ambassadorships. Likewise, those who support the Antichrist will be rewarded with powerful positions.

Speculation: Since the Bible includes the Antichrist's empire as one of the "Great Gentile Kingdoms of the Earth," it is generally believed the Antichrist will be of Gentile descent. Furthermore, since the Antichrist will arise out of Europe, it is speculated the Antichrist will be of Italian descent, since Rome was the capital of the Ancient Roman Empire, from which the nations of Europe arose.

His Covenant with Israel

"Therefore hear the word of the Lord, you scoffers who rule this people in Jerusalem. You boast, `We have entered into a covenant with death, with the grave we have made an agreement. When an overwhelming scourge sweeps by, it cannot touch us, for we have made a lie our refuge and falsehood our hiding place'"
(Isa. 28:14-15).

Early in his career, the Antichrist will befriend the nation of Israel during a time of turmoil and bring an end to Israel's conflicts with its Middle-Eastern neighbors. As such, the Antichrist will set himself up to be the savior (or messiah) of Israel by making a covenant to protect it. This event will mark the beginning of the Tribulation period.

Prophecy: At the beginning of the Tribulation period, the Antichrist will confirm a seven-year covenant (i.e., treaty) with the Jewish people (Dan. 9:27). The Hebrew word for "confirm" is *gabar*, which is not the same word as to "sign." *Gabar* also means to "strengthen" or "make stronger."[2] Therefore, in order to strengthen, make stronger, or confirm something, the peace treaty must already be in existence. As such, it is quite likely that the peace treaty that the Antichrist actually signs with Israel will be an enhanced version of one of the peace treaties already signed or in development. This treaty will bring a perceived peace to the nation of Israel (Ezek. 38:11 describes Israel as a "peaceful and unsuspecting people" at that time, and in 1 Thess. 5:3, the people are quoted as proclaiming peace and safety before the Tribulation overtakes them).

At the midpoint of the Tribulation, he will break the covenant he made with the Jewish people, invade Israel, and take over the Temple (Dan. 9:27, 11:41; Isa. 28:18—see the section on the Abomination of Desolation later in this chapter).

Speculation: It is quite possible that this seven-year agreement or peace deal is what allows the nation of Israel to rebuild the Temple, since rebuilding the Temple prior to such an agreement would be impossible given the current political climate.

His Death and Resurrection

"One of the heads of the beast seemed to have had a fatal wound, but the fatal wound had been healed. The whole world was astonished and followed the beast" (Rev. 13:3).

During the Tribulation period, the Antichrist will be killed and miraculously resurrected. This event will greatly increase the Antichrist's popularity and power. This imitation of the resurrection of Jesus Christ is one of the reasons he is called the Antichrist in the Bible.

Prophecy: Sometime during the first half of the Tribulation period (probably near the midpoint), the Antichrist will be killed by a fatal head wound (Rev. 13:3, 12b, 14b). It's possible this wound might be from an assassination attempt by the forces that oppose him.

The fatal wound the Antichrist receives will be miraculously healed—the Antichrist will essentially be resurrected. This event will amaze the whole world and will lead the world to follow after the Antichrist (Rev. 13:3-4, 17:8).

Speculation: Although not specifically stated, it's quite possible that the Antichrist's death and resurrection will be tied to his indwelling by Satan, the Abomination of Desolation and the worship of the Antichrist (mentioned below). The chain of events could be linked. The scenario would be this: the Antichrist appears as Mr. Nice-Guy for the first half of the Tribulation period and is recognized as a peacemaker after he signs the covenant with Israel. At the midpoint, he is killed. A couple of days later, he is possessed by Satan and miraculously resurrected. It is at this point that he turns on the Jews (perhaps a Jew was responsible for the assassination attempt), desecrates the Temple, and demands that the world worship him as the Messiah. He would point to his death and resurrection as proof of his deity. Many will follow because they will be astonished by his resurrection (an imitation of Christ's resurrection). He will then consolidate his worldwide power by killing three of the ten kings in the European federation, which will lead to the other seven submitting voluntarily to his rule out of fear. This will provide the political basis from which the Antichrist will project his power and start his military conquests. As part of this, those people that chose not to worship the Antichrist will be relentlessly persecuted as traitors against the cause of global unity.

The False Prophet

"Then I saw another beast, coming out of the earth...He exercised all the authority of the first beast on his behalf and made the earth and its inhabitants worship the first beast, whose fatal wound had been healed. And he performed great and miraculous signs" (Rev. 11-13a).

The False Prophet will be the Antichrist's lieutenant or right-hand-man. His job will be to enforce worship of the Antichrist by performing miracles, by making an animated statue of the Antichrist, by sentencing disobedient people to death, and by requiring a mark on the forehead or the hand of everyone in order to buy and sell goods. In essence, he will be the Antichrist's minister of propaganda.

What's interesting about the False Prophet is that he, along with Satan and the Antichrist, form a sort of evil trinity. Just as God, Jesus, and the Holy Spirit make up the Christian trinity, so, too, these three are portrayed in Scripture as satanic trinity. It's well known that Satan has always tried to set himself up to be God (Isa. 14:13-14), so he certainly plays this part. The Antichrist will die and be resurrected similar to Jesus and will be seen as a sort of messiah bringing peace to Israel. Clearly the Antichrist plays the role of Christ. Finally, the False Prophet will speak on behalf of Satan and will compel people to worship the Antichrist. This is similar to the work of the Holy Spirit, who speaks to people's hearts and draws them to a relationship with Christ. Clearly, the Antichrist, False Prophet, and Satan will work together during the Tribulation to achieve their mutual goals.

Prophecy:

• The False Prophet will probably be a religious figure, most likely a Jew (note the phrase "like a lamb" in Rev. 13:11). It's likely that he will have some authority as a political figure (based on the description of him having horns which in prophecy symbolize kingdoms or power—Rev. 13:11).

• He will speak on behalf of Satan (Rev. 13:11).

• He will exercise all the power and authority of the Antichrist (Rev. 13:12).

• His chief job will be to promote worship of the Antichrist (Rev. 12:12b).

• He will be able to perform miracles and supernatural acts, which will deceive the unbelieving world (Rev. 13:13-14).

• He will set up an idol to the Antichrist (that can speak and breathe) and demand that people worship it (Rev. 13:14-15).

• He will kill those who don't worship the idol (Rev. 13:15).

Speculation: While the Antichrist who will arise out of Europe will likely be a Gentile, it's quite possible that the False Prophet will be a Jew. Although this is not definitive, the Bible states that the False Prophet will come out of the land (Rev. 13:11). Frequently, when the Bible uses this phrase, it refers to the land of Israel; so "coming out of the land" would mean that the False Prophet would come out of the nation of Israel. This makes sense in context, because the Antichrist will be a Gentile. Since we know the Antichrist will demand that the world worship him from the Jewish Temple in Jerusalem and will preside over a worldwide religion, it makes sense that his chief lieutenant would have ties to Israel, so that he could deceive the Jewish people into accepting and worshiping the Antichrist as well.

His Indwelling by Satan

"Woe to the earth and the sea, because the devil has gone down to you!" (Rev. 12:12)

The Antichrist will not be a typical man. Rather, he will be personally guided by Satan until the midpoint of the Tribulation period when he will be possessed by Satan himself. This possession (potentially at the time of his death and resurrection) will cause a transformation in the Antichrist. Just as Adolf Hitler transformed during his career from being a likeable politician to a madman bent on destroying the Jewish people, so, too, the Antichrist will change at the midpoint of the Tribulation from being a statesman and peacemaker to a man with a penchant for absolute destruction of Jewish and Christian people. Although Satan indwelling a human being may seem hard to believe, this has actually happened once before in the case of Judas Iscariot—the traitor that betrayed Jesus. The Bible states that "Satan entered Judas" (Luke 22:3; John 13:27), which led to his actions against Christ.

Prophecy: During the first half of the Tribulation period, Satan and his angels will start a war in heaven against the archangel Michael and his angels (Rev. 12:7). Throughout the Bible, examples are given of battles that take place in the spiritual realm similar to battles that take place in the physical realm. For example, when the prophet Daniel was praying to God and awaiting an answer from Him, an angel appeared and informed Daniel that he was late in arriving because he was "detained in a battle against the prince of the Persian kingdom, until Michael, the archangel came to assist" (Dan. 10:12-13). According to the Bible, spiritual warfare is real, so it should be no surprise that during the Tribulation on earth, there would also be a major conflict occurring in the spiritual world as well.

Satan will not be strong enough to overcome Michael and his angels. As a result, he will lose his place in heaven and be cast down to earth along with one-third of all the angels, which are the ones that joined Satan in his rebellion (Rev. 12:4, 8- 9). It is a common misconception that Satan and his angels are imprisoned in Hell at present. This is not true. Although Satan did rebel once before and is considered "a fallen angel," Satan still has access to God in Heaven and is free to roam the earth. Evidence of his ability to converse with God in heaven is found in the book of Job: "One day the angels came to present themselves before the Lord, and Satan also came with them" (Job 1:6), and evidence of his liberty to visit earth includes his appearance to Eve in the Garden of Eden (Gen. 3:1-5) and his appearance to Jesus in the wilderness (Matt. 4:1-11). It will not be until the time of Armageddon (described in a subsequent chapter) that Satan will be incarcerated and will no longer be free to roam the earth or do his own will.

When Satan is cast down to earth:

• There will be great rejoicing in Heaven, because the kingdom of God (i.e., the Millennial Kingdom) will be at hand (Rev. 12:10-12a).

• Satan will be filled with anger because he knows that his time on earth will be short (three and a half years to be exact, Rev. 12:12b). He will use this time to vent his wrath on the inhabitants of the earth before he will be incarcerated and cast into the Bottomless Pit (see chapter twenty-two).

• He will give the Antichrist his power, throne, and great authority (Rev. 13:2).

The Abomination of Desolation

"In the middle of the `seven' he will put an end to sacrifice and offering. And on a wing of the temple he will set up an abomination that causes desolation, until the end that is decreed is poured out on him" (Dan. 9:27)

"He [the False Prophet] ordered them to set up an image in honor of the beast who was wounded by the sword and yet lived. He was given power to give breath to the image of the first beast, so that it could speak and cause all who refused to worship the image to be killed" (Rev. 13:14-15).

The "Abomination of Desolation" is a term used throughout prophecy to refer to an event that will occur at the midpoint of the Tribulation. At this time, the Antichrist will commit the ultimate sacrilege—not only will he defile the Temple in Jerusalem, but he will set up an idol of himself in it, claim to be God, and demand that the world worship him as God.

This event will mark the completion of the Antichrist's transformation. It's from this point on that he will truly be recognized for what he is—a madman opposed to everything that God stands for—a man obsessed with world conquest and with the destruction of all those who stand in his way.

Prophecy: At the midpoint of the Tribulation, the Antichrist will:

• Turn against the false religion (described in chapter sixteen) and destroy this worldwide religious system that flourished during the first half of the Tribulation.

• Kill the two witnesses (described in chapter seventeen).

• Break his covenant with the nation of Israel and invade Jerusalem. The Antichrist will then control the city of Jerusalem for the remaining three and a half years (Rev. 11:2).

• Put an end to the daily sacrifice and offering in the Temple (Dan. 9:27).

• Claim to be God and say blasphemous things against the true God (Dan. 7:8; 11; 25, 11:16, 36; 2 Thess. 2:4, Rev. 13:6).

• Set up a statue of himself in the Temple (Dan. 9:27). This idol, which will be erected by the False Prophet, will be able to speak and breathe (Rev. 13:15).

• The False Prophet and the Antichrist will then demand that everyone in the world worship the statue and the Antichrist (Dan. 112:16, 2 Thess. 2:4, Rev. 13:14-15).

• Everyone on the earth *will* worship the Antichrist—except those who become Christians during the Tribulation period (Rev. 13:8).

• Anyone who resists worshiping the Antichrist will be persecuted. Many will be killed (Matt. 24:16-22, Rev. 13:15).

His Persecution of God's Elect

"So when you see standing in the holy place "the abomination that causes desolation," spoken of through the prophet Daniel... then let those who are in Judea flee to the mountains" (Matt. 24:15-16).

At the midpoint of the Tribulation, after the Abomination of Desolation, the Antichrist will single out Christians and Jews and start a violent campaign of persecution against them. It's at this point that believers will go into hiding to escape the persecution that the Bible forewarned them about. Many Jewish people will flee to a safe place in the desert that God will prepare for them, keeping them safe for the second half of the Tribulation period.

Prophecy:

• The Antichrist will start his campaign of persecution at the midpoint of the Tribulation period (Rev. 12:13).

• Upon seeing and recognizing the Abomination of Desolation as the event prophesied by Daniel and foretold by Jesus Christ, residents of Israel who believe in Jesus will flee for divine protection. They will be transported to a mountainous place in the desert, prepared by God. This place will be out of the Antichrist's reach. Here, they will be taken care of by God for the last three and a half years of the Tribulation (Isa. 26:20-27:1, Matt. 24:16-20, Rev. 12:6, 14). This flight will be reminiscent of Israel's flight from the Egyptians in the days of Moses (compare Exod. 19:4 with Rev. 12:14).

• Satan will try to destroy these Jewish believers in their place of protection by causing a great flood. God, however, will protect the Jews by causing the earth to open up and absorb the water (Rev. 12:15-16).

• Satan will be so enraged by this failed attempt to destroy Jewish believers that he will turn his anger toward those who didn't flee (or who weren't in Israel at the time) and non-Jewish believers. He will then vigorously persecute these people for the last three and a half years of the Tribulation period (Dan. 7:21; 25, Rev. 12:17).

Speculation: Given the general biblical description of Israel's place of refuge and what we know of the Antichrist's conquests, many people speculate that the ancient city of Petra will be the place God will prepare for Israel. The Bible states that when the Antichrist enters Israel to overthrow the countries of Palestine, "Edom and Moab" shall escape out of his hand (Dan. 11:41). Edom is in the wilderness where Israel wandered for forty years, and it is here where the ancient city of Petra exists (in what is now modern day Jordan).

Petra was a great commercial center in the days of King Solomon and was rediscovered in 1812 by a Swiss explorer. In Greek, Petra means "city of rock," which is just what it is—Petra is literally an impregnable fortress made of rock. What makes Petra unique is that it is located in the mountains and is like the crater of a volcano. It has one entrance—through a narrow, winding canyon that ranges from twelve to forty feet wide. The sides of the canyon are at times so close that they almost shut out the sky. The height of the sides varies from two hundred to one thousand feet, and the length of the canyon is about two miles. No other city in the world has such a unique and impenetrable gateway and is protected as well as Petra.

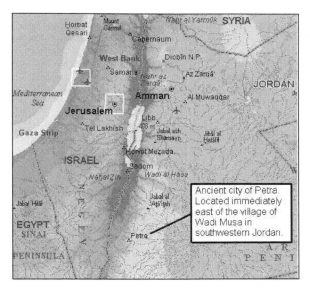

Map 10: The Ancient City of Petra

The Mark of the Beast

"He [the False Prophet] also forced everyone, small and great, rich and poor, free and slave, to receive a mark on his right hand or on his forehead, so that no one could buy or sell unless he had the mark, which is the name of the beast or the number of his name. This calls for wisdom. If anyone has insight, let him calculate the number of the beast, for it is man's number. His number is 666" (Rev. 13:16-18).

Under the direction of the False Prophet, everyone on earth will be required to receive a mark or tattoo which will indicate a person's allegiance to the Antichrist. Those who refuse this mark (i.e., followers of Jesus Christ) will not be able to buy or sell goods and will be persecuted, captured and beheaded. In essence, the mark will be a way of identifying those who have bought into the Antichrist's system of world government and have sworn their loyalty to him as Lord. It will be a way of weeding out and eliminating those who are disloyal to him. As such, this mark will force everyone on the earth to make a decision—are you on the side of the one true God, or are you on the side of the Antichrist? No one on earth will be able to sit on the fence. People will be forced to make a decision—a decision that will have eternal consequences.

Prophecy:

• The False Prophet will force all people of the world to receive a mark on their right hands or on their foreheads. This mark will be required for people to buy or sell goods (Rev. 13:16-17).

• The mark will be a symbol of the Antichrist and a person's allegiance to him (Rev. 14:9-10). In essence, the mark will be a way of exposing those who believe in Jesus Christ and consolidating the Antichrist's economic power over the world.

• The mark must appear on the forehead or right hand (Rev. 13:16).

• The mark will, in some way, be related to the number 666 (Rev. 13:18). For a reason unknown to us, this number will play a role in the identification of the Antichrist in the end-times. Nobody knows exactly how the number 666 will relate to the Antichrist, and it is probably futile to speculate. Numeric schemes have been proposed throughout time that have pointed to people such as Nero, the Pope, Hitler, or Ronald Reagan. Obviously, all of these were wrong. What is significant though, is that the Bible refers to 666 as the "number of man," so it's possible that this number is merely a symbolic reference to the Antichrist. In the book of Revelation, the number "7" is one of the most significant numbers because it is used to indicate perfection.

There are seven Seal judgments, seven Trumpet judgments, seven Bowl judgments, seven thunders, etc. When the Antichrist claims to be God (in the form of the satanic trinity), the number that would be symbolic of this should be 777. What this passage in Revelation might be saying is that "No, you are only 666; you are short of deity."

• There will be no turning back or changing one's mind. Anyone receiving the mark cannot be saved and will ultimately be tormented in the Lake of Fire forever. They will never have rest or relief from punishment (Rev. 14:9-10). The Lake of Fire (i.e., Hell) is God's eternal punishment for those that reject Him (see chapter twenty-three).

• Those who don't receive the mark (i.e., believers in Christ) will be beheaded at the hands of the False Prophet (Rev. 20:4).

• God will bless those who are beheaded for refusing the mark. They will be recognized for their endurance and good deeds and will be resurrected at the Second Coming to reign with Christ during the Millennium (Rev. 14:13, 20:4).

Speculation: Given the nature of the Tribulation judgments, it's probably safe to assume that food and resources will be scarce and that the mark will be instituted as part of some form of worldwide rationing system. Since the Antichrist will probably hold enormous power over the world's resources, he will likely demand allegiance in exchange for food, fuel, etc. Those who don't receive the mark (i.e., Christians) will most likely be branded as rebels, traitors, or troublemakers because they will refuse to buy into the new economic system that the Antichrist created to solve the world's problems. Given the description of the mark, it's quite likely that it will be more than a tattoo. In order to keep people from buying and selling and to prevent the possibility of counterfeits, the mark will most likely employ technology such as a computer chip or a three dimensional bar-code to uniquely identify people and ensure that they are who they say they are (see discussion in chapter eight).

Speculation: Some have speculated that the mark of the beast will be related to the Jewish practice known as gematria. In this system, each Hebrew letter has a particular number assigned to it, since the Greek and Hebrew languages did not have separate numerical systems. Words and names then, could be represented by the sum of the letters used to spell them out. Most people are familiar with the Roman numeral system where Latin letters such as V, X, C, M, and L also function as numbers—V represents a five, X represents a ten, C represents a hundred and so on. The idea is the same in Greek and Hebrew. For example, the Hebrew name for Jesus is Y'shua. The sum of the numbers corresponding to the Hebrew letters for this name would be 749. What's interesting about this is that, in the Bible, the number seven is considered the number of perfection, so the number forty-nine would represent perfection times perfection. So 749 then, would thus be an apt description of Christ. Since the Antichrist's name is said to equal 666, it could be symbolic of the Antichrist's falling short of God. Having said that, there is currently no way, using gematria, to speculate on what the Antichrist's name might be.

His Rise to Power

"Men... worshiped the beast and asked, `Who is like the beast? Who can make war against him?'" (Rev. 12:4)

The Antichrist will rise to power quickly and will be very successful in his effort to become a world dictator. He will however, have opposition. After his rise to power, he will have numerous conflicts that will lead up to the events of Armageddon. The details of these conflicts are explained in chapter twenty-one.

Prophecy:

• After his death and resurrection, the Antichrist will consolidate his worldwide rule by killing three of the ten kings of the European federation, which will lead to the other seven kings submitting voluntarily to the Antichrist's authority. This event will provide the political basis from which the Antichrist will expand his power (Dan. 7:8, 24; Rev. 17:12-13).

• The Antichrist will then be the head of the European federation during the Tribulation period (Dan. 7:7, 24, Rev. 12:3, 13:1, 17:12).

• The Antichrist's conquests will be rapid; he will be very strong and powerful, and there will be an air about him, which is self-assured, and proud (Rev. 13:2—cross reference the descriptions of "leopard, bear and lion" with the descriptions of the Great Gentile Kingdoms of the Earth described in chapter 4 and in Dan. 8).

• God will give the Antichrist power over every nation and people (Rev. 13:7b).

• He will succeed in all that he does, until the time of his demise during Armageddon (Dan. 11:36).

• People will be astonished by the Antichrist's power—they will think that no one will be able to make war with him (Rev. 13:4b).

His Demise

"The beast was captured, and with him the False Prophet...The two of them were thrown alive into the fiery lake of burning sulfur"
(Rev. 19:20).

At the height of Armageddon, the Antichrist will meet his match when Christ returns:

Prophecy: When Christ returns at the Second Coming, the Antichrist (along with the False Prophet) will be cast alive into the Lake of Fire (i.e., Hell, Dan. 7:11, Rev. 19:20). Details of this event are contained in chapter twenty-two.

Notes

1. "Adolf Hitler," Microsoft Encarta 99 Encyclopedia.

2. Jimmy DeYoung, "Preparations for the Potentate," *Countdown to Armageddon,* 125.

CHAPTER 16

THE FALSE RELIGION

"Come, I will show you the punishment of the great prostitute [the false religion]...With her the kings of the earth committed adultery and the inhabitants of the earth were intoxicated with the wine of her adulteries" (Rev. 17:1b-2).

During the Tribulation period, a worldwide religion will arise that will help the Antichrist in his endeavors. This religion will be a false form of Christianity and will most likely be based in Rome. This false religion will have great power, and all the people groups of the world will join together and support this worldwide religion. This religion will be the ultimate completion of the ecumenical movement that began during the twentieth century (see chapter eight).

How could any false form of Christianity get all other religions of the world to join in? Won't true Christians recognize this religion for what it is and be opposed to it? These are good questions, and are one of the reasons that pre-tribulationalists believe the Church will be removed from the earth prior to the rise of this worldwide religion. If true Christians are taken out of the earth, then those left behind would be people who may have an outward form of religion, but no inner or true relationship with God. Given the chaos that will occur during the Tribulation period, it is logical to assume that the people of the world will be looking for answers and will turn to religion. Unfortunately, the religion they will turn to will be a false religion that will exist to deceive them and aid the Antichrist in his conquests. At the midpoint of the Tribulation, however, the Antichrist and ten-nation European federation will turn against this false religion and destroy it. It is at this point that the Antichrist will set up a statue of himself in the Temple and demand that the world worship *him*, instead of the false religion. Although not specifically stated in the Bible, it's logical to assume that the Antichrist will become jealous of the power and membership of the false religion and will overthrow it in order divert the allegiance of the people toward him and away from the false religion.

In the book of Revelation, the false religion is given the name "Babylon the Great, the Mother of Prostitutes." It is called this because the city of Babylon, which name is synonymous with "Babel," was the site of the first great apostasy or false form of Christianity. In ancient days, Nimrod, the great grandson of Noah whose name literally means "rebel," defied God and attempted to unite the world together (both politically and religiously) by building a tower whose top would reach into the heavens. This tower was known as the tower of Babel (Gen. 11:1-9). Its purpose was to facilitate the worshiping of false gods and to serve as a rallying point and symbol of human achievement. This perverted the true form of worship that God desired and marked the beginning of a long history of religions that distorted the message of the one true God. In fact, Herodotus, a Greek historian who lived around 450 BC, claimed that Babylon was the source of all the religions of the world.

Nimrod's wife, Semiramis, was a priestess. After Nimrod's death, she proclaimed Nimrod a god—the sun god who eventually became known as Baal in the Canaanite culture. She had a son, Tammuz, whom she claimed was miraculously conceived after Nimrod's death by a sunbeam which carried Nimrod's sperm to her. Tammuz was said to be Nimrod's reincarnation. Together, they promoted idol worship. Semiramis became known as the Supreme One, or Queen of Heaven, and was worshiped as a god. Tammuz supposedly became god of the underworld after being killed by a wild boar while he was out hunting. The worship of Semiramis and Tammuz soon swept throughout the ancient world and became integrated into other cultures. In Egypt, Semiramis and Tammuz became known as Isis and

Osiris. In Assyria, Ishtar and Baccus; in India, Isi and Iswari; in Asia Cybele and Deoius; in Greece Aphrodite and Eros and in Rome, Venus and Jupiter (a.k.a. Cupid). It was this last form that Antiochus erected an image in the Temple and committed the Abomination of Desolation, as described in chapter two, "Israel, Jerusalem and the Temple." Although the names and cultures have changed, the basic worship of the mother and son remains the same. Even in contemporary culture, the image of Cupid holding a bow and arrow is related to this false religious system—Cupid represents Tammuz (the reincarnated Nimrod), whom the Bible describes as being a "mighty hunter" for the souls of men.

The practice of mother/child worship based on Semiramis and Tammuz became so widespread that it crept into the Christian church. In the city of Ephesus, the mother-goddess was known as Diana and it was in this city in AD 431 that the church council of Ephesus approved the worship of Mary, the mother of Jesus. In fact, the word "Madonna" comes from the Latin phrase, "Mea Domina" ("My Lady"), which was also the title for Baal's wife in the Phoenician culture. Our word "Easter" is a derivative of the Babylonian goddess "Ishtar," the "goddess of sun and spring"—yet another reference to Semiramis. In fact, it's because of this origin that Easter falls on a different day each year – it's scheduled to occur on the first Sunday after the first full moon occurring on or after the vernal equinox, commonly known as the first day of spring. This schedule reflects the pagan celebrations of Ishtar rather than the actual timing of Christ's resurrection from the dead. In the Babylonian culture, the egg was a symbol of fertility, which is where the Easter egg derives. Further, the occasion of lent (which occurs just prior to Easter) originates from the forty days that Semiramis wept after the death of Tammuz during which the Babylonians pleaded with Ishtar for his resurrection. This practice is mentioned in Ezekiel 8:14.[1] Other passages in the Bible referencing Semiramis, the Queen of Heaven, include Jeremiah 7:18 and 44:15-30.

As a result, Babylon was not only the first city to rebel against God and the origin of a movement to a one-world government, but it was also the origin of almost every false religion, occult belief, and form of idolatry. In fact, the concepts that this false religion incorporates, such as the miraculous conception of Tammuz, the death and resurrection, and Tammuz being the father (Nimrod) and son at the same time, should not seem strange—they are counterfeited from the Christian religion.

In prophecy, the words "prostitute" or "whore" refer to false religions that tempt or lead people astray from the true form of Christianity. The reason God was opposed to such a religion is that it focused on mankind and human achievement rather than on the true worship of God. Likewise, the problem with the ecumenical movement of today is that core biblical doctrine has been eroded and discarded in order to reach agreement and unity across the denominations. As churches have sought unity under ecumenical organizations such as the World Council of Churches, they have resorted to a least common denominator set of beliefs for the sake of compromise instead of holding true to what the Bible says. Certainly, this will be the case with the false religion of the Tribulation period as well. In an effort to bring together all of the world's religions under one roof, the resulting theology will likely be so watered down and contrary to the Bible that it will be abhorrent to God, which is why He refers to it as a prostituted form of Christianity.

Prophecy:

• The false religion will be a prostituted form of Christianity (Rev. 17:5-6), but will deny that Jesus Christ (the son of God), came in the flesh to the earth (2 John 7, 2 Pet. 3:4).

• The false religion will have great power and influence during the first half of the Tribulation. In fact, the Bible states that "the kings of the earth" will have committed adultery with her, and that she sits "on many waters...Which are peoples, multitudes, nations, and languages" of the earth. This implies that the worldwide religious system will span across nations and people groups, and will have participation from leaders all over the world (Rev. 17:1-6, 15).

• The false religion will most likely be based in Rome ("the city on seven hills"—Rev. 17:9). Rome has long been known as the city built on seven hills, which were named: Palatine, Aventine, Caelian, Equiline, Viminal, Quirimal, and Capotoline. One cannot be dogmatic about this, though, since there are various interpretations as to the exact meaning of the phrase "seven hills."

• The Antichrist and the false religion will work together during the first half of the Tribulation period. In Revelation 17:3, 8, the false religion is seen riding the Beast, indicating that the religious system will have power over the Antichrist. The fact that the prostitute is on the back of the Antichrist indicates that the Antichrist will support the false religion. In essence, the Antichrist and the false religion will use one another during this time. The Antichrist will find it expedient to go along with the false religion, which will be gaining membership and power from the confusion and chaos that will exist during the Tribulation period; the false religion will find it advantageous to ally itself with the Antichrist, due to his rising popularity and power in the world.

• The Antichrist and the ten-nation European federation will turn on the false religion which had supported them and will destroy it (Rev. 17:16). This will probably happen at the midpoint of the Tribulation period when Satan possesses the Antichrist. It's at this time that he will claim to be God and demand that the world worship him.

Speculation: Many identify the false religion of the end times with the Roman Catholic Church (or, more accurately, what the Catholic Church will become after the Rapture when true believers are removed). Indeed, there is a strong case for making this association. The argument is based on a history of passing on the leadership of the Babylonian Order, and is as follows: [2]

• In ancient days, Noah's grandson Nimrod (whose name literally means "we will revolt"), established himself as the world's first dictator or potentate. Nimrod tried to unite the world's religions together by creating the tower of Babel. It was during this time that the Babylonian Order was created. This satanic cult was based on a system of priesthood, in which a high priest or pontiff had supreme power—power to determine a person's eternal destiny, power to forgive sins, etc. The pontiff was recognized as the high priest of the Babylonian Order and passed down this role from generation to generation. As a result, the city of Babylon became known as the seat or headquarters of Satan in ancient days.

• In 539 BC, the Babylonian Empire fell to the Media-Persian Empire, and the high priest fled to Pergamum in Asia Minor (about eighty miles North of what is now Izmir, Turkey). It's at this time that Satan shifted his capital to Pergamum (Rev. 2:13).

• In 133 BC, Attalus, the king of Pergamum and pontiff at the time, died without an heir and bequeathed his kingdom and the headship of the Babylonian Priesthood to Rome, which had conquered the Media-Persia empire about thirteen years earlier.

• In 63 BC, Julius Caesar was made Supreme Pontiff of the Babylonian Order. Thus, the first Roman emperor became the head of the Babylonian priesthood and Rome became the successor to Babylon. It's at this time that emperor worship became popular, and Caesar demanded that he be worshiped as a god.

• The emperors of Rome continued to exercise the office of Supreme Pontiff until AD 376 when Emperor Gratian, for Christian reasons, refused to accept the office. At this time, Pope Damasus I was elected to the position and, for the first time, the ruler of the Roman church became the head of the Babylonian Order. Thus, the Roman Catholic Church and Babylonian priesthood were united into one religious system. During his tenure as pope (which lasted from AD 366 to AD 384), Damasus made Latin the principal language for services (replacing Greek) and was a strong advocate of the doctrine of Roman primacy—this doctrine stated that the Roman Catholic Church was the one true church of Christ. In addition, Damasus introduced pagan rites into the Roman Catholic Church. These rites prostituted Christianity by mixing pagan practices with Christian practices. These practices and symbols include:

1. Worship of the Virgin Mary as well as other images and symbols, such as the cross. Nowhere in Scripture is there biblical basis for these practices.

2. Celebrating various festivals of the Roman Catholic Church, many of which were of Babylonian origin. Easter, for instance, is not a Christian name—it means "Ishtar," which is the name of the chief goddess of the Babylonians. Ishtar was considered the Babylonian's Great Mother, the goddess of fertility and the Queen of Heaven.

3. The rosary, which is of pagan origin.

4. Celibacy, monks, and nuns, none of which have authority or basis in Scripture. Nuns in fact, are an imitation of vestal virgins, which were the priestesses of the Roman goddess Vesta.

5. Various other religious elements taken from the Babylonian religion, such as the holy days, holy water, etc.

• Since the time of Damasus, the priesthood and headship of the Babylonian Order have been passed down from pope to pope throughout the history of the Roman Catholic Church. In fact, to this day, the pope still carries the title supreme pontiff of the Universal church.

As a result of this history and lineage of passing down the priesthood of the Babylonian religion, many believe that "Mystery, Babylon the Great," described in Revelation 17, refers to the Roman Catholic Church and that the "seat of Satan" still is Rome. Although there are Christians within the Roman Catholic church, it seems likely that when these believers are removed (assuming a pre-tribulational rapture), the Roman Catholic Church will be transformed in the chaos of the Tribulation period and will fulfill the role of becoming the one, worldwide church that the Bible warns about—the perverted form of Christianity known as the false religion.

Further anecdotal evidence for this theory includes the following:

• The "woman" representing the False Religion in Revelation 17:4 is described as being "arrayed in purple and scarlet, and decked with gold and precious stones and pearls." Scarlet and purple are the colors of the papacy and when a pope is installed into office, a vest covered with pearls and adorned with gold and precious stones is worn.

• The false religion, which the Bible describes, will be based in Rome (Rev. 17:9). This is the same location where the Vatican is located today—no other major religion is currently located there.

In addition to the above, it's interesting to note what some non-biblical prophets have predicted about the future of the Papacy and its alignment with the Antichrist: In AD 1140, the Catholic, St. Malachy, predicted the full line of popes, starting in 1143 down to the final pope, using a motto to identify each one. These mottos usually referred to the coat of arms for each pontiff, or to his birthplace, or sometimes to his physical actions, or a major event that occurred during his reign as pope. The pope to reign after John Paul II is identified as "the glory of the olive" (a potential reference to Israel) and the final pope, who is predicted to preside over the Catholic church during the Tribulation period, is identified as Peter of Rome, which is significant given the rise of the revived Roman Empire (i.e., the ten-nation European federation) described in the Bible as giving power to the Antichrist. Pope John Paul II himself predicted that the second pope to reign after him would be aligned with the Antichrist.

Speculation: Another view states that the false religion is not related to the Roman Catholic Church at all, but rather to astrology and the New Age movement. This interpretation has its basis in the fact that the Babylonian priesthood had its roots in astrology and sorcery, which God specifically condemned Babylon for: "Keep on, then, with your magic spells and with your many sorceries, which you have labored at since childhood...Let your astrologers come forward, those stargazers who make predictions month by month, let them save you from what is coming upon you" (Isa. 47:12-13). In this view, the false religion would arise out of the New Age movement and other false religions derived from Semiramis and Tammuz, which emphasize practices such as astrology, witchcraft, and sorcery and is based on centuries-old Eastern mysticism and Gnosticism (a perversion of Christianity that early Church fathers and apostles warned about). Facets of the New Age movement have already permeated society. New Age techniques for self-improvement and the idea that the individual is responsible for and capable of everything have become widespread. These beliefs have made their way into corporate America, health care, the environment, counseling, sports, and the armed forces. Ideas frequently associated with this movement include psychic healing, holistic health, values clarification, inner transformation, reincarnation, extraterrestrial life, biofeedback, chanting, yoga, transpersonal psychology, the occult, astrology, extrasensory perception, acupuncture, massage, tarot cards, Zen, mythology, and visualization. In this theory, the New Age movement would unite the people of the world together under one system of worship based on the tolerance and harmonization of the many different belief systems. This would prostitute Christianity, because in Christianity, there is only one true God. This interpretation holds that the Tower of Babel was primarily a 'ziggurat' or a temple built to the gods and goddesses of the stars. Its primary purpose was an observatory—to better aid the Babylonians in their study of the stars.

Regardless of where the false religion arises, it is clear that during the Tribulation period it will probably include a multitude of belief systems all rolled into one. In essence, the false religion will be the epitome of tolerance and relativism, where any belief system will be welcome as long as it welcomes all other belief systems. There will be no absolutes. As such, the false religion will probably be an amalgamation of beliefs from multiple faiths including Christianity, Catholicism, Islam, Hindu, New Age, etc.

Notes

1. Based in part on Thomas N. Davis, "The Abominable Antichrist," *Countdown to Armageddon,* 190.

2. This argument and logic based primarily on Clarence Larkin, *The Book of Revelation,* 151-152.

CHAPTER 17

GOD'S TWO WITNESSES

"Surely the sovereign Lord does nothing without revealing His plan to His servants and prophets" (Amos 3:7).

The Bible says that the Lord does nothing without first revealing His plan to His servants and prophets. Throughout history, this has been the case. God has repeatedly sent prophets to proclaim His word to His people and warn them of pending disaster. Examples include when Israel was first taken into captivity by Babylon, when God destroyed Sodom and Gomorrah, and when God was set to destroy Nineveh. In each case, God sent a prophet (or series of prophets) to preach that pending judgment would come unless the people repented of their ways and turned to God. In some cases, the people did repent and the pending judgment by God was halted. In most cases however, the people did not repent, and judgment fell just as God forewarned.

The end times will be no different. The Bible indicates that God will send two witnesses to the earth who will prophesy from Jerusalem for three and one-half years. These prophets will warn the nation of Israel (and the world) of God's pending judgments and preach that people should turn from their sinful ways. Unfortunately, the Bible indicates that the vast majority of people will not listen: "The rest of mankind that were not killed by these plagues [the Tribulation judgments] still did not repent of the work of their hands; they did not stop worshiping demons, and idols of gold, silver, bronze, stone, and wood—idols that cannot see or hear or walk. Nor did they repent of their murders, their magic arts, their sexual immorality, or their thefts" (Rev. 9:20-21). "They refused to repent and glorify Him" (Rev. 16:9). "They refused to repent of what they had done" (Rev. 16:11) and "They cursed God" (Rev. 16:21).

This is unfortunate. We can only speculate whether or not God would halt the Tribulation judgments if the people of the world did turn to Him during the last days.

Prophecy:

• The two witnesses will prophesy from Jerusalem for 1260 days (three and one-half years) during the Tribulation period (Rev. 11:3). It is not stated whether the three and one-half years refers to the first-half or to the second-half of the Tribulation period. The first-half seems more likely, however, since the Bible indicates that the witnesses will be killed by the Antichrist after the three and one-half years, which seems to fit better with the midpoint of the Tribulation (when the Antichrist is possessed by Satan, invades Jerusalem, and commits the Abomination of Desolation) than at the end when the Lord returns.

• The two witnesses will be clothed in sackcloth symbolizing that they will be prophets of doom (Rev. 11:3).

• God will miraculously protect the two witnesses from onlookers, hecklers, and the Antichrist. If anyone tries to harm them, fire will come down from heaven and devour them (Rev. 11:5).

• The two witnesses will have power to perform miracles. They will have the power to keep it from raining during the time they are prophesying, the power to turn water into blood, and the power to strike the earth with every kind of plague as often as they want (Rev. 11:6).

• The identity of these two witnesses is not known, but it is likely that these two prophets will actually be forms of Moses and Elijah for the following reasons:

1. The miracles that the two witnesses will be able to perform are identical to the miracles that Moses and Elijah performed. Moses turned water into blood and brought plagues to the earth (Exod. 7:17-21, 8:1-12:29), and Elijah caused it not to rain for three and one-half years and brought down fire to destroy his enemies (1 Kings 17:1, 18:41-45, 2 Kings 1:10-12, Luke 4:25, James 5:17). These are the same miracles the Bible describes the two witnesses performing during the Tribulation period (Rev. 11:6).

2. God promised to send Elijah the prophet "before the great and dreadful day of the Lord comes" (Mal. 4:5-6), which is clearly a reference to the Tribulation period. Elijah's purpose will be to proclaim the Word of God and turn people's hearts toward Him, which is the same purpose the Bible gives for the two witnesses.

3. Moses and Elijah were the only Old Testament prophets who were removed from the earth before their ministries were finished. Moses was prohibited from entering the Promised Land because he disobeyed God and so died with his ministry unfinished (Num. 20:12). Elijah was taken up to heaven in a whirlwind before finishing his ministry.

4. Moses and Elijah both appeared with Jesus when He was on the earth at the Mount of Transfiguration. During this event, Moses and Elijah appeared to Christ and conversed with Him in front of the disciples. This event is widely regarded as a preview of Christ's Second Coming (Matt. 17:1-5). It seems logical that since these two appeared with Christ prior to His death and resurrection, that they might also be the ones to appear prior to His Second Coming.

• At the end of 1260 days of prophesying, God will allow the Antichrist to kill the two witnesses (Rev. 11:7).

• People all over the world will celebrate the death of the two prophets because the prophets will have tormented the people of the world with their words. People will gloat and even send each other gifts to celebrate the deaths of the two witnesses (Rev. 11:10).

• Their dead bodies will lie in the street of Jerusalem for three and one-half days because people from all over the world will refuse to bury them (Rev. 11:8-9).

• After three and one-half days, God will resurrect the two witnesses. Their resurrection will completely terrify people. God will then rapture (or take up) the two witnesses to heaven (Rev. 11:11-12).

• Once the two witnesses have ascended to heaven, a great earthquake will occur. This earthquake will destroy a tenth of Jerusalem and will kill seven thousand people (Rev. 11:13).

CHAPTER 18

TRIBULATION SAINTS

"The Gospel of the Kingdom will be preached in the whole world as a testimony to all nations, and then the end will come" (Matt. 24:14).

"In the last days, God says, `I will pour out My Spirit on all people. Your sons and daughters will prophesy, your young men will dream dreams... and everyone who calls on the name of the Lord will be saved"' (Acts 2:17, 21).

Even while God is punishing the world for its persistent rejection of Him through the Tribulation judgments, He will provide an opportunity for the whole world to hear the Gospel message, and offer a final chance for people to turn to Him (Matt. 24:14). Many will respond. In fact, the Bible states that "a great multitude that no one could count" will come out of the Tribulation believing in Christ (Rev. 7:9, 14). Given that the Bible references the number of "two hundred million" troops in Revelation 9:16, we can only assume that the number of believers coming out of the Tribulation will be far greater than this, so as to be innumerable.

The Tribulation period, while difficult for Christians, will be a time of tremendous revival and witness as millions upon millions come to faith in the Lord. It will be the final and complete fulfillment of the Great Commission, in which Christ instructed His disciples to preach the Gospel to all nations (Matt. 28:19-20). This only makes sense— the people of the world will be looking for answers during this terrible time of judgment and destruction. Although the false religion and the Antichrist will succeed in deceiving many, many will also realize the truth in what is happening around them (either through study of the Bible, the two witnesses, or other believers) and turn to Christ as a result. The mass conversion of people during the Tribulation will start with 144,000 Jews. Just as a group of first century Jews was used to proclaim the Gospel of Jesus to the world after His First Coming, so, too, God will use a group of Jews to proclaim the Gospel message to the world prior to His Second Coming. These Jewish people will be the first to recognize the events of prophecy and turn to Christ during the Tribulation. Most likely, these Jews will be first, because they will be familiar with the prophecies of the Old Testament and will recognize the events that are unfolding around them. Why won't Christians be the first to recognize these events? It's a good question and another reason that pre-tribulationalists believe that the Rapture will happen before the beginning of the Tribulation period. Regardless, the Bible is clear that eventually people from every nation, tribe, people, and language will come to be believers during this time.

Unfortunately, these Tribulation saints as they are frequently called (i.e., people who come to know Christ during the Tribulation period), will be relentlessly persecuted because of their allegiance to Christ and for their refusal to worship the Antichrist. They will be hated and despised and will become outcasts from society and the mainstream economic system. They will not be able to buy or sell any goods because they will refuse to take the mark of the beast (described in chapter fifteen). As a result, many will be beheaded.

The 144,000 Jews

"'Do not harm the land or the sea or the trees until we put a seal on the foreheads of the servants of our God.' Then I heard the number of those who were sealed: 144,000 from all the tribes of Israel"
(Rev. 7:3-4).

The primary responsibility for evangelizing the world during the Tribulation period will fall to 144,000 Jews, which the Bible indicates will plan a special role during this time and will be protected from much of God's wrath.

Prophecy:

• There will be 144,000 people identified or set apart during the Tribulation period. These Jews will be sealed by God, indicating a special purpose or significance (Rev. 7:4).

• The 144,000 will be Jews and will consist of twelve thousand from each of the twelve tribes of Israel (Rev. 7:4-8), with four exceptions:

1. The tribe of Dan is left out. This is probably because the tribe of Dan was guilty of idolatry on many occasions (Gen. 49:17, Lev. 24:11, Judges 18, 1 Kings 12:28-29), and God promised to blot out the name of any tribe that introduced idolatry into Israel (Deut. 29:18-21).

2. The priestly tribe of Levi is substituted for the tribe of Dan.

3. The tribe of Ephraim is left out. This is probably because in 931 BC, this tribe led the way in causing the civil war within Israel. This war resulted in the nation of Israel being divided into two kingdoms—ten tribes of the Northern kingdom that were known as Israel and two tribes of the Southern kingdom that were known as Judah. In addition, the tribe of Ephraim, like the tribe of Dan, was guilty of idolatry (1 Kings 12:25-30).

4. Joseph (Ephraim's father) is substituted for Ephraim.

• The 144,000 will be the first saved during the Tribulation period (i.e., firstfruits, Rev. 14:4). The word "firstfruits" references a practice God gave to the Israelites in which the first fruits of the annual harvest were to be offered to the Lord in thanksgiving to symbolize that the whole harvest belonged to Him (Lev. 23:9-14).

The word used in this verse is used figuratively to describe the first of more people to be redeemed as part of the Tribulation period.

• The 144,000 will precede a much larger group of Israelites and Gentiles who will turn to the Lord during the Tribulation period (see Isa. 2:3 and the description below on the multitude of Gentiles).

• The salvation of the 144,000 will follow the sixth Seal judgment and will precede the Trumpet judgments (Rev. 6:16-7:3). The sixth Seal judgment will consist of great physical destruction. The 144,000 will recognize this as a judgment from God and turn to Him.

• The 144,000 will clearly be identified as followers of the Lord (Rev. 14:1, 3-4). They will receive a seal from God that will appear on their foreheads. This seal will contain the name of the Father and the Son and will be clearly visible (Rev. 7:3-4, 14:1). In essence, these Jews will be marked men for God. There will be no hiding their faith in Christ. This is similar to the mark of the beast described in the previous chapter. Clearly, God's people and Satan's people will be required to choose sides—there will be no secret Christians during this time.

• The 144,000 will be protected from the Tribulation judgments in order to perform service for God during these days (Rev. 7:3, 9:4). Most probably, the 144,000 will be evangelists.

• The 144,000 will keep themselves pure and be blameless before the Lord. They will not lie or "defile themselves with women" (Rev. 14:4-5). This may mean that the 144,000 were unmarried, or it may indicate their state of devotion to God since the Bible frequently uses the terms like fornication and adultery to refer to spiritual purity instead of sexual purity (James 4:1, 2 Cor. 11:2).

• The 144,000 will be hunted down and persecuted because of their refusal to bow down to the Antichrist. They will not be able to buy or sell because they will refuse to take the mark of the beast (see chapter fifteen). As such, they will probably have to depend on other converts to provide for their everyday needs. Many will probably be hungry, sick, and imprisoned.

• When Christ returns and judges the people still alive at the end of the Tribulation period, He will assign eternal life or eternal death on the basis of their treatment of these 144,000, since that will reflect their attitude toward Christ Himself (see chapter twenty-three).

The Multitude of Gentiles

Although the 144,000 Jews will be the first to recognize the events of the Tribulation and turn to God, countless others from every nation and ethnic group will also come to faith in the Lord during this time.

Prophecy:

• The Gospel will be preached to all nations during the Tribulation period (Matt. 24:14).

• God will pour out His spirit on *all* people—many will prophesy and have dreams related to the end times (Acts 2:17-21, Joel 2:28-29). This will be similar to the day of Pentecost in AD 30 when God poured out His Spirit following Christ's ascension into heaven, and multitudes of people started preaching the Gospel and accepting the Lord (Acts 2-3).

• Everyone who calls upon the name of the Lord during this time will be saved (Joel 2:32).

• Everyone will have a final opportunity to accept or reject Christ (until of course, they take the mark of the beast, which will indicate their decision to reject Christ).

• Out of the Tribulation will come an innumerable multitude of people who will be believers in the Lord. These people will come from every racial and geographic group (Rev. 7:9, 14).

There is some disagreement on the exact identity of this great multitude of people and what is meant by the phrase "they will come out of the Great Tribulation" (Rev. 7:14). There are two possible interpretations, which hinge on your view on the timing of the Rapture and your interpretation of the following passage:

> "After this I looked and there before me was a great multitude that no one could count, from every nation, tribe, people and language, standing before the throne and in front of the Lamb...Then one of the elders asked me, `These in white robes— who are they, and where did they come from?' I answered, `Sir, you know.' And he said, `These are they who have come out of the great tribulation; they have washed their robes and made them white in the blood of the Lamb'" (Rev. 7:9-14).

In the first view, the multitude mentioned represents people who become Christians during the Tribulation period (i.e., Tribulation Saints). Those who believe in a pre-tribulation rapture primarily hold this view. Since Christians will be raptured prior to the Tribulation period, this multitude of believers coming out of the Tribulation must be new believers. People who hold to this view believe the 144,000 Jews who first come to Christ will be the ones to evangelize this multitude. This view is supported by the Greek translation of the phrase "ones coming out" (Rev. 7:14), which is a present participle, expressing a continuous and repeated action, not a once-and-for-all action. The second view holds that the multitude represents the raptured Church itself. Those who don't believe in a pre-tribulation rapture hold this view. They believe this multitude represents the Church, which lives through and comes out of the Tribulation at the time of the Christ's Second Coming. They equate the 144,000 as Jews who come to Christ and remain faithful, through the Tribulation period.

CHAPTER 19

THE ATTACK ON ISRAEL

"In that day, when my people Israel are living in safety...I will bring
[Russia and others] against my land...I will display my glory among
the nations, and all the nations will see the punishment I inflict and
the hand I lay upon [them]. From that day forward, the house of
Israel will know that I am the Lord their God"
(Ezek. 38:14b, 16b, 21-22).

At some point during (or even prior to) the Tribulation period, the armies of Russia, Egypt, and the Arab nations will attack the nation of Israel seeking to plunder its wealth. This battle is described in great detail in the book of Ezekiel, chapters thirty-eight and thirty-nine. It is unclear from the Bible, however, exactly when these events will take place. Israel will be at peace when the attack occurs, which may imply that the peace treaty with the Antichrist will be in effect (putting the battle sometime during the first half of the Tribulation). However, some of the events described in this battle are similar to the description of Armageddon, which will occur at the end of the Tribulation period. Perhaps the first part of the battle will begin before the middle of the Tribulation, with successive battles taking place throughout the last half of the Tribulation up to the time of Armageddon.

Regardless of the timing, this battle will be unique in that God will supernaturally intervene and destroy the opposing armies of Israel. Thanks to God, this battle will represent a major victory for Israel and a mass slaughter of Israel's enemies. Consequently, many who are alive during this time will recognize this victory as being from God, and turn to Him.

Prophecy:

• The attack will take place after the people of Israel have been restored to being a nation and after Israel has recovered from a war (Ezek. 38:8).

• Israel will be living at a time of peace and safety, whether real or imagined when the attack occurs (Ezek. 38:11-12, 14).

• Russia and various eastern European countries such as Poland and Czechoslovakia will attempt to invade Israel with the help of Egypt, which will be allied with various Arab nations including Iran, Iraq, and Afghanistan and the countries of northern Africa such as Libya, Ethiopia, and Sudan (Ezek. 38:1-6).[1]

• The motive for the attack will be to loot Israel's great wealth and to capture Israel's strategic position in the Mediterranean (Ezek. 38:12).

• God's purpose for the attack will be for the nations of the world to recognize that He is the one, true God when He supernaturally intervenes on behalf of Israel (Ezek. 38:16, 23, 39:7).

• The armies will invade from the north, riding on horses (Ezek. 38:15, 39:2). It's possible that the reference to horses in this verse is figurative of battle transportation in general. However, it is also quite possible that actual horses might be used. Though it may be hard to believe that modern day armies will ride actual horses into battle, remember that during the Tribulation, there will be a tremendous amount of destruction because of the various Tribulation judgments occurring at this time. As such, established infrastructure such as highways and bridges will likely be destroyed so that the only way an invading army could reach its target may be on horseback.

• God will intervene and supernaturally defeat the invading armies through a great earthquake (so severe that the mountains will be overturned and cliffs will crumble), internal dissension, confusion among the invading armies, and a deadly rain of hailstone and fire (Ezek. 38:20-22). Remarkably, Scripture does not mention any opposing force on the part of Israel. Rather, it appears the defeat of the foreign invaders will be entirely due to God's direct actions. The events described above are similar to the descriptions of the seventh Seal, first Trumpet, seventh Trumpet, and the seventh Bowl judgments. As a result, it's quite possible that God's supernatural intervention described in this attack will be synchronous with one of these judgments.

• The homelands of the invading armies will also be destroyed by fire (Ezek. 39:6). This is significant—not only will God intervene and destroy the invading armies with fire, but He will also destroy the native lands of the invading armies as well.

• The slaughter from this battle will be enormous: Burying the dead from the slaughter will take seven months. In fact, people will be employed to go through the land to ensure that all of the bones have been buried (Ezek. 39:11-15). In the intervening period, the bodies of the dead soldiers will be eaten and picked on by birds and wild animals (Ezek. 39:4). The leftover weapons from the invading armies will supply Israel with fuel for seven years (Ezek. 39:9-10).

• Israel will then proceed to plunder and loot the nations that attacked it (Ezek. 39:10).

• God's supernatural intervention, the enormity of the slaughter, and victory for Israel will lead many nations, including the people of Israel, to recognize and believe in the one true Lord (Ezek. 38:23, 39:21-22, 21-22, 28).

Speculation: The fact that the Bible says Israel will have recovered from war prior to this attack (Ezek. 38:8) implies that there will be a major war between Israel and its enemies at some point in the future (but prior to the Tribulation). The Bible also says Israel will be "living at a time of peace and safety" (Ezek. 38:11, 14), implying that the Antichrist's brokered peace deal will be in effect. If so, the scenario might be this: the current tension between Israel and its Arab neighbors will lead to a major war between these countries. At a time of turmoil, the Antichrist will step in and broker a deal between the Middle Eastern countries that will finally bring peace to the Middle East. This will start the seven-year Tribulation clock. Israel will then live in peace and safety for a couple of years, but would then experience the attack described in this chapter.

Views on the Timing of the Attack

As mentioned above, the exact timing of this attack is not known. The Bible doesn't provide specific details. As a result, there is much debate among scholars regarding when this attack will occur. Following are the various arguments related to the timing of this attack:

Arguments for an Attack Prior to the Tribulation

The passage describing the attack indicates that the burning of the weapons from this attack will supply Israel with fuel for seven years. Since the Jewish people will be persecuted and in hiding for the last half of the seven year tribulation, it can be argued that the attack must happen at least three and one-half years before the beginning of the Tribulation period to allow this time period to occur. The alternative explanation (that the burning takes place during the Millennium) seems unlikely, given Christ's personal presence and provision for Israel during this period.

It is hard to imagine how a revived Roman Empire would come to world power in Europe with the influence of Russia and the Arab countries as strong as they are. An attack prior to the Tribulation period (and perhaps even prior to the Rapture) would help to explain a vacuum in world political power that could lead to the rise of the Antichrist and the revival of the Roman Empire. The scenario would be that Israel will have had a war with an Arab neighbor prior to the attack. Through some form of treaty, Israel would then be in a time of perceived peace. During this time, Russia and the Arab countries would attack Israel, perhaps in retaliation for the prior war in addition to the reasons cited above. These countries would then be completely decimated as described in this prophecy. Because of this, Europe would then be in chaos, which would pave the way for the Antichrist's rise to power and the rise of the ten-nation European federation.

Arguments for an Attack prior to the Midpoint of the Tribulation

The Bible says Israel will be living in security, whether real or imagined, at the time of this attack (Ezek. 38:11-12). This would seem to indicate that the battle must take place before the midpoint of the Tribulation period, while Israel is still feeling secure as a result of its peace treaty with the Antichrist. After the midpoint of the Tribulation, Israel will be invaded by the Antichrist, Jerusalem will be taken over, and Christian Jews will be in hiding as the result of persecution from the Antichrist and False Prophet. As such, it seems unlikely that this attack could happen after the midpoint.

The Bible provides a definite list of nations that will participate in this attack (Ezek. 38:1-6). This list is different than the nations that will take part in Armageddon in which all nations will be gathered against Jerusalem (Rev. 16:14-16). This would seem to argue that this attack and Armageddon are two different events. In the invasion of Israel, the attacking nations will be destroyed by God through acts of nature including an earthquake, hail, and fire (Ezek. 38:20-22). During the battle of Armageddon, the invading nations will be destroyed by the personal return of Jesus Christ. Thus, these would seem to be two different events.

Arguments for an Attack Synchronous with Armageddon

The Bible says that at the conclusion of this battle, birds and beasts will eat the flesh of the warriors. This description is similar to the description of Armageddon given in the book of Revelation, which will occur at the end of the Tribulation (Ezek. 39:17-20, Rev. 19:17-18).

At the conclusion of the attack, the Bible says that nations will understand the judging hand of God and the people of Israel will know that the Lord is their God (Ezek. 39:21-22). This would seem to place the attack at the end of the Tribulation period, which is when the entire nation of Israel will turn back toward God.

The Bible states that the weapons left over from the invading armies will supply fuel for Israel for seven years (Ezek. 39:9-10). As mentioned, some argue that this would have to put the attack at the beginning (or prior) to the start of the Tribulation period. However, Isaiah 2:4 and Micah 4:3 indicate that during the Millennial Kingdom, Israel will "beat swords into plowshares and spears into pruning hooks" which would seem to corroborate the theory that the burning of these weapons will occur during the Millennium.

As can be seen, there are good arguments for each of the different interpretations on the timing of this attack. There is also good reason to believe that multiple views might hold true (i.e., that the first part of the battle will begin before the middle of the Tribulation, with successive battles taking place throughout the last half of the Tribulation up to the time of Armageddon). Regardless of which view a person holds, there is a certainty that these events will be fulfilled as prophesied and in accordance with God's plan.

Notes

1. The countries listed are descended from the nations of Gog, Magog, Meshech, Tubal, Persia, Cush, Put, Gomer, and Beth Togarmah listed in Ezekiel 38:1-6. A full description of the history of these nations and how they became the modern-day nations listed above are beyond the scope of this book. For a complete analysis, however, see Hal Lindsey, *The Late Great Planet Earth,* chapter 5 or Hal Lindsey, *Planet Earth: The Final Chapter,* 175-176.

CHAPTER 20

THE CITY OF BABYLON

"Babylon, the jewel of kingdoms, the glory of the Babylonians pride, will be overthrown by God like Sodom and Gomorrah. She will never be inhabited or lived in through all generations" (Isa. 13:19-20).

Although many passages in the Bible use the word "Babylon" to refer to the coming worldwide government (Rev. 13:3-4), religion (Rev. 13:11-15) or economic system (Rev. 13:16-18) under the Antichrist, there are also many references to a physical, rebuilt city of Babylon that will serve as the capital of the Antichrist's Empire. The Bible is clear that, in the end times, the city of Babylon will rise to world prominence as a commercial and cultural center. Near the end of the Tribulation period, God will then suddenly and violently destroy Babylon once and for all (Isa. 13:6, 9, Rev. 18).

Although the ancient city of Babylon (located just east of the Euphrates River, fifty-six miles south of Baghdad in Iraq) has basically been in ruins for over twenty-five hundred years, the city has recently been rebuilt. In 1987, New Babylon was rebuilt and dedicated by Saddam Hussein as described in chapter eight, "Stage Setting for the Tribulation." Although Babylon certainly can't presently be considered a world commercial or cultural center, it is clear from prophecy that it will be as part of the Antichrist's coming kingdom.

Babylon's Future Prominence

Prophecy:

• Babylon will become one of the greatest cities in the world. The city will have immense power, wealth, and splendor (Rev. 18:3b, 10, 14, 16-18, 23b).

• Babylon will also be a cultural center (Rev. 18:22).

• The city will be full of evil, decadence, self-indulgence, and excessive luxury (Rev. 18:2-3, 12-13).

• The city will be responsible for leading all the nations of the world astray. The language used and the description of the city make it clear that this city will most likely serve as the headquarters for the Antichrist's kingdom during the Tribulation period (Jer. 51:7, Rev. 18:3, 9, 23b-24).

• Merchants will become rich from selling luxury goods to Babylon (Rev. 3b, 11, 15, 17-19).

Although a literal interpretation of the Bible would indicate that the city of Babylon would be rebuilt on the same location as it had existed in centuries past, it is worth pointing out that there are other commonly held beliefs. The first is that the Babylon spoken of in Revelation 18 represents a secular system of commerce and culture in general which is basically alienated from God. By using this interpretation, some believe that this Babylon could represent any great city of the world, such as New York or the world's system of commerce. The other commonly held belief is that this Babylon is actually symbolic for the city of Rome—which is where the false religion will be headquartered and where it seems logical that the Antichrist would have his headquarters. The thinking goes that since Rome was the capital of the Roman Empire, so, too, Rome will be the capital of the revived Roman Empire (i.e., the ten-nation European federation). There are a couple of other arguments in support of this view. The first is that many in the early church viewed Babylon as

Rome. Indeed, the term Babylon was sometimes used as a code name for Rome just as the fish symbol was used to identify Christians. These codes and symbols were used to avoid incriminating writings that might lead to Roman persecution, which was common in the time of John (the author of Revelation). The second point supporting this view is that it seems highly implausible that the European federation would have its headquarters in a non-European country. As such, Rome would be the next, most logical candidate.

There are merits to both of these alternative interpretations because it is difficult to see how a minor city in modern-day Iraq could rise to prominence above the great established commercial cities of the world such as New York, London, and Tokyo. However, God has certainly fulfilled other prophecies, literally, that once seemed implausible (e.g., bringing Israel back together after two thousand years of dispersion, reuniting the nations of Europe, etc.), so it shouldn't be considered outside the realm of possibility that He would fulfill this prophecy literally as well. It should also be noted that a physical, prominent city of Babylon as mentioned in Revelation 18 doesn't have to exist in this form prior to the start of the Tribulation period, just at the end point when it is destroyed by God. It's quite possible that with all of the destruction surrounding the Seal, Trumpet, and Bowl judgments, the major cities of the world could be completely destroyed. This would then lead to the rise of Babylon as a new world center of power.

Speculation: We have seen in the past few years how quickly events can change and how power could easily shift to the Middle East, and Iraq in general, which could lead to increased prominence for the city of Babylon. With Saddam Hussein removed from ruling Iraq and democracy taking hold, one could easily imagine scenarios where Babylon could start to flourish as freedom and capitalism come to this part of the world for the very first time. This is especially true since OPEC continues to maintain tight control of the world's oil supply and Iraq continues to be one of the leading oil producing nations. As China and India continue to develop and demand ever increasing amounts of crude, it's clear that Iraq could be very well positioned to not only gain enormous wealth, but also increased power on the geopolitical stage.

The Destruction of Babylon

"Therefore in one day her plagues will overtake her: death, mourning and famine. She will be consumed by fire, for mighty is the Lord God who judges her. When the kings of the earth who committed adultery with her and shared her luxury see the smoke of her burning, they will weep and mourn over her...because no one buys their cargoes any more" (Rev. 18:8-11).

Although the city of Babylon will rise to world power and prominence, it will be violently and decisively destroyed by God near the end of the Tribulation period:

Prophecy:

• At the time of Babylon's destruction, there will be no light from the sun, moon, or stars (Isa. 13:10). This would put the time of Babylon's destruction after the fifth Bowl judgment, which would probably be in the second-half of the Tribulation period (see chapter thirteen).

• Before the destruction of the city, God will rescue His people and call them out of the city (just as He did in the days of Sodom and Gomorrah—Jer. 50:8, 51:6, 45, Rev. 18:4). The refugees who flee will then go to Jerusalem and tell them of Babylon's destruction (Jer. 51:10, 50).

• Babylon's destruction will come quickly—"in one hour" (Rev. 18:8, 10, 17, 19).

• An alliance of great nations and many kings from the North will be responsible for Babylon's capture and destruction (Jer. 50:3a, 9, 41). Likely, this reference is to the nation of Russia and her allies.

• Babylon will be destroyed by fire in the same way that Sodom and Gomorrah were. The smoke will be clearly visible to the people of the world as a testament to its destruction (Isa. 13:19; Jer. 50:32b, 40; Rev. 18:8, 9, 18).

• Babylon's destruction will be complete. Its walls will be leveled, and it will never be inhabited again (Isa. 13:20; Jer. 50:3b, 13, 24b, 39-40, 51:26, 37, 43, 58; Rev. 18:21-23).

• The king of Babylon (i.e., the Antichrist) will not be present during its destruction (Jer. 51:31).

• The destruction will occur at the same time that the nation of Israel begins to turn back to God, and the destruction will be one of the reasons for this change (Jer. 50:5, 19-20). Again, this would seem to put the destruction sometime around the end of the Tribulation period, probably as part of the campaign of Armageddon.

• The destruction will be from God as retribution for the way His people were treated (i.e., the persecution and killing of God's people at the hands of the Antichrist—Jer. 51:49, 56; Rev. 18:20, 24).

• After the destruction, the kings and merchants of the world—those who profited richly from Babylon's prosperity—will mourn (Jer. 50:46; Rev. 18:9, 11, 15, 17-19).

• The smoke from the fire will rise forever (Isa. 34:10). It's interesting to note that the newly restored city of Babylon was built over an underground lake of asphalt and oil. Because of this, it's quite possible to imagine how this prophecy of continuous fire could be fulfilled—similar to how hundreds of Kuwaiti oil wells burned when Saddam Hussein set fire to them at the conclusion of the Gulf War.

CHAPTER 21

ARMAGEDDON

"Then [the spirits of demons] performing miraculous signs went out to the kings of the whole world to gather them for the battle on the great day of the God Almighty...they gathered the kings together to the place that in Hebrew is called Armageddon" (Rev. 16:14, 16).

The word "Armageddon" conjures up many images. It has frequently been used in movies, books, speeches, and films to connote a final battle or war. Throughout history, people have used the term to describe everything from a nuclear holocaust to a world war and even a meteor collision with earth. Although many current uses of the word are not biblical, the Bible clearly describes an event referred to as Armageddon. Specifically, Armageddon refers to the final war at the end of the Tribulation period, where all of the armies of the world will be gathered together against Jerusalem. It is during this war that the Lord will return to the earth and intervene in history on behalf of His people, the Jews. He will interrupt the battle, capture the Antichrist and the False Prophet, and destroy the armies of the earth (see chapter twenty-two). In essence, the great battle of Armageddon will be over before it even begins; it will be the most anticlimactic battle in history.

The word "Armageddon" is a Greek transliteration (directly translated word) of the Hebrew word *Har-Megiddo,* which means "the mountain of Megiddo." It is a place, specifically a hill overlooking the great Plain of Esdraelon (also known as Jezreel) in northern Israel. This plain spans across the middle of the Holy Land from the Mediterranean to the Jordan. It is about twenty-five miles southwest of the Golan Heights, about twenty miles south-southeast of Haifa, and fifty miles north of Jerusalem.

Map 11: The Plain of Esdraelon, the Site of Armageddon

Megiddo is the site of an ancient city in central Israel that sat between the coastal plain and the valley of Esdraelon. Because of its strategic importance, many famous battles of Israel have been fought in this land including the battle of Deborah and Barak over the Cannanites (Judges 4) and Gideon over the Midianites (Judges 7). It is also in this valley where King Saul was killed and where King Josiah was slain by the Egyptians. Currently, a key Israeli military base occupies this valley.

Technically, the term Armageddon does not refer to a final battle. It is really a campaign, or series of events, that takes place over a wide geographic area, over a period of time. Unfortunately, the sequence of events is not found in one specific passage of the Bible, and a study of all the related passages pertaining to Armageddon reveals a very complex series of battles. Although the basic elements or pieces of the campaign are known, it is unclear how all of these events will fit together or what the timeline would be. A good analogy would be World War II. Imagine seeing individual snapshots of the attack on Pearl Harbor, the battle of Normandy, the air campaign over London, and the final dropping of the atomic bomb over Hiroshima, but not having a clear picture of how all these events were tied together. One would be left to speculate on how the war progressed based on anecdotal evidence, which is exactly what we are left to do with the campaign of Armageddon. As such, there are many different scenarios that could be created to connect these events. Although there are numerous battles, it's quite likely that the final battles (shown as numbers 4 to 6 in the figure below) will actually happen close together.

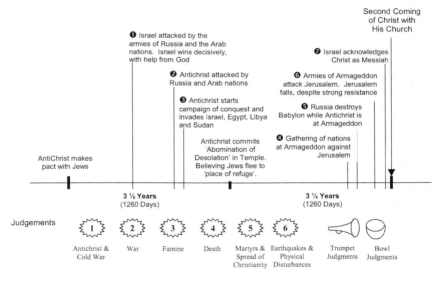

Figure 22: Tribulation Conflicts - One Possible Scenario

Instead of a battle being fought in one location and then a subsequent battle in another, it's likely that the battle will encompass a wide geographic area. The clue that this might be the best way to think of

Armageddon is found in Revelation 14:20, which describes a river of blood 180 miles long and up top four and one-half feet deep. Based on a study of all the relevant passages, below is one possible scenario of how the conflicts of the Tribulation might be played out.

The Attack on Israel (❶)

As described in chapter nineteen, "The Attack on Israel," when Israel is at peace (probably during the first half of the Tribulation period), it will be attacked by the armies of Russia, allied with Iran, Libya, and eastern European countries along with Egypt and the Arab nations of northern Africa. These countries will try to invade Israel to loot Israel's great wealth and capture the strategic position that it holds. God will supernaturally intervene, though, and defeat the invading armies. Israel will then proceed to plunder and loot the nations that attacked it. This event will most likely coincide with the second Seal judgment, where peace will be removed from the earth.

The Antichrist Attacked (❷)

"At the time of the end the king of the South will engage him [the Antichrist] in battle, and the king of the North will storm out against him" (Dan. 11:40).

After a failed attempt to invade Israel, the nations of Russia and Egypt will regroup and try to attack the Antichrist, who most likely will be headquartered in Babylon at the time. The reason this attack must occur *before* the Antichrist's campaign of conquest is because part of the Antichrist's conquests will include Egypt. It's unlikely that Egypt could attack the Antichrist if it is already under his control.

Prophecy: The kings of the South and North (i.e., Egypt, along with the Muslim nations, and Russia)[1] will engage the Antichrist in battle (Dan. 11:40). In essence, these countries will attempt a pincer movement, trying to engage the Antichrist on two different fronts.

Speculation: The motive for the attack is not stated, but given the nature of the third Tribulation judgment (famine), one can assume that resources will be scarce and nations will be desperate for food, fuel, etc. Although the Bible doesn't reveal the results of this battle, it does mention that the Antichrist will then start to invade many countries including Egypt, so it's most likely that Egypt and Russia will be defeated in this battle. It's possible that this pincer movement by Egypt and Russia is what sets off the Antichrist's worldwide campaign of conquest.

The Antichrist's Campaign of Conquest (❸)

"He will invade many countries and sweep through them like a flood"
(Dan. 11:40b).

After being attacked by Russia and Egypt, the Antichrist will then set off on a campaign of conquest throughout the Middle East. His conquests will include the nation of Israel.

Prophecy:

• The Antichrist's conquests will be rapid, he will be very strong and powerful, and there will be an air about him, which is self-assured and proud (Rev. 13:2—cross reference the descriptions of leopard, bear, and lion with the descriptions of the Great Gentile Kingdoms of the Earth described in chapter 4 and in Dan. 8).

• The Antichrist will quickly extend his power and invade many countries including Israel, Egypt, Libya, and Sudan (Dan. 11:41).

• The nation of Jordan will escape from these conquests (Dan. 11:41). Jordan will likely be a place of refuge for the Israeli people during the Antichrist's persecution of the Jews. It is here that Petra is located.

• God will give the Antichrist power over every nation and people (Rev. 13:7b).

• The Antichrist will succeed in all that he does, until the time of his demise during Armageddon (Dan. 11:36).

• People will be astonished by the Antichrist's power—they will think that no one will be able to make war with him (Rev. 13:4b).

• Reports from the `East and North' (i.e. the Orient and Russia) will alarm the Antichrist, and he will set out in great rage to destroy and annihilate many (Dan. 11:44).

Speculation: Although not specifically mentioned together, we can probably assume that the Antichrist's invasion of Israel mentioned here is synchronous with the invasion of Jerusalem that will occur at the midpoint of the Tribulation period. During this invasion, the Antichrist will break the peace deal he made with the Jewish people, invade Israel, take over Jerusalem, and commit the Abomination of Desolation in the Temple (see chapter fifteen). At this time, Christian Jews will flee to the city of refuge as the Antichrist starts his campaign of persecution. The Antichrist will then hold control of the city of Jerusalem for three and a half years (Rev. 11:2).

Gathering of the Nations at Armageddon (❹)

"Then they gathered the kings together to the place that in Hebrew is called Armageddon" (Rev. 16:16).

Upon hearing alarming reports about the armies of the East, the Antichrist will gather the nations of the world together in Israel at the site of Armageddon.

Prophecy:

• To counter a perceived threat by `the armies of the East', the Antichrist and the False Prophet will perform miraculous signs and use supernatural power to gather the nations together in the valley of Armageddon to confront the invading armies (Rev. 16:13-16, Joel 3:9-14). The term "armies of the East" literally translated means *the kings from the rising of the sun.* These are the nations of the Orient (probably led by China).

• The assembling of the armies at the site of Armageddon will begin at the time of the sixth Bowl judgment (Rev. 16:12-16).

• As part of the sixth Bowl judgment, the Euphrates River will be dried up, which will make it easier for the Oriental armies to cross the river bed and invade Israel (Rev. 16:12, 16).

• The nations will gather together at the Plain of Esdraelon, which is the site of Armageddon (Rev. 16:16).

Russia Destroys Babylon while Antichrist is Away (❺)

The destruction of Babylon is discussed in chapter twenty, "The City of Babylon." What's important to note is that the Bible says the king of Babylon (the Antichrist) will not be present during its destruction (Jer. 51:31). Rather, he will hear about the city's destruction through messengers. It is assumed that this is because the Antichrist and the False Prophet will be at the site of Armageddon during this time, gathering the nations together for war.

Speculation: Apparently, while the Antichrist and his army are out of Babylon, the alliance of nations from the North (under the direction of Russia), will take the opportunity to destroy the Antichrist's capital city. This seems like a plausible scenario, given that Babylon's destruction must occur after the fifth Bowl judgment (see chapter thirteen), and the Bible indicates that the gathering at Armageddon will occur during the sixth Bowl judgment. Furthermore, the capture of Russia is not listed as one of the Antichrist's conquests, so this army will probably still be in existence and capable of mounting an attack.

Armies of Armageddon Attack Jerusalem (❺)

*"On that day, when the nations of the earth are gathered against her,
I will make Jerusalem an immovable rock, for all the nations. All who
try to move it will injure themselves. On that day I will strike every
horse with panic and its rider with madness...Then the leaders of
Judah will say in their hearts, `The people of Jerusalem are strong,
because the Lord Almighty is their God.'" (Zech. 12:3-5).*

Once the nations of the world are gathered at the site of Armageddon
for war, they will then attack the city of Jerusalem under the direction
of the Antichrist. God will supernaturally strengthen the people of
Jerusalem, but the city will eventually fall. How did the Antichrist
lose control over Jerusalem, which he invaded at the midpoint of the
Tribulation period and took over? This is a good question. There are
two possible explanations. First, the following list of prophesied
events actually describe the original fall of Jerusalem at the midpoint
of the Tribulation. As mentioned at the beginning of this chapter, all
we see in the Bible are snapshots of these events, so the events
described below could simply refer to the original fall of Jerusalem.
A second explanation is that somehow the Jewish people regained
control of Jerusalem after the midpoint of the Tribulation. The
problem with the first explanation is that it doesn't entirely fit with
the other prophecies which indicate that all nations will be gathered
against Jerusalem, and this will lead the nation of Israel to
acknowledge the true Messiah. These phrases would argue that this
event must occur near the end of the Tribulation and not at the
midpoint. The problem with the second explanation is that a
recapture of Jerusalem is not described in Scripture. Regardless, the
following prophesied events indicate an attack against Jerusalem
during which God strengthens the people to put up a stiff resistance
against the invading armies:

Prophecy:

• All nations will be gathered against Jerusalem to do battle (Zech.
14:2).

• God will supernaturally strengthen the people of Jerusalem and use them to inflict great pain and suffering on the attacking armies:

1. He will strike the invading armies with panic and blindness (Zech. 12:4).

2. God will give strength to the people of Jerusalem ("So that the feeblest among them will be like David"—Zech. 12:8).

3. The people of Jerusalem will inflict severe damages on the surrounding peoples (Zech. 12:6).

4. This will lead to the nation of Israel to acknowledge that they are strong because of God. They will finally recognize Jesus as the true Messiah and weep (Zech. 12:5, 10-14).

• Despite putting up a good fight, the city of Jerusalem will be captured, the city ransacked, and the women raped (Zech. 14:2).

• Half of Jerusalem's people will go into exile; the other half will remain in the city (Zech. 14:2).

• Throughout the Tribulation, two-thirds of the Jewish population will be killed (Zech. 13:8).

Israel Acknowledges Christ as the Messiah (❼)

"When you are in distress and all these things have happened to you, then in the later days you will return to the Lord your God and obey him" (Deut. 4:30).

"And I [Jesus] will pour out on the house of David and the inhabitants of Jerusalem a spirit of grace and supplication. They will look on Me, the one they have pierced, and they will mourn for Him as one mourns for an only child, and grieve bitterly for Him as one grieves for a firstborn son. On that day the weeping in Jerusalem will be great" (Zech. 12:10-11).

Just before the return of Christ, the nation of Israel will realize why the Tribulation has fallen on them. They will see the events that are unfolding (i.e., the destruction of Babylon, God's strengthening of Israel during the fall of Jerusalem, etc.) and recognize this as the fulfillment of prophecy. As a result, the leaders of Israel will acknowledge their national sin and will lead the nation to accept Christ as the Messiah. This confession of national sin will last for two days. The entire nation of Israel gathered at the time will be saved. It's quite likely that this event will occur at the site of refuge described in chapter fifteen. To fully grasp this event, one must imagine the scene and all that has gone on. Jewish author David Brickner writes:

> The world [will have] reached a paroxysm of military conflict. Seven years of tribulation have come to a roaring crescendo of bloodshed and violence. All of the nations of the earth have gathered to fight Israel. The blood of the Jews and Gentiles and the stench of death has filled the valley of Jehoshaphat. The furious screams of the dying fill the ears of all those gathered in this ancient land. A lethal dagger is poised at the heart of the Jewish people, ready for the kill. God, who promised that Israel would be His people forever, is their only hope. At this point all of Israel cries out in the agony of a people who have come to the very end of themselves. There is nowhere left to turn. The hour is upon them. Hope is nearly gone. It is then that the Messiah comes in power and glory.[2]

Prophecy:

• At the time of the end, the entire nation of Israel will turn back toward God. They will go in tears before the Lord and make an everlasting covenant with Him (Deut. 4:30-31, Jer. 50:4-5, Zech. 12:10-14, Isa. 30:19-22, Rom. 11:26).

• This restoration will occur just prior to the Second Coming of Christ (Rom. 11:26).

• The entire nation of Israel will be saved after two days of confession (Hos. 6:1-3, Rom. 11:26, Isa. 66:7-8).

• They will plead for the Messiah to return (Isa. 64, Zech. 12:10, Matt. 24:39).

• God will forgive the people of Israel for their sins (Jer. 50:20, Zech. 13:1).

• All idolatry and false prophesying will cease in Israel (Zech. 13:2).

Clash of the Antichrist's Army and the Army of the East

Although not specifically mentioned in the Bible, it's probably safe to assume that the Antichrist's army will at some point clash with the army of the East. The Bible indicates this army of the East will cross the Euphrates River on their way to Armageddon (Rev. 16:12). This clash (along with the destruction of Jerusalem) will probably represent one of the major battles of Armageddon.

The Second Coming of Christ

In answer to the prayers of the nation of Israel, Christ will return to bring a halt to the battles of Armageddon. He will slaughter the armies arrayed against Israel, capture the Antichrist and the False Prophet, and bring final judgment to the world. It is this slaughter at the hands of Christ, which most people associate with the term Armageddon. The Second Coming of the Lord will bring an end to the fighting and turmoil of the Tribulation period and will usher in a new period of peace and prosperity known as the Millennium. Details of the Lord's return and the Millennium are contained in the chapters that follow.

Summary

Armageddon represents a very complex campaign or series of events. Unfortunately, the details and sequence of these events are not stated definitively in the Bible, so no one should be dogmatic about how these events will unfold. The seven-step timeline described in this chapter represents a plausible scenario for how these events might fit together based upon a thorough study of all of the relevant passages of the Bible. This by no means represents the only possible scenario.

What's important to keep in mind about the battles of Armageddon is that they will usher in a terrible time of war and fighting. Armageddon truly will be World War III. The Antichrist's attempt to bring peace to the world through a global dictatorship will fail. Rebellions will arise and major wars will be fought. Many will die. The situation that mankind will find itself in will be so bad that Christ said "if those days had not been cut short, no one would survive, but for the sake of the elect those days will be shortened" (Matt. 24:22). Mankind will be on the verge of annihilating itself. Fortunately, it's at this point that Christ will step in and keep this from happening. In doing so, Christ will demonstrate that the institutions of mankind (whether they be the United Nations, brokered peace treaties, capitalism, spiritual unity, etc.) are insufficient to bring peace to the world. It's only through Divine intervention that mankind can be saved.

Notes

1. For a great description of how modern day countries descended from the peoples and tribes mentioned in the Bible, see Hal Lindsey, *The Late Great Planet Earth*, chapter 5.

2. David Brickner, *Future Hope,* 86.

CHAPTER 22

THE SECOND COMING OF CHRIST

"At that time the sign of the Son of Man will appear in the sky, and all the nations of the earth will mourn. They will see the Son of Man coming on the clouds of the sky, with power and great glory"
(Matt. 24:30).

"I [John] saw heaven standing open and there before me was a white horse, whose rider is called Faithful and True. With justice He judges and makes war... the armies of heaven were following Him, riding on white horses and dressed in fine linen" (Rev. 19:11-14).

"See, the Lord is coming with fire, and His chariots are like a whirlwind; He will bring down His anger with fury, and His rebuke with flames of fire. For with fire and with his sword the Lord will execute judgment upon all men, and many will be those slain by the Lord" (Isa. 66:15-16).

Almost all of prophecy looks forward to one event—the Second Coming of Christ, when Jesus will return to the earth to judge those who opposed Him and to establish His kingdom of justice and peace forever. His return will mark the final fulfillment and completion of God's plan for the world. This event is so important in Scripture that there are approximately eight times as many prophecies regarding Christ's Second Coming as for His First Coming, and about one out of every twenty-five verses in the New Testament says something about Christ's return to earth. Clearly, the topic of Christ's Second Coming is an important doctrine—second only to salvation (if space

THE TRUTH ABOUT PROPHECY IN THE BIBLE

given to it in the Bible is the measure). In fact, Christ's Second Coming is so central to Scripture that it is mentioned in twenty-three of the twenty-seven New Testament books. Of the four books that make no clear mention of it, three (Philemon, 2 John, and 3 John) are short, one-chapter personal letters.

Christ's Second Coming will be very different from His First Coming. During Christ's First Coming, He presented himself as "a suffering Messiah," coming into the world as a baby and entering Jerusalem riding on a lowly donkey (see chapter five). At His Second Coming, He will present Himself as a "triumphant Messiah," descending from the clouds with His Church during the height of Armageddon to stop the nations from destroying themselves. The world will be at the point of global destruction. The Bible says, "if those days had not been cut short, no one would have survived, but for the sake of the elect, those days will be shortened" (Matt. 24:22). It's at this point that He will return. There will be no mistaking it—Christ will descend from the sky accompanied by a trumpet call and the voice of an archangel. The Bible says, "every eye will see Him" (Rev. 1:7).

Upon making His dramatic entrance, Christ will immediately bring a halt to the battle of Armageddon. He will destroy the armies arrayed against Jerusalem, capture the Antichrist and False Prophet, and bring final judgment to the world. He will then set up His Millennial Kingdom, which will last forever.

His Return

"Look, He is coming with the clouds, and every eye will see Him, even those who pierced Him; and all the peoples of the earth will mourn because of Him" (Rev. 1:7).

Christ's return was so central to His ministry that He referred to it twenty-one times in Scripture. Christ's return will be literal and visible—in fact, the Bible states that He will return in exactly the same way that He left the earth (i.e. visibly descending from heaven to the Mount of Olives—Acts 1:11-12).

Prophecy:

• On the day of His return, there will be no light, no daytime or nighttime, no cold or frost (Zech. 14:6-7, Joel 3:15, Matt. 24:29a). This description is consistent with how the world is described at the completion of the Seal, Trumpet, and Bowl judgments, specifically the fifth Bowl judgment which brings darkness to the Middle East (see chapter thirteen).

• A sign, appearing in the sky, will mark His return. This sign will allow all people and nations to recognize who He is (Matt. 24:30). The Bible is not clear on what this sign will be. Perhaps it will be the sign of the cross appearing in the sky. Perhaps it will be some form of His glory. Regardless, the sign will clearly identify Christ and will be visible to the whole world.

• A trumpet call will announce His return (Matt. 24:31).

• Everyone on the earth will see His return and recognize Jesus as the Messiah (Rev. 1:7, Matt. 24:27, Luke 17:24, Zech. 12:10-14).

• The scars from his crucifixion will be visible to the whole world (Zech. 12:10, Rev. 1:7).

• Christ will be riding a white horse (Rev. 19:11).

• He will be dressed in a robe dipped in blood, which represents the blood of His enemies (Rev. 19:13, Isa. 63:1-4).

• He will descend from the sky in the same way that He left the earth after His First Coming (Dan. 7:13, Matt. 24:30, Acts 1:11). The same way is a reference to Christ's return in the same physical, resurrected, recognizable, and eternal body that he departed the earth with when he ascended to heaven in front of his disciples (Acts 1:9-11).

• An army of believers will accompany Christ. These believers will be the raptured Church and will appear as a "cloud" because there will so many of them (literally billions) and because they will be clothed in white (Dan. 7:13, Rev. 1:7, 1 Thess. 3:13, 4:14, Heb. 12:1, Jude 14, Zech. 14:5, Matt. 26:64, Rev. 19:8, 14).

• People all over the world, and especially Israel, will mourn because they will recognize Jesus as the one they rejected and will recognize that judgment is at hand (Rev. 1:7, Zech. 12:10-14, Matt. 24:30).

• Jesus will return to the Mount of Olives in Jerusalem (Acts 1:11, Zech. 14:4). It should be noted that some scholars believe that the Lord will return to Boraz first (about twenty-five miles southeast of the southern end of the Dead Sea) based on Isaiah 34:1-6, which implies that the Lord will pour out His anger from there. This interpretation holds that the Lord will meet the nations for battle in Boraz and then will travel to the Mount of Olives after this.

Speculation: It's been speculated that the Second Coming of the Lord will occur on the First Day of Tishri (mid-September) to coincide with the Jewish Feast of Trumpets. There are three primary reasons for this. First, throughout the Bible, a surprising number of events in the history of the Jewish people have coincided with the Jewish Feasts (holidays). Second, the Bible indicates that the return of Christ will be accompanied by a trumpet call (1 Thess. 4:16, Matt. 24:31). The Jewish people mark the Feast of Trumpets, which begins the most sacred month in the year, with a trumpet. Third, the prophet Joel precedes his description of Armageddon and the Second Coming with "Declare a holy fast; call a sacred assembly" and "Blow the trumpet in Zion" (Joel 1:14-15, 2:1-2), and the prophet Jeremiah precedes his description of Armageddon with "Sound the trumpet throughout the land!" Both of these are appropriate descriptions for the Feast of Trumpets.

The Demise of the Antichrist and False Prophet

"The beast was captured, and with him the False Prophet...the two of them were thrown alive into the fiery lake of burning sulfur"
(Rev. 19:20).

Upon His return, Christ will immediately do away with the Antichrist and the False Prophet.

Prophecy:

• Upon His return, the Antichrist and False Prophet will be immediately judged and thrown alive into the Lake of Fire (Rev. 19:20). The Lake of Fire is synonymous with Hell. It has been prepared by God as the ultimate residence of Satan, the Antichrist, the False Prophet, and all of the people of the world who have rejected the Gospel. It is described in the Bible as a literal place—a fiery lake of burning sulfur where people will be tormented day and night forever and ever (Matt. 25:41, Mark 9:43, 48, Rev. 19:20, 20:10, 14-15).

• There will be no battle—Christ will simply destroy the Antichrist with "the breath of His mouth" (2 Thess. 2:8, Rev. 19:15, Isa. 11:4b).

The Outpouring of Christ's Wrath

"The Lord is angry with all nations; His wrath is upon all their armies. He will totally destroy them, He will give them over to slaughter" (Isa. 34:2).

After doing away with the Antichrist and False Prophet, Christ will then turn to the armies that were arrayed against Jerusalem and pour out His wrath upon them.

Prophecy:

• Jesus will pour out His wrath from Jerusalem (Zech. 14:4, Joel 3:16).

• He will stand on the Mount of Olives and will split it from East to West (from the North tip of the Dead Sea west to the Mediterranean Sea), forming a very large valley through which believers will flee. Christian Jews, recognizing this as fulfillment of prophecy, will flee into the valley for protection from the coming outpouring of Christ's wrath (Zech. 14:4-5).

• Christ will strike Israel's enemies with a plague, which will immediately cause their flesh to rot (Zech. 14:12-13). This is reminiscent of the Nazis' fate in Steven Spielberg's *Raiders of the Lost Ark* (1981) when the Ark of the Covenant was opened. In fact, it has been reported that Steven Spielberg (a Jew) based this scene in his movie upon this passage in Zechariah.

• The opposing armies will be totally destroyed (Isa. 34:2b).

• The blood from the slaughter will flow 180 miles to a depth of about 4.5 feet. Whether this is literal or an illustration, it's clear that blood will completely soak the surrounding land (Rev. 14:20, Isa. 34:3, 7).

• So great will be the slaughter, that God will call forth all the birds in the air to eat the flesh of those who were killed (Rev. 19:17-18, 21b, Ezek. 39:1-22).

• The bodies of those who were killed will send up an awful stench (Isa. 34:3).

• As the result of the Tribulation judgments and the outpouring of Christ's wrath, the earth will be laid waste. Very few people will be left alive (Isa. 24:6).

The Binding of Satan

"He seized the dragon, that ancient serpent, who is the devil, or Satan, and bound him for a thousand years. He threw him into the Abyss, and locked and sealed it over him, to keep him from deceiving the nations anymore until the thousand years were ended. After that, he must be set free for a short time" (Rev. 20:2-3).

Immediately after the battle of Armageddon and Christ's return, Satan will also be captured and incarcerated.

Prophecy:

• Satan will be captured and bound by an angel of God (Rev. 20:2).

• He will then be cast into the Abyss for one thousand years (i.e., the Millennial period) where he will not be able to deceive the nations anymore (Rev. 20:2). The Abyss is not Hell. It is a phrase used in Scripture to refer to a bottomless pit that is used to confine angels (see description in the Glossary).

CHAPTER 23

THE JUDGMENTS OF MANKIND

"For we must all appear before the judgment seat of Christ, that each one may receive what is due him" (2 Cor. 5:10).

"If God did not spare angels when they sinned, but sent them to hell, putting them into gloomy dungeons to be held for judgment; if He did not spare the ancient world when He brought the flood on its ungodly people, but protected Noah, a preacher of righteousness, and seven others; if He condemned the cities of Sodom and Gomorrah by burning them to ashes, and made them an example of what is going to happen to the ungodly... then the Lord knows how to rescue godly men from trials and hold the unrighteous for the day of judgment, while continuing their punishment. This is especially true of those who follow the corrupt desire of the sinful nature and despise authority" (2 Pet. 2:4-10).

"There is nothing concealed that will not be disclosed, or hidden that will not be made known. What you have said in the dark will be heard in the daylight, and what you have whispered in the ear in the inner rooms will be proclaimed from the roofs" (Luke 12:2-3).

The term judgment day is frequently used in modern day movies, songs, and books. Mankind seems to intrinsically know that at the end of life, there will be a time of reckoning: a time when people will be accountable for the lives they've lived. It will be a time when the Creator will bring everyone's accounts into balance and reward those who are worthy of reward and punish those who are worthy of punishment. While most people are familiar with the concept, very few actually know what the Bible says about it. Although most people hear the phrase Judgment Day and think of a single day or time of judgment, the Bible actually describes three different judgments that will occur to judge all the people of the world (these three judgments will be discussed later in this chapter). In all cases, Christ will be the judge, but the timing of the judgments and the circumstances will be different for different types of people. There are many misconceptions of these judgments. Many believe that these judgments will be based on good deeds and that a person will not know his or her eternal status until judgment day. This is not the case. No person is good enough to meet God's standard (Rom. 3:10-20). All have sinned (Rom. 3:23). Instead, what will determine a person's eternal destiny will be his or her acceptance (or rejection) of Jesus Christ. This is a conscious choice that each person makes while he or she is alive.

To use a legal analogy, all people in the world will stand before Christ and will be guilty of the charges brought against them. Christ will have already paid the penalty for these charges, and everyone will have been offered the opportunity to have Christ represent them at their trial. During a person's life on earth, everyone chooses whether to accept or reject Christ as his or her public defender. If a person accepted Christ's offer of representation, the judge (Christ) will be the same person as his lawyer. Given this favorable situation, the person will get off because he will have found favor with the judge. If a person rejected Christ's offer of representation, he will have no advocate at this trial and will have to defend himself, which, of course, is futile. The hope for believers at this final judgment, then, is not for an innocent verdict (since all are guilty), but rather for an acquittal through the grace of Jesus Christ. Those who rejected Christ during their lifetimes will lose their case, be found guilty of their sins, and sentenced to eternal punishment.

Author Tim LaHaye, in his book *Understanding the Last Days,* tells a story that brings this point to life:

In the archives of the Supreme Court of the United States is the record of a very strange incident that took place during the term of President Andrew Jackson. A man named George Wilson was sentenced to die by hanging for a crime he had committed. Somehow the story came before the President, who granted Wilson a pardon. To everyone's amazement, Wilson tore the pardon to shreds and threw it on the floor of his prison cell. The ensuing legal argument concerned the validity of a pardon that was refused, and the question arose as to whether or not Wilson should be freed or hanged. After great deliberation, the U.S. Supreme Court ruled as follows: "A pardon is a writing, the value of which is dependent upon the acceptance by the individual for who it is intended." It was therefore decreed by the court that George Wilson be hanged until dead—not because a pardon was not offered, but because it was not accepted.[1]

This is a perfect picture of the sinner who hears the gospel of Jesus Christ and knows that God has written a pardon for him, yet rejects Him and thus forfeits his right to the pardon. Not to belittle it, but the "Gospel Message" that Christ instructed His disciples to preach around the world (Matt. 28:18-20) is, in legal terms, essentially advertising that anyone in the world can receive a reprieve or pardon from this sentence of eternal punishment by establishing a personal relationship with the judge prior to the trial at the end of his or her life.

The following is a summary of the three different judgments the Bible describes; the Judgment of Believers, the Judgment of the Nations, and the Judgment of the Unsaved Dead.

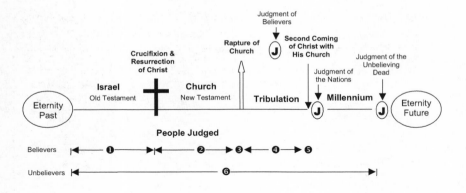

Figure 23: The Judgments of Mankind

	Judgment of Believers	Judgment of the Nations	Judgment of the Unsaved Dead
Nickname	Bema Seat Judgment	Sheep & Goats Judgment	Great White Throne Judgment
Time	After the Rapture, but before the Second Coming	After the Tribulation, but before the Millennium	After the Millennium, but before the Eternal State
Place	In Heaven (before the 'Bema Seat' of Christ)	The 'Valley of Jehoshaphat'	Before the 'Great White Throne' of God
Judge	Christ	Christ	Christ

	Judgment of Believers	Judgment of the Nations	Judgment of the Unsaved Dead
People Judged	❷❸: All believers in Christ prior to the Rapture (does not include Old Testament saints who lived prior to the First Coming of Christ)	❶❹❺: Old Testament saints, those martyred during the Tribulation, and all those living (both Jews and Gentiles) at time of Christ's Second Coming	❻: All unsaved people from the beginning of time, except those living at the time of Christ's Second Coming
Basis for Judgment	Salvation guaranteed. Additional rewards are determined based on a believer's works since time of salvation.	•O.T. Saints – faith in God •Believers who died during Tribulation – faith in Christ •Living Gentiles – faith in Christ as proved by how they treated Israel during Tribulation period •Living Jews – acceptance of Christ	Based on their rejection of the Messiah and their own works
Result	Rewards in heaven given or lost	• Saved ('sheep') – entrance into the Millennial Kingdom • Unsaved ('goats') – cast into Lake of Fire (i.e. Hell)	All will be thrown into the Lake of Fire (i.e. Hell)
Key Scriptures	1 Corinthians 3:11-15, 2 Corinthians 5:10	Daniel 12:1-3, Joel 3:2, Ezekiel 20:34-38, Matthew 25:31-46, Revelation 20:4-6	Revelation 20:11-15, 2 Peter 3:7

Table 9: The Judgments of Mankind [2]

Judgment of Believers

"For God will bring every work into judgment, including every secret thing, whether it is good or whether it is evil" (Eccles. 12:14).

"His work will be shown for what it is, because the Day will bring it to light. It will be revealed with fire, and the fire will test the quality of each man's work. If what he has built survives, he will receive his reward. If it is burned up, he will suffer loss; he himself will be saved, but only as one escaping through the flames" (1 Cor. 3:13-15).

The first judgment will be the Judgment of Believers (also known as the Judgment of the Church). After the Church is raptured and taken to Heaven, all believers in Christ will be judged according to their deeds. Salvation is not at risk, because the people who will have been raptured have already been selected as believers. What is at stake at this judgment are rewards or crowns that Christ will give out based on a believer's deeds. This judgment is frequently referred to as the Bema Seat judgment. The Judgment of Believers will include everyone who has put his or her faith in Jesus Christ and accepted His offer of salvation and as a result, will be taken to Heaven in the Rapture. This includes all believers in Christ throughout the ages— from the time of Christ's First Coming to the time of the Rapture. However, this judgment does not include Old Testament saints (those who believed in God prior to the First Coming of Christ such as Moses and the prophets). These people will not have been raptured with the Church, since the Rapture only includes those who "died in Christ" (1 Thess. 4:16). This later group will be judged as part of the Judgment of the Nations described below.

Prophecy:

• All believers in Christ will appear before Him in heaven for judgment (2 Cor. 5:10).

• Christ will be the judge (2 Cor. 5:10, John 5:22).

• Believers will be judged based on their deeds since the time of salvation and the motives for these deeds. The purpose of this judgment is not to determine salvation, but rather to reveal the quality of each believer's works. These works only include those that were done since the time of salvation (1 Cor. 3:11-13, 4:5, 2 Cor. 5:10).

• Rewards (crowns) will be given or lost based on this judgment (1 Cor. 3:14-15). These `crowns' include the following:

1. The Crown of Life: Given to those who died or suffered for Christ's sake, such as those who were martyred or persecuted in the name of Christ (Rev. 2:10, James 1:12).

2. The Crown of Glory: Given to faithful Church leaders (1 Pet. 5:4).

3. The Crown of Righteousness: Given to those who eagerly anticipate His Second Coming (2 Tim. 4:8).

4. The Crown of Rejoicing: Given to believers who lead other people to faith in Christ (Phil. 4:1, 1 Thess. 2:19).

Note: The `crowns' mentioned above are probably figurative rather than literal. Although the Bible is not clear, many believe these crowns will really indicate a believer's status or authority in Christ's Kingdom. This line of thinking is based on the fact that the Bible says believers will "reign with [Christ]" in His Millennial Kingdom (2 Tim. 2:12) and that crowns are frequently used as symbols of authority. The reason this judgment occurs just prior to the establishment of Christ's Kingdom may actually be to assign Christians their roles and opportunities for service in this Kingdom.

Judgment of The Nations

"I will gather all nations and bring them down to the Valley of Jehoshapat. There I will enter into judgment against them concerning my inheritance, my people Israel" (Joel 3:2).

"But at that time your people—everyone whose name is found written in the book [of those saved]—will be delivered. Multitudes who sleep in the dust of the earth will awake: some to everlasting life, others to shame and everlasting contempt" (Dan. 12:1b-2).

"When the Son of Man comes in His glory, and all the angels with Him, He will sit on His throne in heavenly glory. All the nations will be gathered before Him, and He will separate the people one from another as a shepherd separates the sheep from the goats. He will put the sheep on His right and the goats on His left. Then the King will say to those on his right, `Come, you who are blessed by my Father; take your inheritance, the kingdom prepared for you since the creation of the world...Then He will say to those on his left, Depart from me, you who are cursed, into the eternal fire prepared for the devil and his angels'" (Matt. 25:31-34, 41).

The second judgment will be the Judgment of the Nations. This is the judgment most frequently referred to as "judgment day" by most people. The Judgment of the Nations will occur on earth immediately after the Second Coming of Christ. All people living at the end of the Tribulation period will be gathered together for judgment, and their eternal destiny will be determined. This judgment is frequently referred to as the sheep and goats judgment based on a parable Jesus told. He said He would separate the "sheep from the goats" (Matt. 25:31-46). Also included in this judgment will be all of the believers who were killed during the Tribulation period and all of the Old Testament saints (people who believed in God prior to the First Coming of Christ). New Testament believers (or members of the Church) will not be judged, because they will have been judged as part of the Judgment of Believers described previously.

The question is often asked, "Why are Old Testament saints and believers in Christ treated differently? Why aren't the Old Testament saints resurrected with Christians at the time of the Rapture and taken to Heaven along with the Church prior to this judgment?" It would seem that making a distinction between "believers in Christ" and "believers in God" is arbitrary. The answer to this question is that there is a significant distinction between the two, and God has very different plans for Israel and for the Church. Prior to the First Coming of Christ, God's plan of salvation for people was different than it is today. Salvation was based on belief in God, sacrificial offerings, and obedience to the law. This plan was primarily directed toward the Jews and was based on the covenants God made with Abraham, Isaac, David, and Moses. When Christ came, He died as a sacrifice for sin. His death was a substitute for the sin offerings and obedience to the law required by God in the Old Testament. In essence, His death changed the rules, and now salvation is based solely on faith in Christ. Salvation today, although open to the Jews, is primarily directed toward Gentiles due to Israel's rejection of Christ at His First Coming. As such, the Old Testament Saints and the Church are treated differently by God, both in how they are judged, and the inheritance that they will receive after His Second Coming.

Prophecy:

• At the end of the Tribulation period (immediately following Armageddon), Christ will gather all nations together for judgment in the Valley of Jehoshaphat (Matt. 25:31-36, Ezek. 20:33-38, Joel 3:2, 12, Zeph. 3:8). Although there are several Jehoshaphats mentioned in the Bible, the exact location of the Valley of Jehoshaphat is not known. Most likely, this reference is to the Kidron Valley, which is located between Jerusalem and the Mount of Olives.

• In addition to the people living at the end of the Tribulation period, there will be two additional groups of people resurrected from the dead for this judgment: Old Testament saints who died prior to the First Coming of Christ (Dan. 12:1-2, 13, Isaiah 26:19) and believers in Christ who died during the Tribulation period (Rev. 20:4).

• Christ will be the judge (Matt. 25:31, John 5:22).

• Others will be given authority by Christ to judge and will help in the judging process (Rev. 20:4). Although the Bible doesn't say who these others are (other than to mention that they "sit on thrones"), there are several possibilities for their identity. The first is the twenty-four elders mentioned in Revelation 4:4 that the Bible indicates, "have thrones surrounding the throne of Christ." The identity of these twenty-four elders is not known, but many speculate that they include the twelve disciples plus the patriarchs of the twelve tribes of Israel. The second are the twelve disciples, whom Christ promised would "sit on twelve thrones, judging the twelve tribes of Israel" (Matt. 19:28, Luke 22:29-30). Finally, the Church is a possibility because the Bible says the Church will "judge the world" (1 Cor. 6:2).

• The criteria for judgment will be as follows:

1. Gentiles who were living at the end of the Tribulation period will be judged based on how they treated the 144,000 Jews (which, during intense persecution, is evidence of their attitude toward God—Matt. 25:35-40, Joel 3:2-3).

2. Jews who were living at the end of the Tribulation period will be judged based on their obedience to God and acceptance of Christ as the Messiah (Ezek. 20:37-38, Dan. 12:1-2).

3. Believers in Christ who died during the Tribulation period will be judged based on their faith in Jesus.

4. Old Testament saints will be judged based on their faith in God and their obedience to Him.

• Those who pass judgment will enter the Millennial Kingdom, which Christ will establish following this judgment. They will then reign with Christ for one thousand years on earth (Matt. 25:34; 46, Dan. 12:2, 13, Rev. 20:4, 6). Details of this Kingdom are contained in chapter twenty-four.

• Those who don't pass judgment will be cast immediately into the Lake of Fire (i.e., Hell) for eternal punishment. These people will be separated from the presence of the Lord forever (Matt. 25:41, 46, Dan. 12:2, 2 Thess. 1:8-9).

• This judgment will last for thirty days (see chapter twelve).

Judgment of the Unsaved Dead

"Then I [John] saw a great white throne and Him who was seated on it...And I saw the dead, great and small, standing before the throne, and books were opened...The sea gave up the dead that were in it, and death and Hades gave up the dead that were in them, and each person was judged according to what he had done...If anyone's name was not found written in the book of life [list of those saved], he was thrown into the lake of fire" (Rev. 20:11-15).

The third and final judgment will be the Judgment of the Unsaved Dead. After the Millennium, Christ will resurrect and judge all of the unsaved people of the world who have died since the beginning of time (except those who were living at the end of the Tribulation period—those people will have already been judged and cast into the Lake of Fire as part of the Judgment of the Nations). This judgment is frequently referred to as the Great White Throne Judgment. The resulting judgment will be that all of these unsaved people will be thrown into the Lake of Fire for eternal punishment. Although the description of this event in Revelation 20:11-15 may sound similar to the Judgment of the Nations, it is a different event. The Judgment of the Unsaved Dead will be a terrible time of despair. Imagine the anguish that this judgment will bring as literally billions of people are judged, only to suffer the same terrible fate of being sentenced to eternity in the Lake of Fire. What a horrible sight this will be, which begs the question, "Why must this judgment even happen? If everyone will suffer the same fate, why bother with the judgment? Why doesn't God just immediately throw everyone into Lake of Fire?" The answer to these questions relates to the nature of this judgment. The primary purpose is not to determine guilt or innocence (since all will be guilty of rejecting Christ), but rather to show the unbelievers at this judgment why they are being sentenced to such a terrible, eternal fate. Every sin that a person has committed will be brought before him so that he can see the wickedness of his ways.

People will realize that they are not righteous. They are sinners and guilty of the punishment that will be handed down against them. Since they rejected the pardon that God gave (in the form of Jesus Christ), they will see that God (a God of justice) has no choice but to sentence them to this punishment.

Prophecy:

• All unbelievers who have died since the beginning of time (except those living at the time of Christ's Second Coming) will be resurrected and called before the Great White Throne of the Lord (Rev. 20:13). This will occur after the Millennium. Believers who were living at the time of Christ's return will have already been judged as part of the Judgment of the Nations.

• Christ will be the judge (John 5:22).

• The Bible says that God is recording everyone's deeds in a book. These books will be opened during this judgment to reveal what each person had done (Rev. 20:12-12).

• Unbelievers at this judgment will be judged according to their deeds. Since the deeds of unbelievers are considered evil in God's eyes (as is the case with everyone, Rom. 3:23), the purpose of this judgment is to show the unbelievers that their punishment is deserved (Rev. 20:12b, 13b). As such, unbelievers will have already been condemned prior to this judgment because of their rejection of Christ (John 3:18).

• The result of this judgment will be that all of these unbelievers will be thrown into the Lake of Fire (i.e., Hell) where they will be eternally punished (Rev. 20:14-15).

• At this time, all unbelievers will finally concede that Jesus Christ is the one true Lord, and will bow at the mention of His name (Phil. 2:9-11).

Notes

1. Tim LaHaye, *Understanding the Last Days,* 198.

2. Based in part on Charles C. Ryrie, "A Synopsis of Bible Doctrine, The Future Judgments," Ryrie Study Bible.

CHAPTER 24

THE MILLENNIUM

"'I am coming, and I will live among you,' declares the Lord. `Many nations will be joined with the Lord in that day and will become My people. I will live among you and you will know that the Lord Almighty has sent Me to you'" (Zech. 2:10-11).

"The Lord will be king over the whole earth. On that day there will be one Lord, and His name the only name...Jerusalem will be raised up and remain in its place...it will be inhabited; never again will it be destroyed. Jerusalem will be secure" (Zech. 14:9-11).

The Millennium refers to a thousand-year period during which Christ will physically rule over the earth. During this time, Christ will establish His Kingdom, elevate Israel to a position of prominence, and bring final peace and prosperity to the world. This period of time is so significant that there are more prophecies in the Bible about this Kingdom and its importance than any other prophecy.[1] Although there have been many kingdoms throughout history, the Kingdom of Christ will be different: it will not be ruled by a man. Rather, Jesus Christ Himself will rule the Millennial Kingdom. The Kingdom is what Christ instructed His disciples to pray for when He taught them the Lord's prayer saying: "Your *Kingdom* come. Your will be done *on earth* as it is in heaven."

The Millennial Kingdom will represent the final fulfillment of the promises that God made to Abraham, David, and the nation of Israel. This Kingdom is the heart of the Old Testament prophetic message—

namely, that a Messiah would come to set up an earthly Kingdom over which He would physically rule. When Christ came the first time, the nation of Israel was looking for a king, not a servant; this is why they didn't accept Him as their true Messiah.

The Millennium will start seventy-five days after the Second Coming of Christ (see chapter twelve), following the Judgment of the Nations. The people who will enjoy the Millennial Kingdom will include believers (both Jews and Gentiles) who were living at the time of Christ's Second Coming, people who made it through the Judgment of the Nations (Old Testament saints and believers who died during the Tribulation period) and the Church, which was raptured and returned with Christ at His Second Coming. There are three different views regarding the Millennium (premillennialism, postmillennialism and amillennialism). These views are explained in detail in the *Appendix B*. The view taken in this book is that of premillennialism (the view that Christ will return to earth prior to the Millennium), because it is based on the literal interpretation of Scripture and is the most consistent with the rest of prophecy and the promises God made to the people of Israel.

Characteristics of the Kingdom

"He [Christ] was given authority, glory and sovereign power; all peoples, nations and men of every language worshiped Him. His dominion is an everlasting dominion that will not pass away, and His Kingdom is one that will never be destroyed" (Dan. 7:14).

Christ's kingdom will be unlike any other kingdom on the earth. It will be a time of great joy, peace, and prosperity. The following prophecies describe some of the unique characteristics of this kingdom.

Prophecy:

• The duration will be one thousand years (Rev. 20:3, 4, 5, 6, 7).

• Christ's Kingdom will be an earthly, literal kingdom (Isa. 11, Zech. 14:9-21, Matt. 6:10, Matt. 25:34).

• The Kingdom will never be destroyed; it will last forever (Dan. 2:44, 7:14). Although the physical, earthly Millennial Kingdom will last only a thousand years, Christ's reign as Lord will indeed last forever (see chapter twenty-five).

• Jesus will be physically present; He will live among the people in the city of Jerusalem (Isa. 2:1-4, Ezek. 43:7, Zech. 2:10, 8:3, 22, Micah 4:1-3).

• The Millennium will be a time of restoration from the enormous devastation that occurred to the earth during the Tribulation period (Acts 3:21).

• Knowledge of the Lord will be universal, and all nations of the earth will worship Him during this time (Ps. 22:27; Dan. 7:14, 27; Zech. 8:22-23; Isa. 11:9).

• Foreigners (non-Israelites) will share in this Kingdom just like Israelites (Isa. 56:3-8, Ezek. 47:13-48:29).

• There will be no wars—Christ will bring peace to all nations for this thousand-year period (Isa. 2:4, 60:17b-18, Zech. 9:10, Ezek. 34:27-28, Micah 4:3-4).

• The earth will be free from the influence of Satan, who will be bound in the Abyss during this time (Rev. 20:2-3).

• The Holy Spirit will be present throughout the earth and will indwell all believers (Ezek. 36:27, 37:14, 39:29; Joel 2:28-29; Isa. 32:15, 44:3).

• Righteousness will flourish during this time (Isa. 11:3-5).

• There will be abundant rainfall and water in areas that today are known for their dryness, leading to greatly increased productivity of the earth (Isa. 30:23-24, 35:1-2, 6b-7; Ps. 67:6; Amos 9:13; Joel 3:18).

• Light on the earth will be increased by seven times (Isa. 30:26). This will compensate for the loss of light that occurred during the Tribulation judgments.

• Many physical health problems and infirmities will be eliminated—people who are blind will be able to see; the deaf will be able to hear; the lame will be able to walk, and mutes will be able to speak (Isa. 29:18, 33:24, 35:5-6).

• The length of human life will be extended—to several hundreds of years at least and probably to the length of the entire thousand-year period (Isa. 65:20, 22; Zech. 8:4). The Bible indicates: "He who dies at a hundred will be thought a mere youth; he who fails to reach a hundred will be considered accursed" (Isa. 65:20). The implication in the word `accursed' is that these are unbelievers who will die at one hundred. If this is true, it has enormous consequences. Evidently, people will be given one hundred years to decide whether or not to accept Christ. If they do, their lives will be extended to potentially the length of the Millennium. If they don't, they won't live past their one hundredth birthdays. This would mean that only true believers would be alive to raise children after they reach one hundred.

• The Millennial Kingdom will be a great time of joy (Isa. 51:11, 65:18-19; Jer. 31:12-14).

• The animals around Jerusalem will be tamed. They get along and live in peace, causing no harm to anyone (Isa. 11:6-9, 35:9, 65:25; Ezek. 34:25).

Government of the Kingdom

"The Lord will be king over the whole earth" (Zech. 14:9).

Christ will personally rule the Millennial Kingdom. As such, this kingdom will be a theocracy (government ruled by God). Christ's rule will represent the fulfillment of the promise God made to David (2 Sam. 7:12-16), where He promised that a descendant of David's would establish a kingdom that would last forever. As one would expect, Christ's rule will be righteous and just.

Prophecy:

• The kingdom will be a theocracy. Jesus will rule the whole world and will have the full authority and sovereign power of God (Ps. 2:8-9; Dan. 7:14, 27; Zech. 9:10, 14:9; Isa. 2:3; Mic. 4:7; Luke 1:31-33; Rev. 19:16).

• He will judge between nations and will settle disputes among people (Isa. 2:4, Mic. 4:3). He will be righteous and just as a ruler (Ps. 72:2-4; Isa. 3:5-11, 11:2-3, 29:17-21).

• He will be harsh with any disobedience or outbreak of sin (Ps. 2:9, Jer. 31:29-30, Zech. 14:16-21).

• Christ will be assisted in His rule by:

> 1. David, who will be resurrected along with the other Old Testament saints at the Judgment of the Nations (Hos. 3:5, Jer. 30:9, Ezek. 37:24, Ezek. 34:24-25).
>
> 2. The twelve Apostles (Matt. 19:28, Luke 22:29-30).
>
> 3. The Church (2 Tim. 2:12; Rev. 2:26, 3:21, 5:10, 20:6).
>
> 4. Various others who will arise among the people (Jer. 30:21).

• All people, rulers, and nations in this Kingdom will worship Christ (Dan. 7:14, 27).

• Christ's kingdom will never be destroyed. His rule will last forever (2 Sam. 7:16; Isa. 9:7; Dan. 2:44, 7:14; Luke 1:33).

The Nation of Israel

"You will live in the land I gave your forefathers; you will be my people, and I will be your God" (Ezek. 36:28).

During the Millennium, the glory of Israel that existed during the reign of King Solomon will be restored. The nation of Israel and the city of Jerusalem will be the center, and the envy, of the whole world.

Prophecy:

• The topography of the land in and around Jerusalem will be significantly changed: much of it will be flattened, but the city of Jerusalem, and the land around it, will be elevated (Zech. 14:9-11; Mic. 4:1, 3; Isa. 2:2, 40:4, 49:11).

• God will dry up the northwest finger of the Red Sea that leads to the Suez and the Euphrates Rivers to facilitate the return of His people to Israel (Isa. 11:15-16).

• Israel will expand and possess all of the Promised Land (Ezek. 36:28a, 37:22, 25; Isa. 11:14). Although Israel has been restored to being a nation; it does not currently possess all of the Promised Land, which includes parts of what are now Lebanon, Jordan, and Syria. The Bible indicates that the borders of this land will run from the Mediterranean Sea north of Tyre to a point about one hundred miles north of Damascus; the eastern border will be formed by the Jordan River and the Dead Sea; the southern border will run from a little below the Dead Sea (about one hundred miles south of Jerusalem) to the Wadi of Egypt; and the western border will be the Mediterranean (Ezek. 47:13-23). This land will be allotted to the Israelites for their residences, although the Bible also indicates that Israel will control all of the land from the Wadi of Egypt to the Euphrates River (the land originally promised to Abraham in Gen. 15:18-21).

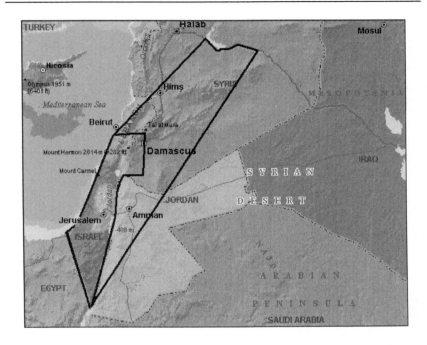

Map 12: The Millennial Israel
(Inner lines represent Israel's residences, outer lines represent total territory)

• The Promised Land will be divided among the tribes of Israel in parallel horizontal sections, except for a square tract of land on the west of the Jordan, which will be reserved for priests and the city of Jerusalem. Although the land will be divided up for the twelve tribes, foreigners will be allowed to live alongside the Israelites and will be treated as equals (Ezek. 47:13-48:29, Isa. 56:3-8).

• A river, beginning as a trickle and becoming a deep river, will flow from the Temple to the south. The source for this river will be a spring, which will be located under the sanctuary. Half of this river will flow into the Dead Sea and half will flow into the Mediterranean. Trees will grow along its banks and fish will live in it. Because of this river, the waters of the Dead Sea will turn to fresh water (Ezek. 47:1-12, Zech. 14:8).

• The land of Israel will bring forth abundant crops, which Israel will be renowned for. There will be no famines or lack of food throughout Israel (Isa. 4:2, 30:23, 35:1-2, 6-7, 55:13; Ezek. 34:26-27, 29; Joel 2:24-26, 3:18).

The Capital of the Kingdom—Jerusalem

"In the last days the mountain of the Lord's temple will be established as chief among the mountains; it will be raised above the hills, and peoples will stream to it. Many nations will come and say, `Come, let us go up to the mountain of the Lord, to the house of the God of Jacob. He will teach us his ways, so that we may walk in his paths.' The law will go out from Zion, the word of the Lord from Jerusalem"
(Mic. 4:1-3).

The capital of Christ's kingdom will be the city of Jerusalem. It will be the center of the world and the focal point of all earthly activity.

Prophecy:

• The capital of the kingdom will be the Temple on Mt. Zion in Jerusalem, from which Christ will physically rule (Isa. 2:1-4, 24:23; Ezek. 43:7; Zech. 2:10, 8:3, 22; Mic. 4:1-3).

• Jerusalem will be the focal point of all earthly activity and worship. Peoples from all nations (including Gentiles) will stream into the city year after year to see and worship the Lord, celebrate the Feast of Tabernacles, and to learn about the Lord and His laws (Zech. 8:20-23, 14:16-17; Mic. 4:1-3; Isa. 2:1-4, 60:3-4, 66:20-20; Jer. 3:17, 33:9).

• Jerusalem will be a city of peace, and its inhabitants will live in safety (Isa. 2:4, 54:13b-15, 60:17b-18, 65:21-23, 66:12; Jer. 23:6, 33:16; Zech. 8:4-5,14:10).

• The city will be ten miles square. It will have a wall around it with three gates on each side named after the twelve sons of Jacob, although the city will expand beyond its walls due to the great number of people living in it (Ezek. 48:15-18, 30-35; Zech. 2:4).

• A highway will lead from the Temple Mount to the main city of Jerusalem. It will be called "The Way of Holiness" (Isa. 35:8). It will be twelve miles long and will be lined with beautiful shade trees.

• The city of Jerusalem will never again be destroyed (Zech. 14:11).

The Temple and Worship

"In that day I will restore David's fallen tent. I will repair its broken places, restore its ruins" (Amos 9:11).

"It is He [Christ] who will build the temple of the Lord, and He will be clothed with majesty and will sit and rule on his throne. And He will be a priest on his throne. And there will be harmony... those who are far away will come and help build the temple of the Lord" (Zech. 6:13-15).

During the Millennium, Christ will build the fourth and final Temple. This Temple will be the focus of the entire world. Israel and the Temple will serve as the center for the priestly rituals and offerings that will provide guidance in the worship of Jesus. The design of this Temple is described in great detail in Ezekiel 40-46, but suffice it to say, this will probably be one of the most beautiful buildings in human history.

Prophecy:

• Christ Himself will build the Millennial Temple along with people who will come from all over to help build it (Zech. 6:11-13,15).

• This Temple will be 875 feet (five hundred cubits) square—making it much larger than any of the previous Jewish Temples. It will sit on land 8.3 miles square (5,312 acres), which is much larger than the current Temple Mount of thirty-five acres (Ezekiel 42:20, 45:1-2).

• The glory of God will be present in this Temple (Ezek. 43:4-5, 44:4; Zech. 2:5, 8:3), just as it was in the first Temple.

• Christ will serve as the high priest of the Temple (Zech. 6:13).

• The Ark of the Covenant will not be present in this Temple—there will be no need because Christ will be present and have His throne there (Jer. 3:16-17).

• It will always be daytime in the Temple because the glory of the Lord will provide brightness instead of the sun or moon (Isa. 60:19, Rev. 21:25).

• There will be a canopy over the Temple Mount—a cloud of smoke by day and a flaming fire by night. This canopy will provide shelter from heat and refuge from storms (Isa. 4:5-6).

• Regular sacrifices will take place (Ezek. 20:40, 40:39, 43:18-27, 45:18-46:24; Isa. 56:7, 66:20-23; Jer. 33:18; Zech. 14:16-21; Mal. 3:3-4), despite the fact that there will no longer be any need for animal sacrifice. The Bible says that Christ was the final and sufficient sacrifice—Heb. 7:26-27, 9:7-28), so these sacrifices will probably serve as a way to look back at the death of Christ, just as the purpose of the Old Testament sacrifices were to look forward to Christ.

• The sacrifices and ceremonies of the Temple will include:

1. A morning sacrifice, but no evening sacrifice (Ezek. 46:13-15).

2. The following ancient Jewish offerings will be given: the burnt, meat, drink, sin, peace, and trespass offerings (Ezek. 42:13, 45:17).

3. The following Jewish feasts will be observed: the Passover feast and the Feast of Tabernacles.

4. The Feast of Tabernacles will be observed by all nations, because all nations will be required to do so. If they do not, the nation will be punished with drought, except Egypt, which will be punished by plague (Ezek. 45:21-24, Zech. 14:16-19).

• There will be a renewed holy priesthood that will serve in the Temple. Only the sons of Zadok (a family within the Levite tribe) will be allowed to offer sacrifices, enter the sanctuary, and minister directly to the Lord in the Temple (Ezek. 40:46, 42:13, 44:15-16). Although Levites (the traditional priesthood of the Temple) shall perform Temple service, they will be barred from priestly duties because of their past sins which included idol worship (Ezek. 44:1-14).

• No unsaved person will be allowed to enter the sanctuary of the Temple (Ezek. 44:9, Zech. 14:21b).

• The twelve gates of the millennial city of Jerusalem shall be named for each of the twelve tribes (Ezek. 48:31-34), and the twelve foundation slabs or sections shall be named for the apostles of the Lord (Rev. 21:14).

The Jewish People

"For if there had been nothing wrong with that first covenant, no place would have been sought for another. But God found fault with the people and said: `The time is coming, declares the Lord, when I will make a new covenant with the house of Israel and with the house of Judah. It will not be like the covenant I made with their forefathers when I took them by the hand to lead them out of Egypt, because they did not remain faithful to my covenant, and I turned away from them, declares the Lord. This is the covenant I will make with the house of Israel after that time, declares the Lord. I will put my laws in their minds and write them on their hearts. I will be their God, and they will be my people' ...By calling this covenant new, he has made the first one obsolete; and what is obsolete will soon disappear" (Heb. 8:7-13, explaining the new covenant in Jer. 31:31-33).

At the beginning of the Millennial Kingdom, Christ will gather the Israelites from among all the nations and bring them back to Israel. God will then make a new covenant with the nation of Israel. This new covenant will replace the Mosaic Covenant broken by the people of Israel (see chapter three). The basis of this new covenant is a restored relationship between God and the people of Israel—the Lord will once again be their God, and they will be His people.

Prophecy:

• God will gather the Israelites from all the nations and bring them back to Israel (Deut. 30:3-5; Isa. 11:11-12, 27:12-13, 43:5-7, 49:22; Jer. 16:15, 23:3, 31:10, 32:37, 33:7; Ezek. 11:17, 36:8, 12, 37:21-28, 39:25-29; Zeph. 3:20; Zech. 10:8-12; Amos 9:14-15; Mic. 2:12; Matt. 24:31).

• The people of Israel will repent of their past sins (Ezek. 36:31, Zech. 12:10-14).

• The Lord will cleanse the Israelites of their past sins and forgive their wickedness (Isa. 1:25; Jer. 31:34, 33:8; Ezek. 16:62-63, 36:25-26, 37:23; Zech. 13:1; Heb. 8:12; Zeph. 3:9).

• The Lord will put His law in their minds and in their hearts so that they will obey His laws and decrees (Deut. 30:6; Isa. 54:13a, 59:21; Jer. 31:33, 32:39; Ezek. 11:19-20, 36:27; Heb. 8:10).

• The Lord will once again be the God of all the tribes of Israel—including the ten lost tribes from the Northern Kingdom as well as the two tribes from the Southern Kingdom. Israel will be reborn spiritually and will serve the Lord (Jer. 30:22, 31:1, 6, 33-34, 32:38; Ezek. 34:25-30, 36:24-30, 37:26-28; Isa. 61:8-9; Heb. 8:10-11).

• All of Israel will know and obey the Lord. The remaining people of Israel will do no wrong (Deut. 30:8; Jer. 31:34; Ezek. 20:40, 37:23-24; Zech. 10:12; Heb. 8:11; Zeph. 3:13).

• God will make Israel prosperous and will bless the nation with abundant crops, riches, honor, and praise (Deut. 30:3, 9; Isa. 35:1-2, 6-7, 60:5; Jer. 30:18-19; Ezek. 34:26-27, 29; Zeph. 3:20; Zech. 14:14).

• God will greatly increase the numbers of Jewish people (Deut. 30:5; Ezek. 36:37-38, 37:26; Isa. 60:22; Jer. 30:19). This is necessary, since very few will have survived the Tribulation period, and there will be a great need to repopulate the earth.

• The Jewish people will receive honor and praise. The glory that existed during the reign of King Solomon will be restored (Isa. 60:5, 15, 66:12; Zeph. 3:20; Zech. 14:14).

• Israel will possess all of the Promised Land forevermore (Ezek. 36:28a, 37:22, 25, 47:14; Isa. 60:21; Amos 9:15).

• All of this will not be for Israel's sake, but for God's—so that His name will no longer be disgraced and ridiculed because of the disobedience and punishment of Israel (Ezek. 36:22, 32, Jer. 23:7-8).

Satan's Final Rebellion

"When the thousand years are over, Satan will be released from his prison and will go out to deceive the nations" (Rev. 20:7-8).

At the end of the Millennium, Satan will be set free from his confinement in the Abyss and will attempt one final rebellion. God will crush this attempt and Satan will be cast into the Lake of Fire, joining the Antichrist and the False Prophet. After this rebellion, the Millennial Kingdom will end. God will judge all unbelievers at the Judgment of the Unsaved Dead (see chapter twenty-three) and then will destroy the heavens and the earth to create the New Heavens and New Earth for eternity. Questions are often asked, "After Satan is freed, why would he once again rebel against God? Why would anyone alive during the Millennium rebel with him?" We can only speculate, but the rebellion seems to show that despite a thousand years of confinement for Satan and a thousand years of humanity living under Christ's perfect rule, Satan and mankind do not change— they are sinful at heart and deserving of the eternal punishment they will receive at the Judgment of the Unsaved Dead.

Prophecy:

• At the end of the Millennium, Satan will be released from his exile in the Abyss and will attempt one final rebellion (Rev. 20:7-8).

• Satan will deceive nations and gather countless people together from all over the earth to march against Jerusalem (Rev. 20:8-9). The question if often asked, "Who are these people? Won't all people who enter the Millennium be Christians? Why would they rebel with Satan?" The answer is that everyone who enters the Millennium will indeed be believers in Christ and will be obedient to Him, but these believers will have children during the Millennium, since the Bible says that the population of the earth will greatly increase during this time (Deut. 30:5; Ezek. 36:37-38, 37:26; Isa. 60:22; Jer. 30:19). Each new child will have to decide whether to accept or reject Christ for him or herself, just as they do today. It's logical then to assume that as the Millennium progresses, there will grow to be a large number of people who are not true believers in Christ. These unbelievers (probably young) will most likely make up the "countless people" to which this passage refers.

• These armies will surround Jerusalem. When this happens, God will immediately destroy them by pouring fire down from heaven (Rev. 20:9).

• Satan will then be thrown into Hell once and for all to be tormented day and night (Rev. 20:10).

Notes

1. Hal Lindsey, There's a New World Coming, 252.

CHAPTER 25

THE ETERNAL STATE

"I [John] saw the Holy City, the new Jerusalem, coming down out of heaven from God, prepared as a bride beautifully dressed for her husband. And I heard a loud voice from the throne saying, `Now the dwelling of God is with men, and He will live with them. They will be His people, and God himself will be with them and be their God. He will wipe every tear from their eyes. There will be no more death or mourning or crying or pain, for the old order of things has passed'"
(Rev. 21:2-4).

Most people believe that when they die, they go to Heaven where they will spend eternity with God. This is actually not the case. When a believer dies, he or she will indeed go to Heaven, but will not spend eternity there. After the Millennium, when God judges all unbelievers at the Judgment of the Unsaved Dead, He will destroy the heavens and the earth and all that is in them with fire. He will then create a New Heaven and a New Earth. In essence, God will cleanse the earth of the evil that occurred during Satan's final rebellion just as he previously cleansed the earth of the evil that existed during the days of Noah. The difference is that, this time, He will destroy (or baptize) the earth by fire instead of by water.

The key difference between Christ's kingdom as it existed during the Millennium and this new creation will be that God will rule instead of Christ. The Bible says that Jesus will "hand over His Kingdom to God" (1 Cor. 15:24-28), who will interact with mankind at a personal level in this new creation. In essence, the Millennium will be just a foreshadow of what life will be like in the Eternal State. Although the Millennium will be very different from the world as it stands today, it will still fall short of the perfection and glory that will exist in the Eternal State with God. The following table shows the differences between the Millennium and the Eternal State.

The Millennium	The Eternal State
• Ruled by Christ. People will have direct interaction with Christ.	• Ruled by God. People will have direct interaction with God.
• An extension of the human history on earth.	• Not associated with human history or the physical earth.
• Set duration of a thousand years.	• Not bound by time – will last forever.
• Sin will still be present.	• No sin will exist.
• Resurrected believers and physical humans will commingle.	• All believers will have resurrected bodies. There will be no physical human beings.
• People will have children, each of which will have a decision of whether to accept or reject Christ as his or her savior.	• No new people will be added to the human race. Everyone's destiny will be settled for eternity.

Table 10: Comparison of the Millennium and the Eternal State

Destruction of the Existing Creation

"But the day of the Lord will come like a thief. The heavens will disappear with a roar; the elements will be destroyed by fire, and the earth and everything in it will be laid bare... That day will bring about the destruction of the heavens by fire, and the elements will melt in the heat" (2 Pet. 10-12).

Prophecy:

• God will destroy the existing heaven (His spiritual creation) and earth (His physical creation) by fire after the Judgment of the Unsaved Dead (Rev. 21:1, 2 Pet. 3:7, 12, Zeph. 3:8).

• The destruction of the earth will be accompanied by a great noise—literally "a big bang" (2 Pet. 3:10).

• Everything in existence will be wiped clean and recreated from new (Rev. 21:5, 2 Pet. 3:10).

• God will then create a New Heaven and a New Earth (Rev. 21:1). These two creations, which had been two different realms in the old order, will be one in the same in the new order.

Characteristics of the New Creation

"Then the end will come, when He [Christ] hands over the kingdom to God the Father after He has destroyed all dominion, authority and power. For He must reign until He has put all his enemies under His feet" (1 Cor. 15:24-25).

Not much is said in the Bible about what life will be like in the new heavens and the new earth. We do know, however, that God will be personally present and that this will be a time of great joy.

Prophecy:

• Unlike the Millennial Kingdom, which will be ruled by Christ, God will rule eternity. Jesus will abdicate His throne and hand over the kingdom to God. Everything will be subject to God, including Christ (1 Cor. 15:24-28).

• God will live with mankind. He will be physically present and will interact with people face to face (1 John 3:2, 1 Rev. 21:3, 22:4).

• The name of God will be present on everyone's foreheads (Rev. 22:4). Just as Satan marked his people during the Tribulation, so, too, God will mark His people for eternity. There will be no unbelievers in the new creation, for they will have all been thrown into the Lake of Fire (Rev. 21:8, 27).

• There will be no sin, for all the powers of evil (including Satan) will have been expelled to the Lake of Fire (Rev. 21:8).

• This will be a time of immense joy—there will be no death, mourning, crying or pain (Rev. 21:4).

• There will be no marriage (Matt. 22:29-30, 1 Cor. 7:29-31).

• There will be no sea (Rev. 21:1). It's not clear why this is, other than that the new creation will be so completely different, that existing elements of creation (such as water, land, etc.) will most likely be unnecessary.

The New Jerusalem

The Eternal State will be centered on the New Jerusalem—a magnificent city that will serve as the residence for all believers for eternity. This is what Christ referred to when He told His disciples: "In My Father's house are many dwelling places; if it were not so, I would have told you; for I go to prepare a place for you. And if I go and prepare a place for you, I will come again, and receive you to myself; that where I am, there you may be also" (John 14:2-3). Just imagine Jesus Christ, a carpenter by trade while He was on earth, overseeing a heavenly construction project for the past two thousand years. How wonderful the New Jerusalem will be!

Prophecy:

• The New Jerusalem will exist for all eternity. It will be the final dwelling place for all believers (Rev. 3:12, 21-22).

• The throne of God and of Christ will be in the city (Rev. 22:3).

• There will be no Temple in the New Jerusalem, because the Lord God and Jesus will be its Temple (Rev. 21:22).

• There will be no night and day or need for the sun, moon, or light. The Glory of God and Jesus will provide light for the Kingdom (Rev. 21:11, 23, 25, 22:5).

• The city will be laid out as either a cube or a pyramid—1,380 miles on every side (length, width and height—Rev. 21:16-17). This would roughly be about two-thirds the size of the continental United States with a height of about 396,000 stories. It has been calculated that even if only 25 percent of this space were used for living space, twenty billion people could be accommodated with plenty of room.

• The city and its streets will be made of pure gold (Rev. 21:18, 21:21b).

• The city will have a great, high wall around it. This wall will be 72 yards thick and will be made of jasper (Rev. 21:17-18).

• The wall around the city will have twelve gates. There will be three gates on each side of the city (north, south, east and west—Rev. 21:12-13). Angels will be stationed at each of the gates (Rev. 21:12). Each gate will be made of a single pearl (hence, the origin of the phrase "pearly gates" – Rev. 21:21). On the twelve gates will be written the names of the twelve tribes of Israel (Rev. 21:12). The gates of the city will never be shut (Rev. 21:25).

• The wall of the city will have twelve foundations. On these will be written the names of the twelve apostles of Christ (Rev. 21:14). The foundations will be decorated with every kind of precious stone (jasper, sapphire, chalcedony, emerald, sardonyx, carnelian, chrysolite, beryl, topaz, chryoprase,, jacinth and amethyst—Rev. 21:19-20).

Note: The fact that the names of the twelve tribes of Israel will be written on the city gates and the names of the twelve apostles of Christ will be written on the city walls shows that, although there will still be a distinction between Jews and Christians in the Eternal State, the two will live together and inherit eternity with God.

The Nations of the Earth

The Bible makes a very curious statement in describing the New Jerusalem. It says: "The nations will walk by its light, and the kings of the earth will bring splendor into it [the New Jerusalem]" (Rev. 21:24). The question that begs an answer is: Who are these nations that the Bible mentions will live outside the city? Won't every believer live inside the New Jerusalem?

Although it's not completely clear, there is evidence to indicate that these nations are the people who lived during the Millennial period. The Bible doesn't state what will happen to the people of the Millennium when the earth is destroyed by fire, other than to say that God will "rescue godly men" (2 Pet. 2:9). It's probably safe to assume that just as God rescued Noah from the flood, so, too, God will rescue His people from the fire that will destroy the earth. He will then return them to the earth to live as they did before, forever.

The view that the nations mentioned are those that lived during the Millennium is supported by the fact that many of God's promises to Israel were said to last forever. For example, God promised that Abraham's descendants would inherit and possess the Promised Land forever (Gen. 13:15, Isa. 60:21, Joel 3:20, Amos 9:15). These promises couldn't be true if the Promised Land was totally destroyed and everyone were to live in the New Jerusalem. Therefore, when God destroys the earth and creates a new earth, perhaps He will also create a new Promised Land and return the people of the Millennium to this land. If this interpretation is correct, then there would be two types of people living throughout eternity—those who will live in the New Jerusalem (i.e., believers that were raptured or died during the Tribulation period) and those that were alive at Christ's Second Coming and inherited the Millennial Kingdom.

EPILOGUE

"I have fought the good fight, I have finished the race, I have kept the faith. Now there is in store for me the crown of righteousness, which the Lord, the righteous Judge, will award to me on that day—and not only to me, but also to those who have longed for his appearing"
(2 Tim. 4:7-8).

Prophecy is complex, mysterious, and frequently confusing. Furthermore, it can be very unsettling—thinking about the events of the Tribulation and end times frequently brings fear to the hearts of many. Just knowing what the world will be like in the end times under the rule of the Antichrist and what the Tribulation judgments will bring is more than most people care to think about.

The purpose of prophecy, though, is not to scare or upset readers. Unlike many doomsday or apocalyptic prophets, the prophets of the Bible paint a wonderful picture of hope and promise for the future. The point of prophecy is not to proclaim the events that are to come, but rather to bring readers closer to a personal relationship with Jesus Christ. God's primary desire is to establish a relationship with a group of people who would reciprocate His love and be obedient to Him. God's desire is that the entire world would come to know Him through His son Jesus Christ. The book of Revelation is so named because the first verse declares that the book is "the revelation of Jesus Christ" (Rev. 1:1). It was written for the sole purpose of revealing truths about Jesus and helping readers see His plan for the world.

The Bible ends with a declaration from Christ that He is coming soon. Although nobody knows the exact time of His return, it is clear that we are indeed very close to the end times described in the Bible. Instead of being worried or fearful about these events, however, believers in Christ should be at peace. After personally witnessing the events of the end times and recording them in the book of Revelation, the apostle John concludes his book with a simple statement of anticipation: "Come, Lord Jesus" (Rev. 22:20). After coming to a full knowledge of prophecy, John was not afraid of the terrible events that would occur during the Tribulation period. Rather, he was eagerly anticipating the return of Jesus Christ and the wonderful events of the Millennium and the Eternal State. So, too, we should eagerly anticipate the return of Christ—if for no other reason than those that do will be awarded the Crown of Righteousness at the Judgment of Believers (2 Tim. 4:8). This is the hope for all believers.

Regardless of your view on the exact timing of the Rapture, the Bible is clear that Christians will not have to endure God's ultimate wrath or the final Judgment of the Nations. Rather, Christians will be rescued from the terrible destruction and wrath that God is going to bring upon the world. Instead of wrath and condemnation, believers are promised eternal blessings and community with God in the Millennial Kingdom and the Eternal State.

For unbelievers, however, the situation is much different. People who reject Christ face the prospect of living through the terrible events of the Tribulation period. Regardless of whether they survive these events or not, the end result for all unbelievers is eternal punishment in the Lake of Fire. Although most people don't like to believe there is a Hell, the Bible describes it as a literal place—a place of isolation from God and torment for those who rejected Him. The English philosopher, John Locke, once said "Hell is truth seen too late." Unfortunately, all too many people will discover that this is the case. Why must there be a hell? Why would such a loving God allow humans to end up in such a place? The answer lies in the nature of Hell itself. Although most people think of Hell as a place of punishment, it really isn't. Hell is not God's way of getting back at people who didn't believe in Him. Rather, it is a place where people who rejected Him will ultimately get their way—they will spend eternity separated from God and separated from the blessings He bestows upon those who trust in Him. If Heaven is the ultimate uniting of God with His people, then Hell is the ultimate separation of God from those who rejected Him. It is for this reason that the message of the Bible must be spread and why the decisions a person makes on earth are so critical—and eternal in nature.

How can one come to know Jesus and be saved from the Lake of Fire? Jesus said: "I am the way and the truth and the life. No one comes to the Father except through me" (John 14:6).

Jesus was making a very narrow and exclusive statement—that no one can be saved except through Him. He was proclaiming that He is the one and only way to salvation. This is what sets Christianity apart from all other world's religions; namely, that salvation is based on *faith in what Jesus did* and not on faith in *what we can do*. This is different than the Old Testament days where salvation was accomplished through blood sacrifices of animals. When Christ came, God's plan for salvation changed. Christ became the ultimate sacrifice. Now, man can be saved simply by accepting the pardon for sin that Christ provided through His death. All people on the earth have already been pardoned—the issue is whether or not a person will accept Christ's pardon.

The obvious question, then, is what must a person do to be saved? The Bible is clear—a person must simply accept the free gift of Christ's sacrifice on the Cross. Salvation is a gift, and all one needs to do is reach out and accept it. The Bible says: "For the wages of sin is death, but the free gift of God is eternal life in Christ Jesus our Lord" (Rom. 6:23). Everyone has sinned. Being good is not enough in God's eyes. The Bible says: "all have sinned and fall short of the glory of God" (Rom. 3:23).

How can one come to know God? The Bible says: "For God so loved the world, that He gave His one and only son, that whoever believes in Him shall not perish but have eternal life. For God did not send

His Son into the world to condemn the world, but to save the world through Him. Whoever believes in Him is not condemned, but whoever does not believe stands condemned already because he has not believed in the name of God's one and only Son" (John 3:16-18). According to Romans 10:9-10, "If you confess with your mouth, `Jesus is Lord,' and believe in your heart that God raised him from the dead, you will be saved. For it is with your heart that you believe and are justified, and it is with your mouth that you confess and are saved." Everyone who acknowledges that he or she is a sinner, believes in Jesus Christ and His sacrifice on the Cross, and puts his or her trust in Him, will be saved. It's that simple. By seeking to establish a relationship with Him through prayer, Bible study, and fellowship in a local church, one can grow in his or her relationship with Christ and further develop as a Christian.

How, then, should Christians respond to prophecy and the events that are still to come? Should we hide in anticipation of the coming rise of the Antichrist and Tribulation judgments? Should we separate ourselves from the world? Should we stockpile food? The Bible is clear on what a Christian's response to prophecy should be:

"But the day of the Lord will come like a thief. The heavens will disappear with a roar; the elements will be destroyed by fire, and the earth and everything in it will be laid bare. Since everything will be destroyed in this way, what kind of people ought you to be? You ought to live holy and godly lives as you look forward to the day of God and speed its coming" (2 Pet. 3:10-12).

"For God did not appoint us to suffer wrath but to receive salvation through our Lord Jesus Christ. He died for us so that...we may live together with him. Therefore encourage one another and build each other up" (1 Thess. 5:9-11).

"The end of all things is near. Therefore be clear minded and self-controlled so that you can pray. Above all, love each other deeply, because love covers a multitude of sins. Offer hospitality to one another without grumbling. Each one should use whatever gift he has received to serve others, faithfully administering God's grace in its various forms" (1 Pet. 4:7-10).

"But in keeping with his promise we are looking forward to a new heaven and a new earth, the home of righteousness. So, then, dear friends, since you are looking forward to this, make every effort to be found spotless, blameless and at peace with him. Bear in mind that our Lord's patience [in returning to earth] means salvation" (2 Pet. 3:13-15).

Live holy lives, encourage one another, be self-controlled, pray, love one another, serve others—these are the traits of a Christian knowledgeable about prophecy who is eagerly looking forward to Christ's return. By knowing and understanding God's plan for the world, we should live better lives, faithfully emulate our savior and spread the good news of the Gospel. In fact, just before Jesus ascended to Heaven, His disciples asked Him about the timing of His Second Coming and the end of the world. His response was quite revealing. He said: "It is not for you to know the times or the dates the Father has set by His own authority. But you will receive power when the Holy Spirit comes on you; and you will be my witnesses in Jerusalem, and in all Judea and Samaria, and to the ends of the earth" (Acts 1:7). When the disciples wanted to talk about the timing of His return, Jesus quickly switched the conversation to evangelism. He wanted them to concentrate on their mission in the world. He said in essence, "The details of my return are none of your business. What is your business is the mission I've given to you–reaching the world with the Gospel message. Focus on that!" Jesus said "And this Gospel of the kingdom will be preached in the whole world as a testimony to all nations, and then the end will come" (Matt. 24:14). If we want Jesus to return sooner, we should focus on completing the mission He has given us!

It is my hope in writing this book that all readers will either come to a personal relationship with Christ, or deepen their existing relationship with Christ by getting a glimpse of His plan for the world and His purposes.

Appendix

APPENDIX A

GUIDELINES FOR THE STUDY OF PROPHECY

"The Bible is the greatest of all books; to study it is the noblest of all pursuits; to understand it, the highest of all goals."

—Charles C. Ryrie

Studying prophecy, and the Bible in general, is the most fulfilling task that a Christian can undertake. Unfortunately, studying prophecy is confusing—relevant passages are frequently found across many different books of the Bible and many symbols and images are used. In addition, the range of prophetic material in Scripture is quite wide—ranging from predictions about the coming of the Messiah, the development of Gentile nations, the life and death of certain individuals, the evolution of the nation of Israel, events to occur during the end times and promises regarding Heaven and the Eternal State. Some of these predictions concern events that will happen thousands of years into the future while others predict events that will occur in just a few days or years from when the prophecy was made. As a result, there are five important guidelines[1] for people to keep in mind who seek to study prophecy in the Bible.

1. Seek the plain and normal meaning of the words and situations described within their historical context: Although symbols and images are frequently used in prophecy, we shouldn't approach prophecy with any preconceived conclusions or agendas. We should seek to understand the grammatical and historical context of each passage and then incorporate that understanding into what we know.

Many symbols and images that are used in prophecy have direct relevance or meaning to the people to whom the prophecy was originally directed. By seeking to understand the historical context, we can better understand prophecy.

2. Compare one prophecy with another: Often, there are overlapping, corresponding or parallel references to prophecies that span several books of the Bible and may have been delivered hundreds of years apart. In addition, various words and symbols that are used in Revelation are defined in Old Testament books such as Isaiah or Daniel. As a result, cross-references and concordances are extremely helpful while studying prophecy to find parallel passages and references.

3. Remember that the timing of the fulfillment may be uncertain: Frequently, prophecies in the Bible don't provide explicit timing. Many prophecies are strung together, so that in one passage of Scripture, there may be references to events that happen during Christ's First Coming as well as Christ's Second Coming. Even though events may appear a couple of verses apart in Scripture, there may be thousands of years separating them in time. Future events may seem to blend into one, as a person looking toward a range of mountains may see two peaks as one, not perceiving the valley between them or its size and unique characteristics (examples include Isa. 9:6-9 and Isa. 11:1-5).

4. Remember the law of double reference (duality): A prophecy may have a fulfillment *both* in the time of the prophecy, *and* another in the distant future. The message of a prophet frequently had meaning both in his own time and for the generations that were to follow. In other words, prophecy, like history, sometimes repeats itself. Something that occurred in the past (or near future) will be seen as a prototype of a later fulfillment. For instance, the prophetic sign given to Ahaz in Isaiah 7:14 refers *both* to the birth of a son by Isaiah's wife (Isa. 8:3) *and* to the birth of the Messiah (Matt. 1:22, Luke 1:27).

5. Remember present tense is often used: Many prophecies in the Bible (especially those of the Old Testament prophets) were delivered in present tense instead of future tense. This was a common literary method used by the prophets to emphasize the certainty of the events they were predicting. For example: "Your country is desolate, your cities burned with fire" (Isa. 1:7) is a prophecy from Isaiah about the future destruction of Jerusalem delivered over one hundred years before the event actually occurred. At the time this prophecy was delivered to the people of Judah, Jerusalem was still very much intact—Isaiah wanted to paint a picture for the people and warn them of what things would be like if they did not turn from their ways.

Notes

1. Four of these points based on Jack W. Hayford, *Until the End of Time: Daniel and Revelation,* 15-16.

APPENDIX B

DIFFERENT VIEWPOINTS REGARDING PROPHECY

There are four different viewpoints concerning the interpretation of the book of Revelation and the timing of Bible prophecy. These different possible interpretations reflect the only possibilities in relation to time—past, present, future, and timeless. There is also a fifth viewpoint that denies prophecy altogether:

Preterists (past):

Preterists believe that most, if not all prophecy has already been fulfilled. They believe that Jesus' Second Coming was in AD 70 at the destruction of Jerusalem, which was the middle of the seventieth seven of Daniel 9:24-27 (see *Appendix D*). His coming was spiritual rather than a physical event. They believe Revelation has already been fulfilled in the early days of the Church (during the Roman Empire and the early Apostolic Church). The beast or Antichrist described in the Bible is usually understood by preterists to be Nero or Domitian, and Babylon is usually understood to be a reference to the Roman government.

Historicist (present):

Historicists believe that much of the current Church age is equal to the Tribulation period (which is not seven years in length). They believe prophecy has already been in large measure fulfilled, but that the Second Coming and events surrounding it have not yet happened. The physical promises God made to the nation of Israel have become spiritual promises to a spiritual Israel. The church became this spiritual Israel when the Jews rejected Christ. Historicists believe the Catholic papacy is the Antichrist and that Daniel's seventieth seven took place immediately after the First Coming of Christ (Christ's coming represents the covenant with the Jews; Christ's death represents the desolation of the Temple at the midpoint, and Stephen's stoning represents the end of the seventieth seven when God gave up on the Jews and transferred His covenant to the Church).

Futurists/Dispensationalists (future):

Futurists or dispensationalists believe prophecies are to be interpreted literally without any transformation from a physical Israel to spiritual Israel. They believe that virtually all prophetic events, including the seventieth seven of Daniel 9:24, have not yet occurred, but will take place in the future. Revelation chapters 4-22 are believed to be prophecy yet to be fulfilled, and the events described will usher in the Second Coming of Christ. Taking this view leads to beliefs such as the restoration of a literal Israel, the mass conversion of Jews during the Tribulation period, a physical Antichrist who forms a worldwide government and signs a peace treaty with the Jews, and a physical battle of Armageddon. The futurist/dispensationalist view is the one taken by this book.

Idealists/Spiritual or Symbolic (timeless):

Idealists believe that the book of Revelation is symbolic—it is a pictorial unfolding of great principles without reference to any actual events, either past or future. They do not believe that the Bible indicates the timing of events or that we can determine their timing in advance.

Historicals/Criticals:

Historicals or criticals deny the truthfulness and inspiration of the Bible. They believe that prophecies, such as those contained in the book of Daniel, are not really prophecy, but that they were written at a later time than stated in the text. Historicals believe that prophecy was designed to act as an encouragement to Israel rather than to forecast the future. They believe Revelation portrays a panorama of history of the Church from the days of John to the end of time. The Antichrist has been identified as Muhammad, the Pope, Napoleon, or some subsequent dictator. This view is primarily taken by skeptics who deny the Bible and try to rationalize the prophecies that it contains.

Different Views on the Timing of the Millennium

In addition to different views on the timing of prophecy, there are also different views on the timing and length of the Millennium:

Premillennialism:

The premillennial view is the oldest and most popular interpretation, and teaches that the Second Coming of Christ will occur before the Millennium. Israel and the Church are seen as two separate and distinct entities throughout all of history, including the Millennium. Therefore, according to this view, there will be a Church era followed by the Tribulation, which will occur at some point in the future. During the Tribulation, persecution will intensify, the Antichrist will arise, and the judgments of Seals, Trumpets, and Bowls will occur. At the end of the Tribulation, Christ will return, defeat the enemy army at Armageddon, set up His Kingdom, and reign on earth for a thousand years from Jerusalem. Christ's reign will be a literal, visible reign on earth. The premillennial view is the one taken by this book.

This view is called premillennial because the Antichrist and the Tribulation come before Christ's return, which marks the beginning of the Millennium. This view is based on the plain, literal, historical, and grammatical method of interpretation. It assumes that God will keep the promises He made to Israel, but that Gentile believers will also be the recipients of these promises as the adopted sons of Abraham. One of this view's major tenets is that the earth is getting worse rather than better, and that the Kingdom age can't begin until Christ returns to destroy those who have led the world in its downward spiral.

There are at least three forms of premillennialism: dispensational, historic, and covenant premillennialism. Dispensational premillennialists hold that Israel and the Church are two separate and distinct entities throughout all of history, including the Millennium. Historic premillennialism regards the Millennium as a further state in the advancement of Christ's Kingdom—an interim stage between the Church age and the age to come. Covenant premillennialists hold that in the Old and New Testament eras, Israel and the Church were the same, but in the Millennium they will be separate.

Amillennialism:

The amillennial view teaches that there is no literal, earthly Millennium (*A-* is a prefix that means "not"). Amillennialists believe that Christ reigns in a Spiritual Kingdom during the current era of the Church and will return to destroy the earth and establish eternity. In essence, the current Church-age *is* the Millennium (which is not a thousand years in length). People who hold this view do not believe in a Rapture. Amillennialism teaches that good and evil will both increase in the world as God's Kingdom parallels Satan's kingdom. The Church age will end in a time of trouble. When Christ returns, the end of the world will occur with a general resurrection and general judgment of all people, followed by eternity. This view is based on the spiritualizing of the promises God made to Israel as a nation and applying these to the Church. It holds that Israel forfeited the promises God made to it because of unbelief; the Church will inherit all these promises originally intended for Israel.

There are several different forms of amillennialism. Some believe that the Spiritual Kingdom is present during the current era of the Church. Other amillennialists believe that the present, spiritual reign of God's Kingdom consists of the influence that the Church exerts through its many, worldwide ministries. Another form teaches that the Millennium is composed of the reign of all dead Christians in heaven. Still a fourth kind believes that the Millennium is equal to the eternal state that will commence at the Second Coming (i.e., that the new heavens and the new earth will equal the Millennium). The amillennial view was made popular by Augustine in the fourth century and has become the dominant view of the Roman Catholic Church as well as large denominations such as today's Presbyterians, Lutherans, and Methodists. Most Evangelical Christians do not hold this view (with some notable exceptions including TV pastors such as James Kennedy and Robert Schuller).

Postmillennialism:

The postmillennial view teaches that the current Church age is the Millennium (which is not necessarily a thousand years in length) and that the Second Coming of Christ will be after the current age. This view holds that there will be an earthly Kingdom, but that Christ will claim it only after the thousand years have expired. This view is based on the belief that Christ is reigning spiritually from His throne in heaven at present. Postmillennialists believe that the Kingdom will gradually be extended through the preaching of the Gospel until eventually the whole world will be Christianized. This will be followed by a period of peace and prosperity known as the Millennium. After Christianity has dominated the world for a long time, Christ will return after (*post-*) the Millennium and usher in the resurrection, the last judgment, and the Eternal Kingdom. Like amillennialists, postmillennialists believe in a general resurrection and a general judgment of all people. The postmillennial view is based on a largely spiritualized interpretation of prophecy. Its major tenet is that the earth is getting better rather than worse and that the kingdom age will be achieved by man through the spreading of the Gospel message.

Postmillennialism was made popular by the writings of Unitarian Daniel Whitby (1638-1726) and was the dominant view in America during much of the nineteenth century. This view relies on achieving a man-made utopian state on earth. World War I greatly decreased the number of people who held this view, and World War II virtually wiped this belief out because it became harder to argue that the earth was getting better and not worse. Because this view spiritualizes the interpretation of prophecy, there is almost no acceptance for this view among Bible-believing Christians.

Literal Interpretation

The futurist/dispensationalist and premillennial views are the ones taken by the vast majority of evangelicals and this book because they are the most consistent with a historical and literal interpretation of the Bible taken as a whole. God has fulfilled prophecy very literally throughout history down to the smallest detail. Examples include the destruction of Jerusalem by Babylon in 605 BC, the seventy years of Babylonian captivity, the prophecies of Daniel concerning the Gentile kingdoms that would arise, the prophecies about the First Coming of the Messiah (including the exact day He would come), prophecies concerning the destruction of Jerusalem a second time and how the Temple would be destroyed, the reformation of Israel, etc.

Throughout history, many have considered the literal fulfillment of these prophecies inconceivable. It was just too hard to imagine how many of these prophecies could be fulfilled in a literal sense. As a result, many Bible scholars tried to spiritualize prophecy to try and create scenarios whereby various prophecies could be fulfilled in the spirit realm without a literal, earthly fulfillment. Time and time again, history has proven these scholars wrong. As God's plan for the world has unfolded, what may have seemed inconceivable to man has become reality through God. The restoration of Israel as a nation, for instance, was thought totally impossible as recent as one hundred years ago, since two thousand years had elapsed since the nation was destroyed and the Jewish people were scattered all over the earth. No other nation in history has ever been destroyed and brought back to its native land to reform the nation it had once lost. Consequently, many believed the promises that God made to Israel were really transferred to the Church or that the fulfillment of God's promises would be a spiritual fulfillment in heaven. God proved these beliefs wrong, however, and in 1948 accomplished the impossible by bringing Israel back together as a nation. This shouldn't be a surprise to students of scripture. The Bible itself states that the promises made to Israel were not nullified as a result of their disobedience. "Again I ask: Did they [the Jews] stumble so as to fall beyond recovery? Not at all! Rather, because of their transgression, salvation has come to the Gentiles to make Israel envious. But if their transgression means riches for the world, and their loss means riches for the Gentiles, how much greater riches will their fullness bring" (Rom. 11:11-12).

Since prophecy has been fulfilled very literally in the past, it is inconsistent and illogical to imagine that the prophecies concerning events yet to come would be the exception. This is especially true in light of the fact that many prophecies concerning the future were written by the same authors and are contained in the same passages as prophecies that have already been fulfilled. Furthermore, the description of the Millennium as given by the Bible (i.e., the duration of one thousand years, the partitioning of Israel for the twelve tribes, the rebuilding of the Temple, etc.) is not consistent with either the present Church age or a Spiritual Kingdom in Heaven. Also, the events of the Tribulation period are described using literal places (Jerusalem, the Plain of Esdraelon, The Dead Sea, etc.) and it's hard to fathom how the Bible could be referring to anything else other than the locations it actually describes. People who hold the postmillennial and amillennial views have had significant problems interpreting Scripture and have had to rationalize what the Bible says and resort to allegorical interpretation in many places in order to sustain their views.

APPENDIX C

DIFFERENT VIEWPOINTS REGARDING THE TIMING OF THE RAPTURE

Because the Bible does not state definitively when the Rapture will occur in relation to the Tribulation period, there has been debate among Christians throughout the ages on precisely when the Rapture will occur. Four main views have emerged. These views are referred to as the pre-tribulation, mid-tribulation, pre-wrath, and post-tribulation positions. The partial Rapture, also described below, is a special case of the pre-tribulation position.

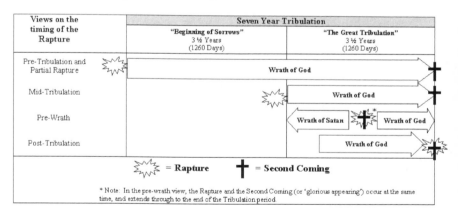

Figure 24: Different Views on the Timing of the Rapture [1]

Pre-Tribulation: This view teaches that the Rapture will occur prior to the seven-year Tribulation period. All members of the body of Christ (both living and dead) will be caught up in the air to meet Christ and then be taken to Heaven. This is by far the most popular view held by mainstream Christians.

Partial Rapture: This view teaches that the Rapture occurs before the Tribulation (similar to the pre-tribulation view), but only spiritual Christians (or those who are worthy) will be taken, while other Christians will remain through the Tribulation period. This view is primarily based on verses such as Hebrews 9:28 which require preparedness (i.e., why would any Christians need to be prepared if all are taken in the Rapture?) However, the Bible makes no distinction between spiritual Christians and other Christians, so this view isn't very widely held.

Mid-Tribulation: This view teaches that the Rapture will occur in the middle of the seven-year Tribulation period. This view is held by a very small group of Christians.

Pre-Wrath: This view blends mid-tribulational and post-tribulational rationale and teaches that the Rapture will occur approximately three-fourths of the way through the Tribulation period at the same time as Christ's Second Coming. This view was developed by a wealthy Christian businessman and was made popular by the 1992 book, *The Sign*. This view has yet to gain any significant following within the Christian community.

Post-Tribulation: This view teaches that Christians will be raptured at the end of the Tribulation. This view is only held by a small group of Christians.

The different views on the timing of the Rapture primarily stem from different interpretations of the phrases "the wrath of God" or "hour of trial" (used in Rev. 3:10, 6:17, 1 Thess. 1:10, 5:9) and the words "elect" or "saints" of God (used in Matt. 24:22, 31, Rev. 12:17, 13:7, 14:13). A sample of some of these verses is included below:

"Jesus, who rescues us from the coming wrath" (1 Thess. 1:10b).

"Since you have kept my command to endure patiently, I will also keep you from the hour of trial that is going to come upon the whole earth to test those who live on the earth" (Rev. 3:10).

"For God did not appoint us to suffer wrath but to receive salvation through our Lord Jesus Christ" (1 Thess. 5:9).

"How awful that day will be! None will be like it. It will be a time of trouble for Jacob, but he will be saved out of it...I am with you and will save you declares the Lord" (Jer. 30:7, 11a).

"If those days [the Tribulation] had not been cut short, no one would survive, but for the sake of the elect those days will be shortened" (Matt. 24:22).

"[During the Tribulation, the Antichrist] was given power to make war against the saints and to conquer them" (Rev. 13:7).

Clearly God promises to keep His Church from the coming wrath, but the Bible also teaches that the elect of God will suffer persecution. Unfortunately, Scripture is not clear on whether the wrath of God refers to the entire seven-year Tribulation period, the last three and a half years (the Great Tribulation) or just the Trumpet and/or Bowl judgments (the most severe of the judgments). In addition, the term "elect of God" has various uses in the Bible. In some places, it refers to Israel (Isa. 45:4), in others to Millennial saints (Isa. 65:22), and still others to Church saints (Col. 3:12) and even angels (1 Tim. 5:21). At question in this context is whether this phrase refers to the Church or to Tribulation saints (people who become Christians during the Tribulation period). Because the Bible is not totally clear on the definition of these phrases, the various different views have arisen regarding the timing of the Rapture.

Following are the most common arguments made for and against each of the different viewpoints. Many of these arguments hinge on the specific meaning of a phrase in Scripture or assume an understanding of end-time events. Having a Bible handy and/or returning to this Appendix after reading the section on Future Prophecy will be helpful to the understanding of some of these arguments.

Arguments for a Pre-Tribulation Rapture

• Very little prophecy actually concerns the Church—almost all of prophecy centers on Israel, Jerusalem, and the Jewish people. Throughout the Bible, clear distinctions are made between God's plan for the Church and His plan for Israel, which are very different. Since the purpose of the Tribulation is for God to pour out His wrath on the people of Israel for their disobedience and to prepare Israel for restoration and conversion prior to setting up His Millennial Kingdom (see chapter thirteen), it makes sense that the Church be removed prior to this judgment. Evidence of this fact is that during the Millennium, the capital city will be Jerusalem, and the nation of Israel will be divided among the tribes of Israel. Although foreigners are mentioned during this time, it is clear that the Millennium will center on Israel and the Jewish people. By mixing these two people groups and believing a view of the Rapture that puts it sometime during or after the Tribulation, the distinction that God created in His plan for these two different people groups is lost.

• Jesus warned several times that no one will know the time of His return—only the Father in heaven will know the date (Matt. 24:36,42, 25:13; Mark 13:33-37). Jesus also warns that the Rapture will come at a time when we are not expecting it to (Matt. 24:44). However, if the Rapture were to happen at the midpoint of the Tribulation, then we would know exactly when it would occur (three and one half years after the Antichrist makes a seven year pact with the Jewish people). Likewise, if the Rapture were to happen after the Tribulation (at the time of Christ's Second Coming), then we would also know when it would occur (three and one half years after the Antichrist desecrates the Temple). More generally, if the Rapture were to happen at any time during the Tribulation, Christians would readily be able to recognize the signs of the times such as emergence of the Antichrist, the ten-nation European federation, the mark of the beast, etc. As such, Christians would be readily anticipating the return of Christ and would not be caught off-guard, as Jesus warns. Therefore, a pre-tribulation Rapture is the most harmonious with the rest of Scripture, which encourages Christians to eagerly await His imminent return (1 Cor. 1:7, Phil. 3:20, Titus 2:13, James 5:7-9, 1 Thess. 5:6, Rev. 3:11, 22:7, 12, 20).

• The Bible makes it clear that the Rapture should be a source of joy and encouragement for the Church (1 Thess. 4:18, 1 Cor. 15:58). Only an imminent, pre-tribulational Rapture would allow this, since any other view would have Christians entering the Tribulation period that would include persecution and suffering for the Church.

• The absence of any instruction to the Church in the Bible to look for events other than the Rapture seems to confirm the fact that the Rapture is the next major event in God's prophetic timetable. The Bible never instructs Christians to look for the Antichrist, the signing of the seven-year covenant, the Seal judgments, the Abomination of Desolation, etc. Instead, the Scriptures only instruct Christians to be prepared for, and anticipate, the Rapture. As such, we can be certain that the Rapture precedes the other prophetic events that the Bible describes.

• The Church is never mentioned in relation to the Tribulation in the Bible (Matt. 24:15-31, 2 Thess. 2:1-11). Although the Church is mentioned nineteen times in Revelation 1-3 (the chapters that precede the description of the Tribulation), it is never mentioned once in the fourteen chapters that describe the Tribulation period. It reappears in chapter 19, after the judgments have been completed, where it is seen in Heaven (Rev. 19:7-9). Such silence about the status of the Church during this period speaks loudly and supports the pre-tribulational view of the Rapture.

• Related to the previous point, it is interesting to note that in Revelation 2 and 3 (chapters that precede the description of the Tribulation) the phrase: "he who has an ear, let him hear what the

THE TRUTH ABOUT PROPHECY IN THE BIBLE

Spirit says *to the Churches*" is repeated seven times, but in Revelation 13, when a warning about the Antichrist is given during the Tribulation, the phrase is shortened to: "if anyone has an ear, let him hear." This is the same warning, except the Church is left out. It seems unlikely that God would omit mention of the Church in a warning about the Antichrist if the Church were still on the earth at this time. As such, this omission tends to further support to the pre-tribulational view of the Rapture.

• The Bible indicates that the "power of the Antichrist" is already at work in the world but is currently being held back by a restrainer (2 Thess. 2:7-8). Most understand this restrainer to be either the Church or the Holy Spirit who is indwelling the Church. According to the pre-tribulational view, the removal of the Church at the time of the Rapture will eliminate this restrainer and will enable the rise of the Antichrist at the beginning of the Tribulation period. Those who hold other views of the Rapture are left to speculate on the meaning of this verse.

• In Revelation 4:1-3, John is taken up to heaven in what many see as a parallel to the Rapture: "I [John] looked, and behold, a door standing open in heaven, and the first voice which I had heard [Christ] like the sound of a trumpet speaking with me, said, `Come up here...'" This event occurs in the book of Revelation prior to the passages that describe the Tribulation. Therefore, if this reference is analogous to the Rapture, then it is consistent with a pre-tribulational view. In addition, the lamps described earlier in the book of Revelation represent the Churches (Rev. 1:12, 20) are now seen by John in Heaven with God (Rev. 4:5). Since the lamps represent the Churches, how did they get moved from the earth to Heaven if it were not for the Rapture? This supports the view that the reference to John in Revelation 4:1-3, does in fact parallel the Rapture of the Church.

• Prior to the outpouring of God's wrath, God instructs His angels: "Do not harm the land or the sea or the trees until we put a seal on the foreheads of the servants of our God. Then I heard the number of those who were sealed: 144,000 from all the tribes of Israel" (Rev.

7:3-4). The seal mentioned in this verse protects these people from various judgments of God that are to come. Why would God describe the servants of God as consisting only of the tribes of Israel and not the Church? It would seem logical that Christians should be protected from the coming judgments just as Jewish believers are. Furthermore, the primary responsibility for evangelism during the Tribulation period is left to these 144,000 Jews (see chapter eighteen and Rev. 7:1-4). Why would Jews be responsible for evangelism around the world unless the Church were no longer on the earth at this time? Both of these questions speak loudly to the fact that the Church must no longer be on the earth during this period, which supports the pre-tribulational view.

• At the midpoint of the Tribulation, intense persecution by the Antichrist will commence (see chapter fifteen). Jesus warns believers by saying "let those who are in Judea flee to the mountains" (Matt. 24:16) and warns, "pray that your flight will not take place... on the Sabbath" (Matt. 24:20). Why would Jesus specifically limit his warning to Judea (i.e., Israel) and not the Church throughout the world or in North America? Why would Christ say that Jews should pray that their flight does not occur on the Sabbath? The reason is that, after the Temple has been rebuilt, the Jewish restriction of a Sabbath day's journey will again be in effect. This Jewish requirement forbids work on the Sabbath including walking (or fleeing) more than three thousand feet (Exod. 16:29). These restrictions have no meaning for Christians, who are not under the Jewish law. It seems unlikely that Christ would primarily address His warning to Jews, unless the Church had already been raptured.

• The pre-tribulational view was the dominant view held in the early Church. Ancient writings by Ephraem the Syrian (AD 373) confirm this fact. This makes it more likely that the pre-tribulational view was the one actually taught by Christ and the disciples, since many of the early Church members were directly exposed to the teaching of Christ and/or to the disciples.

Arguments for either a Pre- or Mid-Tribulation Rapture

When Christ promises to rescue the Church and keep it from the coming wrath, it's not clear in Scripture whether He means the entire seven-year period (Daniel's seventieth seven) or only the last three and one-half years (The Great Tribulation). Since this is ambiguous, the following arguments could equally apply to either a pre-tribulation Rapture, or a mid-tribulation Rapture depending on your interpretation:

• The Bible promises that Jesus will "rescue us from the *coming wrath*" (Rom. 5:9, 1 Thess. 1:10, 5:9) and will "keep us from the *hour of trial* that is going to come upon the whole earth to test those who live on the earth" (Rev. 3:10). Both of these references are to the Tribulation period when God pours out His wrath upon the earth (Rev. 6:17). At issue is if these references are to the whole seven-year Tribulation period, or the last three and one half years ("the Great Tribulation"). Regardless of the interpretation, these promises ensure that at the least, the Rapture will take place at or before the midpoint, not after the midpoint. God is consistent and works in consistent ways. He has never brought judgment without providing a way of escape for His followers.

• Jesus stated that the "coming of the Son of Man will be *just like* the days of Noah" (Matt. 24:37, Luke 17:26). In Noah's case, God removed His people to safety, and *then* judgment fell. He also stated that His coming would be *the same* as in the days of Lot. In Lot's case, Lot left Sodom and *then* God's Judgment came (Luke 17:28-29). Both of these examples argue for a Rapture that will occur prior to the second half of the Tribulation period when the vast bulk of God's wrath will occur.

• At the end of the seven Trumpet judgments, God's Temple is seen in Heaven. In the New Testament, God's Temple refers to the Church (1 Cor. 3:16-17, Eph. 2:19-22). This means that the Church must be in Heaven by at least the midpoint of the Tribulation (Rev. 11:19).

Arguments for a Mid-Tribulation Rapture

• The Great Tribulation refers to only the last half of the Tribulation period when the Antichrist turns on Israel and starts to persecute it. If the Great Tribulation and God's wrath are interpreted to be the same thing, then the Church is only promised deliverance from the second half of the Tribulation (Rev. 11:2, 12:6).

• The resurrection of the two witnesses (described in chapter seventeen) can be seen as synonymous with the resurrection of dead believers at the time of the Rapture. If this is the case, then the Rapture of the Church would have to correspond with the middle of the Tribulation period, because that is when the two witnesses are said to be resurrected (Rev. 11).

Arguments against a Pre- or Mid-Tribulation Rapture

• The pre-tribulational position seems to contradict teaching in Scripture that the elect of God will undergo intense persecution at the hands of the Antichrist (Matt. 24:21-22, Rev. 12:17, 13:7). If the Church is raptured prior to the Tribulation period, this would not be possible. Pre-tribulationalists would argue however, that the elect of God (Matt. 24:22) refer to those who become Christians during the Tribulation period and not the Church, so this apparent contradiction doesn't exist.

• The Bible promises that Jesus will "rescue us from the coming wrath" (Rom. 5:9, 1 Thess. 1:10, 5:9). In the pre-tribulational view, the Church *is* rescued via the Rapture, but people who become believers during the Tribulation are not—they must endure the wrath. Is it fair that *any* believers should have to suffer God's wrath against unbelievers (2 Pet. 7:3, Zeph. 1:17b-18)? This would seem to punish those who held firm to the faith during this terrible time of testing. At issue is whether God's promise to rescue believers applies to all the elect of God or just those who are saved before the seven-year Tribulation period.

Arguments for a Pre-Wrath Rapture

• The pre-wrath view is the only view to harmonize the apparent contradiction in the passages that say the elect of God will undergo intense persecution (Matt. 24:21-22, Rev. 12:17, 13:7), yet God will "rescue us from the *coming wrath*" (Rom. 5:9, 1 Thess. 1:10, 5:9) and "keep us from the *hour of trial*" (Rev. 3:10). A pre-wrath view eliminates this apparent contradiction by defining two different types of wrath—a wrath of God and the wrath of Satan.

• Jesus stated that the "coming of the Son of Man will be *just like* the days of Noah and of Lot" (Matt. 24:37, Luke 17:26-30). In both of these cases, God removed His people to safety, and *then* judgment fell. More to the point, Luke 17:27 states, "the *day* that Noah entered the ark, flood came and destroyed them all." Luke 17:28 states that "the *day* Lot left Sodom, fire and sulfur rained down from heaven and destroyed them all. It will be *just like this* on the day the Son of Man is revealed." This seems to imply that the coming of the Lord will be on the very same day that He rescues the Church from His wrath. Second Thessalonians 6-8 states that "God will... give *relief* to you who are troubled... when the Lord Jesus is revealed from Heaven in blazing fire with powerful angels. He will punish those who do not know God and do not obey the Gospel of our Lord Jesus." This implies that relief (i.e., the Rapture) will occur when the Lord is revealed and pours out His wrath on the world.

• When Jesus was describing the Tribulation period (Matt. 24:4-28, Mark 13:5-23, Luke 21:8-28), He was speaking to the disciples and used the pronoun "you" at least ten times (i.e., "*you* will hear of wars, *you* will be handed over to be persecuted, when *you* see the [Antichrist] standing in the holy place, if someone says to *you*"). This implies that if the disciples were still alive, they would personally go through the events described and not be raptured beforehand.

Arguments against a Pre-Wrath Rapture

• The basic premise of the pre-wrath position—that the Tribulation period can be divided into a wrath of God and the wrath of Satan is not biblical. Nowhere in the Bible is this distinction explicitly made, and nowhere is the transition between the two periods discussed. In fact, in Zephaniah 1:14-17, a number of terms that describe this period are strung together including "the great day of the Lord," "a day of wrath," "a day of distress...anguish...trouble and ruin," "a day of darkness and gloom," "a day of clouds and blackness." The context of these verses supports the conclusion that these all apply to the same period—a time of tribulation and wrath that cannot be chopped into two different segments as the pre-wrath view would advocate.

• The purpose of the Tribulation period is for God to pour out His wrath on Israel for its disobedience and to prepare Israel for restoration and conversion prior to setting up His Millennial Kingdom for saved Jews (Deut. 4:29-30, Zeph. 2:1-3, Ezek. 20:34-35, 22:17-22). It is Christ who opens the scroll at the start of the Tribulation period and sends judgment to the earth (Rev. 5-6), not Satan. Therefore, breaking the Tribulation period into a time of Satan's wrath and God's wrath is inconsistent with the purpose of the Tribulation period as stated in the Bible.

• There is a fundamental flaw in the reasoning behind the pre-wrath view. The pre-wrath view points to Revelation 12:12 when Satan is cast down to earth ("woe to the earth and the sea, because the devil has gone down to you! He is filled with fury, because he knows that his time is short") as the rationale for defining a wrath of Satan. The point at which this occurs, however, (and agreed to by proponents of the pre-wrath view) is at the midpoint of the Tribulation period. The problem with this reasoning is that there are four Seal judgments that the pre-wrath view believes happen during the first half of the Tribulation period. How can this be? If the wrath of Satan doesn't start until the midpoint of the Tribulation period and includes only the fifth and sixth Seal judgments, and the wrath of God only includes the Trumpet and Bowl judgments, then whose wrath are the first four Seal judgments? They can't be either God's or Satan's according to the pre-wrath view. This fundamental flaw in the logic put forth by proponents of the pre-wrath view demonstrates that the Tribulation can't, in fact, be divided into different periods of wrath. There is only one wrath and that is from the Lord. His wrath lasts the entire length of the Tribulation period.

• The apparent contradiction (God's elect will undergo persecution *and* be rescued from the coming wrath) can be eliminated if the elect of God (Matt. 24:22, Rev. 12:17, 13:7) are interpreted to be those who become Christians during the Tribulation (i.e., Tribulation Saints) as opposed to the Church. These believers are discussed in the chapter on "Tribulation Saints."

• In the pre-wrath view, the Rapture and the glorious appearing (what most refer to as the Second Coming), are essentially seen as part of the same event. This contradicts the numerous differences outlined in chapter 11, table 3, which shows that these two events have very different characteristics (e.g., whether believers are transformed into immortal bodies or not, whether everyone will see the event or just Christians, etc.). In general, the Rapture is a movement of believers from the earth to Heaven while the Second Coming is a movement of believers from Heaven to the earth. Making these two events one in the same confuses their many differences. The occurrence of these two events together is based on the similarity between two passages in Scripture: Matthew 24:29-31, which describes the Second Coming of Christ, and Revelation 6:12-17, which describes the Sixth Seal judgment:

> "Immediately after the distress of those days 'the sun will be darkened, and the moon will not give its light; the stars will fall from the sky, and the heavenly bodies will be shaken.' At that time the sign of the Son of Man will appear in the sky, and all the nations of the earth will mourn. They will see the Son of Man coming on the clouds of the sky, with power and great glory. And he will send his angels with a loud trumpet call, and they will

gather His elect from the four winds, from one end of the heavens to the other" (Matt. 24:29:31).

"I watched as he opened the sixth seal. There was a great earthquake. The sun turned black like sackcloth made of goat hair, the whole moon turned blood red, and the stars in the sky fell to earth, as late figs drop from the fig tree when shaken by a strong wind. The sky receded like a scroll, rolling up, and every mountain and island was removed from its place. Then [people] hid in caves and among the rocks of the mountains. They called to the mountains and the rocks, `Fall on us and hide us from the face of him who sits on the throne and from the wrath of the Lamb! For the great day of their wrath has come, and who can stand?'" (Rev. 6:12-17).

It is only by interpreting these two passages as referring to the same event that one can arrive at the pre-wrath view. Unfortunately, there are a couple of problems with this. First, the passage in Revelation that describes the sixth Seal judgment does not mention the coming of the Lord at this time. It would seem that if the Second Coming of the Lord were to occur at this time (the most monumental event in all of prophecy), then the book of Revelation would at least mention it at this point. It does not. This omission speaks loudly to the fact that the passage in Matthew (referring to the Second Coming) and the passage in Revelation (referring to the sixth Seal judgment) are, in fact, describing two different events. Second, according to the pre-wrath view, the wrath of Satan ends after the sixth Seal judgment and the wrath of God begins with the seventh. However, the passage in Revelation, which describes the sixth Seal judgment, clearly indicates that people living at the time of this judgment recognize that the judgment is from God (and not from Satan). If the sixth Seal judgment is clearly recognized as being from the Lord, then it cannot be part of Satan's wrath. With this being the case, the pre-wrath view falls apart.

• In all of the passages in the Bible that discuss the Rapture, there is never a mention for Christians to be looking for something to occur before the Rapture. The Rapture is imminent and could occur at any time. If the Rapture were to occur at any point during the Tribulation, then it would not be a surprise. Christians would then know the Rapture would not occur until after the start of the Tribulation marked by the Antichrist signing a seven-year peace deal with Israel. Therefore, for the doctrine of an imminent Rapture to be correct, the Rapture must happen prior to the Tribulation.

• The Rapture is always mentioned in the Bible in the context of joy for believers. After the apostle John personally viewed the events of the Tribulation, he concludes his book of Revelation with the phrase "Come, Lord Jesus" (Rev. 21:20). John is eager for the return of Christ. The apostle Paul refers to the Rapture as the "blessed hope" for all believers (Titus 2:13) and instructs believers to "encourage one another and build each other up [with the comforting words that Christians will not suffer wrath]" (1 Thess. 5:9-11). Jesus Christ, when instructing His disciples before He died, said "Do not let your hearts be troubled...I will come back and take you with me that you also may be where I am" (John 14:1, 3). Indeed, the Bible promises a reward in heaven for those who "long for his appearing" (2 Tim. 4:8) and instructs believers to "encourage each other with [the description of the Rapture]" (1 Thess. 4:16-18). If the pre-wrath view were correct, it seems odd that Christians would be instructed to be excited about the return of Christ and to comfort one another with the description of the Rapture, knowing that they would have to go through the bulk of the terrible events of the Tribulation period first. Indeed, there would be little hope for believers if the Church had to endure many of the terrible judgments of the Tribulation. By trying to combine the Rapture and the Second Coming into one set of events, the pre-wrath position mixes up God's plan for the Jews and God's plan for the Church. It treats the two entities as one in the same, which they are not. The primary purpose for the Tribulation period is related to the Jews (see chapter thirteen) and in 1 Corinthians 10:32, Paul makes a clear distinction between the two. By combining these two events, the pre-wrath position confuses what God is trying to accomplish through the Tribulation—namely to bring salvation for the Jewish people with His plan for the Church (i.e., to rescue it from the coming wrath).

Arguments for a Post-Tribulation Rapture

• God's promise to protect the Church from His wrath means "supernatural protection" while living on the earth, not deliverance from the period altogether. The analogy is that of Israel during the time of the Egyptian plagues—Israel was supernaturally protected while on the earth, but yet still had to live through the period. They were not actually taken away from the earth.

• The Bible clearly teaches that God's elect will suffer intense persecution under the Antichrist (Matt. 24:21-22, 29-31, Rev. 13:7, 14:13). If the "elect" is interpreted to be the Church, then the Rapture would have to occur after the Tribulation period.

• Verse 15:51 in 1 Corinthians implies that the Rapture will happen "at the last trumpet." The word "last" seems to imply the Second Coming of Christ (i.e., the final event of the Tribulation period), which will be marked by the sound of a trumpet.

Arguments against a Post-Tribulation Rapture

• In order for the post-tribulational view to hold, the Church must go through the wrath of God. This contradicts numerous passages that indicate the Church will be protected (Rom. 5:9, 1 Thess. 1:10, 5:9, Rev. 3:10). To skirt this issue, some post-tribulationalists argue that God's wrath will only fall on the ungodly, but this seems unlikely given the magnitude of destruction and the nature of the judgments that will occur (see chapter thirteen). In addition, this seems to contradict passages that state that the Tribulation judgments will "come upon all those who live on the face of the whole earth" (Luke 21:35).

• When Christ returns at the Second Coming to set up His Millennial Kingdom, He will judge all of the people of the earth (see chapter twenty-three). Those who pass judgment will rule (in physical form) with Christ and will be charged with repopulating the earth during the Millennium. Those who don't pass judgment will enter directly into eternal punishment (Matt. 25:31-46). If the Rapture happened at the same time as Christ's return, then who would be left on the earth in physical form to rule with Christ and repopulate the earth (Isa. 65:20-25)? There would be no mortal believers left, because all believers would have been transformed during the Rapture. In addition, the very judgment itself would be unnecessary because the Rapture would have already accomplished the separation of believers from nonbelievers.

• An interval or gap of time is needed between the time of the Rapture and the Second Coming in order to facilitate the Judgment of Believers, where all of a believer's deeds will be recalled and judged by Christ (2 Cor. 5:10, Rev. 11:18). Since such a judgment would require some passage of time, the Rapture must occur prior to the Second Coming.

• Although the Bible is clear that the elect will suffer persecution, this does not necessarily refer to the Church. Pre-tribulationalists would argue that the "elect" in these verses refer to people who become Christians during the Tribulation period (see chapter eighteen).

• The Bible describes the Wedding of the Lamb (the uniting of Christ with His Church described in chapter 11) as occurring before the Second Coming of Christ (Rev. 19:7-9, 11-21). Since the bride is the Church (Eph. 5:25-27, 32, 2 Cor. 11:2), the Church must be in heaven prior to His Second Coming.

• The "last trumpet" referred to in 1 Corinthians 15:51 that post-tribulationalists point to as evidence for their view could easily refer to the "last trumpet of the Church" as opposed to the "last trumpet of all time." There are many trumpets mentioned throughout end-times prophecy (the seven trumpets of Revelation, the trumpet mentioned in Matt. 24:31, the feast of trumpets, etc.), so the phrase "last" may have a specific meaning as opposed to a more general meaning.

Notes

1. Based largely on Robert Van Kampen, *The Rapture Question Answered*, 39.

APPENDIX D

DANIEL'S "SEVENTY SEVENS"

In 538 BC, during the time that Israel was being held captive by the Babylonians, the prophet Daniel recognized that the time of Israel's captivity would soon be coming to an end. It had been sixty-seven years since Jerusalem was conquered by Babylon, and Daniel had been studying the prophecies that said the captivity would last only seventy years: "I, Daniel, understood from the scriptures, according to the word of the Lord given to Jeremiah the prophet, that the desolation of Jerusalem would last seventy years. So I turned to the Lord God and pleaded with him in prayer and petition, in fasting, and in sackcloth and ashes" (Dan. 9:2-3).

Daniel however, not only expected the captivity to end after seventy years, but also expected an end to the punishments that God had brought upon Israel and the establishment of the Messianic Kingdom. In his prayer, Daniel pleaded with God, confessed the national sin of Israel's people, and acknowledged that the captivity had befallen them because of their unfaithfulness. He then pleaded with God that He would end the captivity and reestablish Jerusalem and the Temple to the people of Israel. During this time of prayer, the angel Gabriel appeared to Daniel. Although the seventy years of captivity would come to an end, the angel of God declared that this would not be the end of Israel's punishment for breaking God's covenant. Rather, the punishment would last `seventy sevens`:

> "Therefore, consider the message and understand the vision: Seventy `sevens` are decreed for your people and your holy city

to finish transgression, to put an end to sin, to atone for wickedness, to bring in everlasting righteousness, to seal up vision and prophecy and to anoint the most holy. Know and understand this: From the issuing of the decree to restore and rebuild Jerusalem until the Anointed One, the ruler, comes, there will be seven `sevens,' and sixty-two `sevens.' It will be rebuilt with streets and a trench, but in times of trouble. After the sixty-two `sevens,' the Anointed One will be cut off and will have nothing. The people of the ruler who will come will destroy the city and the sanctuary. The end will come like a flood: War will continue until the end, and desolations have been decreed. He will confirm a covenant with many for one `seven.' In the middle of the `seven' he will put an end to sacrifice and offering. And on a wing of the temple he will set up an abomination that causes desolation, until the end that is decreed is poured out on him" (Dan. 9:23-27).

In essence, Gabriel was correcting Daniel's misunderstanding concerning when the Messianic Kingdom would be set up. This series of events revealed by Gabriel comprises the most important passage in all of Bible prophecy. It not only defines the timeline and events that would lead to the restoration of Jerusalem, but it also predicts the timing of the coming of the Messiah and lays out the major milestones of the Tribulation period. Although the specific prophecies that are contained in this passage have been explored throughout this book, the entire timeline is presented here so that this prophecy (the "seventy sevens") can be viewed in its entirety.

The first key to understanding this passage (Dan. 9:23-27) is to recognize that the "sevens" mentioned in this passage refer to seven-year periods. This is certainly the case: the original Hebrew translation of this phrase supports this interpretation, and Daniel had clearly been thinking about the years of captivity Israel had endured. Gabriel was using a play on words in the Hebrew text, pointing out that the Messiah's Kingdom would not be established in "seventy years," which is what Daniel had been expecting, but rather "seventy sevens of years" (seventy times seven, a total of 490 years). This is similar to the terminology that Jesus used when Peter came to Him and asked how often he should forgive a brother for sinning against him, "seven times?" Peter asked. Jesus replied "I do not say to you, up to seven times, but up to seventy times seven" (Matthew 18:21 NAS). Jesus was trying to emphasize a point, just as the angel Gabriel was. Therefore, the "seventy sevens" refers to seventy, seven-year periods.

The second important point to note is that the program of seventy "sevens" was for "*your people and your holy city*." The people were Daniel's people, the people of Israel, and the city was Daniel's city, Jerusalem. Therefore, the outline and milestones of the events described pertain mainly to the Jewish people and the city of Jerusalem.

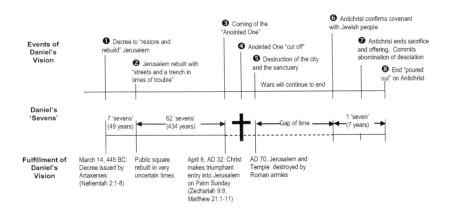

Figure 25: Daniel's 'Seventy Sevens'

The Sixty-Nine "Sevens" (❶,❸)

The first event in Daniel's timeline is "the issuing of the decree to restore and rebuild Jerusalem." This decree was issued by the Persian King Artaxerxes on 14 March 445 BC (see chapter three), which started the countdown of Daniel's seventy sevens. The seventy sevens are divided into three separate units—seven "sevens," sixty-two "sevens" and one "seven." The second block of time is said to immediately following the first, for a total of sixty-nine "sevens" or 483 years (sixty-nine periods of seven years each). From the issuing of the decree in 445, this prophecy says there will be 483 years until the "anointed one, the ruler, comes." Who is this "anointed one?" The Hebrew translation of this word literally means "mashiach" or "the Messiah." Therefore, this is a prophecy about the timing of the coming of the Messiah to the earth.

As was seen in chapter five, "The First Coming of Christ," the 483 years mentioned in this prophecy add up to 173,880 days (using 360-day years, which is based on the Jewish calendar—see *Appendix F*). Remarkably on 6 April AD 32, *exactly* 173,880 days from the issuing of Artaxerxes' decree, Christ made His triumphal entry into Jerusalem on Palm Sunday riding on a donkey and fulfilled this prophecy and the prophecy of Zechariah (Zech. 9:9) just as predicted.

Jerusalem Rebuilt (❷)

The passage then goes on to describe Jerusalem by saying, "It will be rebuilt with streets and a trench, but in times of trouble." Although the passage is a little ambiguous on when this description actually applies to Jerusalem, it seems most likely that it refers to the city after the first "seven," otherwise there would be no reason for Daniel to split the time period described into seven "sevens" and sixty-two "sevens." By 396 BC, forty-nine years after the decree to start the rebuilding process, the public square of Jerusalem was rebuilt to the point where this would be an accurate description of the city. Furthermore, by 396 BC, Israel was still under the control of a foreign power and the Media-Persian Empire was in decline (it would fall sixty-five years later to the Greeks), so the description "in times of trouble" would aptly describe Jerusalem during this time period.

The Gap of Time (❹,❺)

The passage then indicates that various events would happen after the sixty-nine sevens. These events include the cutting off of the Anointed One, the destruction of the city and the Temple, and the continuation of wars. These events were fulfilled just as they were predicted. The Hebrew word "cut off" translated is a common word used in the Mosaic Law and simply means to be killed. The implications of this single prophecy are enormous—this Old Testament passage actually predicted that the Messiah would come in AD 32 and would later be killed. This is fitting with the coming of Jesus Christ and His death on a cross. It is amazing to consider why so many Jewish people ignored this prophecy regarding the coming of the Messiah and rejected Jesus Christ, when they had waited so patiently for His arrival, and their own Scriptures predicted the exact day of His coming. If the Messiah was not on earth 483 years after the decree was issued to rebuild Jerusalem and then was not killed in accordance with this prophecy, then Daniel was a false prophet and his book shouldn't be included in the Hebrew Scriptures. But if Daniel was not a false prophet, then there is no other conclusion but that Jesus Christ was truly the Messiah that the Hebrew Scriptures describe. There is simply no other person that could have fulfilled this prophecy.

The second event the passage describes (which would happen after the sixty-nine sevens) is the destruction of the city and the Temple. This prophecy was fulfilled in AD 70—not long after Jesus was killed (a description of this and the prophecies related to it, are contained in chapter three, "The History of Israel"). Following the destruction of Jerusalem, the passage predicts, "war will continue until the end." Certainly, this has been the case, since there has been no prolonged period of peace on the earth since the coming of Christ.

It's important to note that there is a gap in Daniel's timeline. Daniel talks about the first sixty-nine "sevens," then talks about a series of events that would follow which are said to "continue until the end," and then finally talks about the events of the final "seven." It is in this gap that we find the world in today. The events of the final seven have yet to occur.

The Tribulation (❻,❼)

The passage says that the final seven (known as Daniel's seventieth "seven" or the Tribulation period) will begin with an event. It says "He will confirm a covenant with many for one `seven.'" It is important to know the identities of the parties mentioned in this covenant. The context of this passage clearly indicates that "the many" are the people of Israel. The whole passage concerns the nation of Israel and God's plan for them, so this is the only logical conclusion. Who, then, is the "he" the passage speaks of, who will "confirm a covenant" with the Jewish people around the time of the end? This pronoun relates to the description in the previous verse that describes the ruler whose people destroyed the city and the Temple. Who destroyed Jerusalem and the Temple? The Romans. Therefore, this future ruler must be of Roman descent. What we know from this passage is that this ruler will "put an end to sacrifice and offering" in the Temple in the middle of the final seven year period and will set up an "abomination that causes desolation." This reference can be to no one other than the Antichrist. In describing this event, Jesus Christ warned: "So when you see standing in the holy place `the abomination that causes desolation,' spoken of through the prophet Daniel—let the reader understand—then let those who are in Judea flee to the mountains...how dreadful it will be in those days...for then there will be great distress, unequaled from the beginning of the world until now—and never to be equaled again" (Matt. 24:15-21). Christ is clearly describing the end times in these warnings and is making reference back to this passage in Daniel that describes this event in the middle of the final seven-year period (the Tribulation).

Some people have tried to interpret the "he" as Christ and have tried to fit this final seven-year period into the time of Christ's ministry on earth. This interpretation is often used to support the postmillennial and amillennial views of the end times (described in *Appendix B*).

The argument goes that Christ is the one who made the covenant with the Jewish people at the beginning of His ministry; His death on the Cross represented the abomination of desolation; the rejection of Him by the Jews represented the end of the seven-year period. While interesting, this interpretation has many problems with it. First, the passage in Daniel states, "the people of the ruler who will come will destroy the city and the sanctuary." Clearly, the Jewish people did not destroy their own city and sanctuary; the Romans did. Therefore, this person couldn't possibly be Christ since He was a Jew. Second, if this reference really is to Christ, it's not clear what covenant Christ made with the Jewish people exactly three and one half years prior to His death. Although some explanations have been offered, none of them represent a clear, definitive covenant that would be recognizable in fulfillment of this prophecy. Third, in the discourse Jesus gave concerning the end times (Matt. 24), He warned of wars, famines, earthquakes, and plagues during this period. He then stated that the Jewish people would be persecuted, and that the Gospel would be preached to the whole world. He then warned of the abomination of desolation in the middle of the final "seven." He instructed Jewish people to flee to the mountains because this event would mark the beginning of a terrible time of destruction and persecution. If the middle of the final `seven' is interpreted to be Christ's death on the cross, then the description Christ gave of this time in Matthew 24 doesn't fit. Wars, famines, plagues, and earthquakes didn't happen between the time Christ spoke these words and when He died. Furthermore, Jews were not persecuted, and certainly the Gospel wasn't preached around the whole world before the time of Christ's death. Finally, there was no period of great distress that occurred within three and one half years of Christ's death, which could be described as "unequaled from the beginning of the world until now— and never to be equaled again." Therefore, the only conclusion that can be drawn is that the "he" mentioned in this passage is unquestionably referring to the ruler who has yet to come, but will arise near the time of the end. This person is the Antichrist.

The End of the Antichrist (❽)

The vision of Daniel's seventieth "seven" concludes with the end being poured out on the Antichrist. This is clearly a reference to the Second Coming of Christ, when He will return to banish the Antichrist to the Lake of Fire and usher in His Millennial Kingdom. The details of this are described in chapter twenty-two, "The Second Coming of Christ."

Although Daniel's vision in this passage is somewhat complex and a little difficult to understand, it is the cornerstone of understanding the timeline of God's plan for Israel. These remarkable five verses not only predicted the exact day that the Messiah would come, but also set up the timeline and key milestones for the events yet to occur. God will fulfill the prophecies of the end times mentioned in this passage as accurately and as literally as He fulfilled the prophecies related to the rebuilding of Jerusalem and the First Coming of Christ, which were described in these very same passages.

APPENDIX E

THE SEPTA-MILLENNIAL THEORY

The septa-millennial theory is based on the belief that there would be seven thousand years of time on earth—Christ would return after six thousand years and would reign on earth for an additional one thousand years. This view is based on a model of the creation week, where there were six days of creation followed by a seventh day of rest (Gen. 2:2). This theory then assumes that each day of creation is representative of 1000 years of time based on two verses of the Bible that indicate that a "day is like a thousand years" to God: "For a thousand years in your sight are like a day that has just gone by" (Ps. 90:4). Or, "But do not forget this one thing, dear friends: With the Lord a day is like a thousand years, and a thousand years are like a day" (2 Pet. 3:8).

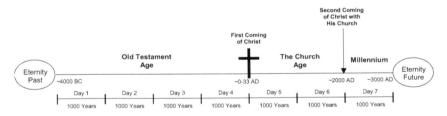

Figure 26: The Septa-Millennial Theory

Since prophecy is clear that the length of Christ's reign on earth (the Millennial period) will be one thousand years (Rev. 20:2-7), septa-millennialists then calculate that the time of man to be six thousand years. The idea is that just as the creation of the earth took six days and then God rested on the seventh day, so, too, there would be six thousand years of time, and then God would rest for one thousand years, which would coincide with the Millennium (Heb. 4:4, 7-9).

The Epistle of Barnabas (a letter written by Barnabas, the first partner of the apostle Paul on his missionary journeys, but not included in the Bible so it can't be considered authoritative), adds credibility to this theory:

> God made the works of His hands in six days, and He ended on the seventh day, and rested on it, and He hallowed it. Give heed, children, what this meaneth; He ended in six days. He meaneth this, that in six thousand years the Lord shall bring all things to and end; for the day with Him signifieth a thousand years...therefore, children, in six days that is six thousand years, everything shall come to and end...and He rested on the seventh day. This He meaneth; when His son shall come, and shall abolish the time of the Lawless One, and shall judge the ungodly, and shall change the sun and the moon and the stars, then shall He truly rest on the seventh day...I will make the beginning of the eight day which is the beginning of another world.

In addition, numerous other writers throughout the ages have also held this view. Examples include Rabbi Elias in 200 BC, Irenaeus, an early Church father in AD 150, Lactantius in AD 300, Bishop Latimer in 1552, Archbishop Ussher in 1650, and Rabbi Ketina in 1817.

Most septa-millennialists believe (based on the Hebrew text of the Genesis 5 and 10 genealogies) that the creation week was around 4000 BC, give or take a decade. If this is the case, the return of Christ would then be around AD 2000 and the Millennium would occur between AD 2000 and 3000. It is difficult to be more precise than this, because there were many serious revisions to the Roman calendar during the past two thousand years. Ultimately, this view will be proved true or false over the next decade or so, as the first decade of the twenty-first century unfolds. Critics of this theory, however, are quick to point out that the genealogies of Genesis 5 and 10 contain numerous gaps (compare Matt. 1:8 to 1 Chron. 3:10-12 where at least three generations are left out). This is because the genealogies given in the Bible are not necessarily complete lists of descendants, but rather tend to focus on the heroes or notable descendants within a family line. Therefore, gaps should be expected. As such, the exact time of the creation week cannot be accurately calculated. In fact, the first Christian missionaries to China experienced shock when it was discovered that Chinese historical records placed the origin of the Chinese nation before 4000 BC. Since then, various people groups have been discovered that date their origins even further back than the Chinese, including the American Indians who date their origin to 9500 BC; the Australian Aborigines, who date back to 25,000 BC; and the Europeans, who date advanced cave art back to 30,000 BC.[1] It may be because of these reasons, that the Bible warns against date setting and specifically states that only the Father in Heaven knows when the return of Christ will be (Matt. 24:36, 42, 44, 25:13, Mark 13:33-37). As such, it seems futile to speculate on the exact date of Christ's return based on anecdotal evidence such as the septa-millennial theory.

Notes

1. Hugh Ross, *The Genesis Question,* 108.

APPENDIX F

THE JEWISH CALENDAR

The Jewish year during biblical times was very different than our own. It was lunar-solar and had only twelve months of thirty days each, for a total of 360 days, as opposed to the solar year used today which consists of 365.25 days. To make up the difference, the Jewish calendar added a "leap month" known as Ve-Adar, seven times during a nineteen-year cycle. This difference in the length of a Jewish year from our own solar year is important to keep in mind when evaluating prophecies in the Bible that have specific, measurable time frames that can be computed. Failure to take this into account has frequently confused people through time and led to miscalculations and misinterpretations of prophecy.

Evidence that the 360-day Jewish calendar was used in prophecy includes Noah's account of the flood in the book of Genesis where 150 days are recorded as five months (from the seventeenth day of the second month to the seventeenth day of the seventh month, Gen. 7:11, 24, 8:3-4), Esther's account of the six-month long feast of King Xerxes (which lasted exactly 180 days, Esther 1:4), and John's account of the end times in Revelation where he describes the last three and one-half years as precisely 1,260 days or forty two months (Rev. 12:6,14, 13:5).

Below are the Jewish calendar months and our equivalent months:

Jewish Month	Equivalent
Nisan, or Abib	Mar – April
Zif, Iyar or Iyyar	April – May
Sivan	May – June
Tammuz	June – July
Ab, or Av	July – Aug
Elul	Aug – Sept
Tishri or Ethanim	Sept – Oct
Bul or Marchesvan	Oct – Nov
Chisleu, Chislev or Kislev	Nov – Dec
Tebeth or Tebet	Dec – Jan
Sebat or Shebat	Jan – Feb
Adar	Feb – Mar
Ve-Adar	The "leap month"

GLOSSARY & PROPHETIC SYMBOLS

Three and One-half Years, 42 months, 1260 days and/or a "time, times and half a time": All of these references are to the same length of time—namely three and a half years or half of the total Tribulation period. The total length of the Tribulation period and its division into two halves is based on Daniel 9:24-27, which is explained in *Appendix D,* Daniel's "Seventy Weeks."

The Number Seven: In the Bible, the number seven represents completion, fulfillment, and perfection. This number occurs fifty-four times in the book of Revelation in reference to the seven churches, seven spirits, seven lamp stands, seven stars, seven seals, etc.

The Number Six (and 666): The number 666 appears in Revelation 13:18 in reference to the mark of the beast. Numerous attempts have been made to identify this number and correlate it to the Antichrist. One view holds that since the number six is mentioned as the number of man in Scripture and since the trinity (or three) is the number of God, the number 666 referred to in Revelation 13:18 is a symbol of man making himself God. An alternative explanation is that since the number seven represents perfection, 777 would represent God's perfection. As such, 666 would represent a number that falls short of God's perfection.

Abomination of Desolation, the: The Abomination of Desolation is a reference to the desecration of the Temple, or committing an unclean act in the Holy of Holies (the inner sanctuary of the Temple). The abomination of desolation happens two times in history: the first was under Antiochus Epiphanes in 168 BC, and the second will be at the midpoint of the Tribulation at the hands of the Antichrist. Antiochus Epiphanes was a forerunner of the Antichrist, as was his desecration of the Temple.

Abomination that Causes Desolation, the (Dan. 9:27): This is a reference to the Antichrist, who will commit the abomination of desolation.

Abyss, the: The Abyss is a phrase used in Scripture to refer to the dwelling place of demons (Luke 8:30-31, Rom. 10:6-8). The Abyss is not Hell or Hades or the Lake of Fire, but rather a bottomless pit, which is used as a place of confinement for demons. The Abyss will be opened during the fifth Trumpet judgment to release demonic creatures upon the earth (Rev. 9:1-2). This is also the place from which the Antichrist will rise (Rev. 11:7) and where Satan will be banished for the thousand-year period known as the Millennium (Rev. 20:1-3). When the Abyss is opened during the Trumpet judgments, smoke will rise from it and will darken the sun and sky. This seems to confirm that the Abyss is a physical place and not just a symbolic reference.

Adultery: In relation to prophecy, the word "adultery" is used symbolically and almost always means spiritual infidelity with a false religion.

Apocalypse, the: This is a reference to the Book of Revelation and/or other biblical books and passages dealing with the end times.

Apostasy: Technically, the word "apostasy" refers to rebellion against God. It is a compound of two Greek words: *apo*, meaning "away from" and *istimi* meaning "to stand." The word literally means to stand away from where one used to stand (i.e., shifting ones' doctrinal beliefs from formerly held biblical teachings). However, it is frequently used to describe the abandoning of sound biblical doctrine, usually as a result of deceiving spirits or false teachers. The New Testament contains repeated warnings against apostasy and warns that apostasy will increase in the last days.

Babylon: This city in modern Iraq was the political, commercial, and religious center of the ancient world empire. It was noted for its luxury and moral decadence. Babylon destroyed Judah and Jerusalem and took the nation of Israel into captivity (see chapter four). To Israel, Babylon symbolized the epitome of a powerful, evil, worldly city destined for destruction. In the context of prophecy, the word "Babylon" has multiple meanings:

• It represents the coming world government and religious system that will be established in the last days by the Antichrist (Rev. 17).

• It represents the physical, rebuilt city in Iraq, which will become the center of the Antichrist's empire (Rev. 18).

Beast, the: The beast is synonymous with the Antichrist and/or his empire, depending on the context.

Bride: The term "bride" is frequently used in Scripture as a reference to the true Church of God. In Scripture, Christians are seen as Christ's bride that will be married to Him at His Second Coming (2 Cor. 11:2, Rev. 19:7).

Day of the Lord: The day of the Lord refers to the period of time during the Tribulation when the wrath of God will be poured out. During this period of unknown duration, God will destroy the wicked inhabitants living upon the earth, and the Lord will be exalted (Isa. 2:17, Zeph. 1:18, Joel 2:20-31, 2 Pet. 3:7-10, Rev. 6:17-17). While some believe this refers to the entire seven-year Tribulation period, others believe it refers to just the second half of the Tribulation period (or even just the Bowl judgments).

Dispensationalism: A system of belief that sees Israel and the Church as separate and distinct entities throughout time and sees the Church age being followed by a literal Millennial Kingdom on earth (see *Appendix B*).

Page 419

Eschatology: Eschatology refers to the doctrine of the end times and the study of it. It concerns the future and the destiny of the whole world.

Gospel, the: The Gospel is the "good news" that Jesus died on the Cross for our salvation; that those who believe in Jesus will be saved from Hell (while those that don't will spend eternity in Hell), and that God will set up a kingdom on earth over which Jesus shall reign (John 3:16, Luke 1:32-33, Rev. 14:6).

Hades: Hades is a place that temporarily holds the souls of unbelievers between their death and their ultimate demise—being cast into the Lake of Fire at the Judgment of the Unsaved Dead, which will occur after the Millennial period. Hades is sometimes called the "place of torments" (1 Pet. 3:18-19, Luke 16:19-31).

Heaven: Heaven is place—a real place where the souls of believers now immediately go upon their death (in Old Testament times, they went to Paradise). Heaven is not a disembodied state or mental state; it is where God resides. The current Heaven is not permanent—it will be destroyed after the Millennium when God creates a "New Heaven and a New Earth" (2 Cor. 12:2-4, Mark 16:19, Rom. 8:34, Phil. 1:23).

Hermeneutic: A system of interpreting the Bible.

Horns: Horns are used frequently in prophecy to refer to kingdoms or kings. They represent power, strength, and authority.

Lake of Fire, the: The Lake of Fire is synonymous with Hell. It has been prepared by God as the ultimate residence of Satan, the Antichrist, the False Prophet, and all the people of the world who have rejected the Gospel. It is described in the Bible as a literal place—a fiery lake of burning sulfur where people will be tormented day and night forever and ever (Matt. 25:41, Mark 9:43, 48, Rev. 19:20, 20:10, 14-15).

Michael: Michael is the only angel explicitly called an archangel in the Bible (Dan. 10:13, 21, 12:1, Jude 9). As such, he holds a position of power above God's other angels. Both Michael and Satan rank below Jesus. Thus, it is fitting that Michael lead the fight against Satan described in Revelation 12:7-9.

Mystery: In biblical terms, a mystery is a plan of God that has been kept secret but has now been revealed.

New Heaven/New Earth: At the end of the Millennium, God will destroy the earth with fire. He will then create a New Heaven and a New Earth. In essence, God will destroy the dividing line between the two so that he can dwell with mankind forever (Isa. 65:17, Rev. 21:1-8).

Olivet Discourse, the: Jesus' discourse to his disciples given on the Mount of Olives near the end of his earthly ministry. This discourse is recorded in Matthew 24:1-44, Mark 13:1-37, and Luke 21: 5-36 and forms the basis for much of prophecy concerning the end times.

Paradise: Paradise is a place where the souls of Old Testament believers went upon their death until the time of Christ's resurrection. Paradise is now empty. When Christ died, He took the souls in paradise to Heaven with him. Believers who die now go directly to Heaven (Eph. 4:8-10, Rev. 1:18). Paradise is synonymous with Abraham's bosom.

Parousia: A reference to Christ's Second Coming.

Pentateuch: A reference to the first five books of the Old Testament: Genesis, Exodus, Leviticus, Numbers, and Deuteronomy.

Prostitute, Great Harlot, or Babylon: The word "harlot" referred to in prophecy commonly represents a religion which prostitutes the true meaning of being wedded to Christ and sells out to all the false religions of man. The "great harlot" is a reference to the worldwide religious system that will exist under the Antichrist. Babylon is a reference to the same—the derivation coming from ancient Babylon when King Nebuchadnezzar set himself up to be God and demanded the world worship him (Dan. 3:4-6). In contrast to the harlot, Christians are seen in Scripture as the bride of Christ (2 Cor. 11:2).

Twenty-four Elders, the (mentioned throughout Revelation): The twenty-four elders in Revelation represent redeemed people who are glorified, crowned, and enthroned around Christ (Rev. 4:4-5). The number twenty-four could represent the twelve disciples of Christ plus the patriarchs of the twelve tribes of Israel.

Whore: The word "whore" used in prophecy is used symbolically (similar to the word "adultery"), and consistently is used to refer to counterfeit religions.

Year: A year in the Bible commonly refers to 360 days instead of 365 days because the Jewish calendar is made up of twelve months, which consist of thirty days each. Julius Caesar added the extra five days to the commonly used calendar in 45 BC.

Zion: Zion was originally the name of the ancient Jebusite hillside fortress, which David captured near the Kidron Valley. After Solomon built the Temple on the adjacent Mount Moriah, the word Zion was expanded in meaning to include the entire Temple area which is now located in the old city of Jerusalem (see chapter two). Eventually the word "Zion" was used figuratively for all of Jerusalem, then the land of Judah, and finally it came to mean the entire nation of Israel. The New Testament writer to the Hebrews gave it another meaning by relating it to the "city of the Living God, the Heavenly Jerusalem" (Heb. 12:22).[1]

Notes

1. Jack W. Hayford, *Until the End of Time: Daniel & Revelation*, 133.

RECOMMENDED READING

Brickner, David, *Future Hope*. San Francisco, CA: Purple Pomegranate Productions, 1999

> Written by a Jewish Christian, this book is unique in that it provides an overview of the end times from a primarily Jewish perspective. As such, this book has many insights into the purpose of the end times as it relates to God's unfolding plan for His people. This book is written in a very easy-to-read format and is targeted at non-Christian Jews, so it is excellent for those that just want an overview of the end times or, are looking for a book to share with their Jewish friends.

Graham, Billy, *Storm Warning*. Word Publishing, 1992

> In Billy Graham's typical style, *Storm Warning* presents the topic of prophecy focused on bringing readers to a decision for Christ. Well-written and filled with personal anecdotes, this book presents prophecy in the greater context of the Gospel message that helps readers see the bigger picture. Highly recommended for non-Christians or new Christians interested in Bible prophecy.

Ice, Thomas, and Timothy Demy, *Pocket Prophecy Series*. Eugene, OR: Harvest House Publishers, 1996

> The *Pocket Prophecy Series* consists of at least ten concise pamphlets, which discuss various aspects of prophecy such as the Temple, the Tribulation, the Rapture, the Antichrist, and the Millennium. They are written in an easy-to-understand Q&A

format and are filled with relevant scripture passages. Published by the Pre-Trib Research Center, this series tends to be overly focused on arguing a pre-tribulational interpretation of the Rapture.

Jeffrey, Grant R., *Armageddon: Appointment with Destiny*. Toronto, Ontario: Frontier Research Publications, 1997

Armageddon is one of the best-researched and most complete books on prophecy around. What makes the book unique is that it goes beyond the typical analysis of the signs of the times and covers new ground by discussing the important role of the Jewish Feasts in prophecy, the role of the Ark of the Covenant, and the time cycles that God seems to plan history around. This book has recently been revised and expanded and is a must read for any person seeking a deeper understanding of prophecy.

LaHaye, Tim, Zola Levitt, Dave Breese and others. *Foreshadows of Wrath and Redemption. Eugene, OR: Harvest House Publishers,* 1999

Similar to *Countdown to Armageddon* (discussed below), this book is a compilation of chapters written by different authors on different topics relevant to the end times. Part One discusses the various prophecies made by Christ in the Olivet discourse, Part Two covers various other signs such as the rebirth of Israel and the rise of Russia, and Part Three discusses various miscellaneous topic such as persecution in America and the problems with the pre-wrath position. This book is well written and organized. Doctrinally, the book supports the pre-tribulational view of the Rapture.

LaHaye, Tim, and Jerry B. Jenkins, *Are We Living in the End Times?* Wheaton, IL: Tyndale House Publishers, 1999

Meant as a companion to the *Left Behind* series (described below under novels), this book outlines the various key doctrines of end time prophecy and provides the biblical basis for LaHaye and

Jenkins' fictional accounts of the end times that have become so popular. Organized topically, this book is a good place to start for those whose first introduction to prophecy was through the *Left Behind* series.

Lindsey, Hal, *The Late Great Planet Earth*. Grand Rapids, MI: Zondervan Publishing House, 1970

Probably the most popular book of all time on Bible prophecy, *Late Great Planet Earth* explains prophecy in an easy to read and understand format. Although outdated (making references to the Cold War and the rise of drugs in the '70s as signs of an imminent return of Christ), this book is still one of the most concise broad overviews of prophecy ever written.

Lindsey, Hal, *Planet Earth: 2000 AD* Palos Verdes, CA: Western Front, Ltd., 1996

Planet Earth: 2000 AD is essentially an update to *The Late Great Planet Earth*. While it doesn't provide the broad overview of prophecy that its predecessor did, it does provide an update on current events and speculates on how they relate to Bible prophecy. Although this book provides good data and background material to help readers see how prophecy might relate to current day headlines, it tends to take an alarmist point-of-view and runs the risk of being quickly outdated just as *The Late Great Planet Earth* was.

Lindsey, Hal, *Apocalypse Code*. Palos Verdes, CA: Western Front, Ltd., 1997

Combining the broad prophetic overview of the *Late Great Planet Earth* and the modern updates of *Planet Earth: 2000 AD*, this book delivers an easy to read, modern overview of prophecy combined with an analysis of current events. Incorporating plenty of Scripture, this book does a better job than Hal's previous books of analyzing what the Bible really says, but as with his other

THE TRUTH ABOUT PROPHECY IN THE BIBLE

books, it runs the risk of being outdated if his analysis of current events proves wrong.

Lindsey, Hal, *Planet Earth: The Final Chapter.* Beverly Hills, CA: Western Front, Ltd., 1998

This book is yet another update to Hal Lindsey's previous books. Although not much new ground is covered, this book does provide a good, high-level overview of the key aspects of prophecy and serves as a good introduction to prophecy for people who haven't studied it before.

Ryrie, Charles, Joe Jordan, Tom Davis and others. *Countdown to Armageddon.* Eugene, OR: Harvest House Publishers, 1999

This comprehensive book, written by many well-respected authors such as John F. Walvoord, Thomas D. Ice, J. Dwight Pentecost, Jimmy DeYoung, Charles C. Ryrie, and others, provides a very good overview of the key events of the end times. Each chapter is written by a different author and focuses on key topics of prophecy such as The Times of the Gentiles, the Revival of the Roman Empire, the Tribulation, the Antichrist, and the Millennium. Written from the pre-tribulational viewpoint, this book also contains an excellent analysis on the "pre-wrath" view of the Rapture and its various doctrinal problems.

Swindoll, Charles, John F. Walvoord, J. Dwight Pentecost and others, *The Road to Armageddon.* Word Publishing, 1999

Written by numerous members of the Dallas Theological Seminary Faculty, this book provides several articles focused on the key events of the end times including the Rapture, the Tribulation, the Antichrist, Babylon, and the Second Coming. Although not very comprehensive, it does provide valuable insight into the end times written by some of the most well-respected scholars in the field.

Novels

BeauSeigneur, James, *The Christ Clone Trilogy.* Rockville, MD: SelectiveHouse Publishers, 1988

> Written by a former intelligence analyst for the National Security Agency and newspaper publisher, this series of three books are very well written and do an excellent job bringing end-times prophecy to life for the average person.

LaHaye, Tim, and Jerry B. Jenkins, *The Left Behind Series*. Wheaton, IL: Tyndale House Publishers, 1995

> The *Left Behind Series* is a best-selling twelve-book series of novels on the end-times. These novels do an excellent job of helping Bible prophecy to come alive in a fictional context, although they tend to draw out the story line too much (and thus, the need for a twelve-book series). Written from the pre-tribulational point-of-view, these books are well researched. The characters in the book are fictional and the authors tried their best to be true to Bible prophecy in the events surrounding the plot line.

Lindsey, Hal, *Blood Moon*. Palos Verdes, CA: Western Front, Ltd., 1996

> *Blood Moon*, Lindsey's first attempt at fiction, is a novel covering prophecy as seen through the eyes of several people who live during the Tribulation period. While the book skims over some important details, it does do a good job of presenting a realistic scenario for how the end times might unfold. What makes the book unique, however, is that it presents fictional accounts of key players throughout history, including Abraham, Noah, Mohammad, and others to tie together past, present, and future prophecy.

Reference Materials

Larkin, Clarence, *The Book of Revelation* and *Dispensational Truth*.
Santa Fe, NM: Sun Books/Sun Publishing, 1996 and 1998

Originally written in 1918, these are probably the original and definitive works on modern prophecy. Written after a twenty-five-year study of prophecy, these books provide countless insights, detail, cross-reference, charts, and tables to explain prophecy from the pre-tribulational point-of-view. What is amazing about these books are when they were written—1918, and the insistence on the literal interpretation of prophetic events such as the future formation of Israel. In 1918, it was outrageous to think that Israel could become a nation again after two thousand years of dispersion. However, by insisting on a literal interpretation of the Bible and not trying to link Scripture to current events, Larkin put a stake in the ground which stands today as a great example of the power of Bible prophecy. *Dispensational Truth* is arranged topically and covers in intricate detail every aspect of dispensational (or future) prophecy. *The Book of Revelation* is an analysis of Revelation chapter-by-chapter. Both books are extremely comprehensive and contain detailed doctrine. As such, they are best suited for those who what to undertake a detailed study of prophecy. They are not intended for the casual reader.

Lindsey, Hal, *There's a New World Coming*. Eugene, OR: Harvest House Publishers, 1973

Unlike Hal Lindsey's other books, which are topical, this book provides a detailed analysis of the Book of Revelation, chapter-by-chapter. As such, it is a good general reference for people who want to study prophecy on their own, while at the same time want some guidance. Much of the content has been re-purposed and appears in some of Hal's other books, including *Apocalypse Code* and *Planet Earth 2000 AD*, but this book is still one of the best commentaries on the book of Revelation written from the pre-tribulational point of view.

Study Guides

Hayford, Jack W., *Until the End of Time*. Thomas Nelson Publishers, 1994

> This study guide walks readers through an insightful self-study of the books of Daniel and Revelation. It is unique because it clearly shows the relationships between Daniel's vision in the Old Testament and the prophetic events and symbols used in the New Testament book of Revelation. Careful not to take a position on the interpretation of passages, Hayford presents the various different proposed interpretations of prophecy. This study guide does a great job in helping individuals (or study groups) get through the complex topic of prophecy.

LaHaye, Tim, *Understanding the Last Days*. Eugene, OR: Harvest House Publishers, 1998

> In this study guide, Tim LaHaye (co-author of the *Left Behind* series), walks a reader through the key passages of prophecy (interspersed with his own opinions and analysis). Filled with many diagrams and insights, this book is valuable for people who want to start digging into prophetic passages themselves, but would like a guide along the way. The book is written with a definite point of view and tends to overly steer readers to the pre-tribulation view of the Rapture.

Navigators, The, *Life Change Series: Revelation*. Colorado Springs, CO: NavPress, 1989

> While equally insightful as *Until the End of Time*, this study guide focuses exclusively on the book of Revelation. Great pains are taken in this book not to take a position on the interpretation of passages—not only on the timing of the Rapture, but also on the timing of the Millennium and the literal interpretation of prophecy as a whole. While this is interesting and helps readers to see the wide range in potential interpretations, it makes a study of prophecy somewhat difficult: for instance, this guide won't

even concede that the Antichrist and False Prophet are human beings as opposed to symbols standing for the ancient Roman Empire, Roman Caesars, or political/religious institutions.

Made in the USA
San Bernardino, CA
24 August 2016